Reading:

The Teacher
and the Learner

CRITICAL READERS

PROFESSOR JOHANNA S. DeSTEFANO
The Ohio State University

PROFESSOR STANLEY I. MOUR
University of Louisville

PROFESSOR PHYLLISS ADAMS
University of Denver

PROFESSOR JOY HESTAND
University of California, Santa Cruz

PROFESSOR SAM SEBESTA
University of Washington

Reading:
The Teacher and the Learner

Jo Ann Dauzat
Grambling State University

Sam V. Dauzat
Louisiana Tech University

JOHN WILEY & SONS
New York, Chichester, Brisbane, Toronto

Library of Congress Cataloging in Publication Data:

Dauzat, Jo Ann
    Reading, the teacher and the learner.

    Includes index.
    1. Reading. 2. Reading, Teachers of. I. Dauzat,
Sam V, joint author. II. Title.
LB1050.D33   372.4′1   80-19435
ISBN 0-471-02668-9

Printed in the United States of America

10 9 8 7 6 5 4 3 2 1

To our Sons
Scott, Jeffrey, Mathew, Christopher

PREFACE

It's what you do that counts, not merely what you know! This is the major premise of this textbook. Because good teachers are measured by what they do in the classroom and not by what and how much they know, the overall goal of this text is to enable you to demonstrate skill in teaching reading to children and youth instead of just amassing enough knowledge about reading to pass a course. Of course, the text is also concerned with helping you to develop theoretical knowledge so that your classroom performance will be based on sound educational principles. But knowledge alone will not result in good teaching. You must apply that knowledge in teaching situations to develop competence as a teacher of reading.

The scope of this book extends to encompass the wide spectrum of skills you will need to be competent as one who teaches reading to children of diverse backgrounds. Competencies developed in the text are designed to span the reading program from prereading, to basic skills, to skills necessary to succeed as independent learners so that you may develop competence for teaching reading at any of these levels. The scope also includes development of competencies for individualizing instruction in reading.

The text is divided into sections comprised of chapters that are devoted to clusters of related competencies. Each chapter focuses on a set of objectives, the attainment of which will result in knowledge, understanding, and performance skills prerequisite for the competent reading teacher.

The specific format was selected because it facilitates instruction that focuses on objectives, thus promoting more goal-oriented and efficient learning behaviors; provides necessary theoretical and practical information while including alternative instructional activities to enrich or remediate gaps in learning; and allows diagnostic-prescriptive instruction at the discretion of the course instructor and the learner. The format for each chapter includes the following components.

1. *Rationale* gives an overview of the chapter, provides reasons for its inclusion in the text, and indicates why it will be of importance to the learner.
2. *Objectives* are stated and are a guide to what is expected for satisfactory completion of the chapter.
3. *Preassessment* instruments are a diagnostic check to identify the areas in which the learner already is proficient and those in which there is a weakness.
4. *Enabling activities* include the basic theoretical and practical information provided in the text and suggest activities in real or simulated classroom settings; *additional enabling activities* refer the learner to other reading reference texts or journals for similar information or

divergent viewpoints and to other field-based activities that can strengthen the learner's skills and understanding.

5. *Reading resources/references* presents a bibliography of current books and journals; some of them are references for the information presented in the chapter, and others may be chosen or assigned as supplementary readings.

6. *Postassessment* instruments, included in a teacher's guide for administration by the course instructor, measure attainment of chapter objectives. Some instruments are written achievement tests, while others require demonstration of a competence in a real classroom or simulated teaching setting.

Using the Text

Each chapter is constructed according to the same basic format to facilitate ease in its completion. Because the chapter objectives are frequently sequenced from simple to complex skills and some of the competencies are prerequisite to success in later chapters, you should proceed through them in the given sequence. However, the chapters included in Section 6 may be pursued in any order, and those in Section 7 may be pursued in any desired sequence after completion of all chapters through Section 5. Steps for completing the chapters are given at the beginning of each section.

To the Instructor

It is indeed difficult to design a book for an intended audience without firsthand knowledge either of the varied and unique characteristics of the audience members or of the instructor who has the responsibility for guiding them. What we have designed is a text that reflects accommodations for the various types of preservice and inservice learners we have taught for more than a decade and the variety of types of children and youth they have gone on to teach successfully. Although we acknowledge that *no* book can be everything to everybody, we have synthesized the best features of traditional classroom-oriented sessions, competency-based sessions, and field-oriented classes into a text that easily adapts to the needs of the audience, the instructor, and the educational program. It lends itself to a variety of instructional uses: the traditional reading methods class structure as a core resource, in a competency-based reading methods course, in field-oriented programs, as a work text to accompany class lectures, as the stimulus for small-group discussion following large-group lectures, and as the basis for independent study for students who need an alternative to the usual class structure. The text also allows the instructor to tailor experiences to the needs of the learner and the restrictions of the program by supplying additional objectives and learning activities and by selecting, from among field-based, simulated, or reading activities included in each chapter, the ones that accommodate the program and students.

Acknowledgments

We wish to acknowledge the efforts and contributions of those who helped us complete this project.

The students in our reading methods courses at Grambling State University and Louisiana Tech University made us keenly aware of the need for such a text and helped us field-test and revise the activities. Theresa Cronan of the University of Arkansas helped us generate ideas and activities for some of the chapters. The creative efforts of Ruth Berlin of the North Louisiana Consortium for Education have been incorporated into Section 12. Finally, we are grateful to Bonnie Collins for her support.

Jo Ann Dauzat
Sam V. Dauzat

OVERVIEW: TOTAL READING PROGRAM

With increased national and international emphasis being placed on literacy, more attention is focused on curricula for promoting development of reading ability, a vital component of literacy. One outgrowth of the concern for reading has been an expansion of the parameters of a total reading program. At one time, educators believed that all necessary reading skills could be taught in the first three grades—that children could spend the first 3 years learning to read but, thereafter, they must read to learn. No longer is this viewpoint widespread, and the reading curricula reflects the growing concern for promoting reading ability at each level throughout the elementary school, junior high school, and senior high school grades.

The total reading program can be viewed as having four component strands. Each strand has a different focus and goal, but each complements the goal of the overall reading program. As depicted in Figure 1, the reason for the total reading program is to help each student develop reading ability to the fullest level of potential. The four strands promote this goal, as shown in their descriptions.

The developmental strand focuses on basic reading skills. (These correspond to chapters in Sections 2, 3, and 4. In addition, Section 6 and portions of Section 7 relate to the developmental strand.) In this strand students are taught all of the basic reading skills in a sequential program.

The goal of the corrective/remedial strand is the alleviation of any difficulties in learning reading skills as sequentially presented in the developmental strand. This strand help the student to bridge gaps in the development of reading skills. (Section 7 deals with some aspects of the corrective/remedial strand.)

The functional reading strand focuses on the development of study skills and their application in reading in the content areas such as science, social studies, and math. Through this strand, students develop the sophisticated reading skills that will enable them to become independent readers and learners. (Section 5 and portions of Section 6 address the functional reading strand.)

The recreational/independent reading strand's goal is the development of a love for reading. Activities in this strand promote wide reading for pleasure, for extension of personal knowledge, to satisfy curiosity, or for some other personal motive. This strand will develop readers who continue good reading behavior long after their schoolwork no longer demands it.

Although it touches on other strands, this text mainly discusses the developmental reading program. After completing the chapters, you should be competent to teach developmental reading activities to children and youth.

J.A.V.D.
S.V.D.

CONTENTS
BY
TOPIC

CONTENTS BY OBJECTIVE

Appendixes

Reading:
The Teacher
and the Learner

Section 1
Introduction to Reading

Certain competencies should be demonstrated by those who teach children and youth to read. Each section of this text is designed to help the teacher develop a set of related competencies. Those for Section I are identified next. The teacher:

- Recognizes characteristics of the learner that can affect reading development.
- Can discuss the strands of a total reading program.
- Demonstrates positive support for the learning efforts of all students (continuous for all sections).
- Demonstrates acceptance and appreciation for the diversity among students (continuous for all sections).
- Recognizes the influence of family and culture on the development of reading skills.
- Demonstrates an ability to establish and maintain rapport with peers (continuous for all sections).
- Understands the physical, psychological, and sociological factors of the reading process.

Using the Chapter in Section I
Follow the listed steps to complete the chapter.

1. Read the introductory information.
2. Read the rationale to get an overview of the chapter contents and an understanding of why the information is important to you.
3. Read the objectives to find out what performance is expected for satisfactory completion of the chapter.
4. Take the preassessment if you desire. (It is included in the appendix.) If you feel that your background in the content is meager, you may want to omit this step. If you do take the preassessment, score it with the answer key to find your weak and strong areas.
5. Read the instructional activity provided for each objective and complete the other activities as directed by the instructor.
6. Select additional enabling activities that you want to pursue. Several options are available for each objective. You may want to do some

supplementary study in the chapter; in this case, see the Reading Resources/References listed as a guide to your independent study.

7. Schedule with the instructor a time to take the postassessment. Prior to this, you may want to retake the preassessment to determine your readiness for postassessment.

8. Meet with the instructor to evaluate your performance on postassessment. If you still demonstrate weaknesses, repeat steps 5 to 7. If your performance is satisfactory, begin work in Section 2.

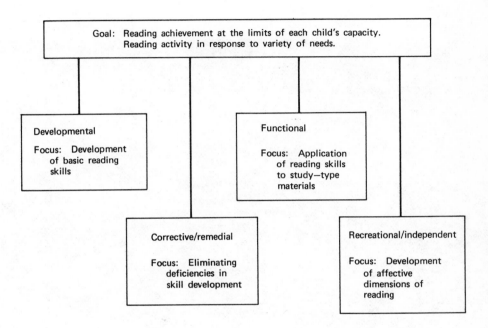

Chapter 1
The Reading Process

RATIONALE

A primary responsibility of teachers is to guide students to become proficient readers. To accomplish this, teachers must know what it means to be a "proficient reader." They must know what elements comprise reading and what factors inhibit or facilitate "proficient reading." This chapter is concerned with such matters. It is designed to develop the concept of the reading process, to identify the facets of reading, and to present the factors that influence the development of reading ability. These understandings are very important, since a person's beliefs about what reading is largely determines his or her teaching behaviors relative to approaches, curricula, and materials.

OBJECTIVES

After completing this chapter, you will be able to:
1. Give a definition of reading that acknowledges reading as a communication process and utilize this definition to decide if reading is taking place in given situations.
2. Identify the major aspects of reading and its relationship to other language skills and utilize the knowledge to make teaching decisions.
3. Identify three factors that influence the development of reading ability.
4. Complete an objective identified by the instructor.

PREASSESSMENT

See Appendix A-1.

Instructional Activity 1

Definition of Reading

Defining Reading
A quick survey of your classmates would probably yield the fact that *all* of them consider themselves readers. Yet you might get vastly different an-

swers if you asked them what they do as they read. How can *reading* be defined?

In developing a definition of reading, the following activities will prove helpful. You are going to interview three different people to get their response to the question "What is reading?" The three people, who represent different role groups, are identified here. But first write your own response to the question.

1. Your response:
2. Response of an *elementary-school child:*
3. Response of a *teacher:*
4. Response of a *peer* (other than a fellow class member):

Examine the four responses. Do you find any common elements? If so, list them. Are you still satisfied with your definition? If not, write a refined definition.

Reading Defined

If you survey the works of recognized authors in the reading field, you will find as many definitions as you find works. However, most of them stress these attributes of reading: a process that involves mental activity, is embedded in other communication abilities, and converts graphic stimuli (letters) into meaning. Acknowledging these components, we may view reading as the process of communication with print as the stimulus. This means that the reader must process the printed stimuli and convert them into meaningful messages.

Utilize this information and write your own definition of reading that focuses on communication.

 Activities

Use the definition of reading to help you make decisions in the following scenes. Compare your responses with those of a peer.

1. Mr. Beta, a first-year teacher, has his students busily engaged in a reading lesson. The first student in row 1 has just read his paragraph from the textbook. Now Mr. Beta has directed student 2 in row 1 to take up where the last student left off. He plans to let all students read this way during the lesson until they complete the story.

    (a) Did student 1 read? Why? _____

    _____

    _____

    (b) Did student 2 read? Why? _____

_____

_____

(c) Did Mr. Beta teach reading? Why? _____

_____

_____

Check: Your responses should include these ideas.

- You do not know if any of the students read.
- You have no evidence that they communicated with the author at all. We only know that they processed the letters into words.
- Mr. Beta's lesson probably did not teach reading because he gave no attention to communication with the author. His lesson only provided for practice in converting print into words.

2. Crissy is on a limited budget, so she is careful with her money. Today she is using the newspaper to find ads from the local markets. She is making her shopping list from the advertised specials. Is Crissy reading?

Why? _____

_____

_____

Check: Your response should include these ideas.

- Crissy is probably reading.
- The ad is communicating to her the items she needs that are on sale.
- She is selecting those items from the ad.

Instructional Activity 2

The Nature of Reading

Interrelationship with Other Language Skills (Knowledge)
Language processes involve the transmitter of messages and the receiver of messages. Reading is one component of the total language processes, which also include listening, speaking, and writing. Of these, reading and listening are processes whereby one receives messages expressed by others. Speaking and writing are processes whereby one transmits or expresses messages to others.

Reading is part of the secondary or printed language system, as is writing.

7

The primary language system is the oral/aural system. This has implications for the way reading should be learned. The child learns his primary language system in an orderly manner. The first language skill is listening. Through this receptive language skill, children acquire ideas as expressed by others. He or she builds a repertoire of meaningful vocabulary and language rules. These bits of auditory input are the base from which perceptions about the phonologic (sound), semantic (meaning), and syntactic (sequencing or ordering words) systems of the language are formed.

From this base, the child develops the next skill in the primary language system—speaking. He speaks the words he has in his listening repertoire. He structures his sentences through the system he developed through listening to others. But, because of the concepts formed as the brain organizes the auditory input, the child can form generalizations about language and generate new expressions instead of imitating those he has heard. The child uses his speech to communicate with others, sometimes in highly creative ways. This competence in primary language abilities is an important resource that the child brings to reading.

The child's experience with audible language helps him to cope with the visible form of language to be used in reading. Initially, he must use the visual bits of input from the page to form perceptions about the orthographic (written symbol) system. From them, the beginning reader constructs a set of rules that enable him to translate the written language (visual symbols) into meaning. According to Smith's interpretation of the reading process, this represents the process of translating the surface structure (the visual symbols used in reading and the auditory stimuli used in oral language) into the underlying deep structure (meaning) (Smith, 1978). It seems to be critical that the child understands that the written symbols stand for speech units and that they carry a message. Without this understanding, the child is unlikely to profit from reading instruction.

Writing should also be based on what the child has experienced in his oral/aural language system as well as in his reading. Listening, speaking, and reading provide foundation skills for the child's development of writing skills.

The preceding discussion is not intended to imply that the language skills must be acquired in the given sequence; it is obvious that some children learn to read a language they will never speak or write and that some children learn to write and read simultaneously. The discussion merely suggests that some language learnings are prerequisite to success in others. The language learnings that enable the child to develop deep, underlying structure necessarily precede those that deal with surface structure of language. Otherwise, the language learner may glibly recite utterances, convert graphic stimuli into sounds, or "hear" a magnificent oration and still entirely miss the objective of language—communication. Viewed in this way, language skills at the deep structure level develop simultaneously for speaking, reading, and writing.

Aspects of Reading (Knowledge and Understanding)

Reading is a process of communication between the author and the reader. No one is quite certain how this process takes place, because little, if any, of the process is of an observable nature. It is primarily (perhaps exclusively) mental activity. Even so, psychologists and linguists have constructed models intended to describe what probably happens in the reading process. The information presented next is a consolidation and interpretation of some of those theories.

What happens when one reads? Read the following passage and then think through exactly what you did. Write down each thing in sequence. Then compare your list with that of a classmate. What did you have in common?

SURVIVING IN COLD WATER

Cold water can be a killer. Exposure to cold water causes the body to lose heat. This can result in loss of consciousness and/or death. Most persons can live in sixty-degree water for about one to six hours. In fifty-degree water, you can live for about one to three hours. In forty-degree water, you can live only about thirty to ninety minutes.

If you are in cold water, do everything you can to save body heat. Don't thrash around. If you can swim to shore, use a back or breast stroke. If it is too far to swim, tread water or use "drownproofing" techniques. If you are wearing a life jacket, hug your knees against your chest to hold in body heat.[1]

There are certain things that everyone must do in order to read. These aspects of the reading process are now discussed.

Mechanical Aspect The first thing the reader must do is respond to some mechanical or psychomotor processes. The reader's eyes must focus on the page of print, but not at random, since we read from left to right and from top to bottom. The reader's eyes must move across the page in a predetermined order as they see the stimuli.

Just what does happen? The following activity will allow you to determine firsthand.

1. Clip out the passage shown in Appendix B-1.
2. Then use your pencil, pen, or other sharp instrument to punch out the dark hole.
3. Choose a partner. Hold the passage up to your eye and sight through the punched-out hole.

---

[1] From *Steck-Vaughn Adult Reading: 2800* by Sam V. Dauzat et al. Copyright © 1978 by Steck-Vaughn Company.

4. Let your partner read the passage as you observe.
5. Write what you saw.
6. Now let your partner do steps 3 to 5.
7. Compare notes. You may want to do steps 3 to 5 again, either now or after you have read the narrative below.

Here is what you should have seen. The eyes begin on the left side of the page to make short, jerky movements and momentary stops. When they reach the end of the line, the eyes make a quick movement back to the beginning of the next line. Where along this journey are you reading? When the eyes are moving? When they stop?

When the eyes stop or *fixate,* they react to the printed stimuli. Then they move to take in another "chunk" of stimuli. It is during the fixation that you read. The *saccadic movements* only get the eyes from one chunk of stimuli to the next. The movement from the end of the line to the beginning of another is called a *return sweep.*

Sometimes the movement of the eyes is characterized by other backward movements. These *regressions* occur when the later information tells the reader that he or she probably did not see what was originally thought to be there. The reader does a double take on the stimuli.

The reader may incur problems in reading if the mechanical aspects interfere. For instance, the child who cannot make a smooth return sweep may lose his place and begin reading on the wrong line of print. Or the child who makes too many fixations becomes a slow reader. The teacher can help this child before he becomes a victim of poor habits.

There are differences between the beginning reader and the independent reader in the mechanical aspect of reading. The beginning reader has more fixations per line of print than the mature reader. Although the duration of the fixation for beginners approximates that of the mature reader, the beginner perceives less per fixation, thereby necessitating more fixations per line of print. The beginner usually has more regression movements because he or she has less skill in anticipating and predicting meanings. The beginning reader also has more problems with losing his place on the return sweep than the more skilled reader. Generally, the beginning reader relies more on the visual stimuli. For the more skilled reader, only part of the total visual information may be necessary for the brain to translate them into meaning.

Word Recognition Aspect Another aspect of the reading process is converting the printed symbol into the words for which they stand—converting the letters into the orally equivalent words. This aspect is also referred to as decoding, word attack, or word analysis. It involves the reader in making correspondencies between the grapheme (written symbol) and its phoneme (unit of sound) and between entire written words and their spoken counterparts. The word recognition aspect results in pronunciation, either vocally, subvocally, or mentally, of the printed words.

Since some word recognition clues to an unfamiliar written word come from familiar words surrounding it in a sentence or paragraph context and are clues only if the reader understands the context, the word recognition aspect of reading is not completely isolated from the comprehension aspect. The reader may be able to make an "educated guess" at an unfamiliar written word only if he or she comprehends the message carried through other familiar words. Thus, although they are two aspects of the reading process, word recognition and comprehension are also interdependent.

It seems that readers at different stages of development have different responses to the word recognition aspect of reading. Whereas the skilled reader may perceive and recognize the words immediately because he or she has stored them in his memory bank, the beginning reader, who lacks such a storehouse of visual patterns and words, engages in intermediate steps to recognize the words. He must scrutinize the word, the features of the letters and letter combinations, and the overall shape of the word that distinguishes it from other words. He may try to match the information with a word he has seen before (a sight word), or try to find known elements of sound and match and blend them to get the new word (apply phonic clues), or he may identify a known base and other word parts (use structrual analysis), or he can use what he already knows about the grammar of his language to predict a word that makes sense (use context clues).

Comprehension Aspect The reading process also involves a comprehension aspect. This aspect involves the reader in converting the words themselves into meaning as well as capturing meaning from the way the individual words are put together to form sentences.

This grasp of the author's message also changes as the reader becomes more mature. The skilled reader makes predictions based on his or her knowledge of language and experience with similar content and verifies them by extracting sufficient samples from the materials to be read. He uses the language cues, such as acceptable word order, inflectional endings indicating number of nouns, tense of verbs, comparison of adjectives, and other language redundancies (information that is duplicated by more than one source)[2] to anticipate meaning and to self-correct where predictions are not verified. The reader uses the previously verified information from the reading and continues to group it into larger units as other predictions are verified.

The beginning reader engages in a similar process, but with more visual stimuli necessary and more on a word-by-word basis. As the beginner decodes the word and determines its meaningfulness, he begins to make predictions about meanings of larger chunks of language. He organizes the relationships of the bits of information about the word and the knowledge

---

[2] For a complete discussion of the function of redundancy in reading, see Smith, 1978.

of language he has stored in his memory bank with current reading experience.

Interpretation/Reaction Aspect This aspect of reading requires high-level thinking skills. It is based on comprehension but extends understanding of the message into a reaction to the message conveyed. The reaction may be a comparison or contrast of this message with a previous one. It might be an affective reaction such as disagreement with, happiness because of, enjoyment of, satisfaction with, or denunciation of the understood message. During this aspect of reading, the reader interacts with the printed message in light of past experiences.

Beyond understanding the message, the reader evaluates and utilizes the new information by incorporating it into his own cognitive and affective structures. This aspect of reading promotes expansion of intellectual growth. The memory storehouse of concepts expands to accommodate the new data and increase the possibility for the reader to generate new ideas.[3]

The aspects of reading just mentioned may be viewed in a sequence as the reading process unfolds. The first aspect is interrelated with the next in that the efficiency of the subsequent aspects is dependent on the efficiency of the previous one. For example, the child who has not completely developed the left-to-right sequence of the mechanical aspect will have difficulty in decoding words and may reverse words such as *no* for *on*. He may have difficulty in the comprehension aspect when he tries to gain meaning from the sequence of words in the sentence.

This relationship is illustrated in the following diagram.

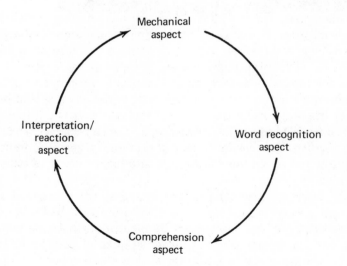

---

[3] For a thorough discussion of the cognitive and affective outcomes of reading, see Robeck and Wilson, 1974.

Now reread the passage on p. 9. Think about the aspects you just learned about. Can you identify them as they occur? How would you change your answer to the question on p. 9?

✳ Activities

Apply the information you have gained in the previous objectives to solve these situations. Compare your responses with those of a peer.

1. Tell why it probably would be difficult for a city-dwelling child to read a passage about the use of *silos*._____

_____

_____

Check: Your response should include these ideas.

- Silos are not seen in the city. It is not likely that the city-dwelling child would have seen one. It is not likely that silos are the topic of conversation in the city.
- If silos are not topics of conversation, it is unlikely that the child will have the word or concept for silo in his listening or speaking language system.
- If the child has no oral language experience with silo, he or she has no foundation for reading about *silos*. He has a barrier to communication with the author of the passage about silos.

2. Using the preceding information, tell why it makes good instructional sense to teach children to read from materials that relate to their own life-styles._____

_____

_____

_____

Check: Your response should include these ideas.

- When one uses materials that relate to the child, part of the vocabulary problem is solved. The materials will use words and concepts familiar to the child. If the child has the words in his or her listening/speaking system, then there is only one unknown, namely what the word looks like in print. The child can draw on his language repertoire to solve the problem of converting the printed symbols back into the oral word that they represent.

3. Miss Alpha calls on Dave Jones to read a paragraph to the class. He

reads orally without missing a single word. When called on to restate what he read, Dave said, "I just read it. I didn't listen." He was unable to relate a single word. Did Dave Jones read that paragraph? Why or why not?_____

_____

_____

_____

Check: Your response should include these elements.

- He demonstrated mechanical aspects and word recognition aspects only.
- Since he failed to demonstrate comprehension or reaction aspects, he failed to complete the reading process. *Therefore* he *called words* but did not read.

4. Christopher opened his mail when he got home from work. His anger became evident as he slapped the notice from the utility company across the desk. He muttered, "I paid that thing last week!"

_____

This is what he saw.

_____

> **Notice:** Electrical services will be
> disconnected unless your
> previous balance is paid by
> February 8.
> Thank you.

Did Christopher read that notice? Why or why not? _____

_____

_____

_____

Check: Your response should include these ideas.

- He *reacted* to the message with anger.
- The preceding aspects must have been in operation to some degree.
- Therefore he probably read the message in the fullest sense of the word.

Instructional Activity 3

Factors that Influence the Development of Reading Ability

Because of the nature of reading, numerous factors can operate at any point in the process to influence a person's development of reading ability. Some of these factors are discussed here. The discussion does not include all possible factors; it merely mentions some of the more important ones.

The factors are organized in categories, but factors from one category can and probably do interact with factors from other categories to influence reading ability.

Physical Factors

Of course, general physical health and stamina are factors that will influence the development of reading ability. The child who is in poor health or who has unfulfilled biological needs will be unable to engage in the mental activity required in reading. He or she may lack the attention span necessary to profit from instruction.

Other physical factors that influence development of reading ability are discussed below.

Vision Reading, under normal circumstances, requires good visual acuity, particularly at near-point, since most reading is done at close range. The child whose vision is poor in general or who suffers from specific visual problems will be handicapped when he or she attempts to see the visual stimuli.

In beginning reading, teachers should be cautious in giving prolonged near-point reading activities. Many children have difficulty with near-point vision until they are 8 years old, when their vision matures. This is because children are born farsighted and gradually develop visual acuity at near-point. Beginners can usually work more easily with large reading charts and chalkboards than with the basal reading texts.

 Activities

1. Survey a set of basal reading materials for kindergarten (prereading) through third grade. What do you notice about the print? _____

   _____

2. Use the preceding information to explain this phenomenon. _____

   _____

   _____

Hearing Another physical factor with implications for reading is the ability to hear. This is important for the child's development of his or her oral/aural language system on which reading skills are based. Poor hearing ability may result in an inadequate primary language system on which to build reading skills. In addition, children whose auditory acuity is poor may have difficulties in profiting from instruction, especially instruction that deals with developing relationships between sounds and symbols.

Psychological Factors

Since reading requires thinking ability and thinking is a mental activity, it is evident that certain mental factors influence the development of reading skills. Some of those factors are discussed here, although the discussion is not inclusive.[4]

Intelligence   It is commonly accepted that intelligence plays a role in the development of reading just as it does in the development of any language skill. However, authorities seem to raise more questions about the relationship than to provide answers. In fact, there is a growing concern for what intelligence really is and what parts of intelligence can really be measured by an intelligence test.

Because of all of the concerns and the unanswered questions, it is necessary to offer some words of caution to the teacher. An intelligence test score does not necessarily predict how well a student will achieve in reading.

- That children from low socioeconomic environments tend to score low on intelligence tests does not necessarily mean they lack intelligence and/or ability to read.
- There is no "magic IQ score" required before a child can profit from reading instruction.
- IQ does not seem to be a "one-time hereditary gift" that either you *get* or you *do not get*. It does seem to be greatly influenced by environment and can change.
- Do not use a low IQ score as an excuse for your failure to teach a child to read. Adjust your techniques until the child learns.

Attitude/Motive/Self-Concept   These factors strongly influence the amount of energy the student will expend in pursuit of reading skills. Furthermore, they are vital factors in determining what types of materials a student will read after he or she has developed initial reading skills.

In order to develop his potential reading ability, the child must have a positive attitude toward reading; he must want to learn to read initially and to strengthen his reading ability subsequently; and he must see himself as a reader. These factors are so intertwined that they cannot be dealt with individually because they impact each other. For instance, the child who has been read to in his home and has pleasant associations with the expe-

---

[4] For further discussion, see Ekwall, 1973, Chapters 3 to 7.

rience will quickly develop the desire to read for himself and will profit from reading instruction. The success he experiences as a result of the instruction promotes the concept of himself as a reader and strengthens his positive attitude toward reading.

Because of the extreme importance of these factors, the teacher should do everything possible to foster positive attitudes, stimulate motivation, and develop positive self-concepts in the beginning reader and in the child who falters in the development of his reading ability. Key things to remember in this regard are to:

Help children discover that books are sources of pleasure and knowledge.

Provide reading activities that are stimulating themselves.

Provide as many success experiences in reading as possible.

Avoid all verbal and "body language" expressions that might communicate to the child that he is not "smart."

Teacher Expectation

Closely related to the factors just discussed, teacher expectation can also positively or adversely influence the student's attainment of reading ability. There is clear and ample evidence to suggest that when teachers have favorable expectations of students, the students perform in accord with those expectations. Conversely, teachers who have unfavorable expectations of students get unfavorable performance from the students. This has been termed "the self-fulfilling prophecy" and proposes interesting implications for educators.

For further discussion see Robert Rosenthal, "Self-Fulfilling Prophecies in Behavioral Research and Everyday Life," in Eldon Ekwall, Reading Resources/References.

 ### Activities

Using the preceding information, respond to these situations. Compare your responses with those of a peer.

1. Mr. Macho, a first-grade teacher, believes that boys are innately more adept at recognizing words. He carefully avoids telling this to them however. At the end of the 9-week period, he tested all of the children to determine the number of words they could recognize from a list. Predict what he found and why. _____

_____

_____

_____

Check: Your response should include these ideas.

- The boys will probably do better.
- The self-fulfilling prophesy is in effect.

2. Precious Patty, a second-grade nonreader, told her tutor, "You're wasting your time. I can't learn to read and I don't want to, anyway!" What

   factors will inhibit her learning to read?_____

   _____

   _____

   _____

Check: Your response should include these ideas.

- She has a poor self-concept. She does not see herself as a reader; therefore, she does not want to try.
- She has developed an unfavorable attitude toward reading.

Sociological Factors

Whereas the financial circumstances of a child's family has little direct bearing on a child's success or failure as a reader, socioeconomic factors do stimulate conditions that may advance or hinder the learning progress of the child. For example, both the quality and the quantity of available reading materials usually vary with socioeconomic status, with the meagerest offerings being at the lowest end of the income scale. Generally, families in the lowest income brackets have the least educational experiences and are so totally involved in day-to-day living that little time remains to pursue cultural interests or establish recreational reading habits. This is not to say that good readers always come from middle- and upper-income families or that poor readers come from low-income families, because this is not necessarily the case. Some good readers come from families of the poorest economic means. But the key factor seems to be the type of family itself. Children tend to be successful in reading when the family sets a value on reading, the family has good reading habits, and the children are exposed to reading situations that stimulate positive feelings about reading. Parental influence shapes the child's frame of reference toward reading and either motivates him or her toward or against reading tasks.

The child from a low socioeconomic background frequently is unsuccessful as a reader because of teacher attitude. There are often conflicts between the mores of the lower-socioeconomic-level child and the middle-class values of the school that can contribute to learning problems for the child (McDermott, 1976). In some instances it manifests itself in low expectations for success in language learnings by minority children. As indicated in a previous section, low expectations result in low achievement. Certainly, then, low expectations contribute to failures in reading-related activities.

Educational Factors

There are certain things that one learns from personal experiences, whether they entail formal education or not, that influence the development of reading ability. The teacher should be aware of such factors.

Visual Discrimination Under normal circumstances one must be able to see adequately before one can read. This is a physical factor. But just being able to *see* does not guarantee being able to process the printed symbols. The reader must have the power to see likenesses and differences in letters and words. For example, he or she must be able to tell the difference between *u* and *n* and among *p* and *b* and *d* before recognizing words in which they appear. This is called *visual discrimination,* and it is usually prerequisite to success in reading. In fact, many activities in a prereading program are designed to teach this ability.

Auditory Discrimination This, too, is a learned ability to hear likenesses and differences in spoken words and sounds. It goes beyond the mere physical ability to hear. Auditory discrimination is also influential in the child's success in reading, particularly when he or she is learning phonics as a word analysis skill. The reader must be able to hear the difference in *pen,* and *pet, sell* and *bell,* or *pit* and *pet* in order to be successful in learning phonics.

Background Experience All life experiences impact on a person's development as a reader. These experiences may be rich or they may be meager. They may be directly related to what is expected in a classroom, or they may have little relationship, as in the case of many "culturally different" children. Their experiences differ from those normally recognized in instructional materials and even instructional methods.

The "world" that the person experiences determines his or her *language development.* Some children experience rich language environments, and others receive limited verbal stimulation. Differences in experiences result in differences in language development—meanings for words themselves, length of sentences uttered, sophistication of sentence structure. Acknowledging the interrelationship of reading with the other language skills, it becomes evident that language development in oral/aural skills has an important influence on the development of reading skills.

Language Differences

A smile or embrace communicates greetings across cultures whereas the word *hello* may not. Shared experiences and associations contribute to the universal understandings of the smile. Lack of shared experiences block communication. This is also true in reading. For reading to be a communication process between author and reader, some basic understandings are necessary. For instance, it is assumed that the writer and reader share a language with similar orthographic, semantic, and syntactic systems (and perhaps the phonologic system). They must also share some life experiences. When this is not the *case,* communication can break down. This is a reason for concern about learners who have different oral/aural language systems from the one predominant in the materials used to teach reading. The child with a linguistic variation may speak a dialect of English or may speak another language as his or her native language.

There is presently insufficient evidence to conclude that dialectal differences actually interfere with learning to read standard English material. (Venezky and Chapman, 1973). Most children who speak dialects of English have been exposed to standard English through radio and television. They are receptive to standard English even though they do not actually use it.

Dialect differences do precipitate indirect interference in the development of reading. Much of the potential interference is of a social nature. Dialects carry status. The dialect of the larger cultural group becomes the standard and the highest-status dialect. Other dialects become nonstandard and have lesser status. This fact, plus lack of understanding that different dialect does not mean deficient language, contributes to potential negative attitudes toward the nonstandard dialect during instruction. In many instances, this is interpreted by the nonstandard speaker as negativism toward himself or herself. Certainly this feeling on the part of the learner is an obstacle to the development of reading skills. For the child to continue his efforts to become a reader, it is important that the interpersonal relationships between the student and teacher be rewarding (Robeck and Wilson, 1974, p. 43).

Some of the negative and stereotypic responses to minority children who speak nonstandard English result from lack of basic understanding of the nature of language and its development in children and the adequacy of different languages or different forms of language to communicate ideas. The following information may clarify some of the most prominent and interfering misconceptions (Carroll, 1973).

1. Different forms of a language are called dialects. Although one form may acquire higher status than others, it is not better than the others.
2. Other dialects are highly structured and are as capable of communicating thought as standard dialect. Speaking a nonstandard dialect is not a sign of deficiency in thought or mental development. Minority children, blacks, Puerto Ricans, Chicanos, Indians, are not victims of underdeveloped language codes.

Teachers must assess their own attitudes and understandings to be certain that they do not have responses that interfere with the learning of children from any racial, cultural, religious, or economic background.

✳ Activities

Complete the following sets of activities. Compare your responses with those of a peer.

1. Read the following sentence.
   The dog jumped on the man's trunk.
2. Now depict that sentence in a sketch.
3. Print the sentence on an index card or blank sheet of paper.
4. Have two peers (other than classmates) read the sentence and draw a picture of what they read. Ask them:

    (a) What kind of dog is it?_____

    (b) What kind of trunk is it?_____

5. Now share your three pictures with a classmate. Compare and contrast what you found with his or her findings.

    (a) What were the similarities?_____

    _____

    _____

    (b) What were the differences?_____

    _____

    _____

6. Using the information in this chapter, explain the phenomenon. _____

    _____

    _____

    _____

Check: Your responses should include these ideas.

The differences occur because of the differences in a person's background of experiences. What he has experienced in the past interacts with information he processes in the present. His understandings of the printed message are dependent on his past associations with the words/concepts for which the print stands.

7. Using the information in this chapter, respond to the following sentence:

    "There is no meaning on a page of print, only in the reader." _____

_____

_____

_____

ADDITIONAL ENABLING ACTIVITIES

1. This is a reading-study activity. Read and take notes on at least one of the following sources for each objective. The objective that relates to the source is listed after the reference. (See Reading Resources/References for complete bibliographic information.)

    (a) Burns and Roe, Chapter 3 (Objective 2); Chapter 1 (Objective 3).
    (b) Dallmann et al., Chapter 3 (Objective 1); Chapters 1-2 (Objective 1)
    (c) Goodman, "Comprehension-Centered Reading," in Ekwall, Chapter 3 (Objective 1).
    (d) Smith, 1978, Chapter 1 (Objective 1); Chapters 2-3 (Objective 2).

2. Attend class session(s) Time _____

    Date _____

    _____

3. An activity selected by your instructor.
4. An activity of your choice.

READING RESOURCES/REFERENCES

1. Burns, Paul C., and Betty D. Roe. *Teaching Reading in Today's Elementary Schools*. Chicago: Rand McNally, 1976.
2. Carroll, John B. "Language and Cognition: Current Perspectives from Linguistics and Psychology," *Language Differences: Do They Interfere?*, James L. Laffey, and Roger Shuy, eds. Newark, Del.: International Reading Association, 1973, pp. 173-188.
3. Dallmann, Martha, Roger L. Rouch, Lynette Y. C. Chang, and John L. DeBoer. *The Teaching of Reading,* 5th ed. New York: Holt, Rinehart, & Winston, 1978.
4. Ekwall, Eldon, ed. *Psychological Factors in the Teaching of Reading*. Columbus, Ohio: Charles E. Merrill, 1973.
5. Gross, Alice Dzen. "Sex-Role Standards and Reading Achievement: A study of an Israeli Kibbutz System," *The Reading Teacher* (November 1978), pp. 149-156.
6. Harris, Albert J., and Edward R. Sipay. *How to Teach Reading: A Competency-Based Program*. New York: Longman, 1979.
7. Laffey, James L., and Roger Shuy, eds. *Language Differences: Do They Interfere?* Newark, Del. International Reading Association, 1973.

8. McDermott, Roy P. "Achieving School Failure: An Anthropological Approach to Illiteracy and Social Stratification," *Theoretical Models and Processes of Reading,* 2nd ed., Harry, Singer and Robert Ruddell, eds. Newark, Del.: International Reading Association, 1976, pp. 389-428.
9. Pflaum-Connor, Susanna. *The Development of Language and Reading In Young Children,* 2nd ed. Columbus, Ohio: Charles E. Merrill, 1978.
10. Robeck, Mildred C., and John A. R. Wilson. *Psychology of Reading: Foundations of Instruction.* New York: Wiley, 1974.
11. Smith, Frank. *Psycholinguistics and Reading.* New York: Holt, Rinehart, & Winston, 1973.
12. Smith, Frank. *Understanding Reading: A Psycholinguistic Analysis of Reading and Learning to Read,* 2nd ed. New York: Holt, Rinehart & Winston, 1978.
13. Spache, George D., and Evelyn B. Spache. *Reading in the Elementary School,* 4th ed. Boston: Allyn and Bacon, 1977.
14. Venezky, Richard L., and Robin I. Chapman. "Is Learning to Read Dialect Bound?", *Language Differences: Do They Interfere?,* James L. Laffey and Roger Shuy, eds. Newark, Del.: International Reading Association, 1973, pp. 62-69.

Section 2
Prereading Experiences

The competencies desired for Section 2 focus on the teacher of students who have not yet begun to read. These competencies reflect the skills necessary for the teacher to help pupils get ready to read with optimum chances for success. As a result of experiences in Section 2, the teacher:

- Knows the characteristics of those pupils who are ready for instruction in reading and those who are not.
- Develops lessons designed to teach reading readiness skills.
- Understands reading readiness in terms of maturational and educational factors.
- Provides experiences that facilitate maturation and otherwise foster readiness for reading.
- Establishes the stimulating and supportive climate in which positive attitudes toward reading flourish (continuous for all sections).
- Demonstrates an ability to provide constructive critiques of self and others (continuous for subsequent sections).

Using the Chapters in Section 2

The chapters in this section are designed to provide knowledge and understanding as well as actual performance competencies. Follow the listed steps to complete the chapters.

1. Read the rationale for an overview of the chapter contents and for an understanding of why it is important for you as a teacher.
2. Read the objectives to find out what you must do to be successful in the chapter.
3. Take the preassessment if you desire. If not, proceed to step 4. If you take the preassessment, use the answer key to score your performance. On items that require a demonstration of teaching competence (Chapter 3), you must schedule a meeting with the instructor and complete the activity.
4. Read the instructional materials for each objective and complete the other activities as directed.
5. Select additional enabling activities that you need as indicated in the preassessment. Use the Reading Resources/References section of the chapter for your independent study. Other activities are included in the suggested teaching activities for Chapter 3. Use these as directed by your instructor.
6. Schedule a meeting with the instructor and take the postassessment. You may choose to retake the preassessment to diagnose your readiness for postassessment.
7. Evaluate your performance with your instructor. Repeat steps 4 to 6 if necessary, or begin work in Section 3.

Chapter 2
Understanding Reading
Readiness

RATIONALE

In the development of each child there is a time when his or her language facility, experience, and social development indicate that the child is ready for beginning reading instruction. But before he may begin reading, the child must be systematically prepared for the meaningful interpretation of printed or written verbal symbols. The purpose of this stage of development—the readiness stage—is to lay a foundation on which reading success can be built.

This readiness, or prereading, period is most important for the child. Everything he is exposed to at this time will greatly affect the extent of future learning. No one factor guarantees readiness to read. A child is ready to begin reading only when he is at least fairly well-adjusted emotionally, has acquired certain attitudes, has profited from some background experiences, and has developed considerable verbal facility in oral communication. Other important influences include physical health and self-concept.

All of these factors, along with certain physical skills such as auditory and visual acuity and left-to-right orientation, help to determine the child's readiness for beginning reading instruction. This chapter will enable you, as a teacher of young children, to identify these factors and skills and to observe their significant relationship to reading readiness.

OBJECTIVES

After completing this chapter, you will be able to:
1. Identify the relationship of the following factors to reading readiness instruction.
   (a) Mental age or intellectual development.
   (b) Physical condition.
   (c) Social and emotional development.
   (d) Experiential background.
2. Identify the skills prerequisite to success in beginning reading.
3. Complete an objective identified by the instructor.

PREASSESSMENT

See Appendix A-2.

See Appendix A-2.

**Instructional
Activity 1**

Factors Associated with Reading Readiness

Reading readiness means the attainment of the level of development that enables a child to learn to read through regular classroom instruction by a competent teacher. In attaining this level of development, many inter-relating factors are involved. However, it is impossible to determine the precise degree to which the child must possess these factors before he or she can be said to be ready to begin formal reading instruction. Children are extremely complex and vary from one another in many ways. Furthermore, a particular child's readiness will depend to some extent on the program of instruction that he encounters in school.

This means that he may be ready to begin learning to read if, for example, the program focuses on whole words instead of sound-symbol associations or uses a language experience approach instead of commercially prepared materials. Readiness for learning to read is partly determined by the approach used to teach reading. Viewed in this context, most children who enter school are ready to begin instruction in reading, provided that the teacher is ready to adjust that instruction so that it is suited to the child's current level of development.

Physical Factors

Readiness for reading is also influenced by the general health status of the child. A child with low general health is likely to be listless, readily fatigued, and to have a greatly shortened attention span. He or she usually does not retain what he learns as well as he would if he were in ordinary good health. Every child should be helped, if necessary, to secure as good health and as high a level of physical efficiency as possible.

Maslow's belief that before any learning can take place, the physiological needs of a child must be met also applies to readiness for learning to read. These needs include rest, shelter, and food. The nutrition of the child should be especially guarded as a factor in physical well-being, because in the early years especially malnutrition causes inefficiency in the organism. The presence of vitamin B in the diet should be assured; a deficiency of vitamin B often results in injury to the nervous system and consequently causes an inferior learning capacity. Since reading is dependent on an efficient nervous system, we can expect that the child with good nutrition will have a better chance to learn to read than one who is malnourished.

Every child should have a complete physical examination before entering school. If difficulties are discovered that cannot be corrected, instructional procedures should be adjusted to the child's needs. To expect a sick or physically handicapped child to take pleasure in learning in the regular classroom situation is unrealistic unless adaptations are made.

Visual Acuity (Vision)   Reading demands that visual stimuli be received for interpretation. It is then quite necessary that the organs for their reception be normal or that adjustments be made before the child is ready to read. Some kind of screening test for visual acuity should be used by the school nurse or other qualified person to detect the pupils who should be referred to a specialist for diagnosis and correction. It is important that the visual screening include vision at both near and far points. Some screening tests (such as the Snellen E) fail to detect problems with near-point vision (ability to see objects at close range) and, therefore, are not useful for screening for reading distance vision. Be certain that the information is useful. Many signs of discomfort that may be symptoms of visual disability may be noticed by the teacher: excessive watering of eyes, squinting, squirming about, tilting the head while reading, holding material too close or too far away from eyes, and complaints of headaches after reading. When symptoms persist, the teacher should recommend a visual examination by a professional.

Auditory Acuity (Hearing)   Because the child first learns to attach meaning to printed symbols through the medium of spoken language, hearing is an important factor in reading readiness. The child needs the ability to perceive and reproduce sounds correctly, the ability to fuse sounds into words, and the ability to sense or perceive the sounds characterized by certain auditory frequencies. For measuring auditory acuity, the watch tick or whisper test may be given to detect severe hearing difficulties. But the most reliable measure can be made by an audiometer.

Certain signs that may indicate that a child may be hard of hearing should be noted by the teacher, who should refer the child for professional testing. Symptoms may include inattentiveness, tilting the head, turning one ear toward the speaker, requests that statements be repeated, and reports of buzzing in the head. Also suspect a hearing loss if the child is noticeably slow to come when called, turns the record player louder than is reasonably necessary, or prefers very loud and noisy toys.

Social-Emotional Factors

In addition to physical factors, a child should possess a certain degree of emotional and social stability before beginning reading instruction. Poor environmental background during the child's early years may make it quite impossible for him or her to meet the new and difficult situations without emotional strain. Difficulty in adjusting to the school situation may cause behavior to take a form that prevents learning to read.

The attitudes that can be seen in a child at the time he begins school must also be considered. It is very important that he shows a positive and accepting attitude toward the school, the teacher, the opportunities to read, and toward himself. A good self-concept is most important. The teacher should provide an atmosphere for children that will lessen criticism, hostility, and ridicule and will stimulate tolerance, encouragement, and acceptance. Most first graders are eager to start reading. However, if they fail to experience success in activities prior to reading or are frustrated in their early reading lessons, they may develop a lasting dislike for reading. Instruction should be arranged so that every child can experience some success from his first reading experiences on.

The background experiences of the child very definitely affect his chances for success in reading. The child who is able to converse well and understand the interchange of thoughts by spoken words has already achieved a state of language development at which most of the words he will meet in beginning readers will be familiar. He will be able to make effective use of past experiences as he derives meaning from the printed page.

Language Factors
Emphasis should be placed on general facility in language as an important requisite for progress in reading. Since one best learns to talk by talking, the development of oral language depends largely on opportunity, stimulation, and encouragement to talk.

Listening to others talk will also help to prepare the child for reading. Conversations heard between adults or other children or the oral reading of a storybook to the child will greatly enrich the experiences associated with printed symbols.

Although most children have sufficient language competence (deep structure) to be ready to read without intensive language training, some lack language performance (surface structure). The teacher should not mistake this for a lack of mental development. Since children learn the language of their home in a pattern that is the same, regardless of the particular language, they accomplish the same learning processes. Even so, when children come to school from homes where English is not the dominant language or where nonstandard English is spoken, they may need special guidance from the teacher. The teacher should be sensitive enough to pupil needs to use materials of instruction that will make learning easier for the children. The teacher should also provide opportunities for the children to expand their aural/oral skills by listening to others, following directions, expressing ideas, and retelling stories or events in logical sequences.

Prereading Concepts
Children need certain concepts about print before they experience success in learning to read. The concepts, as identified by Clay (1977) include the following.

1. Print, not pictures, carries the message.
2. Print carries directional constraints. The print must be read from left to

right (although recognition of the names for the directions is unnecessary) and from top to bottom. The behavior of reading from left to right and top to bottom should be modeled by the teacher as the child develops the concepts.

3. The sequence of print is related to a sequence of spoken words.
4. A word is the pattern of marks, made up of letters.
5. Words must be approached from left to right.
6. Segmentation for words in print is signaled by spaces on the page.

Clay points out that whereas these concepts are learned very quickly by some children, it takes the average child about 6 months to learn the concepts and use them to behave consistently. She suggests that the use of language experience lessons helps children to establish these basic concepts firmly. (See Chapter 15 for further discussion of the language experience approach to teaching reading.)

Another significant element in a child's readiness for reading is interest in reading and desire to read. Of course, this factor is closely related to attitude. The child with a positive attitude toward reading is more likely to be interested in learning to read. This motivation is a powerful force in actually learning to read when other factors are favorable.

Sex of the child also is an aspect of reading readiness. In the United States, girls are more likely to possess a high degree of reading readiness than boys. This is not the case in some other countries. Various theories have been advanced to account for this and for the superior achievement in reading by primary-level girls over boys at the same levels. One (and there is some evidence to support it) is that female teachers' attitudes toward male children create the difference (Dwyer, 1974); other contributing factors are the conforming attitudes of female Americans and the small number of male teachers at primary levels (Johnson, 1973–1974). This results in male children who stereotype reading as feminine and, consequently, do more poorly in reading situations.

❋ Activities

Use the information in this chapter to respond to these situations. Check your responses with those of a peer.

1. Miss Jones has taught first grade for years. She firmly believes that all children should be taught to read as soon as they enter school. She wastes no time with "frills" such as reading to the children or engaging them in discussions. She teaches at least three words on their first day (whether or not they learn them!). The words are *do not talk*.

   (a) What does Miss Jones fail to understand? _____

   _____

   _____

(b) What would you do in this classroom situation? _____

_____

_____

2. Mrs. Mater, an irate mother, demands an answer to this question about her 7-year-old son who is the bully of the first grade. Why is Mike not reading? He says he only gets to do "baby" things at school such as listening to stories, making up stories, or matching stupid shapes. He says that is why he cries every day when I bring him to school. He is an only child, you know, and is alone. He needs to be reading now. What

   explanation would you give? _____

_____

_____

3. Identify at least six factors that contribute to readiness for reading.

   _____   _____

   _____   _____

   _____   _____

4. Every year Current Katie sends home a note to the father or older male sibling of every boy in her kindergarten class. The note says:

   Take time to read to _____ everyday. It is important for him to see you in settings where you read. He needs you to model reading to him.

   Using the information in the chapter, tell why she does this. Tell what

   you think about this practice. _____

_____

_____

   Compare your answers with those of a peer.

5. Mr. Noe Know has a child who frequently says she cannot see the board even though she sits close and squints and holds her book almost on her nose. Mr. Know knows that the child is faking because the health record says that the child has 20/20 vision.

   (a) Did Mr. Know analyze the situation correctly? Why? _____

   _____

   _____

   (b) What does it tell us about reading and about distance reading?____

   _____

   _____

**Instructional
Activity 2**

Skills Prerequisite to Success in Reading

Reading readiness is a composite of many factors—physical, intellectual, environmental, maturational, and educational. But a child can be taught certain skills that will contribute to his or her readiness for reading. These skills include visual discrimination, auditory discrimination, listening comprehension, sequencing, left-to-right orientation, color discrimination, and knowledge of alphabet letters. The importance of giving attention to each will be discussed here.

Visual discrimination refers to the ability to perceive likenesses and differences between visual forms, such as shapes, letters, and words. Some students lack skill in this area and need instruction before formal reading instruction can be successfully undertaken. Some children can be systematically taught to match like shapes and identify unlike ones. For example, the children may be asked to select the letters that are like the key letter in the following sequence.

Visual discrimination ability seems to be a good predictor of success in beginning reading if the method involved relates to teaching words as wholes. Since this method requires the student to attend to the visual clues of first-last letter, letters above-below the line, and overall patterns or outlines (configuration), it makes sense that good visual discrimination ability would contribute to success with such tasks.

Before giving instruction in visual discrimination, the teacher must alert the child to the focus point of his attention. Even though he may be familiar with print from his experiences, he may not know which "things" on the page to attend to. Other visual discrimination skills related to reading include perceptions of up and down and left and right.

Readiness for reading requires not only that the child have a normal sense of hearing (auditory acuity), but that he or she also be able to distinguish readily between the sounds of spoken words. This is *auditory discrimination* ability. Training in auditory discrimination involves producing the sounds of a word as it is pronounced and discriminating the sounds as they occur in the initial, middle, and final parts of the word. Auditory discrimination ability is especially important if the methods of teaching reading focus on sound-symbol correspondencies.

As noted, children who speak nonstandard dialects and those whose first language is not English sometimes do poorly on auditory discrimination tests. This is partially because they are tested with tests that measure differences in pairs of words with minimal differences. In some instances

33

the example words exist for them as homophones (words with the same sounds) when they may be different words in standard English. For example, *him,* and *hem* are pronounced exactly the same way in some dialects. To some Spanish speakers, *ship* and *sheep* sound as the same word. When faced with such circumstances, the teacher may decide to concentrate on the contrasts and teach the discriminating features or to accept the differences and go on with instruction. The first decision seems to cause undue hardship on the child and the teacher. The second decision may be the most sensible since, as soon as the child knows some words and focuses on meaning in print, he will be able to get the correct word from the context. The lack of discriminations makes a difference only when context is ambiguous (Melmed, 1973).

Along with auditory discrimination comes another related skill—*auditory* or *listening comprehension*. This does not involve the distinguishing of sounds, but the understanding of spoken words. Again, the words must have meaning for the child while he is developing the skill of responding to or acting on them. The child must use his memory and thinking abilities in order to comprehend what is said. Following oral directions is one activity that requires proficiency in these areas.

Closely related to the auditory comprehension skills just identified are skills in retelling a story, directions, or other information in a sequence. These also involve skill in remembering, which may be fostered when the teacher helps the children maintain attention in the task of listening to the information supplied.

The left-to-right sequence of perception in reading has to be developed. It may be learned by teaching the child to identify his right and left hands and to grasp the concept of left and right in relation to the sides of objects in the schoolroom, such as the chalkboard, the desks, or a page of a book. This particular skill is not easily taught through incidental learning or games instead of by formal drill. Establishing the habit of moving the eyes from left to right may be facilitated by having the teacher sweep his or her arm in a left-to-right motion when reading things from the board and by drawing attention to writing from left to right on the board and having the child do some writing, making sure that the left-to-right sequence of movement is maintained.

Another skill that can be taught in the reading readiness program is knowledge of the names of the letters of the alphabet. This means that the children learn the name of the letter and match it with the visual form. It should not be confused with learning the alphabet "jingle," which does not necessarily reflect knowledge of letters.

Although there is no research evidence that one must know the alphabet before reading, the practice of teaching the alphabet is grounded in history. It does seem practical that a label for a letter provides a common referent for it. The label may help the child attend to the critical features of *p* that make it what it is and distinguish it from *d* or *b*. In any event, knowledge of the alphabet has been shown to correlate positively with subsequent reading achievement. Knowing the alphabet does not cause achievement in reading, but it still is sensible to teach the letters before the child learns to read. On the other hand, it is not sensible to delay reading instruction until the child masters knowledge of the letters of the alphabet.

❋ Activities

Apply the information you learned in this chapter to respond to these situations. Compare your responses with those of a peer.

1. Ms. Cherie is providing the following lesson for her beginning first-grade children.
   "I'm going to read a story about a rat. You must listen carefully because when I say a word that rhymes with *rat* you must hold up your thumb. Suppose I said, 'He sat in an old chair.' What would you do? Great! You'd hold up your thumb because *sat* rhymes with *rat*."

   (a) What readiness skill is she teaching? _____

   _____

   (b) Do you think this is a good activity? Why? _____

   _____

2. Each child in Mr. Collins' class has a set of cards on which a different letter is written. As he says a letter, the children hold up the appropriate card.

   (a) What skill is he working on? _____

   (b) Do you think this is a good activity? Why? _____

   _____

3. Bonnie is telling a story to her kindergarten children, but she tells only one part at a time. After each part, she asks questions that check the children's understanding.

   (a) What skill is she teaching? _____

   (b) Is this a good activity? Why? _____

   _____

ADDITIONAL ENABLING ACTIVITIES

The activities listed here are designed to help you meet the stated objectives. Each activity includes a notation for the objective to which it relates.

1. This activity is a reading activity for Objective 1. Read and take notes on at least three of the listed sources. Check the Reading Resources/References for the chapter for complete information on the sources.
   (a) Barufaldi.
   (b) Emans.
   (c) Larrick.
   (d) Lundsteen.
   (e) McCormick.
   (f) Nevius
   Also, choose one of the following textbook readings.
   (a) Burns and Roe, "Readiness Concepts and Factors," pp. 75–80.
   (b) Harris, *Effective Teaching of Reading,* pp. 23–36.
   (c) Spache and Spache, "Research on Readiness," pp. 148–166.
2. This is a reading/study activity for Objective 2. Read and take notes on at least three of the listed sources. Check the Reading Resources/References for the chapter for complete information on the sources.
   (a) Evans.
   (b) Montgomery.
   (c) Paradis.
3. Observe a child in a preprimary classroom setting for 1 to 2 weeks. Complete the checklist in Appendix C-1. Work with the child on an individual basis and note the relationship of the checklist factors to his reading readiness ability. Turn in your checklist and observation notes for critique by instructor or a peer (Objective 1).
4. Observe a child in a preschool setting. Use the checklist in Appendix C-2. Work with the child individually to determine her performance in the skills given (Objective 2).
5. Attend class session(s) Time _____ Date _____ .
6. An activity of your choice. _____
7. An activity selected by your instructor.

READING RESOURCES/REFERENCES

1. Barufaldi, James P., and Jennifer Wallenfels Swift. "Children Learning to Read Should Experience Science," *The Reading Teacher* (January 1977), pp. 388–393.
2. Blackhurst, J. Herbert. "The Nature of the Reading Process," *Language Arts* (February 1977), pp. 183–186.
3. Breiling, Annette, "Using Parents as Teaching Partners," *The Reading Teacher* (November 1976), pp. 187–192.
4. Burns, Paul C., and Betty D. Roe. *Teaching Reading in Today's Elementary Schools.* Chicago: Rand McNally, 1976.
5. Clay, Marie M. *Reading: the Patterning of Complex Behavior.* London: Heinemann Educational Books, 1977.

6. Dallmann, Martha, Roger L. Rouch, Lynette Y. C. Chang, and John J. DeBoer. *The Teaching of Reading,* 4th ed. New York: Holt, Rinehart & Winston, 1974.
7. Downing, John, and Peter Oliver. "The Child's Conception of 'a word'." *Reading Research Quarterly, 4* (1973–1974), pp. 568–582.
8. Dwyer, Carol A. "Influence of Children's Sex Role Standards on Reading and Arithmetic Achievement," *Journal of Educational Psychology 66* (December 1974), pp. 811–816.
9. Emans, Robert. "Oral Language and Learning to Read," *Elementary English* (September 1973), pp. 929-934.
10. Engel, Rosalind. "Literature Develops Children's 'I's' for Reading," *Language Arts* (November/December 1976), pp. 892–898.
11. Engmann, Arthur M. "A Look At Early Reading," *The Reading Teacher* (April 1971), pp. 616–620.
12. Evans, James R., and Linda Jones Smith. "Psycholinguistic Skills of Early Readers," *The Reading Teacher* (October 1976), pp. 39–43.
13. Harris, Albert J., and Edward R. Sipay. *Effective Teaching of Reading,* 2nd ed. New York: David McKay, 1971.
14. Harris, Albert J., and Edward R. Sipay. *How to Increase Reading Ability,* 6th ed. New York: David McKay, 1975.
15. Johnson, Dale D. "Sex Differences in Reading Across Cultures," *Reading Research Quarterly, 9* (1973–1974), pp. 67–86.
16. Karlin, Robert. *Teaching Elementary Reading,* 2nd ed. New York: Harcourt Brace Jovanovich, 1975.
17. Laffey, James L., and Roger Shuy, eds. *Language Differences: Do They Interfere?* Newark, Del.: International Reading Association, 1973, pp. 70–85.
18. Larrick, Nancy. "Home Influence on Early Reading," *Today's Education* (November/December 1975), pp. 77–79.
19. Levenson, Dorothy. "Where Do They Belong?", *Teacher* (March 1977), pp. 54–56.
20. Lowes, Ruth. "Do We Teach Reading In the Kindergarten?" *Young Children* (July 1975), pp. 328–331.
21. Lundsteen, Sara W. "On Developmental Relations Between Language-Learning and Reading," *The Elementary School Journal* (January 1977), pp. 192–203.
22. McCormick, Sandra. "Should You Read Aloud to Your Children?", *Language Arts* (February 1977), pp. 139–143.
23. Melmed, Paul Jay. "Black English Phonology: The Question of Reading Interference," *Language Differences: Do They Interfere?* Newark, Del.: International Reading Association, 1973, pp. 70–85.
24. Montgomery, Diane. "Teaching Prereading Skills Through Training in Pattern Recognition," *The Reading Teacher* (March 1977), pp. 616–623.
25. Nevius, John R., Jr. "Teaching for Logical Thinking is a Prereading Activity," *The Reading Teacher* (March 1977), pp. 641–643.

37

26. Paradis, Edward, and Joseph Peterson. "Readiness Training Implications from Research," *The Reading Teacher* (February 1975), pp. 445–448.

27. Pickarts, Evelyn M. "Learning to Read—with a Parental Assist," *Today's Education* (February 1973), p. 31.

28. Pikulski, John J. "Parents Can Aid Reading Growth," *Elementary English* (September 1974), pp. 896–897.

29. Price, Eunice H. "How Thirty-Seven Gifted Children Learned to Read," *The Reading Teacher* (October 1976), pp. 44–48.

30. Roberts, Kathleen Piegdon. "Piaget's Theory of Conservation and Reading Readiness," *The Reading Teacher* (December 1976), pp. 246–250.

31. Rupley, William H. "Reading Readiness Research: Implications for Instructional Practices," *The Reading Teacher* (January 1976), pp. 450–453.

32. Smith, Frank. "Learning to Read by Reading," *Language Arts* (March 1976), pp. 297–299.

33. Spache, George D., and Evelyn B. Spache. *Reading in the Elementary School,* 4th ed. Boston: Allyn and Bacon, 1977.

34. Tinker, Miles A., and Constance M. McCullough. *Teaching Elementary Reading,* 4th ed. Englewood Cliffs, N. J.: Prentice-Hall, 1975.

35. Todd, Charles C., Jr. "Should Reading be Taught at Home?", *The Reading Teacher* (May 1973), pp. 814–816.

36. Tovey, Duane. "Children's Perceptions of Reading," *The Reading Teacher* (March 1976), pp. 536–540.

37. Weiser, Margaret. "Parental Responsibility in the Teaching of Reading," *Young Children* (May 1974), pp. 225–230.

Chapter 3
Teaching Reading Readiness Skills

RATIONALE

With a background knowledge of the factors and skills affecting readiness for reading instruction, the teacher of young children should be able to implement specific plans for developing these skills and, at the same time, attempt to broaden the horizons of limited background experience and lead the child in benefiting from his or her experience.

Readiness instruction should be characterized by its flexibility. Each child is situated at a different position in his or her readiness to read, and the instructor must find out where he is and work with him from there. Planning is needed in preparation for the actual teaching of an activity and in the careful selection of an activity appropriate to the needs of the individual. This chapter gives the student experience in identifying and participating in planned activities designed to develop or reinforce specific readiness skills.

OBJECTIVES

After completing this chapter, you will be able to:
1. Identify at least one procedure for fostering readiness in each related area.
2. Identify the skill to be taught or reinforced by a specified learning activity given a series of readiness activities or settings.
3. Prepare a plan for teaching or reinforcing a given reading readiness skill. The plan must meet given criteria.
4. Implement a plan to teach a given readiness skill in a peer or small group setting.
5. Complete an objective identified by the instructor.

PREASSESSMENT

See Appendix A-3.

**Instructional
Activity 1**

Procedures for Fostering Reading Readiness

There is no conclusive evidence that children should have a reading readiness program in the school before they are taught to read. Many children will be ready when they come. But it is practical to provide for children who lack one or more readiness ingredients while allowing others to begin formal reading instruction.

The teacher may determine the readiness of the individual child for reading instruction in several ways. Some of these, as discussed in Chapter 17, are formal tests, informal tests, and teacher observation. Experienced teachers are competent to assess the child's reading readiness by his or her *performance* behaviors in the classroom. Some of the criterion behaviors that indicate readiness for reading instruction are identified in the checklists in Appendixes C-1 and C-2.

For children who have special weaknesses, there are activities that the teacher can direct to promote readiness in a number of areas. Some of the suggested activities or procedures relate to multiple areas of reading readiness and general readiness for other learning tasks as well.

Intellectual Development

This is hard to work with, and time is needed for mental maturing. Some experiences that involve thinking and reasoning abilities may promote the intellectual development necessary for success in beginning reading instruction. Some activities include:

- Giving a title to a picture that is presented.
- Drawing conclusions, given several pictures leading to a conclusion.
- Making comparisons.
- Matching uppercase and lowercase letters.
- Responding to precise labels and descriptive terms.
- Associating consonant sounds with alphabet letters.
- Knowing own address and phone number.
- Playing games that require thinking and reasoning (e.g., checkers).

If the teacher is doubtful that the child's level of intellectual development is sufficient to enable him to be successful in beginning reading, the teacher should work with the child's general readiness, with little emphasis on reading.

Physical Condition

Motor coordination is important to success in reading and writing. Some classroom activities for developing good muscle coordination include cutting out pictures, pasting, painting, coloring, weaving, construction, copying shapes, working with clay and sand, learning to tie shoes and button buttons, and using manipulative toys such as a pegboard.

Some large motor activities that may improve and maintain physical condition include free play outdoors, running, hopping, skipping, and jumping, and jumping rope, tumbling, climbing monkey bars, throwing and bouncing balls, and using hula hoops.

The teacher may also want to include discussions of foods that provide proper nutrition to alert the children to good eating habits. Activities should vary frequently to include those that require fine motor skills and those that involve gross motor skills.

Social and Emotional Development

The teacher may choose to structure activities that promote social and emotional development while simultaneously structuring reading activities. The child who lacks social/emotional development may progress in this area as a result of the efforts necessary in a beginning reading program. Some classroom activities follow.

- Enjoying stories—the teacher should motivate the child to read by helping stories come to life with puppets, visual aids, and the like.
- Entertaining parents with a program.
- Engaging in dramatic play—puppets—dress-up.
- Playing with other children—social interaction.
- Celebrating child's birthday.
- Accepting opportunities for independence and responsibility, such as special jobs in the classroom.
- Establishing pride in good work.
- Learning respect for adult authority.
- Acquiring some basic personal health habits.
- Sharing with others.

The teacher should provide numerous opportunities for the child to experience success and should reinforce a job well done. In addition, the teacher should give assurance that the child is respected and valued.

Experiential Background

All of the activities in school expand the child's background, but there are some special experiences that the teacher should seek to provide.

- Field trips.
- Opportunities to learn about the child's world by seeing and doing things.
- Discussions about experiences.
- Dictating sentences about observations and experiences (for more suggestions in this area, see Chapter 14).
- Opportunities to dramatize familiar stories or recent experiences.

- Opportunities for free and spontaneous oral expression.
- Encouragement to use new words.
- Activities that help the child recognize concepts of shape (square, round, triangle).
- Opportunities to interpret different emotions in pictures (happy, angry, sad).
- Opportunities to recognize concepts of size (big, little, tall, short).

Interest in Reading

A powerful way to motivate a child to read is to make a task interesting. Teachers who want to spark interest in reading may structure a stimulating classroom environment. Things such as signs and labels around the room and children's names on their own desks are helpful. Teachers use the labels to call the children's attention to the fact that objects have words (names) and that spoken words have a written counterpart. Reading interesting stories to children and providing many easily accessible picture books for children's use are other ways of promoting interesting in reading.

Furthermore, labeling items with the appropriate written word while calling children's attention to it helps to clarify the meaning of some of the terms used in beginning reading instruction such as, word, begins with, letter, and ends with. There is evidence to indicate that many students who are approached with beginning reading tasks fail to understand even the vocabulary used by the teacher as reading is taught (Downing and Oliver, 1973–1974). Also, young children may not know what reading is and what one reads for, further contributing to their confusion during initial reading instruction.

Attitude

All of the experiences that the teacher provides should have as a secondary objective the development of a positive attitude toward reading. The teacher should help each child discover that reading can be a source of pleasure as well as a tool for learning. Most of the previously mentioned activities (reading to children, having them dramatize the stories, etc.) can be helpful in fostering a positive attitude toward reading. In addition to activities *per se,* the teacher should ascertain that the child is successful in reading-related endeavors. Children, as well as adults, tend to like to do the things in which they experience success.

Sex

The teacher might want to provide opportunities for the fathers or other male figures to read stories to the children. This can be done by providing books to be read and audiotaped by fathers or older male siblings. The rationale for such activities is that children will not view reading as a feminine activity.

Activities

Complete the activities and compare your list and other responses with those of a peer.

1. Observe a preschool classroom setting. Make a list of all formal and informal activities that foster readiness. Identify which factor is being affected (optional).

2. Mrs. Bonnie Blue has a boy in her first-grade class who is mentally bright, physically well-developed, has traveled extensively, and gets along well with other children. The problem is that the boy will not become interested in learning to read anything, although his progress in math and other areas is exceptionally good. He says that he needs to know math because he wants to be a carpenter just like his dad.

    (a) What factor(s) seems to be interfering with this boy's learning to

    read? _____

    _____

    (b) What would you suggest that Mrs. Blue do to overcome the problems?

    _____

    _____

3. Terrible Tony is a first grader who is normal in just about every way, but he cannot sit quietly in a group without pinching, jabbing, or otherwise disturbing others. His teacher cannot decide whether or not to take him out of his reading group and delay reading instruction until

    he can display more maturity. What would you suggest? Why? _____

    _____

    _____

Instructional Activity 2

Activities for Teaching or Reinforcing Reading Readiness Skills
Certain skills that contribute to the child's readiness for reading can be taught. These skills have been identified in Chapter 2. The skills include visual discrimination, auditory discrimination, listening comprehension, sequence left-to-right orientation, and knowledge of alphabet letters.

Activities and/or procedures for fostering readiness skills are identified next.

Visual Discrimination
Children who have a weakness in visual discrimination should be given help in this skill. The focus probably should be on letters and their distin-

guishing features. Teachers should call attention to the critical differences, and they may also want to highlight a *different* feature with colors. For example, to teach discrimination between *p* and *b*, the distinctive feature of the *p*, the "stick" below the line, might be highlighted in red for initial presentation and gradually faded away (Ross, 1976).

Although most children already possess the skill of matching objects by shape, teachers may want to provide experiences for those who do not. In such cases, provide activities in sorting objects by shape, matching like pictures on cards, and observing likenesses and differences in pictures or objects. Other activities include:

- Matching like letters on pairs of cards.
- Matching like words on pairs of cards.
- Sorting word cards that begin with the same letter.
- Working simple puzzles.
- Assembling component letters to match a given word.

Visual Memory

Visual memory refers to the ability to retain mental images of words. Some activities to improve this skill include finding other letters that match one presented visually and finding other words that match one presented visually.

Auditory Discrimination

Children who speak divergent language may be wrongly assessed as deficient in auditory discrimination. Because of the phonology (sound system) of some dialects, certain sounds that are distinguished as different in standard English are not different at all in those dialects. Teachers should be aware of this both in assessing and in teaching auditory discrimination skills. This knowledge should influence the choice of example sounds to be presented for discrimination. Caution should be maintained to omit activities that involve the nonstandard speaker in hearing differences that are nonexistent in his or her dialect.

Activities that may help a child sharpen auditory discrimination skills include the following.

- Sorting pictures of objects with names that begin alike.
- Sorting pictures of objects with names that rhyme.
- Listening to pairs of words and giving a signal for same or different, for example, can-can and can-ran.
- Listening to pairs of sounds, such as ă-ă and ă-ĕ, and giving a signal for same or different. (The teacher may either give the children specially coded response cards such as + for same and − for different or ask them to show thumbs up for the same sound and thumbs down for different sounds.)

- Responding to a key word by generating another that has the same beginning or ending sound.

Listening Comprehension

Listening comprehension is closely related to reading comprehension and can be promoted by similar techniques. The teacher can greatly enhance listening comprehension by using this sequence in reading a story to children: (1) establish a set for listening ("Listen to find out . . . ."); (2) stop periodically to ask questions about the story; (3) have the children use the accumulated information from the story to make predictions about what might happen next; (4) use those predictions as a set for listening to the next part of the reading; and (5) repeat the sequence until the story is complete.

Additional activities for listening comprehension include:

- Predicting outcomes from stories read aloud without an ending.
- Recalling details after listening to a story.
- Following oral directions.

Sequencing

- Sequencing a set of pictures in correct order to tell a story.
- Relating events of the school morning/afternoon in the order in which they occur.
- Describing how to make or build something, such as a snowman or Koolaid.

Left-to-Right Orientation

- Arranging scrambled story pictures in sequence from left to right.
- Remembering order of shapes (or letters of alphabet) as arranged from left to right.
- Writing.
- Labeling left and right sides of things in room (chalkboard, bulletin board, etc.).

Knowledge of the Alphabet

- Matching like letters and naming them.
- Choosing letters on printed cards after the letters have been called out.

Instructional Activity 3

Planning for Teaching Reading Readiness Skills

Study the steps involved in preparing a plan for teaching a reading readiness skill as presented here. You may also want to study the "Design for a Successful Lesson" in Appendix E.

Lesson Plan

1. *Statement of the Objective.* The learner will correctly sequence a set of picture cards.
2. *Materials.* Two large sets of teacher-made picture cards (for use by the whole class) and three or four smaller sets (for use by an individual or a small group).
3. *Procedure of the Lesson.*
   (a) *Introduction.* Encourage discussion of things we do each day at home to prepare for school. Elicit several responses from the children. Call their attention to the fact that certain events come before or after others and that, in telling a story, we must tell the events in order.
   (b) Tell a story to the children using four large picture cards such as the following:
      (1) Picture of a banana.
      (2) Picture of banana partially peeled.
      (3) Picture of child taking a bite of banana.
      (4) Picture of partially eaten banana.
   Place the cards in correct order on the chalk tray. Discuss the order of events and why certain events could or could not occur before or after others. Retell the story.
   (c) *Comprehension Check.* Ask questions that lead the children to use correct sequence. "What happened first, . . . next, . . . last?" "What did Rita have to do before she could eat the banana?" "Could she eat it before it was peeled?" Display the picture cards in mixed order. Have the children tell which card should be first, next, and so on. Allow the children to place the cards in correct sequence.
   (d) *Guided Practice.* Display a second set of picture cards in mixed order. Write on the chalkboard, spaced apart, the numbers 1, 2, 3, and 4. Have one child select the correct card to begin the story and place it under the number 1. Continue through the fourth card, allowing a different child to place each card. Have a volunteer tell the story from the cards in the order they are placed. If the cards have not been sequenced correctly, it should be obvious to the group. Allow several different children to tell the story from the cards.
   (e) *Independent Practice.* Let the children work in groups and then alone to sequence small sets of picture cards. If working in pairs, the children can tell the story to each other. Some suggestions for sequenced pictures are filling a glass with milk, building a snowman, and drawing a picture. The cards may be self-checking if picture keys are prepared that show the correct sequence.

A sample teaching episode for visual discrimination is shown next. The teaching procedure follows the steps in a "Design for a Successful Lesson" in Appendix E.

1. *Anticipatory Set.* Hold up two identical cookies and ask, "What do you notice about these cookies?" (Elicit response that they are just alike.)

Then hold up the same two cookies and one of a different flavor and ask, "What do you notice about these cookies?" (Elicit response that one is different from the others. It is still a cookie, but not identical.) say, "Today we will be working with objects that look just alike."

2. *Objective.* You will be able to find things that look just alike. You need to be able to do this to tell one word from another when you learn to read.

3. *Input.* Look at the things I have on the board. Decide which one is just like this.

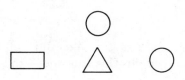

(Point to it) Can it be the first one? Why not?
(Point to it) Can it be the second one? Why not?
(Point to it) Can it be the third one? Why? Right, they look just alike.
Now look at these. Let's decide which are alike.

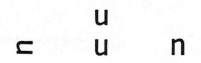

4. *Modeling.* How can I tell which is just like the top letter? Watch as I decide. (Trace the letter with finger and verbalize the direction of the key letter. Then begin the process with the bottom letter.) Can this one match? No. It does look like the key letter. Just as all three cookies were a little alike, these are too. But they are not exactly alike. (Use the same process on the next form and identify it as the same. Use the process on the third letter and reject it as not being the same.)

5. *Check on Comprehension.* Either project sets of letters on an overhead projector or write them on the chalkboard. Give these directions to children: "As I show you a form, if it exactly matches the key form, hold your thumbs up. If not, put your thumbs down." Expose the following series as you observe pupil responses and help child make the necessary corrections.

49

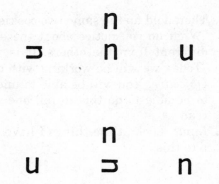

6. *Guided Practice.* You did well on this. Now I want you to do some more as I watch. Use this sheet and draw a line between the two that match.

u

n   n   u

——————————————

n

u   u   n

——————————————

u

ᴐ   u   u

——————————————

n

ᴖ   n   u

——————————————

7. *Independent Practice.* Provide cards for the child to match like forms by joining them with colored yarn.

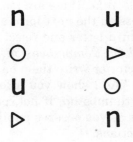

    Choose a reading readiness skill from those identified in Chapter 2. Prepare you own plan for teaching the skill. Utilize the sample lessons provided in this chapter and the "Design for a Successful Lesson" (Appendix E) to assist you in your preparation. The "Criteria for Teaching a Lesson," Checklist C-3 in Appendix C, may also be used.

The following tips for teaching may be helpful in planning your lesson.

1. Know what you are going to do and be well prepared, yet flexible.
2. Plan activities that are challenging and interesting to each child.
3. Give the children time to become familiar with you and you with them.
4. Make allowances for pressures and distractions.
5. Allow the children the opportunity to express their own ideas.
6. Help each child to experience some success.
7. Most important, ENJOY THE CHILDREN.

When reading aloud from a picture book:

1. Gather the children closely around either on low chairs or on the floor.
2. Sit in a low chair or on the floor yourself.
3. Take your time to encourage a relaxed, happy atmosphere.
4. Build some background for the story by relating it to their experiences.
5. Ask questions to be answered by listening or give purposes for listening.
6. When showing pictures, move the book slowly and hold it as close to the children as possible.
7. Try to "tell" the story so that you do not have to keep your eyes on the book all the time.
8. Point out minute deails in the pictures so that the children will look for them when they handle the book later.
9. Stop periodically to ask questions such as, "What do we already know about . . . ?", and "What do you think might happen next? why?"
10. Show them that you are enjoying the story, too.
11. After the book has been completed, ask the children questions about the content and about the parts they enjoyed most. (See Chapter 8 for some model questions at different levels of understanding.)
12. Make the book available for them to handle later.

Instructional Activity 4

Teaching Reading Readiness Skills

Implement a plan for teaching a readiness skill in a peer or small group setting. Refer to the plans for teaching that you prepared in Objective 3 or use instead one of the sample plans for teaching provided in Objective 3. **Suggested Activities:** (1) Observe a preschool classroom setting. Make a list of all formal and informal activities that foster readiness. Identify which skill is being developed for each activity. (2) Refer to the suggested teaching activities for this chapter. Choose one of the reading readiness activities. Prepare the materials and implement the activity with a small group.

SUGGESTED TEACHING ACTIVITIES

The activities presented are designed to provide students with practice in one or more reading readiness skills. You may develop the activities and teach them in a peer or actual classroom setting as suggested by your course instructor.

1. *Skill:* Developing speaking vocabulary.
   Materials: Common objects such as a ball, comb, rock, toy animal, eraser, or crayon and two large paper bags.
   Procedures: The teacher collects common objects, places them in a large paper bag, and then removes one object from the bag and places it in the second bag without the children seeing the object. One child reaches in the bag, feels the object, and describes it in every way he or she can without looking at it. Another child tries to guess what it is. If he is unsuccessful, others try. Then the child takes the object from the bag and shows others. The children discuss what it is called, what they can do with it, and if it is the same color as something else in the room.
   Variation: Items used could belong to some group, such as vegetables, fruits, or toys.
   Number: Whole class.
2. *Skill:* Identifying missing items from a group of observed objects (visual discrimination).
   Materials: Various objects such as chalk, eraser, pencil, or book.
   Procedures: The teacher collects materials beforehand and places them in an orderly manner on a table. The children study the objects, look away as the teacher removes one, and then try to recall the missing object.
   Variation: Allow one child to remove the object and another to identify the missing object.
3. *Skill:* Matching like shapes and shapes of same color (visual discrimination).
   Materials: Construction paper of various colors.
   Procedures: The teacher cuts from construction paper a red circle, a blue circle, a red square, a blue square, a green oval, an orange oval, a green triangle, and an orange triangle. The teacher presents the shapes, one by one, and has the children review names—circle, triangle, oval, and so forth. The teacher holds up the shapes again and has the children name the colors. He or she then asks the children to match the shapes and match the colors.
   Variation: Change the colors and shapes.
   Number: Whole class, small group.
4. *Skills:* Motor coordination, body awareness, oral language development, and remembering sequence.
   Materials: Poem
   Touch your nose.

Touch your shin.
That's the way the fun begins.
Touch your eyes.
Touch your knees.
Now pretend you're going to sneeze. (finger under nose)
Touch your head.
Touch one ear.
Touch your two pink lips right here. (lips together)
Touch your elbows
Where they bend.
And that is where the fun will end.

Procedures: The teacher leads the pupils in saying the poem. (They need not memorize it the first day but should do so with repeated practice.) He or she demonstrates the actions directed in the poem. The teacher repeats the poem and the actions several times as the children follow along.

Number: Whole class or small group

5. *Skill:* Identifying rhyming words (auditory discrimination).

Materials: Pictures of rhyming words mounted on index cards and one index card with an *x*.

Procedures: The teacher puts objects on cards, making rhyming pairs, and assembles and shuffles them. He or she deals three to five cards to each player. The child matches cards with rhyming pairs and says the words. Then he or she draws a card from other child, trying to make rhyming matches. The children put all matched pairs out of play and continue until all possible matches have been made and discarded, leaving one child holding the *x* card (played like Old Maid).

Variation: Play the game like Fish without using the *x* card.

Number: Small group.

Example:

ADDITIONAL ENABLING ACTIVITIES

Select one of the following activities for each objective.

1. This is a reading study activity. Choose at least one reading from the listed textbook sources and at least one of the journal articles from the Reading Resources/References. Read the selections and take notes on activities to promote the reading readiness factors identified in Objective 1.

      (a) Burns and Roe, "Activities to Promote Readiness," pp. 80–107.

      (b) Harris, "Developing Reading Readiness," pp. 45–54.

      (c) Spache and Spache, "Readiness Training," pp. 183–222.

2. Attend class session(s), Time _____ Date _____ .
3. An activity of your choice.
4. An activity selected by your instructor.

READING RESOURCES/REFERENCES

1. Burns, Paul C., and Betty D. Roe. *Teaching Reading in Today's Elementary Schools.* Chicago: Rand McNally, 1976.
2. Dallmann, Martha, Roger L. Rouch, Lynette Y. C. Chang, and John J. DeBoer. *The Teaching of Reading,* 5th ed. New York: Hold, Rinehart & Winston, 1978.
3. Foulke, Patricia. "How Early Should Language Development and Prereading Experiences be Started?", *Elementary English* (February 1974), pp. 310–315.
4. Harris, Albert J., and Edward R. Sipay. *Effective Teaching of Reading,* 2nd ed. New York: David McKay, 1971.
5. Hood, Joyce. "Sight Words Are Not Going Out of Style," *The Reading Teacher* (January 1977), pp. 379–382.
6. Kales, Eva, and Sharon Nizolek. "Growing with Words," *Childhood Education* (March 1973), pp. 311–315.
7. Karlin, Robert. *Teaching Elementary Reading.* New York: Harcourt, Brace, Jovanovich, 1971.
8. Kerber, James E. "The Tasks of Teaching Reading," *Language Arts* (April 1976), pp. 414–415.
9. McDonald, Dorothy. "Music and Reading Readiness," *Language Arts* (September 1975), pp. 872–876.
10. Robison, Helen F., and Sydney L. Schwartz. *Learning at an Early Age,* Vol. 2. New York: Appleton-Century-Crofts, 1972.
11. Ross, Ramon Royal. "Frannie and Frank and the Flannelboard," *The Reading Teacher* (October 1973), pp. 43–47.
12. Ross, Alan O. *Psychological Aspects of Learning Disabilities and Reading Disorders.* New York: McGraw-Hill, 1976.
13. Spache, George D., and Evelyn B. Spache. *Reading in the Elementary School.* Boston: Allyn and Bacon, 1977.
14. Valmont, William J. "Creating Visual Activities to Enhance Predictive Behaviors," *Language Arts* (February 1977), pp. 172–175.
15. Weiser, Margaret. "Awareness—One Key to Reading Readiness," *Young Children* (September 1970), pp. 340–344.

Section 3

Basic Reading Skills: Word Recognition

This section is concerned with developing competencies necessary for teachers who work with children at the beginning stages of reading development. The teacher:

- Knows the characteristics of different facets of word recognition skills.
- Can develop lessons that teach these skills.
- Uses inductive teaching sequences to meet given objectives.
- Evaluates his or her own teaching effectiveness and that of peers.

Using the Chapters in Section 3

The chapters in this section deal with knowledge, understanding, and application skills. Follow the listed steps to complete the chapters.

1. Read the rationale for an understanding of the importance of the chapter content for teachers.
2. Read the objectives to determine what is expected for satisfactory completion of the chapter.
3. Take the preassessment if you think you have sufficient background to be successful. If not, begin work at step 4. If you take the preassessment, score it and pursue the indicated learning activities.
4. Read the information for each objective and pursue the activities as directed.
5. Select from the additional enabling activities those that will strengthen the areas of noted weaknesses. Use the Reading Resources/References and supplementary study as directed by your course instructor and your own needs. The chapters that relate to teaching methods include suggested teaching activities. Use these as suggested by your course instructor.
6. Schedule a meeting with the course instructor and take the postassessment. The preassessment may be used to diagnose your readiness for this step.
7. Meet with the course instructor to evaluate your performance. If your progress is satisfactory, begin work in Section 4. If not, pursue steps 4 to 6 again.

Chapter 4
Identifying Word Recognition Skills

RATIONALE

Word recognition refers to the skills the reader applies as he or she develops a correspondence between the written word and its spoken counterpart. The skills include sight recognition, use of context clues, identifying the unknown word by analyzing its structure, analyzing sound-symbol relationships (phonics), and consulting a dictionary.

Reading involves many skills other than word recognition, but the learner starts with words because they are the visual units that make up the message that must be understood. Word recognition skills are thought of first when reading skills are discussed. Growth in the ability to recognize words in print is the most *basic* skill in learning how to read.

Word recognition includes the identification of words that a reader already knows by sight and also the reader's ability to "attack," "unlock," or "decode" unfamiliar words. Children must learn to apply the appropriate word recognition skills when they are needed. They must realize that a number of different word recognition skills can be used to help them arrive at a conclusion about the word.

This chapter will help the student identify the word recognition skills so he or she might understand the theory and background behind teaching them. The student will also discover the advantages, disadvantages, and appropriate times to apply the various skills to unknown words.

OBJECTIVES

After completing this chapter, you will be able to:
1. Identify at least five broad categories of word recognition skills.
2. Identify at least two meanings of the term *sight words*.
3. Identify at least two sources of sight words.
4. Identify the types of context clues.
5. Identify the elements (subskills) involved in structural analysis.

6. Identify the subskills involved in the use of the dictionary.
7. Complete an objective identified by the instructor.

PREASSESSMENT

See Appendix A-4.

Instructional Activity 1

Categories of Word Recognition Skills

You already know word recognition techniques and use them as you read. The following exercise will help you learn to identify and label various word recognition skills. Answer the questions presented and read the explanatory information.

DIRECTIONS.   Read each item and respond as indicated.

1. Read the word in the box.

> look

If you responded accurately and immediately, which word recognition skill did you use? _____

You have used sight words (i.e., whole words recognized immediately on sight) without having to analyze the word elements. Sight words may be recognized by the distinctive shape, or configuration, of the word. They may be functional words used repeatedly. They may be frequently used words that are not spelled as they sound. Children learn to recognize them as whole words instead of attempting to sound them out.

2. (a) Read the sentence in the box.

> The soft bark came from a little brown *puppy*.

Assume that the italicized word is unknown to you in printed form. If there was a picture of a puppy next to the sentence, it would help you to identify the word. You might use known words in the sentence as clues. You would be using context clues. You would be able to supply the correct word (puppy) even if you had not seen it in print before by associating it with the *meaning* of the known words in the sentence—bark, little, brown. The word puppy fits into the context of the sentence.
(b) Read the sentence in the box.

> The owner of the *games* was *unknown*.

Assume that you are seeing the italicized words for the first time in printed form. You know the root words *game* and *known*. You correctly identify the words with the use of some structural analysis skills. You used the structure, or parts of the word such as its root, prefixes, and/or suffixes, to derive word meaning.

The following learning experience will allow you to see how the various word recognition skills can be applied practically in a reading situation. Read the following sentence:

Mendicant friars were collecting money for charity.

Try to pronounce and think of a synonym for the italicized word in this sentence. (Assume this is not a sight word. You do not recognize it immediately.)

1. (a) What meaning did you derive for the word "mendicant?"

_____

(b) Did you arrive at this meaning by using the known words in the

sentence? _____

(c) If so, you have used a form of _____
clues. These clues are very helpful in deriving meaning in this particular situation.

2. (a) If you were able to get meaning from context clues, your next step may have been to look at the *structure* of the word to find familiar parts.

(b) Parts such as root words, prefixes, and/or suffixes are often helpful in deriving word meaning. In using word parts to derive meaning,

you are using _____
skills. Perhaps the word parts were not as helpful to you in this particular reading situation as they may be in others.

The child might often be in a similar situation, since *all* the word recognition skills will not apply in each instance.

> Knowing the various word recognition skills will enable the learner to have *more than one* resource to draw on and apply when reading independently. He or she will learn to attempt to use the different skills and use those that apply. He will become *flexible* in the use of word recognition skills.

3. (a) Did you pronounce the italicized word (men' di kənt)?

    (b) If so, you probably applied *phonics* skills. (Phonics is included as one of the five broad categories of word recognition skills. Phonics skills are presented in detail in Chapters 6 and 7 but are mentioned here because they can be applied in pronouncing the word.)

4. (a) If you were still unable to derive meaning from the sentence, what skills would enable you to pronounce and find the meaning of the word?

5. (a) Locate in the dictionary the word in the box.

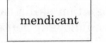

mendicant

    (b) What skills enabled you to locate a word?

    (c) What skills helped you to pronounce the word?

    (d) Could you use the precise meaning of the word in a sentence?

    (e) What skills helped you do this?

The use of alphabetical order and guide words has enabled you to _____ the word. You may have used diacritical markings, the pronunciation guide, syllabication, and accent in _____ the word. You had to _____ in order to use the precise meaning of the word in a sentence.

The major skills involved in the use of the dictionary are *locating the word, pronouncing the word,* and *selecting the appropriate meaning.*

> You have made use of various word recognition skills to help you derive meaning from the sentence. The child will become an *independent* reader by learning to make use of the appropriate word recognition skills as needed, in the same way that you have just done.

The steps for applying word recognition skills to an unfamiliar written word include using the *context* to get clues from surrounding words, using structural analysis skills to identify known elements of the word, using phonics to get the oral counterpart for the written word, and using the dictionary if the other skills fail.

This order is often used by the independent reader in applying skills to unknown words. Words *already known* and recognized in a split second are referred to as sight words.

Instructional Activity 2

Meanings of the Term *Sight Words*

The term *sight words* refers to all the words a reader can recognize immediately on sight. The configuration or shape of words, their length, and features such as ascending and descending letters are clues that children can use in building a sight vocabulary. Look at these two words. Decide which might be easier for the child to learn.

was   elephant

Examine the words again.

was	elephant	was

Did you change your mind? Why? A word such as "elephant" has a distinctive appearance that makes it easy to recognize. Words very similar in size and shape such as "was" and "saw" may be difficult for beginning readers to recognize.

The first sight words introduced should be meaningful, functional words. A child's name should be one of the first sight words he or she learns. Days of the week, months of the year, and names of school subjects are examples of useful sight words.

Many of the most frequently used words in English are irregularly spelled words—those not spelled the way they sound. Some examples are "of", "through", "two", and "know". Instead of trying to sound them out, children must learn to recognize them as whole words.

A potential sight word may be initially identified for the learner. A teacher may show the printed word as he or she points to it and pronounces it. The children then "look-and-say" the word.

Sight words are the words that are recognized by the child on sight as whole words, possibly because of their configuration or repeated use. Sight words include selected words that appear frequently in basal readers and are often categorized in lists. They need to become part of the child's sight vocabulary as they are useful, functional words and are often spelled irregularly.

The term *sight words* could then refer to specific words in sight word lists or all of the words recognized on sight whether or not they are part of selected word lists.

 Activities:

After you have read the preceding material, respond to the questions. Compare your responses with those of a peer.

1. Name at least two meanings of the term sight words.

    (a) _____

    (b) _____

    Your answer may have included (a) the words recognized immediately on sight, possibly by the shape (configuration) of the word or other distinctive features that allow the child to recognize the whole word, (b) those functional words used repeatedly, (c) look-say words or whole words, and (d) words from basal lists or sight word lists.

2. Give a specific meaning of the term sight words that will answer the questions.

    (a) Sally remembers that l-o-o-k is "look" because the two o's remind her of eyes. Which meaning of sight words is this? _____

    (b) The teacher has labeled the children's desks with their names. Which meaning of sight words is this? _____

    (c) The teacher is holding up a card with the word "come" printed on it. She identifies the word for the children. Which meaning is this? ___

    _____

Instructional Activity 3

Sources of Sight Words

Authors of reading textbooks have attempted to choose words that are a part of the understanding and speaking vocabulary of the child for inclusion in the basal readers for the primary grades. Since it has not been possible to include the many dialects and linguistic variations used in different parts of the country, an effort has been made to find a common denominator (Dallmann, 1978).

Authors of reading textbooks have generally felt that it is unwise to try to teach beginning readers to read unfamiliar words when there are several thousand words in their understanding vocabulary that they cannot recognize in print. It is later on in the primary grades that most authors of basal texts try to introduce words that will extend the child's understanding vocabulary. In an attempt to provide the child with a vocabulary with which to begin reading, the authors of reading series base their vocabulary selections in part on carefully compiled lists of words, some based on frequency of occurrence in language, others based on sound-symbol correspondencies.

A Reading Vocabulary for the Primary Grades by Authur I. Gates offers one of the lists widely used by authors of textbooks for grades one to three. It provides 1811 words frequently used in primary-grade reading materials. Gates based his list partly on studies done by Edward L. Thorndike and Irving Lorge. (In the studies, words were selected from a variety of sources of reading material—for adults and children—placed in groups by frequency of use.)

A Basic-Sight Vocabulary by E. W. Dolch is also often used. Dolch included 220 words (excluding nouns) used with the greatest frequency in primary-grade reading books. Dolch also has a separate list of 95 nouns commonly used in the lower grades in basal readers. According to Dolch, approximately two-thirds of the words in primary reading materials are among the 220 words of his list. Also, a large percentage of words in the intermediate readers examined in his study are on the list. Dale D. Johnson used 220 words from the Kučera-Francis word list and provides statistical evidence that these words are used more commonly by children in the lower primary grades today than those on the Dolch Basic Sight Word List. (See Appendix D-1.)

The Harris-Jacobson Core List was compiled after a check on the vocabulary in books for the first six grades of 16 basal reading series widely used in 1970.

Some additional sources of word lists are *The American Heritage Word Frequency Book,* and Otto and Chester's *Great Atlantic and Pacific Sight Word List.* Other sources of word lists are available. (See Lowe, 1974; Gates, 1935; and Hillerich, 1974 if additional information is desired.)

Activities

Complete the following activities. Compare your responses with those of a peer. You will need basal readers on the primary level to complete these activities. Select basal readers from three different publishers.

1. Write in the names of the readers here.
   (a) (Title) _____

   (Publisher) _____

   (b) (Title) _____

   (Publisher) _____

   (c) (Title) _____

   (Publisher) _____

2. Consult the vocabulary listings in the teacher's editions to determine at what level each of the sight words listed here is introduced.

WORD	BASAL 1 LEVEL	BASAL 2 LEVEL	BASAL 3 LEVEL
to			
with			
the			
has			

You may have found that the sight words included in the basal vocabularies are introduced at the same or near the same level. The appearance of the same words in the various basal readers seems to indicate that they are useful words for the child to learn. The teacher is justified in teaching the words as sight words.

3. Compare the word lists from the primary level basal readers with the Kučera-Francis word list in Appendix D-2. List the words from the reader that are not included in the Kučera-Francis list. _____

_____

_____

Do the words you have listed have anything in common? If so, what?

_____

_____

_____

You may have found that many of the words not included in the word list are proper nouns or special vocabulary words. They were needed to understand a particular story but not necessarily intended to be reused immediately or recognized as sight words.

4. Read a page or selection from the following sources:
A magazine (Example: *Reader's Digest, Good Housekeeping, Redbook*)
(Write in the name of the magazine you select.)

_____

A newspaper editorial: _____
(Title of Editorial)

A paperback novel or bestseller: _____
(Title)

(a) List some of the words that are found in common in *all* three sources.

_____

_____

_____

_____

Are any of these included in the Kučera-Francis word list? Check off those on your list that are also on the Kučera-Francis word list.

(b) What does this lead you to think about the use of word lists in primary level teaching? _____

_____

You have found that the words included at the primary level become functional words at all stages of reading. Your findings would seem to justify the teaching of a certain set or core of words as the child's sight word vocabulary.

Instructional Activity 4

Context Clues

The following information will help you label and understand the use of the different types of context clues. You are given practice in using context clues along with information on how to use the skill with the child in the learning situation.

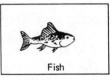

Fish

1. *Picture Clues (Visual Context)*.
   Look at the information in the preceding box.

   (a) What is in the picture? _____
       If the child was asked the same question, he or she might readily reply, "fish." However, he might respond with the word "goldfish" instead.
   (b) If he responds with "goldfish," what could you, the teacher, have him

       do next? _____

   You could ask the child to look carefully at the beginning of the word. He might then correctly respond "fish." In this way, the child will learn to use picture clues along with clues in the printed word.

   > The teacher should encourage the use of picture clues *along with* the clues present in the printed word.

   Picture clues may be useful in the first stages of reading but should not be relied upon too heavily as reading skills continue to develop. This is so the child will learn to develop word analysis skills.

Picture clues become less and less useful to the child as he advances to more difficult material. (Burns and Roe, 165).

2. *Verbal Context (Semantic or Meaning and Syntactic or Sentence Structure Clues).*

(a) In the act of reading, unfamiliar words are identified with the help of known words used in the same context (sentence or group of sentences) (Durkin, 1974). Read the following information and answer the questions.

Suppose the word *scissors* is at first unfamiliar to the child in printed form. He may meet the word in the reading situation.

> The paper chains were cut with a new pair of scissors.

In reading this sentence, the child will usually be able to identify the word *scissors* by using information from the known words. The meaning of the known words (paper chains, cut, pair of) may have caused the child to expect the new word to be *scissors*.

The use of known meanings and other clues (to be discussed in part b) often results in the identification of unknown words.

In the previous example, we can say that the unknown word was identified by using *semantic cues*. Read the following passage. Words have been omitted in order to emphasize the importance of semantic cues.

"Little xxx, little xxx, let me come in," said the xxxx. "Not by the xxxx of my xxxxxx xxxx xxxx," said the xxxx. "Then I'll xxxx and I'll xxxx and I'll blow your house in!" yelled the xxxx.

Were you able to supply the missing words? How? _____

_____

_____

_____

You may have found that the *use of the known words* in the sentence assisted you in supplying meaningful words in place of the x's—the unknowns. Perhaps the lengths of the unknown words also provided useful clues. Background experiences were probably helpful to you in this particular selection, since you are likely to have heard it before. (It is in your listening-speaking vocabulary.)

Meaning clues are therefore very useful in word recognition. The teacher must note the importance of helping children learn that what they read should make sense (Durkin, 1974).

(b) Read the following sentence. Supply a word for the blank.

The sn＿＿ is a creature that often goes unnoticed in the garden.

By using semantics (meaning clues) alone, the answer is ambiguous (snail? snake?).

The *snail* is a creature that often goes unnoticed in the garden.

What other clues besides semantics can be applied in identifying

the italicizied word? ＿＿＿＿＿＿＿＿＿＿＿＿＿＿＿＿＿＿＿

＿＿＿＿＿＿＿＿＿＿＿＿＿＿＿＿＿＿＿＿＿＿＿＿＿＿＿＿＿＿＿

Letter-sound relationship cues (clues present in the word itself—also called phonological clues) are often applied along with semantics in the same way that they were applied with the picture clues (See Part 1).

More information from the sentence is that the underlined word must be a *thing,* not an action or description. This information is also used by the child in identifying the word. This is so even though the child may not be aware that he is using the information. He is using *syntactic cues,* another type of verbal context clue.

> The child will often use semantic, phonological, and syntactic cues in identifying words through verbal context.

3. *Reinforcement.* You will need two student copies of basal readers. One of the readers should be on the first or second reading level. The other reader should be on the fourth or fifth reading level.

(a) Choose and read 6 to 10 pages of the lower-level basal reader. Observe the information present in the pictures of the pages. Many of the words in the reading may be identified with the help of pictures. This allows the child to make use of *picture clues* (visual context). List some of the words in the text that the child might identify with

help from the information in the picture. ＿＿＿＿＿＿＿＿＿＿＿

＿＿＿＿＿＿＿＿＿＿＿＿＿＿＿＿＿＿＿＿＿＿＿＿＿＿＿＿＿＿＿

＿＿＿＿＿＿＿＿＿＿＿＿＿＿＿＿＿＿＿＿＿＿＿＿＿＿＿＿＿＿＿

> The information gained from pictures in identifying words is known as picture clues or visual context clues.

(b) Read three to four pages of the fourth- or fifth-level text.

(1) Can picture clues be relied on to identify *any* of the words in the

reading that may be unknown to the child? _____

(2) Can the child rely solely on picture clues for the identification of all of the unknown words?

_____

(3) What other clues are available in the text that may help the student identify the unknown words?

_____

_____

You may have found that a word can often be identified by its context and the way it is used in a sentence. For example, assume that the italicized word is unknown to the child.

The small brown cub returned to its home in the *forest.*

The child may realize that *forest* makes sense in the sentence. He is using *semantic cues* (meaning clues). He also knows from the sentence order that the word is a thing. It cannot be a descriptive word, action word, or another part of speech. He is using *syntactic cues.* The child can combine semantic and syntactic cues with the sounds known in the word (phonological cues).

> Semantic and syntactic cues are types of *verbal context* clues.

(c) Note that in the lower-level reader, picture clues are more heavily relied on for helping in word identification than in the higher-level text.

> The beginning reader makes extensive use of picture clues, but the child must learn to make use of verbal context (semantic and syntactic cues) in order to become an independent reader.

Instructional Activity 5

Subskills of Structural Analysis

The narratives and exercises in this activity will help you become aware of the elements (subskills) involved in structural analysis.

Structural analysis skills allow the child to decode unknown words by using units larger than single letters (Durkin, 1974; Burns and Roe, 1976).

1. *Inflectional Endings.* The words *steward(s)* and *steward(ess)* are variants of the noun *steward. Steward* is the root.

   A word variant is a word that deviates from the root according to the case, number, and gender of nouns; tense, voice, and mood of verbs; and comparison of adjectives and adverbs (Dallmann et al., 1978).

   Endings added to a root to make variants are called *inflectional endings.* The variant form of a word can then be called the inflected form.

   (a) The circled endings of the preceding words are called _____ .

   (b) The words *talks, talked,* and *talking* are variants of the verb _____ .
   (c) The _____ of the adjective *great* are *greater* and *greatest.*

   (d) What are the inflectional endings? _____
   Some common inflectional endings are *s, es, ing, ed, er,* and *est.*

2. *Prefixes, Suffixes, and Roots.* Word *derivates* (derived forms) are words formed by adding prefixes and/or suffixes to roots (bases) (Dallmann et al., 1978).

   Some derived forms of the root *comfort* are *comfor(table)* and *(uncom-fortable).*

   Affixes are sequences of letters added to roots to change their meanings and/or parts of speech (Burns and Roe, 1976).

   (a) The circled letters on the derived forms of the word *comfort* are called

   _____ .

   (b) *Prefixes* are affixes added at the beginning of a word. *Suffixes* are affixes added at the end of a word.

   (c) The word *uncomfortable* has both a _____ and a _____ .

   (d) The affix _____ is a suffix because it is added at the end of the word *uncomfortable.*

   (e) The affix _____ is a prefix because it is added at the beginning of a word.
   Affixes are very useful to the child in decoding word meaning when he is familiar with the root. (Refer to Burns and Roe, *Teaching Reading in Today's Elementary Schools* p. 154, for a table of useful affixes and their meanings.)

3. *Compound Words.* Compound words are two (sometimes three) words joined together to form a new word. The pronunciation and meaning of the individual words are usually carried over to the compound word. Identifying a word as a compound word will help the child to quickly decode it.

   Match the words in list 1 with those in list 2 to form compound words. Write the new words in the blanks at the right.

List 1	List 2	Compound
every	ground	(everywhere)
sun	room	
play	where	
bed	tan	

Burns and Roe, pp. 160–161

4. *Contractions*. Contractions are two words written in shortened form to make one word. They are indicated by the use of apostrophes within the contraction. The apostrophe in a contraction shows that letters are omitted.

Two words—can not

Contraction—can't

The apostrophes represent the omitted letters *n o* in the contraction *can't*.

Match the contraction in list 1 with the correct meaning in list 2.

List 1	List 2
don't	will not
can't	I am
won't	can not
I've	I have
I'm	do not

Can you list other contractions and the words they represent? Write them here.

Contraction	Words represented

Check the correct spelling of the contraction in a dictionary. Were your apostrophes in the correct places?

5. Review the elements presented in parts 1 to 4. These are the subskills involved in structural analysis. List the five elements.

Reinforcement Activity

Structural analysis skills "enable the child to decode unfamiliar words" by using units larger than single letters. Structural analysis skills are often used together with phonics skills (Burns and Roe, 1976). (Phonics and related skills are presented in Chapter 6.) Children must learn to apply structural analysis skills in order to become independent readers.

There are many important elements (subskills) involved in structural analysis. The following activities and explanations will help you to become aware of the subskills of structural analysis.

1. Read the following story.

The family of *Rabbits* was *unhappy* and *discouraged*. The Joseph family had already moved out of the big yellow house. There would be no one to plant the summer garden! Why *couldn't someone* like the farmer at Hobson Hill be *moving* in?

Unknown to Father Rabbit, a deal was *being* made that very moment. Farmer Pedro *needed* a *bigger* house for his *growing* family. Several *weekends* ago, the Pedro *boys* had *started* plants from seed and *placed* them on their *bedroom windowsill*. They were ready to start *planting* that very week!

2. Words italicized in this story can be categorized in the table that follows. You may not be familiar with all of the terms heading the columns. Examples have been filled in using words other than those italicized in the story. Study the words under each column. Try to determine the unique characteristics of the word that place it in the column. Arrange all of the italicized words in the story in the appropriate column. (Some words may fit more than one column.)

Elements of Structural Analysis

Inflectional Endings (used in word varients)	Compound Words	Contractions	Prefixes (used in word derivatives)	Suffixes (used in word derivatives)	Roots (list the root of the words in all the other columns except contractions and compounds)
toys	beehive	won't	regain	comfortable	toy
managed	_____	_____	_____		manage
reading	_____		_____		read
smaller	_____				small
_____	_____				gain

Elements of Structural Analysis (continued)

Inflectional Endings (used in word varients)	Compound Words	Contractions	Prefixes (used in word derivatives)	Suffixes (used in word derivatives)	Roots (list the root of the words in all the other columns except contractions and compounds)
_____					comfort
_____					_____
_____					_____
_____					_____
_____					_____
_____					_____
_____					_____
_____					_____

Instructional Activity 6

Subskills for the Use of the Dictionary

Because of the complexity of the skills to be learned in using the dictionary, the teacher should have a clear understanding of the subskills that should be taught (Dallmann, et al., 1978).

In order to use the dictionary, you must be able to *locate* the word, *pronounce* the word, and *select the appropriate meaning* of the word. What subskills will enable you to accomplish these tasks? The following sequence will help you obtain a clearer understanding of the subskills involved in the use of the dictionary. You will need a copy of a dictionary to complete the exercise.

1. In order to use a dictionary efficiently, you must know *alphabetical order*. Use of the *guide words* at the top of a dictionary page helps you find the word quickly. Next, you must be familiar with the *pronunciation guide* and the *diacritical markings,* which allow you to correctly say the word.
   (a) Look at the pronunciation key and diacritical markings used in a dictionary. Use them to help you correctly pronounce the words represented by the phonetic respellings given here.

Phonetic Respelling	Word
əb-'sȯr-ban(t)s	_____
'käm-paund	_____
'strək-chər	_____
'pōz	_____

(b) Skill in using the pronunciation guide is an important part of using the dictionary. Selecting the appropriate meaning of a word in the dictionary is another task which the child must become skilled in. Write your own definition for the word "hand."

_____

_____

(c) Read the sentences that follow and check the one that illustrates the meaning of the word "hand" as you have defined it.

_____ Hand me that newspaper.

_____ The audience gave the pianist a big hand.

_____ Give me a hand with this suitcase.

_____ We didn't get any allspice because the store manager said he had none on hand today.

(d) Was your meaning used in one of the sentences? You can see that there are several meanings for the word. What does this mean for the child using the dictionary?

_____

_____

_____

The reader must be able to select the appropriate meaning of a word from all of those given in the dictionary. He or she chooses the one that fits a given context.

2. Locate the word "ethereal" in a dictionary.

(a) What skills enabled you to locate it quickly? _____

_____

_____

(b) What skills helped you to pronounce the word? _____

_____

(c) How would you go about selecting the meaning for the word used in a particular sentence? Look at the dictionary again to be sure you have answered correctly. _____

_____

(d) How are the words arranged on the page? _____

_____

(e) What are the two words at the top of the page called? _____

_____

Of course, the words are arranged *alphabetically*. The words in bold print at the top of the page are the *guide words,* since they guide or assist you in quickly locating the word.

(f) What helps you to pronounce the words? _____

_____

The *pronunciation guide* and the *diacritical markings* assist you in correctly sounding words.

(g) What helps you to arrive at the meaning? _____

_____

The word is usually followed by its pronunciation, then the meaning or various meanings of the word are given. Synonyms of the word might be given. The *specific meaning* of the word is often demonstrated in a sample sentence following the definition. In this way, you use the *context* of the known words in the sentence to help you understand the meaning of the new or unknown word. Pictures or diagrams often accompany the text to provide further understanding of the meaning.

You can see that there are several subskills involved in using the dictionary. The child must have a clear understanding of each subskill in order to become independent in reading.

ADDITIONAL ENABLING ACTIVITIES

1. This is a reading-study activity. See p. 76 for a reading-study guide.
2. Read and take notes on at least three of the following sources for supplementary information on Objective 2. (See Reading Resources/References for complete information.)
   (a) Burns and Roe, pp. 128–129.
   (b) Dallmann, pp. 139–141.

(c) Durkin, pp. 190.

(d) Heilman, pp. 226–231.

(e) Spache, p. 415.

(f) Tinker, p. 154.

Read to identify two meanings of the term *sight words*.

3. For supplementary work on Objective 3, select a minimum of two readings from the sources listed. (Check the list of Reading Resources/References for complete information on the books.) Read to identify at least two sources of sight words. Take notes on the readings.

(a) Burns and Roe, pp. 134–135.

(b) Dallmann, pp. 163-168.

(c) Dolch, pp. 373–374.

(d) Durkin, p. 197.

(e) Groff, pp. 572–578.

(f) Harris and Sipay, p. 278.

(g) Hillerich, pp. 353–360.

(h) Hood, pp. 379–382.

(i) Johnson, pp. 449–457.

(j) Lowe, pp. 40–44.

(k) Otto, pp. 54–57.

4. Read and take notes on two of the sources listed for supplementary work on Objective 4. Read to identify the types of context clues. Be able to identify the different terms used in the texts to refer to the same context clues.

(a) Dallman, pp. 142–144.

(b) Burns and Roe, pp. 164–170.

(c) Tinker and McCullough, pp. 169–175.

5. Read and take notes on at least one of the following sources for supplementary information for Objective 6.

(a) Burns, pp. 170–178.

(b) Dallmann, pp. 292–296.

(c) Dechant, pp. 394–395.

(d) Heilman, pp. 499–501.

(e) Spache, pp. 426–427.

(f) Zintz, pp. 260–262.

6. Attend class session(s), Time _____ Date _____

7. An activity of your choice. _____

_____

_____

8. An activity selected by your instructor. _____

_____

_____

Reading-Study Guide for Enabling Activity 1 (Optional)

Read and take notes on at least one of the following resources.

1. Read Dallmann's text, *The Teaching of Reading,* pp. 131–168, to identify at least four broad categories of word recognition skills and to obtain an overview of the skills. To identify the fifth category, read pp. 291–298. [*Alternate* readings that provide the same information are: (a) Burns and Roe, Chapter 5, pp. 127–186; (b) Smith, Chapter 7, pp. 138–184; (c) Spache and Spache, Chapter 11, pp. 361–406.]

2. List the five broad categories of word recognition skills.

   (a) _____

   (b) _____

   (c) _____

   (d) _____

   (e) _____

3. Complete if you have read Dallmann. You may need to refer to the reading in Dallmann again to answer these questions.

   (a) Briefly explain the justification for teaching words as wholes. _____
   _____
   _____

   (b) What is an obvious advantage claimed for the whole-word method?
   _____
   _____
   _____

   (c) Explain briefly why it is necessary for a child to have an adequate background of experiences for success in the use of context clues.
   _____
   _____
   _____

   (d) Briefly tell how structural analysis differs basically from phonic analysis. _____
   _____
   _____

   (e) True or False.

      _____ (1) Alphabetization and guide words help you locate a word quickly.

_____ (2) The pronunciation of a word can be learned from the dictionary.

_____ (3) Ability to select the specific meaning for a given context is one of the meaning skills in the use of a dictionary.

Reading-Study Guide for Supplementary Information on Objective 5 (Optional)

1. Read Dallmann, *The Teaching of Reading,* p. 150–155, to identify the elements of structural analysis that are frequently considered important enough to be taught in the elementary school. Read also to understand the principles of teaching structural analysis. When you have completed the reading, proceed with the next part of this activity, which is concerned with information in the reading.
2. It is stated in Dallmann that structural analysis deals with both word variants and word derivations.

   (a) Briefly tell what is meant by *word variant.* _____

   _____

   _____

   _____

   The endings added to root words to make variants are called *inflectional endings*.

   Give examples of word variants. _____

   _____

   (b) Briefly define *word derivatives.* _____

   _____

   Contractions are also types of derived forms.
   (c) Read this statement.
      A teacher should not bother to teach children to use structural analysis of words when phonic analysis could be used.

   Briefly explain why this statement is false. _____

   _____

   _____

   _____

   (d) True or False.
      Test your understanding of the principles of teaching structural anal-

ysis. Do not look back in the reading to answer these questions (Dallmann, pp. 151–153).

_____ (1) Structural analysis should be overemphasized when it is used along with other word recognition methods.

_____ (2) Usually the reader should try to analyze a word structurally before using phonics.

_____ (3) The analysis of new words should not be isolated from reading as a meaningful process.

_____ (4) The sequence in teaching a new word by structural analysis should usually be from the whole word to the word part and then back to the whole word.

_____ (5) Generalizations about structural analysis should be developed with the pupils.

Refer again to pp. 151–153 of Dallmann to check your answers. If any errors were made, be sure to read the explanation for that item.

3. The subskills of structural analysis may be categorized by these headings.
   (a) Inflectional endings.
   (b) Compound words.
   (c) Contractions.
   (d) Prefixes.
   (e) Suffixes.
   (f) Bases or roots.

READING RESOURCES/REFERENCES

1. Burns, Paul C., and Betty D. Roe. *Teaching Reading in Today's Elementary Schools.* Chicago: Rand McNally, 1976.
2. Dallmann, Martha, Roger L. Rouch, Lynette Y. C. Chang, and John J. DeBoer. *The Teaching of Reading,* 5th ed. New York: Holt, Rinehart, & Winston, 1978.
3. Dechant, Emerald V. *Improving the Teaching of Reading,* 2nd ed. Englewood Cliffs, N.J.: Prentice-Hall, 1970.
4. Dolch, Edward W. *Methods in Reading.* Champaign, Ill.: Garrard, 1955.
5. Durkin, Dolores. *Teaching Them to Read,* 2nd ed. Boston: Allyn and Bacon, 1974.
6. Gates, Arthur I. *A Reading Vocabulary for the Primary Grades.* New York: Teachers College Press, Columbia University, 1935.
7. Groff, Patrick. "The Topsy-Turvy World of Sight Words," *Reading Teacher* (March 1974), pp. 572–578.

8. Harris, Albert J., and Edward Sipay. *Effective Teaching of Reading.* New York: David McKay, 1971.
9. Harris, Albert J., Edward Sipay, and Milton D. Jacobson. *Basic Elementary Reading Vocabularies.* New York: Macmillan, 1972.
10. Heilman, Arthur W. *Principles and Practices of Teaching Reading.* Columbus, Ohio: Merrill, 1972.
11. Hillerich, R. L. "Word Lists—Getting It All Together," *Reading Teacher* (January 1974), pp. 353–360.
12. Hood, J. "Sight Words Are Not Going Out of Style," *Reading Teacher* (January 1977), pp. 379–382.
13. Johnson, Dale. "The Dolch List Reexamined," *The Reading Teacher* (February 1971), pp. 449–457.
14. Lowe, A. J. "Comparison of the Dolch List With Other Word Lists," *Reading Teacher* (October 1974), pp. 40–44.
15. Otto, Wayne, and Robert Chester. "Sight Words for Beginning Readers," *Journal of Educational Research* (July-August 1972), pp. 435–443.
16. Smith, Richard J., and Dale D. Johnson. *Teaching Children to Read.* Reading, Mass.: Addison-Wesley, 1976.
17. Spache, George D., and Evelyn B. Spache. *Reading in the Elementary School,* 4th ed. Boston: Allyn and Bacon, 1977.
18. Tinker, Miles A., and Constance M. McCullough. *Teaching Elementary Reading,* 4th ed. Englewood Cliffs, N.J.: Prentice-Hall, 1975.
19. Zintz, Miles V. *The Reading Process,* 2nd ed. Dubuque, Ia.: William C. Brown, 1975.

Chapter 5
Teaching Word Recognition Skills (Excluding Phonics)

RATIONALE

The sequence for teaching word recognition skills is not determined solely by grade level, but the teacher must be able to identify a logical sequence for teaching the skills. Students' needs, the existence of several known words from which examples may be drawn, and the complexity of the skills to be taught must be considered. Acknowledging these factors will enable the teacher to identify a sequence for teaching word recognition skills and for applying this knowledge to planning and teaching.

It is also necessary that the student, as a prospective teacher of reading, be able to identify the word recognition skill being demonstrated by a child in a given reading setting. This will enable the teacher to determine the decoding strategies being used successfully by the child and those in which the child needs further practice.

The student should be aware of the elements involved in plans for introducing or reinforcing a given word recognition skill and use this knowledge in preparing a plan.

According to the prepared plans, the student should be able to teach the lesson following given criteria. As an observer the student can critique the teaching of another student. This practice will enable the student to become aware of the importance of the knowledge of word recognition skills, the results of effective planning, and the effects of and need for competence in the teaching of reading. The importance of including word recognition skills in the elementary reading program has already been established (Chapter 4). It was seen that the student as a potential teacher needs a basic understanding of word recognition skills. The student must be equally competent in implementing methods of teaching the material if he or she is to become an effective teacher. This chapter will help you to develop such competence.

The techniques discussed in this chapter are primarily intended to form the base from which the beginner may become a fluent reader. Word identification as discussed here refers primarily to what Smith (1978) refers to as mediated word identification. This occurs when the reader encounters a word he or she has not seen in print before. He uses the word identification technique of phonics, structural analysis, context clues, and the dictionary to help decode the word. This type of mediated word identification occurs frequently with the beginning reader, at least until he builds up an adequate store of words in his memory bank.

When the reader is familiar with the word, he identifies it immediately by using the configuration or distinguishing features. However, until the reader has the word stored as a sight word, he uses the mediated word identification techniques as discussed in this chapter.

OBJECTIVES

After completing this chapter, you will be able to:
1. Determine levels at which specific word recognition elements are taught.
2. Identify the word recognition skill being demonstrated by a child in a given reading setting.

3. Prepare a plan for introducing or reinforcing a given word recognition skill.
4. Teach at least one lesson designed to enable children to develop a word recognition skill (excluding phonics). The lesson must satisfy given criteria.
5. Critique (either orally or in writing) the teaching of another student (Objective 4) according to given criteria.
6. Complete objective identified by the instructor.

PREASSESSMENT

See Appendix A-4

Instructional Activity 1

Sequence for Teaching Word Recognition Skills
The first step of any beginning reading program should be to teach children to recognize a certain number of whole words or sight words. Sight words are words that the reader can identify immediately without any help. There are several reasons why it is important to teach sight words.

1. To expedite the child's reading.
2. To prepare for word recognition instruction by teaching words that can serve as models of language patterns used in word attack.
3. To teach irregularly spelled words that cannot be successfully recognized by analysis.

Instruction in sight words may be appropriate at any grade level when you find it necessary to teach specific sight words to expedite a learner's reading. Children are able to begin analyzing words and using other word recognition skills if a basic core of sight words is learned. Before sight words are taught, children must have developed visual discrimination skills—they must be able to see likenesses and differences among printed words.

However, the sight word skills are not sufficient alone; the reader must remember each individual word. The child must become equipped for reading by learning the various word recognition techniques.

Once the beginner has enough words that he can recognize in print, teachers should help him focus on "sense" as a guide to decoding new words. This can be done by asking, "What word would make sense there?" After the child applies skills to predict the word, ask "Does the word make sense there?". This helps the child realize that reading is supposed to make sense. Reading is supposed to communicate a message. It is not merely a matter of converting the symbols into their sounds. An early focus on context to give clues to visually unfamiliar words is highly desirable. Of course, these should be combined with other visual clues so that reading does not become a "wild guess". Even when the child is focusing much of his energy on decoding the graphic form of words, the teacher must keep *meaning* in the foreground. Not to do so may promote word calling instead of reading.

The readiness activities for use of context clues and structural analysis begun in kindergarten are reinforced at the first reading level. Labeling objects, signs posted in the classroom and dramatic interpretation of meaning are some of the prerequisites for use of context clues. Ear training, comparisons, and inductive reasoning are some prerequisites for structural analysis skills (Tinker, 1975).

Picture clues are heavily relied on in beginning reading, but the child must learn to use clues present in the printed word. Some structural analysis skills—compound words, contractions, root words, and endings—are presented during the first reading level. More root words with prefixes and suffixes and more difficult plural forms are included at the second reading level. (Otto, 1976).

As the child advances in the use of other word recognition skills, he will develop the use of verbal context. Additional structural analysis skills are used as the words met in print become more and more complex structurally (Burron, 1972). From the third level on, prefixes, suffixes, and roots are taught extensively (Tinker, 1975). Verbal context use also becomes more advanced. Syllabication, accent, and possessive forms are also used (Otto, 1976).

When considering the order for teaching structural analysis skills, several factors should be considered. The occurrence or presentation in the reading textbook of words that represent a form to be studied is one factor helpful in determining order of development. The teacher's manual usually provides definite guidance for the word recognition program. Also, the difficulty of the point to be taught should be considered before determining the order of teaching.

Other things being equal, points that are easier to learn and apply should be taught first (Dallmann, 1978).

Grade level cannot be a satisfactory determiner for sequence or word recognition skills. The sequence to follow should be logically organized from the simple to the more complex. The sequence should be adapted to the pupil's level of achievement (Tinker, 1975).

Before the child can use a dictionary, he must be able to locate a word with reasonable ease. The skills necessary for locating words are knowledge of alphabetical order and the ability to use guide words. Children first learn alphabetization by the first letter of the word. Gradually, they learn to alphabetize by the first two, three, and more letters and learn that sometimes it is necessary to work through every letter in a word.

Children should learn that the two words at the top of a dictionary page are called guide words and that they indicate the first and last words on each page. After they are proficient in the use of alphabetical order, children should be able to decide whether or not a word will be found on a particular page by checking to see if the word falls between the two guide words alphabetically.

After the words have been located, the child must be able to interpret the diacritical markings through use of the pronunciation guide. There should be a pronunciation guide or key somewhere on every page spread of a good dictionary. Different dictionaries use different markings; therefore it is not necessary for the child to memorize the marks.

The teacher has the choice of the order in which to teach word recognition skills. However, no one sequence is appropriate for all children. The children's needs determine the sequence of the skills to be taught. The following guidelines are helpful.

1. A core of sight words should be taught before the skills of structural analysis are applied.
2. The child should be able to locate, name, and blend word parts before attempting to use structural analysis.
3. The child should have learned several word recognition skills before attempting to apply a variety of skills.
4. Dictionary skills become more important as the child encounters more complex words. These skills are usually stressed more in the intermediate grades; however, primary children should be able to locate a word in a simple dictionary.
5. The important thing to remember about sequence is that you do not expect a child to master a given skill unless he has the foundation skills. To do so may frustrate him and help him develop negative attitudes that will inhibit his ongoing learning and, perhaps, future learning in reading. Sequence relates to level of difficulty; the learner is ready to learn only the information that fits directly on what he already knows. For example, the child who lacks understanding of bases is unlikely to be successful in dealing with this objective: Identifies common suffixes on

base (words). In such a case the child could only be successful if he were taught to identify the base first.

✳ **Activities**

You may work with a peer in completing the following activities to help you determine a logical sequence for teaching word recognition skills.

1. Publishers of elementary reading texts often provide schools using the texts with charts listing the skills covered in the series. The skills are arranged according to the levels at which they are taught. These charts are called scope and sequence charts.

   You will need two reading scope and sequence charts from two different publishers. Each chart must cover the kindergarten through the elementary levels. You may obtain the charts from your instructor or school system.

   The charts will include all of the reading skills, but you will be concerned with word recognition skills only (as indicated in Chapter 4).
2. Skim each scope and sequence chart and locate skills that could be included as word recognition skills. Compare the charts. You will notice slight variations or omissions from one chart to the other. Overall, the charts will give you a general idea of the sequence for teaching word recognition skills. Levels at which certain skills are placed may vary. Note these variations.
3. *Synthesize* the findings into your own chart to show sequence of word recognition skills. Fill in the following chart (or use poster board or other material of your choice).

Scope and Sequence for Word Recognition Skills (Excluding Phonics)

Skill	Level

Scope and Sequence for Word Recognition Skills (Excluding Phonics)

Skill	Level

You have learned from your reading that the teacher must consider the needs of the child in identifying the sequence for teaching word recognition skills.

In your attempt to determine an idea about sequence of teaching word recognition skills, you should realize that certain skills are generally taught *before* or *after* other skills.

On your own you can obtain a third chart if you wish to make further comparisons with the chart you have compiled.

Instructional Activity 2

Identifying Word Recognition Skills Applied in Reading Situations
Use your knowledge of word recognition skills (Chapter 4) to identify the skill being utilized by readers in the following simulated situations from reading lessons. You will identify the word recognition skill being utilized by the child in each situation.

1. The teacher is holding up a card with the word "harbor" printed on it.

She pronounces it, and the children look at the word and repeat it. Which word recognition skill is being used in this situation?

2. The teacher writes a sentence on the board. "Sam played _____ (ball, boy, bat, work, sing) with his brothers." One of the students chooses the word "bat" for the blank. Which skill is being used?
3. The boys and girls are making lists of words containing a given root such as "walks, walked, walking". Which word recognition skill are they utilizing?
4. The teacher has written the letters in the alphabet with some letters missing. The students are to supply the missing letters. Which sub-skill of dictionary use is this?
5. The students are practicing pronouncing words according to the dictionary respellings. Which skill are they practicing?
6. Chris is reading a story in his primary-level reader about a trip to the zoo. The picture on the page shows a tall, slender giraffe munching on leaves from the treetops. Chris reads the sentence, "The giraffe is one of the animals in the zoo." He has not seen the word giraffe in print before now, yet he correctly identifies the word. How does he do this?

Suggested Activity: Observe *both* a primary-level and an intermediate-level reading lesson in an elementary school. Briefly describe the method used by the children to decode words in the lesson. List all the techniques you observe. For example,

Intermediate-Level Lesson	Grade _____
Skill:	Discription:
(Structural analysis-context clues)	(Child read sentence orally, "Cut out the picture with your scissors." Did not know word "scissors" at first; reread sentence for meaning and correctly read scissors.)

 Activity

You will need a primary- or intermediate-level teacher's manual to complete this activity. Study the manual and determine the word recognition skills to be taught in at least three lessons. List the skills and read the examples for teaching. Summarize the teaching example for each skill. Using this information, decide how you could determine that the child was using that particular decoding skill in the reading situation (Adapted from Zintz, 1975).

Grade
Name of reader _____   Level _____

Publisher _____

Skill	Teaching Example	Use by Child
Lesson 1 1. Using context.	Sentences put on board, words underlined; discussion of how meaning is derived by using known words.	Child could correctly pronounce new word and tell the meaning derived from sentence.

_____

_____

_____

Skill	Teaching Example	Use by Child

_____

_____

By listing the skills and examples for teaching, you can see that the lessons were carefully planned to introduce and provide practice in word recognition skills. Since we cannot always know the particular situation the child will meet in his or her reading, we want to provide instruction in the skills and determine if the child is able to effectively use them so he will be equipped for reading on his own. The importance of eventually teaching several word recognition skills to equip the child for independent reading is illustrated by this practice.

Instructional Activity 3

Planning for Teaching Word Recognition Skills

Planning a Lesson

In planning a lesson the teacher must keep in mind the purpose (objective) for teaching and know the pupils (needs, level, previous learnings assumed). It is understood that the teacher must know the subject matter to be taught. A guide for general planning is outlined here.

1. *Objective.* Identify the skill to be taught. State the objective that reflects the skill to be mastered. State the objective in terms of what the learner will do. "The student will . . . ."
2. *Material.* What materials will be needed during the lesson (overhead projector, chalkboard, work sheets, etc.)?
3. *Procedure.* What will the teacher do? What will the learner do?

4. *Evaluation.* How do I know that students have profited from instruction? Which students have met the objective? Which students need further instruction?

Background Information

Information for teaching particular skills is presented here. Read all of the information before preparing your own plan.

Teaching Sight Words   In basal readers, sight words are introduced in a simple context and repeated frequently in different contexts so that a student has repeated exposures to a word he is to learn by sight in a given book in a basal series. The repeated exposure is designed to help the student master the word by sight. Additional workbook practice exercises on the words may be used for reinforcement. Even so, some children fail to master the words and need supplemental teaching procedures.

The approach to teaching sight words described here can be used to supplement the work done in the basal reader, to teach additional sight vocabulary, and as the basic way to teach sight words in a language experience approach.

There are usually five steps involved in teaching sight words, but not necessarily in the following order (Smith and Johnson, 1976).

1. *Seeing.* The word is printed on the chalkboard or flash card, or is used as a label or picture caption.
2. *Discussion.* After the word has been read by the teacher and repeated by the children, a short discussion is held to relate the word to the lives and experiences of the group.
3. *Using.* Pupils are asked to use the word in a sentence or to think of a synonym.
4. *Defining.* After the students have used the word in several sentences, ask "What does this word mean?"
5. *Copying.* Many teachers have their pupils keep a personal dictionary of new words.

Games may be used to teach or reinforce the learning of sight words. There are a large number of commercially prepared games available, or they may be teacher constructed. [For lists see DeBoer (1970); Gallant (1970); and Zintz (1975).].

Three approaches can be used to get the child to say a word when he or she first sees it in print.

1. *Look-Say Approach.* You tell the child how to pronounce the word and then have him repeat it.
2. *Visual Approach.* You tell the child how to pronounce the word by associating it with a visual, such as a picture or object. Generally, you do *not* pronounce the word. (This approach often results in a *better* retention of sight words).

3. *Experience Approach.* You tell the child how to pronounce the word by relating it to a sentence he has previously memorized. Generally, you do *not* pronounce the word. You might write on a chart a story dictated by the child. Then have the child pronounce a specific word by recalling the memorized sentence. (This approach often results in the *BEST* retention of sight words.)

Teaching Principles for sight words include:

1. Eliciting the response (Use one of the three preceding approaches).
2. Providing practice of the response.

(*Hint:* Set short-term goals that the pupil will be able to achieve, such as learning 1 or 2 new sight words each day. Increase this goal on a very gradual and individual basis.)

Sample Plan—Sight Words
1. *Objective.* The student will immediately pronounce three of the pronouns on the *Dolch List of 220 Sight Words: we, they, I.*
2. *Materials.* Word cards with *we, they, I* printed on them. A set for each child.
3. *Procedure (Look-Say Approach).*
   (a) Teacher tells students the objective and why it is important.
   (b) Teacher says a sentence using the key pronoun word.
      I went to the store. Tom and I went to the store.
   (c) Have students say the word after you.
   (d) Repeat steps 1 and 2 for other two words.
   (e) Give each student a set of the three word cards.
   (f) Give a sentence illustrating the word and have pupils respond by holding up the appropriate word card.
      Where can *I* (students show "I" card) go?
      We want to go to town. *They* want to go, too.
   (g) Hold the word card and get responses from pupils.
   (h) Let students work in pairs, showing the word cards and responding.
4. Work with an individual child to determine if the child knows all three words at sight. Do this while children are working in pairs.
5. *Independent practice.* Have students take the word cards home to pronounce each one to parents or siblings.

Sample Teaching Plan—Structural Analysis
1. *Objective.* The learner will identify the pronunciation and meaning of the prefix *re.*
2. *Materials.* Word cards containing words with known base words and the prefix *re,* and a page containing example words in a new context.
3. *Procedure.*
   (a) Tell the student the reason for the lesson and why it is important.

     (b) *Context examples.* Use examples of *re* with a known base word in a context setting. As you say the key word, hold up the word card.

       (1) Tom's paper was messy so he had to *redo* it.

       (2) Maria spilled water on her letter. She had to *rewrite* it.

       (3) Orlando had to *reread* a page.

     (c) *Whole word examples.*

       (1) Put key words on the chalkboard.

       (2) Lead pupils to see and hear likenesses in the words.

       (3) Lead pupils to understand likenesses in meaning of words.

     (d) *Word part examples.*

       (1) Help pupils analyze the word.

       (2) Separate the prefix from the base.

       (3) Lead pupils to see that *re* is a common element. It is called a prefix.

       (4) Lead them to understand the change it produces in the base word.

     (e) *Whole word examples.*

       (1) Reconstruct the whole word by attaching prefix to base words.

       (2) Supply other examples.

     (f) *Examples in context.* Give students examples in a new context or supply the whole word and have pupils generate a sentence.

4. *Evaluation.* Have pupils apply information in new context. For example:

     (a) Juan had to bring the book back to school.

       He had to (redo, return, rewrite) it today.

     (b) Mrs. Estes wanted every child to do well on the test.

       She helped them (return, review, redo) the information.

     (c) Jeff liked his visit to the fire station. He wants to (revisit, review, return) it next year.

Sample Teaching Plan (Compounds)

Study the structural analysis skill being taught in the following plan.

1. *Objective.* The student will decode words by recognizing that they are compound words.

2. *Materials.* Chalkboard, reinforcement activity/worksheet.

3. *Procedure.* ·

     (a) *Introduction.* The teacher will use the words in oral context.

          The bedroom window was closed.

          The homemade pie was hot and fresh.

          The captain saw a signal from the lighthouse.

          The plumber fixed the kitchen drainpipe.

     (b) Present the whole words on the board: bedroom, homemade, lighthouse, drainpipe.

     (c) The teacher will analyze the words. The children should be made to realize that there are component words in the compound: bed/room.

(d) The teacher will present the words again as wholes: bedroom.

(e) The teacher will allow the children to apply all the words in context and will record responses on the chalkboard.

(f) The teacher will provide reinforcement (enrichment) through teacher-made activities or workbook pages, such as the following.

Matching

every	cake
never	more
hot	side
out	where

(See Durkin, p. 342–343, for additional practices.)

A matching exercise is also a useful practice in teaching contractions to show that the contraction represents two words.

4. *Evaluation.* Matching exercises may be used in evaluation. Also the teacher may make a checklist to note from observation during activities which children need further practice.

Sample Teaching Episode Using Induction

In teaching structural analysis skills, the teacher should present activities in such a way that the students observe and form generalizations from the practices. Students should not be presented only with rules to memorize. This can be done as follows.

Write on the board nouns such as these ending in *y* and their plurals.

boy, boys
lady, ladies
day, days
candy, candies
toy, toys

Allow the pupils to observe how the plural is formed. They may write in one column the singular nouns ending in *y* preceded by a vowel. The other column will contain singular nouns ending in *y* preceded by a consonant. Allow the pupils to summarize their observations. The students should be helped to become aware of the application of these observations in reading and spelling (Dallmann 1978, p. 153).

> Generalizations about structural analysis skills should be developed with the student, not presented as rules to memorize.

Preparing a Plan for Teaching

Read the directions given for preparing a plan for teaching a word recognition skill. Choose *one* of the skills and prepare a plan as directed.

1. *Sight Words.* Design a plan to teach sight words. Use the following objective.
   Objective. The children will be able to instantly pronounce these three words: _____ , _____ , and _____ . Write the steps you will take to elicit the response, and the steps you will take to have the child practice the response.

2. *Structural Analysis.* Prepare a plan for teaching the inflectional ending *s, ed,* or *ing,* or choose another structural analysis skill. Use the sample plan previously given as a guideline. Some suggested words for teaching the inflectional ending *s* are:

   boy (boys), girl (girls), jar (jars), coat (coats)
   table (tables), barn (barns), desk (desks), seat (seats)

   Be sure to implement your own ideas, materials, and activities into the lesson. Think through the actual teaching in order to be prepared. Consider the observations made in Objective 2 that might help you present the material in a meaningful way. (Several useful activities for teaching or reinforcing structural analysis skills are suggested by Burns and Roe (1976, pp. 155–161).

   Alternatively, refer to the preceding sample plans. Taking the same considerations as in teaching structural analysis, prepare a plan for teaching the use of context clues (picture or verbal).

   Keep in mind what you know about the context clue selected. For example, the use of picture clues is generally used at the primary level, specifically at the readiness and beginning reading levels. (You would not teach picture clues as a technique for recognizing sight words already in the meaning vocabulary to sixth graders.)

3. *Choose a Word Recognition Skill to Teach.* After you have chosen the skill to be taught, state your objective. You must be familiar with your purpose, procedure, materials, and students and know what level you will be teaching.

Some GENERAL CONSIDERATIONS in preparing your plan apply to most word recognition skills.

Make sure your plan allows the pupils to make conclusions about the information you present. (See the sample teaching episode on p. 92.)

Plan to have all the pupils respond or participate in some way.

Plan reinforcement activities. (Have a variety of games or materials available for reinforcement. It is better to over-prepare than to run out of interesting activities.)

Instructional Activity 4

Teaching Word Recognition Skill Lessons

Teach at least one lesson designed to enable children to develop a word recognition skill (excluding phonics.)

The lesson must satisfy given criteria.

This activity is used in conjunction with the activities in Objective 3.

Refer to the plans for teaching in the previous objective. You may choose to teach either the sample lesson or the lesson you have prepared.

In order to have an effective presentation, you must satisfy the criteria in Appendix C, Checklist 3. You may wish to make copies of the checklist for use in other teaching activities.

Instructional Activity 5

Critiquing Word Recognition Skill Lessons

Critique (either orally or in writing) the teaching of another student (Objective 4) according to given criteria. Use Checklists 3 and 4 in Appendix C as criteria to critique the teaching of a peer.

SUGGESTED TEACHING ACTIVITIES

1. *Skill:* Sight words.

   Materials: Fish cut from poster board with sight words on them and a staple on the mouth, pole, string with magnet.

   Procedures: The teacher places fish in a box "pond" and has the student insert magnetic "hook" on the line into the pond to catch a sight word fish. The student names the fish and keeps it if he or she successfully pronounces the word.

   Variations: Instead of fish, prepare whales and put phrases on them.

   Number: Small group.

   Level: First, second.

   Examples:

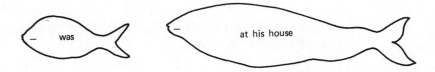

2. *Skill:* Structural analysis, prefixes and suffixes.

   Materials: Broomstick or curtain rod, metal rings, white oaktag rectangles (for root words), green oaktag squares (for prefixes), red oaktag squares (for suffixes), and worksheets.

   Procedure: The teacher punches holes in each oaktag square and puts all the prefix cards on one metal ring, all the suffix cards on the third metal ring, and all the root word cards on the center metal ring. Then the broomstick or curtain rod is inserted through the rings. The student flips through the cards and sets up correct combinations. Students may use this as an independent activity for review of root words, prefixes and suffixes.

Number: Individual or small group.

Level: Third.

Example:

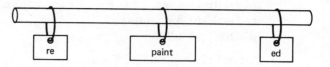

3. *Skill:* Use of guide words (dictionary).

   Materials: Sheets with guide words, cards with words, envelopes.

   Procedure: The teacher prepares worksheets with pairs of guide words, selecting some words that would be on the same dictionary page as the guide words and some that would not and writing them on word cards. The teacher places the words in envelopes to distribute to the students. The students take the word cards from the envelopes and alphabetize them as they would occur on the dictionary page. They discard words that would not be included between the given guide words.

   Number: Individual and group.

   Level: Fourth, fifth.

   Example:

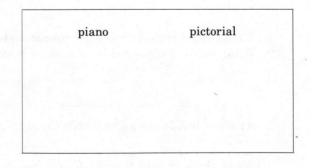

Sample Sheet

pica phyton	physical piccolo	picot picture	pick piece	pink pickle

Sample Word Cards

ADDITIONAL ENABLING ACTIVITIES

1. This reading-study activity is for additional information on Objective 1. Read the following sources to obtain an overview of the sequence and levels of teaching word recognition skills. Take notes on your reading. See the following page for the reading-study guide.
   (a) Tinker, pp. 189–191 (general sequence, include phonetic analysis).
   (b) Dallmann, pp. 153–155 (structural analysis).
   (c) Dechant, pp. 260–264.
   (d) Otto, pp. 52–56.

2. Attend class sessions. Time _____ Date _____

3. An activity of your choice. _____

   _____

   _____

4. An activity selected by your instructor. _____

   _____

   _____

Reading-Study Guide for Enabling Activity 1

Read the following questions to set your purposes for reading the assigned selections. After you have completed the readings, respond to the questions in writing.

1. Which word recognition skill should be taught first? _____
2. What skills are needed by the child before sight words are introduced?

   _____

   _____

3. At what levels are sight words taught? _____

   _____

4. What skills should the child have before he or she can locate a word in the dictionary (Chapter 4)? _____

   _____

5. At what level and in what order are these dictionary skills taught?

   _____

   _____

   _____

6. What skills are needed for pronouncing a word once it has been located (Chapter 4)? _____

_____

7. When are these pronunciation skills taught? _____

_____

8. A set sequence for teaching significant structural analysis elements cannot be stated authoritatively for all grades. What factor(s) can help determine the order of development in teaching structural analysis?

_____

_____

_____

If you need further understanding of the material, refer back to the reading to find the correct response.

Suggested Activity: Consult the teacher's manuals of a basal reader series and make an outline of the sequence of word recognition skills taught. Begin at the primary level and work through the intermediate-level readers.

READING RESOURCES/REFERENCES

1. Burns, Paul C., and Betty D. Roe. *Teaching Reading in Today's Elementary Schools.* Chicago: Rand McNally, 1976.
2. Burron, Arnold, and Amos L. Claybaugh, *Basic Concepts in Reading Instruction.* Columbus, Ohio: Charles E. Merrill, 1972.
3. Dallmann, Martha, Roger L. Rouch, Lynette Y. C. Chang, and John J. DeBoer. *The Teaching of Reading,* 5th ed., New York: Holt, Rinehart & Winston, 1970.
4. DeBoer, John J., and Martha Dallman. *The Teaching of Reading,* New York: Holt, Rinehart & Winston, 1970.
5. Dechant, Emerald V. *Improving the Teaching of Reading.* 3rd ed., Englewood Cliffs, N.J., Prentice-Hall, 1970.
6. Durkin, Dolores. *Teaching Them to Read.* Boston: Allyn and Bacon, 1974.
7. Emans, Robert. "When Two Vowels Go Walking and Other Such Things," *The Reading Teacher* (December 1967), pp. 262–269.
8. Gallant, Ruth. *Handbook in Corrective Reading: Basic Tasks.* Columbus, Ohio: Charles E. Merrill, 1970.
9. Greene, Harry A., and Walter T. Petty. *Developing Language Skills in the Elementary Schools,* 4th ed. Allyn and Bacon, 1971.

10. Harris, Albert J., and Edward R. Sipay. *Effective Teaching of Reading*. New York: Holt, Rinehart & Winston, 1972.
11. Harris, Larry A., and Carl B. Smith. *Reading Instruction Through Diagnostic Teaching*. New York: Holt, Rinehart & Winston, 1972.
12. Heilman, Arthur W. *Principles and Practices of Teaching Reading*. Columbus, Ohio: Charles E. Merrill, 1972.
13. Heilman, Arthur W. *Phonics in Proper Perspective*. Columbus, Ohio: Charles E. Merrill, 1972.
14. Otto, Wayne, and Robert D. Chester. *Objective-Based Reading*. Reading, Mass: Addison-Wesley, 1976.
15. Smith, Frank. *Understanding Reading: A Psycholinguistic Analysis*, 2nd ed. New York: Holt, Rinehart & Winston 1978.
16. Smith, Richard J., and Dale D. Johnson. *Teaching Children to Read*, Reading, Mass: Addision-Wesley, 1976.
17. Spache, George D., and Evelyn B. Spache. *Reading in the Elementary School,* 4th ed. Boston: Allyn and Bacon, 1977.
18. Tinker, Miles A., and Constance M. McCullough. *Teaching Elementary Reading,* 4th ed. Englewood Cliffs: Prentice-Hall, 1975.
19. Wallen, Carl J. *Competency in Teaching Reading*. Chicago: Science Research Associates, 1972.
20. Zintz, Miles V. *The Reading Process,* 2nd ed. Duboque, William C. Brown, 1975.

Chapter 6
Phonics and Related Skills: Content

RATIONALE

It is nearly impossible for anyone to become an independent reader without developing a procedure for learning symbol-sound associations. An organized program for learning these relationships is a vital component of any good reading program. Phonics, a system of sound-symbol associations, is one method whereby the reader may decode print (i.e., pronounce the printed word). Phonics is valuable tool for recognizing words in print. It is not a method of teaching reading, because decoding is only one aspect of reading skills.

The reader is presented with a series of visual symbols (the graphemes). His or her task is to determine the auditory symbols (the phonemes) that those graphemes represent. Knowledge of the reasons for these associations is an aid to the reader in making predictions about the auditory counterpart for the visual symbols. This information generally forms the content of phonics commonly taught in elementary schools.

As you will see in the next chapter, there is still some question as to how much of the phonics content is actually useful to the reader as he decodes visually unfamiliar words. Many of the issues remain unresolved. For this reason, the content of this chapter is intended to be broad. You may use your knowledge of the needs of the children you teach and the results of future research to decide how much of this content should be presented as an aid to word attack skills of students.

Technically, letters (graphemes) have no sounds. Instead, they stand for sounds (phonemes). Sounds have letters that represent them. In some cases it is a single letter; in others multiple letters represent a sound. If you glance at suggested lessons in the teacher's guides of basal readers or in workbook materials, you may get the idea that the opposite is true. The terminology implies that letters make sounds. The intent is not to teach faulty information but to promote the understanding of the learner whose task is to convert the letter into the sound represented by it.

Unlike other word recognition skills, phonics and related skills have a body of content. One cannot teach phonics to children without first knowing that content. This chapter will facilitate your acquisition of the content of phonics. Chapter 7 will help you to become an effective teacher of phonic elements.

OBJECTIVES

After completing this chapter you will be able to:
1. Identify phonic principles (or elements) present in a series of real or nonsense words. (i.e., consonant sounds, variant consonant sounds, consonant blends, consonant digraphs, silent consonants, short vowels, long vowels, schwa sound, r-controlled vowels, special vowel sounds, diphthongs, and vowel digraphs).
2. Divide real or nonsense words into syllables and state appropriate generalizations (i.e., *CVC, VCCV, c + le* patterns.)
3. Specify the probable pronunciation of the component graphemes in a series of nonsense words that conform to given phonic/syllabication generalizations (i.e., vowel sounds in open syllables and closed syllables, in words ending in silent *e,* and in words with two vowels together).
4. Complete an objective identified by the instructor.

PREASSESSMENT

See Appendix A-6.

Instructional Activity 1

Phonics Elements
In order for you to engage in teaching phonics skills to children, you must first meet, become acquainted with and get to know well terms that sound strange and technical.

Terminology of Phonics
1. *Phonics*—This is a word recognition skill that is concerned with the association between symbols and sounds.

Sound — 2. *Phoneme.* This is a *unit* of minimally constrastive *sound* in spoken words; that is, it makes a difference in meaning. For example, *pet* and *pat* are minimally contrastive. A phoneme may be a consonant or a vowel.

written symbol on page — 3. *Grapheme.* This is the symbol (usually a letter of the alphabet) used to represent a phoneme. For example, the letter *p* represents the first sound you hear in the word *pat.*

4. *Phoneme-Grapheme Correspondence and Phoneme-Grapheme Associa-*

tion. These refer to the relationship between the phoneme (sound) and grapheme (symbol).

5. *Consonants*. These are sounds (phonemes) produced with obstruction of the breath stream by the tongue, teeth, or lips. Consonants are represented by letters such as *b, c, d, f,* and *g*. There are 19 consonant letters in the English alphabet.

6. *Vowels*. These are phonemes produced without obstruction of the breath. The letters *a, e, i, o,* and *u*, represent vowels. The letters *y* and *w* may also represent vowel sounds.

7. *Semivowels*. These are letters that may serve both vowel and consonant functions under certain conditions. Both *w* and *y* are semivowels. They serve as vowels in *cry* and *blow* but as consonants in *yell* and *wind*.

8. *Consonant Blend*. This refers to a two-or three-consonant letter combination in which the sounds merge or blend together but *each* is distinguishable. There is no clear break from the ending of one consonant sound to the beginning of the next. For example, in the word *spring* the *s, p,* and *r* are said in such rapid succession that their sounds blend together, but one can still hear the sound of the *s,* the sound of the *p,* and the sound of the *r*. This is sometimes referred to as a consonant cluster.

> *[handwritten: Both]*
> *[handwritten: you hear the sounds of the letters]*

9. *Consonant Digraph*. This is a two-consonant letter combination that represents a single sound. The sound is a unique sound, one that is different from the sound that could be represented by either letter by itself. For example, in *shell* the *sh* represents a single sound.

10. *Diphthong*. This refers to a two-vowel letter combination in which the sounds partially merge but are distinguishable. For example, in *boy* the *oy* forms a diphthong. There are two commonly accepted diphthong sounds: (1) *oy, oi,* as in *joy* and *soil,* and (2) *ow, ou* as in *now* and *loud*.

11. *Vowel Digraph*. This is a two-vowel letter combination that represents a single sound. For example, in *country,* the *ou* stands for a single sound. (Note that the *ou* in *country* does not stand for a diphthong as it does in *county*.) There are long vowel digraphs as in *boat, clean,* and *deed:* and there are short vowel digraphs as in *deaf, thread,* and *would* (o͝o).

12. *Short Vowel*. This is the vowel sound heard in *ham, let, if, hot,* and *run*. The sound is marked with a ˘ (breve) over the vowel letter in the dictionary and other pronunciation guides.

13. *Long vowel*. This refers to the vowel sound heard in *ate, meet, ice, loaf,* and *mute*. The sound is the same as the vowel letter name. The long vowel sound is shown by a ˉ (macron) over the vowel letter in the dictionary and other pronunciation guides.

14. *Schwa*. This refers to a neutral vowel sound heard in *unaccented* syllables. This symbol (ə) is used to represent the schwa in the dictionary and other pronunciation guides. The schwa is heard in the words *soda, collect,* and *minium*. All vowel letters may represent the schwa sound.

15. *Syllable.* This is an uninterrupted unit of speech containing one vowel sound. For example, *legal* has two syllables—*le,* and *gal.* There is one vowel sound for the first syllable and one vowel sound for the second. Each syllable must have one and only one vowel sound.
16. *Phonetics.* This is a science of speech sound.
17. *Glided Vowels.* This term is used in some basal reading materials to refer to the long vowel sounds.
18. *Unglided Vowels.* This term is used in some basal reading materials to refer to the short sounds of the vowels.

Elements of a Phonic Program
The elements comprising the content of phonics are given in Tables 6-1 to 6-17. Study the information in each table and the accompanying explanatory material.

Table 6-1 Single Consonants

Letter/ Symbol	Common Sound in Word Context 1[a]	2[b]	3[c]
1. b	bat	ribbon	knob
2. d	dish	body	lid
3. f	fish	before	leaf
4. h	hand	behave	
5. j	jar	enjoy	bridge
6. k	kite	hiking	book
7. l	lion	pilot	fall
8. m	man	hammer	jam
9. n	nut	funny	can
10. p	pig	happy	mop
11. r	ring		
12. t	top	little	cut
13. v	valentine	oven	five
14. z	zero	dozen	size

[a] Initial position.
[b] Medial position.
[c] Final position.

Discussion for Table 6-1
1. The examples given represent the most common sound associated with the given consonant letter.
2. Note that no example is given for the *h* in final position. The reason is that when it does occur as a single consonant in final position, it does not represent a consonant sound. For example, hurr*ah*.
3. Note, also, that not all consonants are treated in Table 6-1. The conso-

nants that represent frequently occurring multiple sounds are given in Table 6-2.

Table 6-2 Single Consonants Representing Multiple Sounds

Letter	Sound	Sounds in Word Context
1. c	1. k (hard)	cat, cone, cub
	2. s (soft)	city, cell, cyst
2. g	1. g (hard)	gate, gone, guess
	2. j (soft)	gem, giraffe, gyrate
3. s	1. s	bus, so, safe
	2. z	busy, rose, is, his
	3. sh	sugar, sure
4. qu	1. kw	queen, quiet, quart
	2. k	antique, technique, quay
5. x	1. ks	box, mix, tax
	2. gz	exam, exact, exit
	3. z	xylem, xylophone, anxiety
	4. sh	anxious

Discussion for Table 6-2

1. Note the letters *c, qu,* and *x.* Read the examples given for the letters. These letters represent no new sound. They merely spell the sounds that are already represented by other letters. They make no unique contribution to the English sound system.
2. Look at the examples given for the letter *q.* Do you see a pattern? What is special about the *q?* In the English language, the *q* is always followed by a *u.*
3. Look at the examples given for the hard *c* (*k*). How are they alike? Look at the examples given for the soft *c* (*s*). How are they alike? Compare the two groups of words. State a generalization that predicts when *c* will represent the soft sound. State a generalization that applies to the hard sound represented by *c.*
4. Compare your predictions with this. *C* represents the soft sound *s* when it is followed by *e, i, y. C* has its hard sound when it is *followed* by *a, o, u* (and other consonants.)
5. Look at the examples given for the hard and soft sounds of *g.* Note likenesses. State a generalization.
6. Compare your generalization with this one. The generalization in point 4 also applies to the *g.* However, *g* is less consistent than the *c* in yielding its soft sound. This is particularly true when the *g* is followed by *i,* as in *girl, gift, give, gill,* and *girdle,* all of which illustrate the hard

105

sound, of *g* in defiance of the rule.

Table 6-3 shows sounds represented by clusters of consonants.

Table 6-3   Two-Letter Consonant Blends

Letters	Examples in Context
Group I. R blends	
1. br	brown, broom, bight
2. cr	crown, cracker, cream
3. dr	dress, drill, drum
4. fr	fright, from, fresh
5. gr	great, grin, grape
6. pr	proud, April, prune
7. tr	tree, train, trust
Group II. L blends	
1. bl	blue, blow, blend
2. cl	clown, cloud, clay
3. fl	flame, fly, flower
4. gl	glue, glow, glass
5. pl	play, plow, plain
Group III. S blends	
1. sc	scar, scope, scum
2. sk	skate, skill, sky
3. sn	snake, snail, snow
4. sm	small, smile, smoke
5. sp	spill, sport, spoil
Group IV. Miscellaneous	
1. dw	dwell, dwarf, dwindle
2. tw	twinkle, twelve, twin

Discussion for Table 6-3

1. Note that the blends are grouped for ease in remembering them. There is no absolute grouping of the blends, and the groups overlap.

Blends that are represented by three consonants grouped together are shown in Table 6-4.

Table 6-4   Three-Letter Consonant Blends

Letters	Examples in Context
1. scr	scrape, script, scream
2. spr	spray, spring, sprite
3. str	string, stray, straight
4. shr	shrill, shread, shrink
5. spl	splash, splint, splice
6. squ	squid, squirrel, square
7. thr	three, thrill, throw

Discussion for Table 6-4

1. *Squ* qualifies as a three-letter consonant blend because of the (kw) sound represented by the *qu,* even though *u* is not a consonant letter.

Sometimes consonant letters recurring together represent a single sound instead of the blend sounds already shown. These are presented in Table 6-5.

Table 6-5   Consonant Digraphs

Letters	Examples in Context
1. ch	choice, chair, church
2. sh	shoe, shower, wish
3. wh	whistle, whale, what
4. (a) th (unvoiced)[a]	thin, thumb, with
(b) th (voiced)[a]	this, that, bathe
5. ng	ring, finger, hang
6. nk (sounds ngk)	bank, ink, sunk
7. ph (sounds f)	telephone, phony, trophy
8. gh (sounds f)	enough, laugh

[a] In *ether,* the vocal cords do not vibrate to produce the *th* sound. The voiced *th* sound is produced with vocal cord vibration, as in *either.*

Discussion for Table 6-5

1. Note that the consonant digraphs in Table 6-5 are separated by a dotted line. Many authorities consider the first five digraphs (*ch, sh, wh, th* and *ng*) as the true digraphs because they produce unique sounds. Although those below the dotted line (*nk, ph,* and *gh*) represent a sound that could not be represented by either of the single letters acting alone, they do not stand for new *sounds.* They duplicate the sounds already represented by other letters.
2. The *wh* digraph sound is no longer present in some English dialects. The *wh* sound has been replaced with the *w* sound in these dialects so that *witch* and *which* have the same sounds.
3. The *th* represents two different digraphs. Although the sounds are articulated alike, one receives voice while the other does not. The presence of voice as you produce the word *teethe* enables you to distinguish it from the word *teeth* when you hear it.
4. The digraphs *ng* and *nk* never occur in initial position in a word or syllable. The *wh* never occurs in final position in a word or syllable.
5. The *ng* digraph has been dropped from some dialects, particularly as the *ing* ending. In such dialects, the digraph sound has been replaced by the consonant *n* sound so that *going* may be pronounced *go-in.*

6. When *nk* occurs in a word, the digraph sound *ng* and the *k* sound are usually heard.
7. Although *gh* sometimes represents an *f* sound, it does not do so consistently. For example, in *eight,* the *gh* represents no sound.
8. In ghost, the *h* represents no sound. In *though,* the *gh* represents no sound.
9. In some words, particularly those with foreign origins, the *ch* represents the *sh* digraph sound. For example, *chef, chalet, chandelier.*

Sometimes consonant letters occur together but represent the sound of only one. The spelling patterns for these are presented in Table 6-6.

Table 6-6   Consonant Sounds with Variant Graphemes

Sound	Grapheme	Examples in Context
1. n	kn	knight, knife, know
2. n	gn	gnat, gnaw, gnome
3. n	pn	pneumatic, pneumonic
4. s	ps	psyche, psalm
5. r	wr	write, wrestle
6. m	mb	lamb, thumb, plumber
7. m	mn	solumn, column
8. m	lm	calm, salmon, palm
9. k	ck	black, stick, lock
10. k	lk	walk, stalk
11. t	bt	doubt, debt
12. ch	tch	catch, pitcher

Note. *gh* may occur in words and represent no sound. In words such as fight, caught, bough, and high, the *gh* is only part of the spelling pattern.

Discussion for Table 6-6

1. In addition to single-letter representation, some sounds may be represented by multiple combinations. The student needs to know this so that he or she will not attempt to convert the individual letters into sound. He also must realize the possibilities for variant spellings of sounds so as not to experience frustration in trying to find a word such as *gnu* in the dictionary when he knows it only by sound.
2. These combinations represent sounds that could have been represented by a single consonant letter. For example, the *n* sound in *knave* could have been written *n + ave.* This is unlike a consonant digraph, which can rarely be represented by one one of its component letters. In the word child, *ch* together represent the sound heard in the beginning of the word. This is different from the sounds usually represented by the *c* alone or the *h* alone.

Table 6-7 Semivowels: Consonant Functions

w Examples	y Examples
wind	yes
wake	yell
will	yoga
forward	yogurt
witch	yoyo
	canyon

Discussion for Table 6-7

1. Note that *w* and *y* are semivowels. This means that they serve both consonant and vowel functions. (See Table 6-14 for examples as vowels.)
2. The examples in Table 6-7 illustrate *w* and *y* as consonants. Look carefully at the examples. Formulate a generalization that predicts when *w* and *y* will be consonants and represent consonant sounds.
3. Check your generalization with this one. Both *w* and *y* serve as a consonant whenever they occur in *initial position* in a word or syllable.
4. Can you give other examples which apply? If so, write them down and check your answers in a dictionary.

Common sounds represented by vowel letters are shown in Table 6-8 to Table 6-10.

Table 6-8 Vowels: Short and Long Sounds

Letter	Examples	
	Short (unglided)	Long (glided)
1. a	add, cap, man	aid, lake, say
2. e	etch, pet, shell	each, meet, pea
3. i	if, sit, him	idol, mite, tie
4. o	ox, rock, not	oak, hope, go
5. u	up, hut, funny	use, music

Table 6-9 Vowels: Schwa Sound

Letter	Schwa Sound	Example
1. a	ə	sof*a*
2. e	ə	op*e*n
3. i	ə	pol*i*cy
4. o	ə	rand*o*m
5. u	ə	circ*u*s

Table 6-10   Vowels: r-Controlled

	Letters
Group I. ar, or	
1. car, star, mark, far	ar
2. nor, for, storm	or
Group II. ir, ur, er	
1. fir, bird, stir	ir
2. fur, curl, hurt	ur
3. her, were, perk	er

Discussion for Tables 6-8 to 6-10

1. Note that *any* vowel letter may represent the schwa, provided that the letter occurs in an unaccented syllable.
2. Can you think of other examples of words with the schwa sound? If so, write them down and check your answers in a dictionary.
3. Note that Group I words represent one *r*-controlled sound while Group II words represent another *r*-controlled sound in Table 6-10.
4. When the vowel and *r* occur in the same syllable, the *r* influences the preceding vowel sound. This influence on the vowel sound is not present *if* (1) the *r* does not occur in the same syllable as the preceding vowel [e.g., *irate* (i rate)], or (2) the *r* does not follow the vowel [e.g., *rose* (r o s e)].
5. Note that each vowel letter represents at *least* four sounds.
   (a) short,
   (b) long,
   (c) schwa, and
   (d) *r*-controlled.

Table 6-11   Special Vowel Sounds

Letters	Example
1. *al* (or all)	*a*lso, b*a*ll, t*a*ll, *a*lmost
2. *aw*	saw, awful, paw
3. *au*	automobile, caught, haul
4. *ou* (ght)	bought, thought, ought, cough

Discussion for Table 6-11

1. Note that the four different letter combinations represent the same special sounds.

Table 6-12 Diphthongs: Vowel Blends

Letters	Examples
1. (a) oi	boil, joint, soil, coin
(b) oy	boy, royal, coy, oyster
2. (a) ow	how, crowd, shower
(b) ou	proud, blouse, shout

Discussion for Table 6-12

1. There are two commonly accepted diphthong *sounds* represented by four groups of letters. The diphthong sound heard in *choice* may be represented in print by *oi* (usually within the word) and *oy* (usually at the end of the syllable or word.) The diphthong sound heard in *pound* may be represented in print by *ou* (usually within the word) and *ow* (usually at the end of syllable or words).
2. The same letter combinations *may* also represent vowel digraphs (especially *ou* and *ow*). For example, the *ow* is a vowel digraph in *blow* but a diphthong in *cow;* the *ou* is a vowel digraph in *thought* but a diphthong in *count.*

Table 6-13 Vowel Digraphs: Common Combinations

Letters	Long (glided) Sound	Example	Letters	Short (unglided) Sound	Example
1. ai	$\bar{a}$	rain, bait	1. ou	$\breve{u}$	touch
2. ay	$\bar{a}$	day, play	2. ea	$\breve{e}$	head, thread
3. ea	$\bar{e}$	each, beat	3. ee	$\breve{e}$	been
4. ee	$\bar{e}$	keep, beet	4. oo	$\breve{oo}$	book, hood
5. oa	$\bar{o}$	toast, coat			
6. oe	$\bar{o}$	toe, hoe			
7. oo	$\overline{oo}$	moon, groom			

Discussion for Table 6-13

1. Note that there are both long and short vowel digraphs.
2. Note that the same letter combinations may represent different vowel digraph sounds.

Both w and y can represent either consonant or vowel sounds. Conditions under which they function as vowels are given in Table 6-14.

Table 6-14   Semivowels: Vowel Function

		W		
	Digraph			Diphthong
	Examples	Sound		Examples
	1. yell*ow*	$\bar{o}$		1. h*ow*
	2. cr*ow*	$\bar{o}$		2. cr*ow*d
	3. bl*ow*	$\bar{o}$		3. fl*ow*er
	4. f*ew*, st*ew*	$\bar{u}$		4. p*ow*er
	5. thr*ew*, bl*ew*	$\overline{oo}$		5. pr*ow*l

		Y		
Digraph	1. End of one-syllable word 2. End syllable within word	End multi-syllable word	Only vowel mid-syllable	Diphthong

Examples	Sound	Examples	Sound	Examples	Sound	Examples	Sound	Examples
day	$\bar{a}$	1. cry,my by, fry	$\bar{i}$	baby	$\breve{i}$ or $\bar{e}$	cyst	$\breve{i}$	boy, joy, loyal
they	$\bar{a}$			happy	$\breve{i}$ or $\bar{e}$	cymbal	$\breve{i}$	
pulley	$\bar{e}$	2. myopia (my-o-pi-a)	$\bar{i}$	funny	$\breve{i}$ or $\bar{e}$	cymbal	$\breve{i}$	
buy	$\bar{i}$	nylon (ny-lon)	$\bar{i}$	gravy	$\breve{i}$ or $\bar{e}$	mystic (mys-tic)	$\breve{i}$	

Discussion for Table 6-14

1. Look carefully at the examples for two vowel functions served by the *w*. Do you see a pattern? Can you form a generalization which predicts when the *w* will be a vowel? If so, write it here.
2. Compare your generalization with this one. (1) The *w* is a vowel when it occurs in medial or final position in a syllable or word. (2) The *w* is a vowel only when it occurs immediately after another vowel. It is not a vowel on its own.
3. Look carefully at the examples for the five conditions under which the *y* may serve as a vowel. Do you see a pattern here? In what way is the *y* as a vowel different from the *w* as a vowel? Can you state a generalization that applies?
4. Compare your generalization with this. The *y* serves a vowel if it is in a medial or final position in a word or syllable, either in a word combination with another vowel or alone acting as the only vowel in a word or syllable. The *y* may represent three different sounds: (1) the $\bar{i}$ as in try; (2) the $\breve{i}$ or $\bar{e}$[1] as in gravity, or (3) the $\breve{i}$ as in crystal (crystal).

---

[1] $\breve{i}$ or $\bar{e}$ is dependent on the pronunciation of the individual.

Sounds represented by vowel letters vary, but they are governed by some rules or generalizations as shown in Table 6-15 and Table 6-16.

Table 6-15   Long Vowel Generalizations

Condition 1. Two vowel letters together		
Vowel Sound	Symbol/Spelling	Example
1. $\bar{a}$	ai	rain
2. $\bar{o}$	oa	boat
3. $\bar{e}$	ea	peach
4. $\bar{\imath}$	ie	pies
Condition 2. Vowel, consonant, final e		
1. $\bar{a}$	a c+e	ape
2. $\bar{o}$	o c+e	smoke
3. $\bar{\imath}$	i c+e	side
4. $\bar{u}$	u c+e	cube
5. $\bar{e}$	e c+e	concrete
Condition 3. Vowel ends a syllable		
1. $\bar{a}$	a	apron (a pron)
2. $\bar{a}$	a	label (la bel)
3. $\bar{u}$	u	human (hu man)
4. $\bar{u}$	u	music (mu sic)
5. $\bar{o}$	o	hotel (ho tel)
6. $\bar{e}$	e	legal (le gal)
7. $\bar{\imath}$	i	bison (bi son)

Discussion for Table 6-15   Table 6-15 shows three conditions under which a vowel may belong.

1. Look at condition 1. Look carefully at the examples. Do you see a pattern? Can you state a generalization that applies to vowel sounds in words such as those given in condition 1?
2. Compare your generalization to this one. In a word or syllable, when two vowels occur side by side, the first generally represents a *long* sound and the second represents no sound. The two vowel letters stand for one sound.
3. Look at condition 2. What likenesses do you see in the example words? Form a generalization that applies.
4. Compare generalizations. In words containing a final *e* separated from

113

the preceding vowel by a consonant, the preceding vowel generally represents a long sound and the *e* represents no sound. The vowel plus the consonant and *e* stand for the long vowel sound.

5. Look at the examples in condition 3. What likenesses do you observe? Can you form a generalization?
6. Compare your generalization with this one. When a syllable ends in a vowel (an open syllable), the vowel sound is generally long.

Table 6-16 Short Vowel Generalization

Example	Vowel Sound
1. rot	ŏ
2. bottle (bot tle)	ŏ
3. had	ă
4. hammer (ham mer)	ă
5. tub	ŭ
6. huddle (hud dle)	ŭ
7. sip	ĭ
8. mitten (mit ten)	ĭ
9. crest	ĕ
10. elbow (el bow)	ĕ

Discussion for Table 6-16

1. What likenesses do you see in the example words or syllables? What causes them to have short sounds? State a generalization that applies.
2. Compare your generalization with this one. When a word or syllable ends in a consonant (a closed syllable) the vowel sound is usually short.

Generalizations which apply to vowels depend on the vowel positions in syllables. Consequently, dividing words into syllables is important in determining vowel sounds. Table 6-17 presents some common syllabication patterns.

Table 6-17 Syllabication Generalizations

1. VC/CV	
Example	Syllabic Division
1. involve	in volve
2. under	un der
3. survey	sur vey
4. person	per son
5. common	com mon
6. alter	al ter
7. member	mem ber

8. inform	in form
9. support	sup port
10. rescue	res cue

2. V/CV

Example	Syllabic Division
1. private	pri vate
2. secret	se cret
3. local	lo cal
4. student	stu dent
5. major	ma jor
6. cement	ce ment
7. elect	e lect
8. unique	u nique
9. music	mu sic
10. recent	re cent

3. C + le

Example	Syllabic Division
1. gentle	gen tle
2. uncle	un cle
3. multiple	mul ti ple
4. syllable	syl la ble
5. wiggle	wig gle
6. stable	sta ble
7. bundle	bun dle
8. struggle	strug gle
9. stifle	sti fle
10. people	peo ple

Discussion for Table 6-17

1. Look at the first group of 10 examples. Examine the syllabic division. Do you see any pattern? If so, write a generalization that applies.
2. Compare your generalization with this one. When two consonants occur between two consonants: *VC/CV* (Remember that you cannot separate consonant digraphs and consonant blends when making syllabic division. Additionally, keep the base and separate at the suffix, for example, *want-ed* or *list-ing*.)
3. Look at the second group of 10 examples. Examine the syllabic divisions. Do you see likenesses among the words? Write a generalization that predicts how words that fit the pattern should be divided into syllables.
4. Compare your generalization with this one. When a single consonant occurs between two vowels, the syllabic division may be made so that the consonant begins the next syllable: *V/CV*. Look at example 2 under group 2. Tell why the syllabic division did not occur between *c* and *r*.

5. Look at the third group of 10 examples. Look carefully for a pattern in the way the words are divided into syllables. Write a generalization for such words.
6. Compare your generalization with this one. When a word ends in *le,* the *le* plus *the* immediately preceding consonant form the final syllable: *c* + *le.*

ADDITIONAL ENABLING ACTIVITIES

The following are designed to extend your knowledge of phonics. Because the objectives are interrelated, you may be able to accomplish one or all three by engaging in only *one* of the given activities. You and your instructor should decide the activity or activities that are best suited to your own needs and time commitments.

1. This enabling activity requires your reading and taking notes on one or more of the following resources.
   (a) Harris and Sipay, Appendix B. This gives good background information.
   (b) Heilman, 1976. Entire book gives good background.
   (c) Durkin. Entire book gives a good treatment.
   (d) Heilman, 1972, Chapter 7.
   (e) Study the workbooks and/or activity pads that accompany the basal readers.

2. Attend class session(s) Time _____ Date _____ .
3. An activity of your choice.
4. An activity selected by your instructor.

READING RESOURCES/REFERENCES

1. Anderson, Verna D. *Reading and Young Children.* New York: Macmillan, 1968, Chapter 8.
2. Bush, Clifford L., and Mildred H. Huebner. *Strategies for Reading in the Elementary Schools,* 2nd ed. New York: Macmillan, 1979, pp. 75–87.
3. Dallmann, Martha, Roger L. Rouch, Lynette Y. C. Chang, and John J. DeBoer. *The Teaching of Reading,* 5th ed. New York: Holt, Rinehart & Winston, 1978.
4. Dechant, Emerald V. *Improving the Teaching of Reading,* 2nd ed. Englewood Cliffs, N.J. Prentice-Hall, 1970, pp. 302–360.
5. Durkin, Delores. *Strategies for Identifying Words.* Boston: Allyn and Bacon, 1976.
6. Harris, Albert J., and Edward R. Sipay. *Effective Teaching of Reading,* 2nd ed. New York: David Mckay, 1971, Appendix B.

7. Heilman, Arthur W. *Phonics in Proper Perspective,* 3rd ed. Columbus, Ohio: Charles E. Merrill, 1976.
8. Heilman, Arthur W. *Principles and Practices of Teaching Reading,* 3rd ed. Columbus, Ohio: Charles E. Merrill, 1972. Chapter 7.
9. Wilson, Robert M., and Mary A. Hall. *Programmed Word Attack for Teachers.* Columbus, Ohio: Charles E. Merrill, 1968.
10. Zintz, Miles V. *The Reading Process: The Teacher and the Learner.* Dubuque, Ia. *William C. Brown, 1970, pp. 168–174.*

Chapter 7
Teaching Phonics Skills

RATIONALE

Phonics is an important word analysis technique. As such, it has a place in the reading curriculum, particularly in the primary (grades 1 to 3) reading program. Contrary to what one might read or hear in nonprofessional (perhaps even some professional) media, phonics is not a method for teaching reading to children. It is a skill that we teach children so that they may become independent and proficient in their ability to convert print into its oral counterpart. This chapter will help you teach phonics skills to children. Specifically, it is concerned with enabling you to develop and implement plans for teaching phonics through inductive approaches, assess phonic generalizations as to utility, sequence phonic skills, and distinguish between approaches to teaching phonics.

OBJECTIVES

After completing this chapter, you will be able to:
1. Identify an appropriate sequence for presenting phonic elements to children.
2. Assess phonic generalizations as to utility.
3. Distinguish among different approaches to teaching phonics.
4. Develop and implement a teaching plan for phonics that meets given criteria.
5. Identify an activity to reinforce a given phonic element.
6. Complete an objective identified by the instructor.

PREASSESSMENT

See Appendix A-7.

**Instructional
Activity 1**

Sequence for Presenting Phonics Elements

Recall the phonic skills you learned in Chapter 6. There are so many elements that they need organization and sequencing so as not to overwhelm and awe the student and thereby interfere with his or her learning. Just where should one begin? With the first letter of the alphabet? Although some persons advocate just that, most reading authorities propose an orderly sequence for the presentation of the phonics skills that proceeds from simplest to most complex. This rationale is generally employed in the way phonic skills are presented in basal reader series. Still, it will be helpful for you to know what authorities recommend, particularly when you want to select materials or to depart from the basal reading series in use in your school.

You may want to do this as you address the individual needs of the pupils and as you use alternative approaches to basal readers.

A key factor to remember when teaching phonic skills is that they should be kept in a meaningful context. Phonic principles should be applied to words children already know, so that when they can recognize in print 3 to 5 words that illustrate a phonic principle you think they are ready to learn, they probably can learn it then. You would want to use common sense, of course, and teach the simpler skills before you introduce the complex ones. Use the sequence suggested in this chapter to help you make your decision.

You learned in previous chapters that good auditory and visual discrimination abilities are necessary for success in phonics instruction. Thus development of those abilities should form the basis for other phonics instruction.

Most authorities recommend the following sequence for phonics instruction.

1. Teach *consonants* sounds first. Teach those that do not represent multiple sounds first: *b, j, m, p, t, f,* and *v.* Teach the sounds as they occur in the initial, then final, and then medial position. Introduce consonants with multiple sound associations later (*c, g, s,* and *x*).
2. Teach common consonant digraphs.
3. Teach common consonant blends (also referred to as clusters).
4. Teach sounds of short (unglided) vowels.
5. Teach useful generalizations.
6. Teach sounds of long vowels (glided).
7. Teach vowel digraphs.
8. Teach diphthongs.
9. Teach silent letters.
10. Teach rules governing short vowel sounds.
11. Teach rules governing long vowel sounds.

There are some common sense reasons supporting the sequence. You can discover these by completing the following activities.

120

Activities for Sequence—1 (Consonant Sounds)

1. Look over the list of sight words. Note how most of them begin. More words start with consonants than with vowels.
2. Read these words. Write what you noticed about the vowels sounds and the consonants sounds.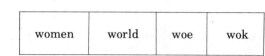

| women | world | woe | wok |

Consonant letters more consistently represent the same sound. Vowels are highly variable in sounds.

3. Using the letters given, see if you can decide on the whole word.

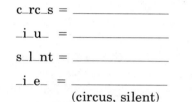

c_rc_s = _____

_i_u_ = _____

s_l_nt = _____

_i_e_ = _____

(circus, silent)

Consonants usually comprise more easily identifiable features of words than vowels do.

Comments About Sequence in Phonics

The sequence in which phonic elements are introduced is important. Still, deviations are sometimes warranted. A real need for one skill may arise in a classroom before its preceding skill has been introduced. In such instances, it may be wise to introduce the needed skill. Also, a child probably does not have to have been taught *all* of the initial consonant sounds before he or she is introduced to some of the short vowel sounds. In fact, for phonics to be meaningful and useful as a word analysis tool, children probably should be introduced to certain vowel sounds (ă as in *cat*, ŏ as *hop*) early in the program so that they can apply their newly acquired skills to analyze new words. A good rule to guide the teacher in this decision is as follows. As soon as the child has three to five words that illustrate a phonic element in his sight vocabulary, it is time to teach that skill. For example, once the child has mastered the sight words *am, and, at,* and *as,* it may be profitable to teach him the short vowel sound for *a*.

Activity for Sequence—4 (Short Vowel Sounds)

Look at a sight word list. Out of the first 20 words, record the number of words with a short vowel sound and the number of words with a long vowel sound. Short vowels occur more in beginning reading material.

121

Although it does not appear in the sequence just described, another useful step in learning phonics is learning common phonograms. This step can be inserted at any point after the child has a stock of initial consonant sounds. For example, the child who has knowledge of the sounds *b, f,* and *m* and their representative letters and who knows the word *at* as a sight word has the basics to profit from instruction in the phonogram *at.* Armed with this information, the child may decode three new words—*bat, fat,* and *mat.*

❋ Activity

Using the scope and sequence chart from a basal reading series, compare the sequence for the introduction of the phonic skills with those just given. Compare your responses with those of someone who chose a different series. Give a possible rationale for deviations.

Series _____ .

Deviations _____ .

Instructional Activity 2

Assessing the Utility of Phonics Generalizations

Of what real value is the phonics instruction provided for children? Is the English language so unphonetic that the teaching of phonics is impractical? Several researchers set out to answer these questions. In the first study, Clymer (1963) identified 45 generalizations commonly taught in the primary-grade basal readers and checked the words included in the readers against the generalizations. The result was a percentage of utility for the generalizations. Some generalizations were found to have percentages of utility that were so low that they were useless and even confusing to children. Some were found to have high percentages of utility (75% and above). The original research was extended by Bailey (1967) and Emans (1967) to include words above the fourth-grade level, substantiating some of Clymer's findings but finding differences in others. The results are presented in Appendix F.

As you read about the three research projects, keep these points in mind.
- Some of these rules should not be taught, since they are not useful. Consider 75 percent utility generalizations as helpful to children.
- Some of the differences found by the researchers may be due to their regional pronunciation of words in their sample.
- Clymer worked with basal reader words in grades 1 to 3. Bailey compared words from eight basal readers in grades 1 to 6.
- Emans compared words that he sampled from the *Teachers Word Book of 30,000 Words* by Thorndike and Lorge.
- The first word in parentheses represents an example that conforms to the generalization, while the second is an example that deviates from it.

122

Activities

Using the preceding information, respond to these situations. Compare your responses with those of a peer.

1. Ms. Perfect, a second-grade teacher, has a pet principle that she teaches to perfection to all her pupils. It is, "When two vowels go walking, the first does the talking and it says its name. But the second is silent."

    (a) Which principle is she teaching? _____

    _____

    (b) Explain why her pupils read the following words as they did.

    (1) bread = /brēd/_____

    (2) field = /fīld/_____

    (3) build = /būld/_____

    (c) If you wanted to help, what would you tell Ms. perfect about her

    phonics content? Why? _____

    _____

    _____

    _____

Check: Your responses should include these ideas.

- Ms. Perfect taught the generalization "When there are two vowels side by side, the long sound of the first is heard and the second is usually silent."
- But she did not consider that the principle is less than 45 percent useful. This means that the children who learn and apply the rule will probably be wrong in their pronunciation of words 55 percent of the time.
- Assess the value of a given generalization before you teach it.

2. You are a new teacher in the school and you want to do a good job in your school, which has a "heavy-on-the-phonics" philosophy. As you prepare to teach a reading lesson, you note that a phonic generalization is to be emphasized. You want to teach it just right and give many examples, but you can only think of words that are the exception to the

    rule. What should you do? Why? _____

Check: Your responses should include these ideas.

- Check the generalization for utility. It may not have a high enough utility value to warrant teaching it.

123

Instructional Activity 3

Approaches to Teaching Phonics

In the history of reading instruction in the United States, phonics instruction has been prominent and neglected in cycles. Much of the "rise and fall of the phonic empire" has been precipitated by the methods used to teach phonics at various periods.

The first emphasis in phonics embodied techniques of teaching the name of the letters of the alphabet and the corresponding sound it represented and combining these into syllables and then into words. The learner *synthesized* the sounds into words, with little attention given to meaning. This synthetic method of teaching words, while not prominent today, is still advocated by some people and is evident in some instructional materials.

With the decline of the synthetic phonics methods came the advent of the whole-word approaches to teaching beginning reading. Soon phonics crept back into the instructional scene, but with a different emphasis that reflected the influence of whole-word methods. An *analytical* approach to phonics developed. Instead of teaching the letter, the sound it represented, and how to combine them into syllables and words, teachers began with the whole word to show how it was composed of phonic elements.

Phonics today shares instructional time and effort with the other word attack skills and the meaning skills, some teachers would like to see synthetic phonics as "king" once more. A critique of the two approaches is now presented.

Synthetic phonics involves teaching the sounds associated with the individual letters and then combining them to form words.

- Isolating individual consonant sounds produces distortion. Kuh-a-tuh does not equal the word *cat*.
- Children frequently have problems in blending the sounds to form words.
- The method requires repetitive drills that may become boring.
- Getting meaning is deemphasized and can produce mere "word calling."

Analytic phonics involves teaching the sounds of letters as they occur in known words.

- Distortion of sounds is avoided.
- The child's use of phonics as a skill to analyze words as they occur in reading is facilitated.

Other terms associated with phonics instruction are *inductive* and *deductive*. These relate to how the teacher goes about teaching a particular phonic element or generalization. In the inductive approach, the teacher presents examples that illustrate a given element or principle and then leads children to formulate a generalization that might apply. This approach is illustrated in the procedures used in Chapter 6. In a deductive approach, the teacher states the generalization and then has the student apply it to words.

In most circumstances the inductive approach is preferable to the deductive approach. The inductive approach requires the student to concentrate on likenesses and differences in words; this is a most useful technique to apply in real-life reading, when one must decide how the new word is similar to one already known and apply what is known to the decoding of the new word. The inductive approach fosters independence in word attack, since the student can form his or her own "rules" from the examples encountered. Furthermore, learners tend to be able to apply generalizations better and to remember them longer when they have been developed inductively.

Phonics and Language Differences

Research on children who speak nonstandard dialects has created concern for the poor auditory discrimination abilities (factors that are associated with success in phonics instruction) of these children. However, some inherent weaknesses in the tests themselves have contributed to the findings, which should be interpreted in this light. All of this has an influence on phonics instruction.

Several authors have acknowledged other linguistic variables that could contribute to interferences in instruction in phonics. (Weber, Melmed, and Seymour in Laffey and Shuy, 1973). Certain phonological differences occur between nonstandard and standard English. For instance, some nonstandard speakers tend to produce words as homophones (words with the same sounds). Examples are *pen-pin* or *more-mow*. There is no constrast in the vowel sounds. Not only do the speakers not produce a contrast in the sounds, they also tend not to hear the contrast. If these words or similar words occur on a test of auditory discrimination, they would likely find no difference in the pairs. This cannot be interpreted to mean that they have poor auditory discrimination abilities, however. They are giving correct responses according to their dialect.

This has other implications for phonics instruction. Teachers who seek to give phonics instruction to speakers of nonstandard dialects must use caution in the choice of illustrative words. For instance, the teacher who works with some Black-dialect or other Southern-dialect speakers should not use the word *ten* to illustrate the short sound of *e*. For these groups, there is no contrast between the vowel sounds in *ten* and *tin,* even though they would identify them as words distinct in meaning if spoken in an appropriate context.

This means that the teacher has a responsibility to learn as much as possible about the language of his or her children. If the teacher does not do so, he is apt to fail in efforts to teach them phonics and, perhaps, other reading skills.

Activities

Use what you have learned to make decisions in these situations. Compare your responses with those of a peer.

1. You are observing in Mr. Rote's second-grade classroom. Mr. Rote points to a letter on a chart—*d*—and the children respond /d/ in unison. What

   type of lesson is this? _____

   _____

2. Mrs. Right, the second-grade teacher across the hall, is teaching the same content. She asks the children to pronounce the sight words *do* and *down*. She calls their attention to the beginning sound, then to the

   beginning letter *d*. What type of lesson is this? _____

   _____

3. Mr. Moody is presenting this lesson to his third-grade students. "A single vowel usually represents the short sound if it is in a closed syllable. Now, as you read p. 17, I want you to write down each word that follows

   this rule." What type of lesson is he presenting? _____

   _____

Check: Your responses should include these ideas.

- Mr. Rote is presenting a synthetic phonics lesson.
- Mrs. Right is presenting an analytic phonics lesson. It is also an inductive lesson.
- Mr. Moody is presenting a deductive phonics lesson.

Instructional Activity 4

Planning for Teaching Phonics Lessons

In presenting a phonics lesson that is inductive, the following steps should be used. These steps correspond to steps 2, 3, and 4 of the daily plan you worked with in previous chapters.

Step 1. Auditory Discrimination—Noting Likenesses.

The teacher says words that illustrate the principle to be developed. These should be words in the child's oral/aural language system and could be words in his or her sight vocabulary.

The teacher helps students determine how the words are alike (regarding sound).

Step 2. Visual Discrimination—Noting Likenesses.

The teacher then records on the board the same words as in step 1.

The teacher asks children to find parts that look alike and has a child frame in (using hands as the frame) the part that is alike.

Step 3. Auditory Discrimination—Noting Differences.

The teacher pronounces another group (three to five) of words, one of which does not illustrate the key principle.

The teacher asks the children to identify the word which does not belong and to tell why.

Step 4. Visual Discrimination—Noting Differences.

The teacher places the second group of words (step 3) on the board. The teacher calls for a child to locate one that does not belong in the group and to tell why.

Step 5. Blending—Forming New Words from Known words.

The teacher writes on the board a known sight word from which a new word can be formed by substituting or placing in the key principle. For example, if the teacher is teaching the *ch* digraph in initial position, he might place the word *in* on the board.

The teacher shows how the new sound and the known sight word can combine to form a new word: *ch* + *in* = *chin*.

Variation. If the teacher places the word *will* on the board, a substitution process must take place to form the new word: will → chill

This step helps children apply their phonic knowledge in the analysis of other words.

Step 6. *Application*. The teacher takes newly generated words and places them in context for the child to choose the one that makes sense.

For example, using step 5 and the *ch* digraph, the following words can be formed from the basic sight words list.

ch + at = chat   ch + now = chow   ch + best = chest
ch + eat = cheat   ch + walk = chalk

These words can then be placed in meaningful sentences for application of skill. For example: She uses (chat, chest, chalk) to write on the board.

The teacher provides opportunities for other reading (silent or oral) that requires the student to apply the skill in a variety of contexts.

A sample lesson is presented here for the initial sound of *b*.

Skill: Initial *b* sound

1. *Objective*. Given oral presentation of real or nonsense words, the learner identifies the letter that stands for the initial *b* sound or supplies another word that begins with the *b* sound.

2. *Introduction*. Different instruments can make different sounds. Our language also has different sounds. The letters of the alphabet stand for different sounds.

3. *Development.* Listen as I say these words. They are words you already know.

   best   big   back

   How are they alike? Right, they begin with the same sound.
   Now look at these words I put on the board.

   best   big   back

   How do they look alike? Right, they all look alike at the beginning.
   Come frame the part that is alike in each word, Bob.
   Now listen as I say these words.

   best, big, hot, back.

   Which word is different? Right, *hot.* Why is it different?
   Yes, because it doesn't sound like the other words at the beginning.
   Watch as I write these words.

   best, big, hot, back.

   Which word does not belong? Why? Good, *hot* doesn't belong because it doesn't begin with the same letter.

   I am writing a word you already know. The word is *us.* Now watch what happens when I put our new letter in front—*bus.* Use your new sound and say the new word. Do it with these words.

   at → *b*at   all → *b*all

   Here are some other words you already know.

   get   take   far

   Now watch what happens when I change the first letter to our new one.

   *g*et → bet   *t*ake → bake   *f*ar → bar

   I am going to give you an activity. What you must do is decide which word is best in the sentence and draw a line under it. There may be some words that you do not know *but,* if you do what we already did in this lesson, you can figure them out.
   (a) Dan left his (look, book) at home.
   (b) Meg had a new (felt, belt) on.
   (c) Sue feels (bad, had) now.
   (d) Mother must pay the (will, bill).

4. *Summary/Evaluation.* I am giving each of you three cards. One says *Yes.* Hold up the *Yes* card. One says *No.* Hold up the *No* card. One has a question mark—?. Hold up the ? card.

   Now I am going to call out some words to you. If the words have our new sound in the beginning, hold up your *Yes* card. If the word does not, hold up your *No* card. If you do not know, hold up your ? card.
   Here are your words. (Teacher calls out words and notes responses of children).

   Now let's look at what we learned today. Who can tell me? Good, we learned that the letter *b* stands for the sound we hear in the beginning of *bat.*

Activities

1. Observe the preceding lesson carefully and answer these questions. Compare your responses with those of a peer.

   (a) Does the lesson represent an inductive approach to phonics? Why?

   _____

   _____

   _____

   _____

   _____

   (b) Does the lesson represent a synthetic approach to phonics? Why?

   _____

   _____

   _____

   _____

   _____

   _____

   _____

   Check: Your responses should include these ideas.

   - The lesson is *inductive* because it presents examples and leads children to form the symbol sound relationship for *b*.
   - The lesson is *analytic* because it presents words and focuses on sounds as they occur in words.

2. Look at the lesson again. Certain parts are followed by blank spaces. Read the paragraphs so marked and describe what step the teacher is trying to present. You may want to refer to the *Plan for Teaching a Phonic Element* on pp. 126–127.

3. (a) Choose any phonic element listed in Chapter 6. Write a plan for teaching the element that incorporates the basic plan format presented in Appendix F and the procedure for teaching a phonic element presented in this chapter.

   (b) Submit the plan for critique by a peer.

   (c) Submit the plan for critique by your instructor.

   (d) Revise your plan as indicated by the critiques.

   (e) Implement that plan in at least one of these settings while being observed by the instructor or a peer.

(1) With a small group of children

                                      Date   Time

---

(2) To the entire class

                                        Date   Time

(f) Critique your performance with a peer and/or the course instructor.

Instructional Activity 5

Reinforcement Activities for Phonics Skills

Remember that although they are a part of a lesson, reinforcement activities differ from other activities. Some activities are intended to introduce a new skill and may be called developmental activities. Other lessons may be designed to have the student practice a skill that has already been introduced by the teacher. These are called reinforcement activities.

In teaching phonics, a reinforcement activity might differ in structure from one designed to develop the skill initially. For instance, you learned to prepare a lesson for introducing a new phonics skill to children. You did this through an inductive approach. In planning a reinforcement activity, you may use a deductive approach. This means that you may use a deductive reinforcement activity to follow up a skill that was initially taught through an inductive approach.

The following is a sample deductive reinforcement lesson for the initial *b* sound.

Skill: Initial *b*

The teacher states the following.

The letter *b* stands for the sound we hear at the beginning of the word *book*. I have some pictures in this envelope. The names of some of these pictures begin with the same sound as *book*. I'll give each of you a picture, and you must tell if the word for the picture begins with our *b* sound.
Note. In the envelope are pictures of, for example, a box, a baby, a boy, a girl, a ball, a bugle, a bicycle, a bird, and a man. Each child takes his or her turn to tell if his pictured word begins with *b*.

SUGGESTED TEACHING ACTIVITIES

1. *Skill*:   Initial consonant substitution.
    Materials: Various shapes cut from poster board.
    Procedures: The teacher prints a common phonogram or familiar sight word on the shapes and cuts a hole in the shape large enough for a beginning letter to be placed there. He or she prepares a long strip of poster board with appropriate consonants on it, secures it to the back of

the shape where the hole is cut by making a sleeve that allows the strip to move freely, or prepares a wheel with the consonants so that it can be secured to the shape with a brass fastener and the letter will show through the hole in the shape.

The student manipulates the wheel or the strip so as to expose the consonant and form a word and then pronounces the word and turns to form a new one.

Variation: Make the consonant stationary and put different phonograms on the movable parts.

Number: Individual or small group.

Example:

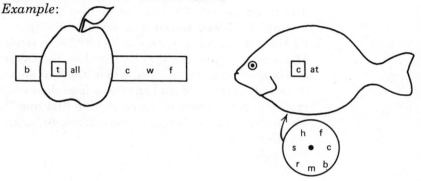

2. *Skill*: Short and long vowel sounds.

Materials: Sheet with example long and short vowel words, crayons.

Procedures: The teacher prepares a sheet as shown in the example and has students follow these directions. If the word has a short vowel sound, color its space blue. If it has a long sound, color the space pink. (Any contrasting colors will work.)

Example:

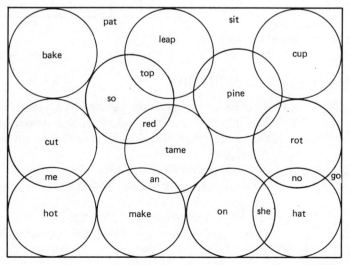

131

Variation: Use words with diphthongs and digraphs or consonant blends and consonant digraphs.

Number: Whole class, small group, or individual.

3. *Skill:* Consonant blends.

Materials: Playing board made from cardboard or an open manilla folder, a circular spin disc cut from cardboard, word cards, and playing tokens such as buttons.

Procedures: The teacher constructs a game board and disc as shown in the example. He or she cuts 3 × 5 inch index cards in two pieces and writes words on them illustrating the *r* blends, such as in *crow, braid, dream,* and *great.* The teacher divides the word cards into stacks illustrating the blend sound and divides the spin disc into four sections, labeling the sections with the blends being studied: *cr, br, dr, gr.*

The student spins the dial on the disc and takes a card from the stack corresponding to the area in which the dial stops. He or she pronounces the word on the card and advances his token a space if he is correct, but remains in the space if incorrect. The first one "home" wins.

Variation: Use different blends, digraphs, or other phonic elements.

Number: Small group.

Example:

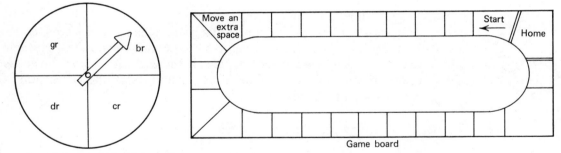

Spin disc with spinner attached with brass fastener

Game board

ADDITIONAL ENABLING ACTIVITIES

1. This enabling activity relates to Objectives 1, 2, and 3 of the chapter. You may extend your skill in the stated objectives by pursuing any of these readings. Read and take notes on at least two of the following references.

    (a) Burns and Roe, pp. 136–153.

    (b) Dallmann, et al., pp. 144–150.

    (c) Zintz, pp. 247–253.

    (d) Lapp and Flood, pp. 205–239.

2. This enabling activity relates to Objectives 4 and 5. It is probable that

you will need to pursue more than one for each objective, particularly since these objectives require you to demonstrate specific teaching competencies.

(a) Observe a primary-grade teacher present a phonics lesson.

                    Date   Time   Place

_____

(b) Observe as a peer presents a phonics lesson. Critique the lesson with the peer according to given criteria (given in Instructional Activity 4).

3. Attend class session(s) Time _____ Date _____ .
4. An enabling activity of your choice.
5. An enabling activity selected by your instructor.

READING RESOURCES / REFERENCES

1. Burns, Paul C., and Betty D. Roe. *Teaching Reading in Today's Elementary Schools.* Chicago: Rand McNally, 1976.
2. Dallmann, Martha, Roger L. Rouch, Lynette Y. C. Chang, and John J. DeBoer. *The Teaching of Reading,* 5th ed. New York: Holt, Rinehart & Winston, 1978.
3. Lapp, Diane, and James Flood. *Teaching Reading to Every Child.* New York: Macmillan, 1978.
4. Laffey, James L., and Roger Shuy. *Language Differences: Do They Interfere?* Newark, Del.: International Reading Association, 1973.
5. Zintz, Miles V. *The Reading Process,* 2nd ed. Dubuque, Ia.: William C. Brown, 1975.

Section 4
Basic Reading Skills: Comprehension

The competencies for this section are necessities for any good teacher, regardless of the level or subject matter taught. These competencies relate to skill in stimulating thinking abilities.

The teacher:

- Knows the characteristics of different facets of reading comprehension.
- Develops questioning strategies that promote critical reading skills.
- Implements questioning techniques that stimulate complex levels of thinking in students.

Using the Chapters in Section 4
Follow the listed steps to complete the chapters.

1. Read the rationale to get an overview of the contents and an understanding of why the chapter is important to a teacher.
2. Read the objectives to learn the expected performance for the chapter.
3. Take the preassessment if you choose. If not, proceed to step 4. If you take the preassessment, score it to determine your strong and weak points relative to the objectives.
4. Read the information provided by the text and complete the activities as directed.
5. Select from additional enabling activities those that correspond your needs. Use the Reading Resources/References to extend your understandings.

   The chapters that relate to teaching techniques include supplementary activities. Complete these as suggested by your instructor.
6. Schedule a meeting with your instructor and take the postassessment.
7. Evaluate your performance and proceed to chapters in Section V or repeat steps 4 to 6, accordingly.

Chapter 8
Identifying Comprehension Skills

RATIONALE

Word recognition skills are vital in the reading process; however, they are merely tools whereby a person can decode the graphic symbols, which is a prerequisite for comprehension of meaning. A child must be able to decode a word before he or she can apply meaning to it and before he can understand the relationship of the word to other words. Word recognition is a tool for reading and is meaningless in the absence of comprehension. Word recognition without comprehension is "word calling" and does not fulfill our definition of reading as the association of experience with given written symbols.

Reading comprehension consists of a series of skills ranging from very simple to highly complex. In order to read, there must be understanding of words, phrases, sentences, paragraphs, and larger units. There must be skills in understanding in various degrees and for various purposes. The reader must be taught to read *between* the lines or comprehend implied or inferential meanings or to read *beyond* the lines by being stimulated to think of applications beyond those suggested by the author.

Since the development of comprehension skills is one of the main tasks of teachers of reading, teachers must be able to identify and teach comprehension skills to children. This chapter will enable you to identify specific comprehension skills, categorize the skills according to levels of understanding or thinking required, and assess questions according to type of skills required for response.

OBJECTIVES

After completing this chapter, you will be able to:
1. Identify the written units for reading comprehension.
2. Identify the levels of reading comprehension.
3. Classify given reading comprehension skills according to level.
4. Classify questions according to comprehension skill required to answer correctly.
5. Complete an objective identified by the instructor.

PREASSESSMENT

See Appendix A-8.

Instructional Activity 1

Units for Reading Comprehension

Introduction

Some authorities believe that comprehension is an entity, that it cannot be broken down into components. In contrast to this holistic view, we maintain that there are critical components of the comprehension process and that these components can be taught. The components are viewed as subskills of the comprehension process (Lapp and Flood, 1987, pp. 299–317), which requires the simultaneous application of many skills.

Reading Comprehension Units

One way to think of reading comprehension is in terms of the written units of understanding. This dimension of comprehension can be depicted from the smallest to the largest component. In this view, the basic units for reading comprehension are the words, phrases, sentences, paragraphs, and whole passages.

Word Meaning. This aspect of comprehension deals with getting meaning from the written words. It includes skill in utilizing word structure to drive meaning from words. Examining the unknown word for known prefixes, suffixes, or base words can be an aid in discovering the word meaning. For example, the reader who knows the base word *plant* and the prefix *re* may be able to apply this knowledge to understand the meaning of the new word *replant*. The use of structural analysis skills (as discussed in Chapter 4) for understanding can be and should be taught in the reading program.

Word meaning relates to what Smith (1978, p. 122) calls mediated comprehension. It requires extra processes to figure out what a word means before other meaning can be extracted. This may be a difficult process, since most words have multiple meanings. Word-by-word comprehension of a sentence is difficult to process and may yield a meaning unlike that intended by the author, since word-by-word meaning does not account for the relationships intended between and among the component words.

Another tool for getting meaning from words involves the use the context. Some types of context clues with examples are given next.

1. *Use of Parentheses.* There was a slight fissure (crack) in the bone.
2. *Use of the word or (appositives).* The cement began to solidify, or harden, too quickly.
3. *Use of another sentence to restate word meaning or give examples.* His writing was illegible. No one could read the prescription he had written.

4. *Use of comparison or contrast.* Jane abominates washing dishes. But she loves to do the cooking.

Phrase Meaning. Just because a reader understands the meanings of the individual component words does not necessarily mean that he will understand a phrase such as "out of her head" or "by the same token." The language contains figurative expressions that are not a composite of the meanings of the individual words. This is true of most phrases that require an understanding of the relationship of the component words to each other as well as an understanding of the word meanings.

Perhaps not much instructional time need be given to phrase reading particularly for those children who are progressing well in reading. Most good readers organize their reading into meaningful phrases. But poor readers tend not to do so, and comprehension suffers. For these children, exercises in understanding phrases and in breaking sentences into meaningful phrases may be fruitful.

Sentence Meaning. Just as it is possible for a reader to understand the meanings of words in phrases and *not* comprehend the meaning of the phrase, it is also possible to miss the meaning of a sentence even if one knows the meaning of each component word. Getting meaning from a sentence is one integral step in the reading process. Sentence meaning is gained from understanding specific details, understanding sentence organization, and attending to word order.

Difficulty in understanding sentence meaning reflects the complexity of the sentence itself. For example, simple sentences written in the active voice would be the easiest to understand; sentences containing more than one clause and prepositional phrase would be the most difficult to comprehend, particularly if they were in the passive voice. In fact, sentences in passive construction seem most difficult to comprehend, perhaps because children attend most carefully to word order (Gleason, 1969).

But sentence meaning cannot be separated from paragraph meaning. In fact, the context in which a sentence is placed contributes to the meaning of the sentence itself, just as sentence context contributes to the meaning of words. For example, read the following sentence and think about what it means.

He put his arms down.

Does the meaning match the one conveyed in the following paragraph?

The robber held the police at bay with his gunfire for several minutes. Suddenly he heard the voice of one of the policemen behind him. At that moment, the robber realized that escape was hopeless. He put his arms down. A policeman moved in and kicked the guns aside while another handcuffed the robber.

Does the meaning match the one conveyed in this paragraph?

Tom was playing "Simon Says" with a group of friends. The leader said,

"Arms down" without saying "Simon Says." He put his arms down. Tom was the first one out.

Paragraph Meaning. Paragraphs are groups of sentences organized around a central theme. Within the paragraph are sentences that denote relationships to each other and to the central theme. However, all paragraphs that the reader will encounter may not follow "the rules," and the reader will be expected to get meaning from them, too.

In addition to the topic organization of a paragraph, other types of organization are evidenced in reading materials of students. Other paragraph patterns that imply relationships are given next.

1. Comparison/contrast patterns present ideas that are related for comparison or contrast. The relationship may be of degree or of equality.
2. Time-order patterns present sequences of ideas that cannot be altered without changing meaning. Signals include before/after; first/last; while/later.
3. Cause-and-effect patterns indicate a relationship of one group of ideas as dependent on another idea. This relationship may be signaled by such markers as *if/then; because . . . therefore;* since x happened . . . then y took place; or the relationships may be implied.
4. Enumeration patterns usually consist of a statement with a listing of supporting topics or items. Signals for this pattern include *one type, another type; one, two, three,* and the like.
5. Question-and-answer patterns give a question with the answer following.

Longer Passage Meaning. The ability to comprehend all smaller units is a prerequisite to understanding entire passages. The ability to understand passages is enhanced by the reader's perception of the structure that unites groups of words, groups of sentences, and groups of paragraphs. The groups of paragraphs do not stand alone. Each one contributes in some way to the central theme of the passage.

The reader must be able to follow the author's thinking in order to comprehend the longer passage. To do this, he or she needs to recognize the organization of the selection and the functions of the various types of paragraphs.

- Introductory paragraphs introduce a passage or introduce a new idea within a selection.
- Illustrative or explanatory paragraphs give information or examples or provide support for an author's idea. The paragraph may contain a signal word that relates it to previous paragraphs.
- Descriptive paragraphs provide description of places, things, or events that are relevant to the passage.
- Narrative paragraphs explain actions of characters in a story-type passage.

- Transitional paragraphs signal a shift from one idea to another.
- Concluding paragraphs complete the passage. Frequently they include a brief restatement of the important ideas in the form of a summary.

 Activities

Use the information in the chapter to respond to the question or situations. Compare your responses with those of a peer.

1. Identify one way to classify or think of the reading comprehension skills.

   _____

2. According to the preceding information, place the reading comprehension units where they would occur along the continuum.
   Longest   Length of Unit

   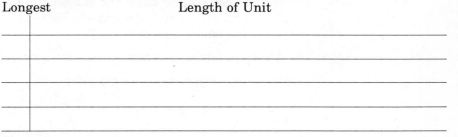

   Shortest

3. A well-meaning third-grade teacher, Mary Meaning, preteaches the meaning of every word to the children before asking them to read a certain sentence. She is thoroughly frustrated when 4 children from her group of 10 are unable to tell her what the sentence means. Use what you learned to explain why this might happen. _____

   _____

   _____

   _____

4. Use what you have learned to solve this problem. In working with her second-year students, Naive Natalie found that some of them had extreme difficulty in understanding the following sentence.

           The boy was hit by a girl.

   Here are some of the answers given to her questions about the sentence.

       Who did the hitting?   The boy.
       Who got hit?   A girl.

Natalie tried to explain the sentence, but to no avail. Then, out of frustration, she rewrote the sentence as follows.

A girl hit the boy.

Imagine her surprise when the same children who consistently answered incorrectly had no trouble at all correcting their error. Explain this. _____

_____

_____

Check: Your response should include these points.

- The first sentence was in the passive voice, so the subject *received* the action. But young readers respond to the word order. In this case the readers predicted that the first in order would be the *doer* of the action, as indicated in their responses.
- In changing the construction from the passive to the active voice, Natalie made the subject the *doer* just as the children who attend to order expect. Therefore they were able to understand the sentence.

5. Use all of the given information to form a true statement about using

passive voice constructions with children. _____

_____

_____

_____

6. Select a passage from a newspaper, magazine, or pamphlet. Analyze each paragraph according to function. Then label the paragraphs as introductory, illustrative/explanatory, descriptive, narrative, transitional, or concluding. Share your work with a peer. Have the peer critique your labeling.

Instructional Activity 2

Levels of Reading Comprehension

In addition to thinking about reading comprehension in terms of the units of learning, one can also think about it in terms of complexity of skills involved. Although there is no clear consensus about these levels of reading comprehension, there does seem to be agreement that some skills are easier to perform while others are more difficult. This continuum of complexity is paralleled by understanding at literal, inferential and critical reading levels.

Literal Comprehension Level

At the easiest level one will find the reading comprehension skills that require recall of details and fact specifically mentioned in the passage. At this level, the important data are provided by the author. The reader receives "surface" messages.

Skills at this level correspond to Bloom's *Taxonomy of Cognitive Domain* in the following ways. Both knowledge and comprehension levels are involved. At the *knowledge* level, the reader is required to recall specific information—facts, details, ideas—from the passage. All understanding at this level is passage dependent. At the *comprehension*[1] level, the reader must have a basic understanding of the facts, details, ideas in the paragraph. The reader may demonstrate the understanding by giving examples or by paraphrasing the information.

Inferential Comprehension Level

Inferential comprehension, although based on literal comprehension, is at a higher level of thinking than literal comprehension. At this level the reader is required to use the information given in the passage in combination with his or her relevant background of experiences and get meanings that are not directly stated but are implied. The reader needs to "read between the lines," or receive messages deeper than those at the surface.

Skills at this level corresponds to Bloom's *Taxonomy* at the *application* level. The reader must use the stated facts, details, and other passage-given information to apply to a situation in which all of the information is not supplied.

Critical Comprehension Level

At this, the most complex level of reading comprehension, the reader must utilize the literal meanings and the inferential meanings in a passage to relate them to concepts beyond what was given in the passage. In the language of Bloom's *Taxonomy,* the skills at this level require *analysis,* or breaking down the whole selection into its parts to find the relationships; *synthesis,* or constructing new possible parts or relationships for the selection; and/or *evaluation,* or judging the materials by some criteria.

Comprehension at this level requires divergent or evaluative thinking. Divergent thinking involves thinking of a diversity of possibilities, using the passage information as the catalyst of thought. Evaluation involves determining the correctness, acceptability, value, or goodness of the information or a conclusion.

---

[1] *Comprehension* as defined for Bloom's *Taxonomy* has a much more specific meaning than the meaning discussed in Chapter 1, in this Chapter and in Chapter 9. In the *Taxonomy, comprehension* refers to a specific kind of thinking, not to a broad category of understanding that can encompass all reading comprehension skills and levels. For a complete discussion of the *Taxonomy,* see Bloom, 1956.

143

What is another way to think about or classify reading comprehension skills?

The two ways of thinking about reading comprehension, by written units and by complexity of thinking skills involved, are depicted in the following figure. As indicated by the figure, the complexity of the comprehension skill cuts across the length of the written segment. For instance, the reader of an entire passage may understand it only in terms of its facts and details, reflecting the simple level, or may have justified conclusions about the worth of the material itself, reflecting complex comprehension. He or she may do the same for a paragraph, sentence, phrase, or even a word, as illustrated by this process. The reader decodes the word *red*. At the literal level, he understands that *red* stands for one of the primary colors. At an inferential level, he understands that red is used to refer to a particular political inclination. At the critical level, he makes a decision that *red* is bad because it is in opposition to the democratic process in which he believes strongly.

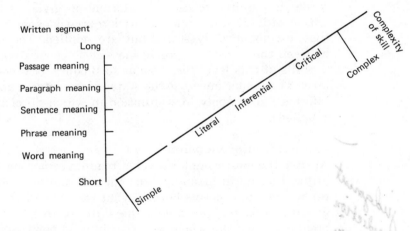

Activities

Use what you have learned to respond to these situations. Compare your responses with those of a peer.

1. Janice is a conscientious seventh-year student who thinks of herself as a good reader. After she reads her social studies text, she can always remember who did something, what they did, where they did it, and when they did it. But, unless it is stated, she does not know why they did it, nor can she tell whether or not it was the right thing to do. What might be concluded about Janice's level of reading comprehension?

_____

_____

_____

_____

2. What makes you think that Janice does a fine job with understanding
   at the literal level? _____

   _____

   _____

3. What helps you understand that she does not function well at inferential
   reading comprehension levels? _____

   _____

   _____

4. What supports the conclusion that Janice does not do well with critical
   comprehension? _____

   _____

   _____

   _____

Check: Your responses should include these ideas.

- Janice did fine as long as the understanding dealt with surface messages of fact or detail—all relating to the literal level. When she tried to find meanings below the surface, she ran into trouble.
- She was unable to take the facts and apply them to decide why something happened—an inferential level skill.
- She also could not evaluate the action, which indicates a weakness at the critical comprehension level.

Instructional Activity 3

Classifying Comprehension Skills
Within each of the comprehension levels, there are various skills that become a focus for instruction. These skills are now explained.

Skills at the Literal Level
1. *Identifies Facts, Details.* The reader knows who, what, when, where about the selection.

145

2. *Sequences Events, Actions.* The reader relates details to each other in a logical sequence when sequence is specified by sequence markers. Some markers are temporal.
   (a) First, last.
   (b) Before, after.
   (c) Calendar names such as morning, noon, afternoon, night; yesterday, today, tomorrow; names of days of week, months of the year, or actual dates.
   (d) Next, then, later, soon, finally, until, while.
   (e) Meanwhile, at the same time, during.
   Others are markers of order.
   (a) In order of importance.
   (b) In consecutive order.
   (c) First in the series.
3. *Identifies Main Idea at Literal Level.* Frequently the reader will encounter a selection in which the main idea is directly stated. In this case, understanding the main idea occurs at the literal level. If, however, the passage gives supportive details without directly stating a main idea, the reader is required to infer a main idea and is comprehending beyond the literal level. Types of skills for identifying main idea at the literal level include:
   (a) Identifying the general topic of the paragraph.
   (b) Determining whether given details support or are irrelevant to the central theme.
   (c) Identifying a main idea statement within a passage. (This statement is usually in the introduction or at the conclusion of the selection, but it may occur in the middle.)
4. *Follows Written Directions.* The reader must be able to identify important facts and details, follow them in sequence, and have a general idea of what the whole thing is about before he can be skillful in following directions.

Skills at the Inferential Level
1. *Draws Inferences from Printed Statements.* This may involve inferring a main idea when one is not explicitly stated or a sequence when clues are implicit.
2. *Identifies Relationships that Are Not Explicitly Stated.* Relationships such as cause and effect, interpersonal, and time and place occur at this level.
3. *Identifies characterizations from traits that are implied.* The reader forms an impression of the personality or the underlying motives of a character.
4. *Identifies setting from stated facts.* The reader utilizes the facts from the selection to form an idea as to where the story is taking place.

Skills at the Critical Level

1. *Predicts Outcomes*. The reader goes beyond the stated information to make possible predictions.

2. *Separates fact from fiction or fact from opinion*. The reader must decide if the information presented can be verified by observation, written records, or experimentation. Beyond this, he must weigh the worth of opinions—those based on facts, those that are unsupported.

3. *Identifies authors mood, tone, or purpose*. The reader decides why the author wrote the materials—to inform, to persuade, to entertain, and the like. He decides what mood the author tries to create by the words employed—emotion-laden terms or figurative language. The reader assesses the tone of the passage by the way the author presents the messages and the words he chooses.

4. *Forms Conclusions*. The reader notes specific instances and utilizes them to form a warranted conclusion. He must use his logical reasoning powers to reach a conclusion that seems sensible to him based on his own knowledge and his interpretation of the selection. The reader should be able to support his conclusions with passage-based evidence.

5. *Recognizes Persuasive Techniques*. The reader recognizes the persuasive techniques commonly used by propagandists.

   (a) *Name calling*. Applying a negative label to a person, an idea, or a whole organization to discredit the person or thing. Such labels include *alien, warmonger,* and *radical*.

   (b) *Glittering Generalities*. Using general terms without providing any details. Frequently, "glowing" terms are used to convey positive feelings so that the audience will accept the idea without careful evaluation. Such emotional words as *peace, brotherhood, prosperity* are frequently used.

   (d) *Testimonials*. Quoting well-known persons as favoring the idea.

   (c) *Transfer*. Using the reputation of a respected person or organization to attach to the idea.

   (e) *Plain Folks*. Portraying oneself as one of the common people to appeal to the public.

   (f) *Card Stacking*. Using facts to give positive or negative impressions, by using only those facts which support the impression intended.

   (g) *Bandwagon*. Urging acceptance of an idea because everyone else has.

   (h) *Other persuasive techniques used in advertisements in varying combinations*. Some are identified here.

      (1) *Sex Appeal*. Using attractive people to help sell a product.

      (2) *Fear*. Using examples to frighten people by indicating that bad things may happen if they do not use a product or service.

      (3) *Identification with Prestige*. Using prestigious terms and settings such as elegant, distinguished, and luxurious to build an image for a product.

(4) *Personification.* Using a person as a symbol of an idea and applying that to a product or service.

6. *Compares/contrasts elements (facts, details, conclusions, etc.) of the selection to each other or to other selections.*

7. *Evaluates the selection according to criteria.* For example, the reader may utilize this skill by deciding whether or not Goldilocks was justified in eating Baby Bear's porridge and supporting that decision. The reader carefully weighs all information in keeping with his own value system and responds accordingly. He may like, dislike, approve, disapprove, appreciate, or not appreciate.

 Activities

Use what you have learned to respond to the situations. Compare your responses with those of a peer.

1. Reading comprehension skills are grouped in the following diagram. Decide which level of comprehension corresponds to the group and label it in the blank space.

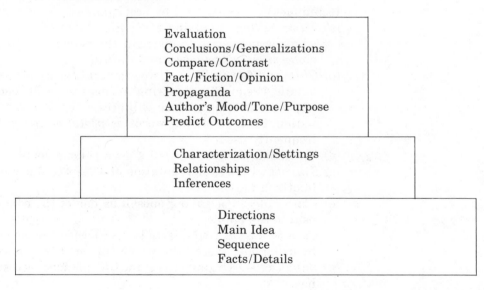

Evaluation
Conclusions/Generalizations
Compare/Contrast
Fact/Fiction/Opinion
Propaganda
Author's Mood/Tone/Purpose
Predict Outcomes

Characterization/Settings
Relationships
Inferences

Directions
Main Idea
Sequence
Facts/Details

2. Cindi Simple just read *The Biography of Peter Perfect,* her favorite rock star. She shared some of the highlights with her friend Judy and concluded by stating, "Peter is the most fantastic singer of all time."

Judy commented, "Oh? I really don't agree!"

Cindi quickly responded, "I'll prove it to you," as she grabbed her book and thumbed through.

In a minute she began reading to Judy, "Peter Perfect has to be the most fantastic singer of all time."

(a) At which *level* is Cindi comprehending? _____

(b) Which *level* of reading comprehension is required in this situation?

_____

(c) Which specific skill does Cindi seem to lack? _____

_____

Check: Your response should include these ideas.

- Cindi is assuming that everything in the book is fact.
- She is functioning at a literal level.
- She needs to function at the *critical* level to distinguish fact from opinion.

3. Select several advertisements from a magazine. What terms, phrases, or labels are used to describe the product or tell what the product can do for you? Use the terms to help you decide the persuasive technique(s) being employed by the sellers of the product in each instance.

Name of Product	Description	Technique
1. Sleek Look Hair Spray	Used by Hock E. Puck, star hockey player	Sex appeal, identification with prestige to build image of product (sleek)
2. _____		
3. _____		
4. _____		

Why is it important for the readers to be able to understand reading material at the critical level? _____

_____

_____

You can see that the reader will often need to read beyond the literal level. He will need to be able to use high-level thinking skills that may go beyond the information explicitly stated. He often uses this ability to make decisions about the material read.

**Instructional
Activity 4**

Classifying Comprehension Questions

Reading comprehension can be stimulated by questioning. The type of question itself determines the type of comprehension it stimulates. Therefore the teacher should be aware of the skills that are stimulated by a given type of question.

Questions at the Text-Explicit Level.

The answers to some questions may be found stated explicitly in the passage. These correspond to the *literal* level of comprehension, but some are more difficult than others because they require a paraphrase or restatement response instead of recall of bits of information.

- Fact/detail questions ask who, what, where.
- Sequence questions ask when.
- Main idea questions ask about the central theme. For example, "What is the topic of the selection?"

Questions at the Text-Implicit Level.

Questions at a higher level require that the reader will generate answers when the information is implied in the material but not explicitly stated. These questions call for responses at the *inferential* comprehension level.

- *Relationships.* What caused *x* to happen? What happened as a result of *y?* Why did *x* occur? How are *x* and *z* alike? Different?
- *Characterizations/Settings.* How did Tom *feel* about . . . ? What evidence shows that Ellen is (lazy)? In which section of the U.S. could this have happened? What makes you think so?

Questions at the Experience Level.

Some questions require a mixture of understanding at text-implicit and background experience levels for adequate responses. These questions stimulate comprehension at critical reading levels.

- *Outcomes.* What might happen because of . . . ? What might have happened if . . . ?
- *Author's Mood/Tone/Purpose.* Why did the author write this passage?

  How did the author want you to feel about _____ ? What words did he use to convey that mood?
- *Propaganda Techniques.* Why does the ad for Savings and Loan Association use a picture of Thomas Jefferson? What words does the ad use to cause you to buy the product?

- *Fact/Fiction; Fact/Opinion.* Could _____ have really happened? How do you know? Which of these statements can be verified?

  Which statements show what the author thinks about _____ ?

- *Comparison/Contrast.* How are _____ and _____ alike in their motives? What were the differences beween two authors' articles on (same topic)?
- *Conclusions/Generalizations.* What conclusions can you draw about the story plot? What evidences support your conclusion?

- *Evaluation.* Did _____ do the right thing when he _____ ? Why do you think so? Would you recommend this article to your friend? Why?

❋ Activities

Use what you have learned to answer these questions.

1. Pretend that you have just read the story "Little Red Riding Hood." Now your teacher asks some comprehension questions. Analyze each question and write the level (literal, inferential, critical) and type of specific skill (fact, conclusion, outcome, etc.) required for successful response.

   (a) What was the little girl's name?

   Level: _____

   Skill: _____

   (b) What might have happened if the woodcutter had not been nearby?

   Level: _____

   Skill: _____

   (c) What makes you think that Red Riding Hood had not met a wolf before?

   Level: _____

   Skill: _____

   (d) Could this story really have happened? Why?

   Level: _____

   Skill: _____

   (e) What caused the wolf to be able to find Grandma's house?

   Level: _____

   Skill: _____

   (f) What happened just before Red Riding Hood got to Grandma's?

   Level: _____

   Skill: _____

   (g) Where was Red Riding Hood going?

Level: _____

Skill: _____

(h) What evidence supports that this took place before Bell invented the phone?

Level: _____

Skill: _____

(i) How is Red Riding Hood like you?

Level: _____

Skill: _____

(j) Why did the author use the sequence: "Oh Grandma, what great big eyes you have." "The better to see you with, my dear," etc.?

Level: _____

Skill: _____

(k) Did Red Riding Hood do the right thing when she stopped to pick the flowers in the woods? Why?

Level: _____

Skill: _____

(l) How can you describe the personality of the wolf?

Level: _____

Skill: _____

(m) What conclusion can you make about the importance of doing exactly what your parents tell you? Why?

Level: _____

Skill: _____

(n) What is the story mainly about?

Level: _____

Skill: _____

ADDITIONAL ENABLING ACTIVITIES

1. Read and take notes on both sources for additional work on any objective in this chapter.
   (a) Dallmann et al., Chapter 7A.
   (b) Lapp and Flood, Chapter 9.

2. Attend class session(s). Time _____ Date _____ .

3. An activity of your choice. _____

_____

4. An activity selected by your instructor. _____

_____

READING RESOURCES/REFERENCES

1. Bloom, Benjamin S., ed. *Taxonomy of Educational Objectives.* New York: David McKay, 1956.
2. Dallmann, Martha, Roger L. Rouch, Lynette Y. C. Chang, and John J. DeBoer. The Teaching of Reading, 5th ed. New York: Holt, Rinehart & Winston, 1978.
3. Gleason, J. B. "Language Development in Early Childhood," in *Oral Language and Reading,* edited by J. Warden. Champaign, Ill.: National Council of Teachers of English, 1969.
4. Karlin, Robert. *Teaching Elementary Reading: Principles* and *Strategies.* New York: Harcourt Brace Jovanovich, 1971.
5. Lapp, Diane, and James Flood. *Teaching Reading to Every Child.* New York: Macmillan, 1978.
6. Smith, Frank. *Understanding Reading: A Psycholinguistic Analysis of Reading and Learning to Read,* 2nd ed. New York: Holt, Rinehart & Winston, 1978.
7. Tatham, Susan Masland. "Comprehension Taxonomies: Their Uses and Abuses," *The Reading Teacher* (November 1978), pp. 190–193.

Chapter 9
Teaching Reading Comprehension

RATIONALE

As noted in Chapter 8, we believe that reading comprehension involves many processes, from very simple to highly complex, and that these processes are facilitated by learning specific comprehension skills. We further maintain that comprehension can be taught by providing direct learning experiences with the specific comprehension skills. Teachers can help the reader comprehend by providing purposes for the reading, pointing out cues to the reader, and guiding discussion of the content by asking questions that probe at the surface meaning and beyond.

This chapter is concerned with teaching procedures for fostering development of reading comprehension skills. It is designed to enable you to develop these competencies.

- Skill in preparing comprehension questions.
- Application of questioning techniques to facilitate reading comprehension.
- Designing of lessons to stimulate comprehension.
- Implementation of activities that reinforce comprehension skills.

OBJECTIVES

After completing this chapter, you will be able to:
1. Identify two purposes for comprehension questions.
2. Construct questions that stimulate the development of specific comprehension skills and meet other given criteria.
3. Prepare a plan for stimulating reading comprehension that meets given criteria.
4. Implement a reading comprehension lesson in either a peer-teaching or actual classroom setting while being observed or videotaped.
5. Complete an objective identified by the instructor.

PREASSESSMENT

See Appendix A-9.

Instructional Activity 1

Purposes for Comprehension Questions

Techniques for Questioning

Comprehension can be stimulated by questions. Because of this, teachers should learn how to formulate stimulating questions. Two types of questions serve this function: those asked before reading the selection (preview questions) and those asked after reading the selection. Preview questions are discussed in the next section.

Preview Questions

Questions stimulate comprehension after one has read and also help the reader to form a mind set before he or she reads. The reader who undertakes the task with a clear purpose in mind tends to understand the material better and retain the information longer. Questions help the reader identify purpose for reading and select a reading style and rate to match this purpose. Questions also help the reader break the reading task into manageable chunks for selective processing. For example, if the preview questions focus on fact and detail, the reader sets his rate for slow, detailed reading without undue reflections about the meanings below the surface. If the preview questions focus on identifying the author's purpose, the reader may not be as attentive to what the facts are as he is to the way the facts are stated.

Preview questions can focus the student's reading comprehension. Because of this, teachers should structure preview questions that stimulate the type of thinking necessary to understand the materials at one or more levels—literal, inferential, and critical. Furthermore, teachers should vary the purpose questions to encourage students to tap their thinking skills at each level.

The purpose-setting questions form a basic step in a directed reading activity, as discussed in Chapter 13. It should be included as part of a teaching plan that involves students in reading any materials, regardless of the content. The same applies to lessons in which the pupil is required to listen. When the student is given a clear purpose for reading or listening, he tends to comprehend more and recall it longer than if no purposes are established. Note that the more advanced reader can be taught how to formulate his own preview questions, as shown in Chapter 11.

Activities

Use what you know to respond to these situations. Compare your responses with those of a peer.

1. Mr. Parrot, an eighth-grade social studies teacher, always provides preview questions for the students. As he assigned the reading of Chapter 16, he said, "I want you to find out when the war began, when it ended;

the names of four major leaders, where the major battles were fought, etc."

The next day he began asking questions such as, "How was this war like the Civil War? What might have happened if the war had not ended when it did?"

Mr. Parrot was perturbed because no one even attempted to answer his questions. Still, the students assured him that they had read the assignment. Write an explanation for this. _____

_____ *- preview end questions -* _____

_____

2. What would you tell Mr. Parrot to do to keep this from happening?

_____

_____

3. What purpose is served by preview questions? _____

_____

_____

Check: Your responses should include these items.

- Mr. Parrot gave the students a mind set for facts and details (literal comprehension) as they read by the type of preview questions he supplied. But when he used questions to check comprehension, he switched types. He asked for critical comprehension (comparison, predicting outcomes). The students' purpose for reading did not match the postreading questions.
- Mr. Parrot should give prereading purposes that correspond to the type of comprehension he wants the students to develop and to the types of postreading questions he asks.
- Prereading questions help the reader focus his comprehension.

Postreading Questions

The various types of postreading questions were discussed in Chapter 8. They were divided by comprehension level into literal, inferential, and critical questions. They were further divided according to the skill they stimulated from factual recall to making evaluations. In this chapter, you will apply your knowledge of comprehension questions to actually writing questions for a given passage. Some guidelines for doing this follow.

Guidelines for Preparing Questions

1. Keep questions brief and to the point.
2. Use language the students understand and use.

3. Structure questions so that they are <u>passage dependent or relate to</u> the <u>materials</u> and cannot be answered correctly without first reading the selection. Be careful that the question does not merely measure the student's background of experiences.

4. Make sure that the question requires the desired skill for successful responses.

5. Avoid questions that require mere yes/no or true/false responses. They tell you very little about the student's skill, since he has a 50 percent chance of answering correctly with either choice whether he has read the selection or not. No Closed end questions -

6. Be certain to prepare questions at a variety of levels instead of focusing only on the literal level. This applies regardless of the level of the student; for primary-grade students need stimulating questions at inferential and critical comprehension levels just as older students do.

✳ **Activities**

Apply what you have learned by responding to these situations. Compare your responses with those of a peer.

1. Evaluate these questions. Read the situation, then respond by telling which guideline for preparing questions the teacher is using or abusing.

(a) Who was George Washington? _____

_____

(b) "When George was just 5 years old, he did something that influenced his whole life. Remember what it was? He didn't know then that it would make a difference, but it really did change his life. Now, who can tell me how his life was changed by that event?" _____

_____

_____

(c) Tune in as Mr. Oblivious questions his third graders as to what attitudinal characteristics pervaded George's behaviors. _____

_____

_____

(d) We talked about three important things that happened. Think what each told us about. This is the main idea. Now, who can tell what the main idea of the story is? _____

_____

_____

_____

2. Observe in a classroom as a primary-grade teacher is asking comprehension questions. Use a listing of the types—literal, inferential, critical, and tally the number of questions asked in each group.
3. Observe in a classroom as an intermediate- or upper-grade teacher is asking comprehension questions about materials read. Using the same listing as in Activity 2, tally the number asked in each group.
4. If you have no access to a classroom setting, use a basal reader (teacher's edition) and categorize the question used in a lesson according to type.

Instructional Activity 2

Constructing Reading Comprehension Questions
In this section you will apply what you learned in previous activities to develop questions to measure or stimulate reading comprehension skills.

Writing Comprehension Questions

 Activities

1. Use the passage to write comprehension questions that follow the given guidelines and reflect the identified skill.

SHARKS!

Watch out for sharks in your supermarket. Several stores have started selling shark steaks. Much to everyone's surprise, the shark meat is receiving positive reactions, particularly from young adults.

Those who try the meat say that it has a taste much like that of redfish. Because it has cartilage rather than bones, it is easier to eat. Shark can be broiled, baked, fried, poached, smoked, and even grilled on skewers. The firmness of the meat also makes it suitable for use in salads, soups, and gumbos.[1]

(a) Fact or detail. _____

_____

Verification: _____

_____

(b) Main idea *(note that the main idea is not explicitly stated)*. _____

_____

_____

Verification: _____

_____

[1] From *Steck-Vaughn Adult Reading: 2800* by Sam V. Dauzat et al. Copyright © 1978 by Steck-Vaughn Company.

(c) Comparison or contrast (be sure that you don't merely ask for the one explicitly given in the passage). _____

_____

_____

Verification: _____

_____

(d) Cause-and-effect relationship. _____

_____

Verification: _____

_____

(e) Author's purpose. _____

_____

Verification: _____

_____

(f) Predict outcome. _____

_____

Verification: _____

_____

(g) Making conclusions or generalizations. _____

_____

Verification: _____

_____

2. Submit your questions to a classmate who decides if they actually assess the identified comprehension skill. Note that you were not asked to prepare comprehension questions for each possible skill. Why not? Look at the passage again. Can you write a sequence question for the selection?

_____

_____ Can you write a characterization question? _____

_____ What about fact/opinion? _____ Some passages are appropriate for dealing with certain reading comprehension skills. The materials may be inappropriate for other skills. The wise teacher will match the comprehension questions to the selection for reading.

3. Use the passage in Appendix B-2 to write comprehension questions that follow the given guidelines and reflect the identified skill.

(a) Fact or detail. _____

_____

Rating: Self: _____ Peer: _____

(b) Drawing inferences. _____

_____

Rating: Self: _____ Peer: _____

(c) Sequence of events. _____

_____

Rating: Self: _____ Peer: _____

(d) Characterization. _____

_____

Rating: Self: _____ Peer: _____

(e) Distinguishing fact from fiction. _____

_____

Rating: Self: _____ Peer: _____

(f) Predict outcomes. _____

_____

Rating: Self: _____ Peer: _____

(g) Conclusions. _____

_____

Rating: Self: _____ Peer: _____

(h) Author's tone. _____

_____

Rating: Self: _____ Peer: _____

(i) Cause-and-effect relationship. _____

_____

Rating: Self: _____ Peer: _____

(j) Fact or Opinion. _____

_____

_____

Rating: Self: _____ Peer: _____

4. Now let a classmate read your questions *and* answer them. Then evaluate the question together to see if it does stimulate the type reading comprehension described and if it is well stated. Each of you assign a rating according to the given scale.

    4—well done

    3—adequate

    2—needs improvement

    1—unacceptable

Instructional Activity 3

Planning for Teaching Reading Comprehension

In this section you will learn how to put what you learned in Chapter 8 and the other parts of Chapter 9 into practice. The section deals with planning for teaching and expanding reading comprehension through questioning.

The Basic Plan.

The steps involved in the basic plan are described for you here. [The entire Directed Reading Activity (DRA) plan is given in Chapter 13.]

1. Select your comprehension objectives. Be thoroughly familiar with the selection you will use to stimulate comprehension. Decide which comprehension skills could best be developed through the passage. Then state the objectives in terms of the skill the student will demonstrate as a result of the lesson.
2. Get the student ready for the lesson. Help the reader bring his old learnings that relate to the new selection to a conscious level. Introduce any words that may cause him difficulty. Give the reader a purpose for reading. (Use your prereading questions here.)
3. Have students read the passage silently.
4. Ask your comprehension questions that stimulate the skills identified in the objective. Be certain to use guidelines for constructing as well as for asking questions.
5. Provide opportunities for the student to reread any part that he may not understand sufficiently to answer a given question. You may have him read a part of the selection orally to satisfy a given purpose, such as to support a stated conclusion with facts.

Activities

1. Use the passage given in Appendix B-3 to construct your reading comprehension lesson plan. Fill in the basic elements of the format.
   A. Objectives. (Identify at least three—one for each level of comprehension.)

   (1) _____

   (2) _____

   (3) _____

   (4) _____
   B. Initiatory activities (getting student ready for lesson).
   (1) Relationship of previous experiences to present learning. (Identify what you will do to accomplish this.) _____

   _____

   _____

   (2) Introduce new words. (Identify at least three words you will introduce and give the context you will use.)

   (a) _____

   (b) _____

   (c) _____
   (3) Give prereading questions. (Make sure that they cannot be answered by reading only the first or second paragraph, etc.) Identify at least two.

   (a) _____

   (b) _____
   C. Developmental activities (what learner will do to develop the objectives).
   (1) Silent reading of passage.
   (2) Development of comprehension through questions. (Identify the questions to be asked. Write at least two for each level—literal, inferential, and critical—and identify them by *skill*.)
   Literal

   (a) Skill: _____

   Question: _____

   (b) Skill: _____

   Question: _____

Inferential

(c) Skill: _____

    Question: _____

(d) Skill: _____

    Question: _____

Critical

(e) Skill: _____

    Question: _____

(f) Skill: _____

    Question: _____

Others

(g) Skill: _____

    Question: _____

(h) Skill: _____

    Question: _____

(3) Extension of comprehension through rereading. Identify at least three questions for purposeful rereading (oral or silent).

    (a) _____

    (b) _____

    (c) _____

D. Evaluation. Evaluate students by responses to questions.

2. Submit your plan to a peer and then to your instructor for critique. Make whatever changes you so desire and resubmit the plan to your instructor for approval.

Instructional Activity 4

Teaching Reading Comprehension Lessons
Before you are ready to implement the plan you developed for a reading comprehension lesson, there are some things you should consider that will help you become more effective in actual teaching settings when you use questions.

Guidelines for Asking Questions
How you construct your reading comprehension questions and how you ask questions are both important. The following guidelines will help you utilize questions that will stimulate and extend reading comprehension.

1. Allow students time to think about the answers. Do not let the first student who raises his hand respond then. Encourage all children to think of an answer before calling on one child.

2. Present questions in a nonthreatening manner.

3. Give immediate feedback for a response. If the response is the one desired, make a positive comment, such as "Good for you." If the response is not the one desired, do not reject the response. Dignify it by stating, "I see how you might think so. x and y are alike. Let me rephrase the question."

4. When a student is unsuccessful in answering a question at a critical level, begin questioning at a more basic level and then build up to the critical comprehension question.

5. Ask the question before naming a student to respond. The intent is to get maximum pupil participation in thinking about the reading materials. Naming a student before asking the question tells the other students that they are "off the hook," and participation decreases.

6. Allow a student to pass on an opportunity to answer a question, but tell him or her you will be back later for a response.

7. Periodically, have students prepare the questions for the selection and ask peers and the teacher the questions.

General Guidelines for Teaching Comprehension Skills

1. Make certain that the materials are at an appropriate level of difficulty for the student. If the material is too easy, the student will not be challenged. But if it is too difficult, he or she will be frustrated and unable to succeed. (See Chapter 17 for a description of techniques for determining the instructional reading level of the child.)

2. The materials should be of interest to the child. Research indicates that the interest of the material to the reader has a direct effect on comprehension.[2] The greater the level of interest in the material, the greater the comprehension of the reader.

3. Be sure to probe the reader's thinking with questions that delve into the kinds of comprehension desired.

Activities

1. Evaluate these teacher responses. Read the situation, then tell which guideline for asking questions the teacher is using or abusing. Work with a peer and critique your answers.

   (a) "John, what is the best title for this story?"

   _____

   (b) "Yes, that's part of the answer. Can you add anything else to ___ ?"

[2] For additional reading on this subject, see Belloni and Jongsma, 1978.

(c) "No he did not! Are you sure you read this?"

_____

(d) "Fine! Now tell me why you think he did _____ ."

(e) "I need to see that a few more people have an answer before I call on anyone."

_____

2. This requires either an actual classroom or a peer-teaching setting. Schedule a meeting with your instructor.

Time _____ Date _____ Place _____

Implement the plan you prepared in the preceding section. Be sure that you follow the guidelines for asking questions. Critique your performance with your instructor and/or peers.

SUGGESTED TEACHING ACTIVITIES

1. *Skill:* Identifying explicit and implied character traits.
   Materials: A game board, word strips.
   Procedures: Construct a game board as shown in the example. After students finish reading a story, have them identify characterizations of one of the story characters. For each characteristic that can be verified from the story, write the trait on the strips of paper and mount them to the board.
   Number: Whole class or individual, depending on the board.
   Level: Fifth and sixth grades.
   Example:

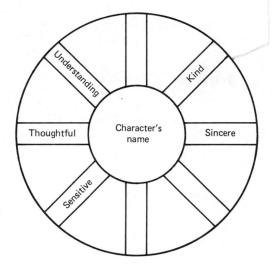

2. *Skill:* Following directions.
   Materials: Ditto sheets, as shown.
   Procedure: The teacher prepares two ditto masters, one with the directions and the other with the snowman outline. The student completes the exercise.
   Example: Follow these directions.
   1. Color the eyes blue. Cut them out and paste them on the face.
   2. Draw a big smile on the face.
   3. Color the carrot orange. Cut it out and paste it on for a nose.
   4. Color the hat black and the ribbon green. Cut it out and paste it on the head.
   5. Color the pipe brown and paste it at the right corner of the smile.
   6. Color the buttons red and paste them on the stomach.

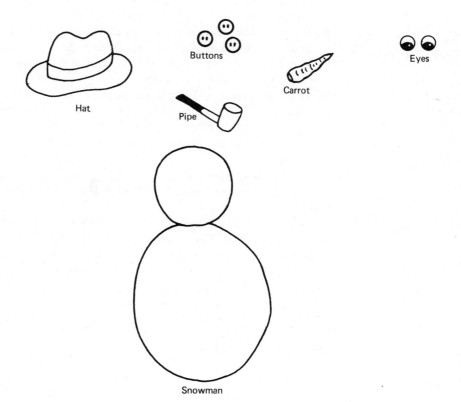

Hat

Buttons

Carrot

Eyes

Pipe

Snowman

3. *Skill:* Following directions.
   Materials: Ditto master or transparency and overhead projector.
   Procedures: The teacher prepares a ditto master or transparency. The student follows directions.
   Variation: Put in science facts or social studies facts as the alternatives.

Level: Fourth, fifth, and sixth grades.

Example:

Follow these directions.

1. If Christmas comes in December, fold a sheet of paper in half from top to bottom (crosswise).
2. If *l* comes before *j*, fold the paper in half from right to left (lengthwise). If not, draw a large circle on the bottom half of the folded sheet.
3. If birds fly south in summer, draw another large circle to the left of the first circle. If not, draw a circle about half as large as the first on top of the large circle.
4. Draw three small, unconnected circles from top to bottom in the larger circle if the water in the sea is salty. If not, draw a flower in the lower left corner of the page.
5. If cats bark, draw a square on top of the smaller circle. If not, draw a funny hat on top of the smaller circle.
6. If fires burn, draw a carrot in the center of the smaller circle. If not, draw a square at the bottom of the page.
7. If pillows are soft, place a nice smile below the carrot. If not, place a large frown below the carrot.
8. Draw two eyes above the carrot if a dime is worth twice as much as a nickel. If not, write your name in the larger circle.
9. If the earth is larger than the sun, write the word *error* beside the larger circle. If not, write the word *snowman* underneath the larger circle.

4. *Skill:* Distinguishing fact from opinion.

Materials: Two boxes, one labeled Facts and the other Opinions, and card strips.

Procedures: The teacher prepares strips that reflect both statements of fact and opinion. The student selects a strip, reads it, decides whether it is fact or opinion, and places the strip in the appropriate box.

Variation: The teacher prepares statements of fact and opinion that relate to a previously read selection or allows students to prepare the fact and opinion statements to be used.

Level: Fourth, fifth, and sixth grades and junior high.

Number: Whole class or individual.

Example:

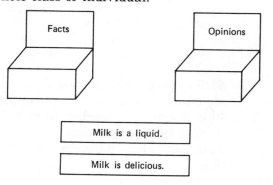

ADDITIONAL ENABLING ACTIVITIES

1. Observe a directed reading activity in an elementary or junior high school. This will be especially helpful for Objectives 3 and 4.

2. Attend class sessions. Time _____ Date _____

3. An activity selected by your instructor.

READING RESOURCES / REFERENCES

1. Belloni, Loretta Frances, and Eugene A. Jongsma. "The Effects of Interest on Reading Comprehension of Low Achieving Students," *Journal of Reading* (November 1978), pp. 106–109.
2. Burns, Paul C., and Betty D. Roe. *Teaching Reading in Today's Elementary Schools*. Chicago: Rand McNally, 1976.
3. Dallmann, Martha, Roger L. Rouch, Lynette Y. C. Chang, and John J. DeBoer. *The Teaching of Reading*, 5th ed. New York: Holt, Rinehart & Winston, 1978.
4. Gerhard, Christian. *Making Sense: Reading Comprehension Improved Through Categorizing*. Newark, Del.: International Reading Association, 1975.
5. Hittleman, Daniel R. *Developmental Reading: A Psycholinguistic Perspective*. Chicago: Rand McNally, 1978.
6. Pearson, P. David, and Dale Johnson. *Teaching Reading Comprehension*. New York: Holt, Rinehart & Winston, 1978.
7. Smith, Richard J., and Thomas C. Barrett. *Teaching Reading in the Middle Grades*. Reading, Mass.: Addison-Wesley, 1974.
8. Spache, George D., and Evelyn B. Spache. *Reading in the Elementary School,* 4th ed. Boston: Allyn and Bacon, 1977.

Section 5
Work-Study and Specialized Skills

The competencies for Section 5 relate to those required for success as a teacher of reading skills required for student success in the content fields. The teacher:

- Lists the work-study skills that an elementary-junior high school student needs for independence as a learner.
- Develops lessons to teach the work-study skills in reading or content fields.
- Develops plans designed to facilitate application of reading skills in a variety of settings.

Using the Chapters in Section 5
Follow the listed steps to complete the chapters.

1. Read the rationale, which provides an overview of the contents and an explanation of its importance to teachers.
2. Read the objectives, which are stated as skills that you must demonstrate.
3. Take the preassessment and score it if you choose. Otherwise, proceed to step 4. Proceed to step 4 or 5, depending on your preformance.
4. Read the information for each objective provided in the text and engage in activities as directed.
5. Select other enabling activities that will help you supplement your knowledge and skill. Use the Reading Resources/References and suggested teaching activities as directed by your instructor.
6. Schedule a meeting with your instructor and take the postassessment.
7. Evaluate your performance with your instructor and proceed to chapters in Section 6 or 7 or repeat steps 4 to 6 accordingly.

Chapter 10
Identifying Work-Study Skills

RATIONALE

It has been said that a major weakness of elementary schools is their failure to develop effective and efficient study habits in young children. In fact, many elementary school teachers may be so preoccupied with teaching the mechanics of reading skills that they overlook the necessity of teaching techniques for the use of those skills in various types of study situations. Work-study skills designed to aid children to study successfully are an essential part of a comprehensive elementary reading program.

The overall goal of the work-study skills is to develop a reader who is not dependent on the teacher for learning. Work-study skills taught to students will enable them to become independent readers. From the broadest viewpoint, the goal of helping students to be independent readers is really the ultimate aim for all learning, both in and out of school.

The importance of work-study skills to the learner is not always paralleled by the effectiveness with which they are taught. One of the reasons for this is that these particular skills cut across all subject areas, while responsibility for them may be left vague. Every teacher should shoulder the responsibility for teaching the work-study skills in his or her content area.

Ideally, helping children develop efficient study skills should be an integrated part of teaching in all content areas.

This chapter will familiarize you with the various work-study skills and subskills and the importance of these skills in enabling children to become independent readers.

OBJECTIVES

After completing this chapter, you will be able to:

1. Identify and categorize work-study skills into subskills as
   (a) locational and organizational,
   (b) study techniques,

(c) rate, and
(d) specialized skills.
2. Complete an objective identified by the instructor.

PREASSESSMENT

See Appendix A-10.

**Instructional
Activity 1**

Location, Organization, Study, Rate and Special Skills

Locational and organizational skills
Harris (Harris and Sipay, 1971) states that developmental reading, although not an end in itself, lays the foundation for success in utilizing reading. The skills learned are put to use for two main purposes—reading to learn (functional reading) and reading for pleasure (recreational reading).

The work-study skills, or study skills, are sometimes referred to as the functional skills of reading and deserve greater emphasis in the developmental reading program (Zintz, 1975).

Children cannot succeed in school without learning to read for information; however, this ability requires more than simply applying the skills learned in the developmental aspect of the total reading program.

Beyond success in school, readers who master the work-study skills can continue their learning in life long after they have a teacher to guide them. In effect, mastery of the work-study skills facilitates independence as a learner.

Consider your task as a student as you approach the assignment of writing a brief report on a given subject. Assume that you have evaluated the subject and have selected an appropriate topic narrow enough to be dealt

with in a brief report. What will your next step be? _____

_____

You will need to *locate* information about your topic.

Locating information. There are various sources available to you in this phase of your research. List all the possible sources you can think of that

might assist you in locating information. _____

_____

_____

_____

You may have listed an atlas, almanac, encyclopedia, newspaper, dictionary, card catalog, and the *Reader's Guide to Periodical Literature*. The parts of a book you may have included are the title page, table of contents, glossary, appendix, and index. (See the outline at the end of this instructional unit for a brief description of the sources for locating information.)

When you have selected the appropriate source from those just suggested, you will have to locate the information in each one that pertains to your choice. You will probably not read all of the material at hand in detail at this point, since your purpose is to *locate* the information and it is not essential that you read each word. What will you do? You will probably do some rapid partial reading of the information. You will skim and scan the materials as necessary.

In *skimming,* the reader glances over material to get an overall impression of what it contains. He or she does a telegraphic type of reading by responding only to the important words. The reader might read titles in heavy print, subheadings, italicized words, initial sentences in paragraphs, and summarizing statements. The purpose in reading is probably to get the main idea and a few supporting facts.

In *scanning,* the reader uses a rapid reading technique. By letting the eyes move vertically on the page, the reader can isolate a single fact or locate the answer to a specific question. He responds only to key words that may help him achieve his purpose.

Some situations in which scanning is the best technique to achieve a purpose include:

- Checking a table of contents to find the page number on which a chapter begins.
- Surveying a dictionary page to locate a given entry word rapidly.
- Locating a specific telephone number in the directory.
- Surveying an index to find where a particular topic is treated in the book.

These skills will help you locate the information so that you can evaluate it and make decisions concerning its appropriateness.

To evaluate the material, you must read the information more carefully, your purpose now is to get a full understanding of the content of the paragraph, selection, chapter, etc. (Adjusting rate to purpose is presented in more detail later.)

Now that you have *located* the information, read the contents, and made decisions on its appropriateness, what will be your next step? _____

_____

You will need to *organize* the material in a coherent form that makes sense to you and can be used later to serve your study purposes.

Organizing Information You will probably use one or more organizational skills during and/or after reading. You might take some notes on the material. This may be in *outline form, summarization* of the material read, or whatever form is most useful to you. It might be helpful to *underline* the important points in a content textbook if this is permitted or it is your own copy.

In note-taking, you should use (and encourage your students to use) a form that helps you most. Notes should be made only on the most important things, and they should be written in your own words using phrases or sentences.

In outlining, you are recording information from the reading material in a way that makes clear the relationship between the main ideas and the supporting details. Two types of outlines that students may find useful are the sentence outline and the topic outline. Each point in a sentence outline is stated in the form of a complete sentence. The points in a topic outline are written in the form of key words and phrases. The sentence outline is generally easier to master, since the topic outline involves an extra task— condensing main ideas, already expressed in sentence form, into key words and phrases.

In summarizing, you must restate in a more concise form what the author has said. The main ideas and essential supporting details of a selection should be preserved in a summary; illustrative material and statements that merely elaborate on the main ideas should not be included.

Often there is a need to use the organizational skills in combination with each other. Constructing an outline as an overall framework for your report can help you to organize the subject matter in a logical fashion. Then, when you have made summaries and/or an outline from the various sources used, you can fill in the information from your note-taking in the appropriate slots in the master outline.

At this point in your task, you will determine if the information you have is sufficient to meet the requirements of the assignment. If it is felt that further work is needed, you may want to accomplish more locating and/or organizing. If no further locating and organizing is necessary, you will take the information from your note-taking and organize it into logical sequence.

Children at the elementary level need much teacher-assisted practice in gaining an understanding of the work-study skills presented before they can actually utilize the skills independently.

It is possible that you would need to use specialized work-study skills, such as interpretation of maps, charts, graphs, and diagrams, to obtain information. (These skills will be presented in detail later.)

Another aspect of work-study skills involves the use of techniques that aid in studying material such as in the content area subjects (see pp. 178– 180).

Overview The functional skills of reading—the work-study skills—can be categorized in these five major headings.

Locational skills.

Organizational skills.

Adjusting rate to purpose.

Study techniques.

Specialized skills.

Some of the uses for locational and organizational skills have been presented as you viewed the task of a student in the process of beginning an assignment. The remaining skills are presented in the following sections of the chapter.

Listing and Definition of Locational Sources

1. Within a book.
   (a) *Title Page.* The title page of a book tells the title, author, publisher, and location of the publisher.
   (b) *Table of Contents.* The table of contents is a guide to the kind of material contained in a book and a help in locating the pages on which the information begins.
   (c) *Index.* The primary technique in using an index is in determining key words to locate a topic. Topics are arranged in alphabetical order.
   (d) *Appendix.* The appendix contains helpful information that may appear in the form of a bibliography or tabular material.
   (e) *Glossary.* A glossary is in the back of a book before the index. It is an alphabetical listing of special words found in the book and their meanings.
2. *For locating sources.*
   (a) *Card Catalog.* Title, author, and subject cards for all books in the library are placed in alphabetical order in a card catalog. Guide letters on each drawer indicate between which sets of letters the information will be located.
   (b) *Readers' Guide to Periodical Literature.* A book in which articles from approximately 160 popular magazines are indexed.
3. *Special reference books.*
   (a) *Atlas.* A collection of maps in a volume.
   (b) *Almanac.* A book containing a calendar of days, weeks, and months, to which astronomical data and various statistics such as the times of sunset and sunrise and changes of the moon are often added.
   (c) *Encyclopedia.* A set of volumes containing summaries of knowledge on various topics (organized in alphabetical order).
   (d) *Dictionary.* A book in which the words of language are entered alphabetically and defined.
   (e) *Newspapers and Magazines.* These can be used to develop a variety of work-study skills such as (1) flexible rate, (2) reading graphs, charts, tables, and maps, and (3) summarizing.

Study Techniques

The importance of setting a purpose for reading has been presented in sections of previous chapters. In the same way, having an organized strategy for reading longer selections, such as chapters in content areas, can greatly aid in comprehension and retention of the material read. Various study techniques have been devised to assist students in approaching study-type reading in an organized manner. The SQ3R technique is described and several others listed in order for you to gain an understanding of the procedures involved. As you become familiar with the techniques, note which elements, if any, are common to all of them. (You might want to take notes or underline as you read.)

SQ3R The first technique is presented through the following guided discovery. Complete the activity for a clear understanding of the study technique.

✳ Activities

1. Obtain a social studies or science textbook on an intermediate-grade level. Write in the name of the book here. _____

_____

Title _____

Publisher _____
    Select a chapter for study-type reading. Write in the name of the chapter here: _____

                                                       Name   Pages
    Follow the steps described in reading and studying the content of the chapter.

(a) _____
    Glance over the headings in the chapter to see the main points that will be developed. Read the final summary paragraph if the chapter has one. This step should not take more than a minute and will show the core ideas contained in the chapter. This step is an orientation to help you organize the ideas as you read them later.

(b) _____
    Turn the first heading into a question. This arouses your curiosity and in so doing increases your comprehension, giving you a purpose for reading. Having a question in mind as you read will make the important points stand out from the explanatory detail. It is not difficult to turn the heading into a question; however, it does require a conscious effort to read to find the answer.

(c) _____

Read to answer the question posed in the previous step. Read to the end of the first section. This requires active reading, in search of an answer.

(d) _____

Look away from the book and try briefly to recite the answer to your question, using your own words along with an example. If you have comprehended the material, you will be able to carry out this step successfully. If you are unable to do this, glance over the material again. It is very helpful to do this from memory by jotting down the cue phrases in outline form.

(e) _____

When you have read the complete lesson and carried out the steps *a* to *d* for each heading of the chapter, review your notes to get an overview of the main points and their relationship. Also check your memory of the content by reciting the major subpoints under each heading (Zintz, 1975).

You may find that this procedure permits better comprehension of the chapter content than merely reading the material with no set purpose in mind. Look back over the five steps you have just completed. Think of *one word* that best summarizes or describes what you have done. Write in the appropriate word next to the number of the step it describes.

Your choices probably include these words, or synonyms for them.

1. Survey.
2. Question.
3. Read.
4. Recite.
5. Review.

These are the key words that describe the components of the SQ3R study method.

S—Survey.

Q—Question.

3R—Read, Recite, Review.

The SQ3R technique is used to illustrate the strategy behind most of the other study techniques. The SQ3R formula, developed by Francis Robinson in 1946, has proven useful in helping students in study-type reading tasks. It can also be used by the student when the teacher has not set specific purposes for reading the chapter (Dillner and Olson, 1977).

Some of the other techniques developed are listed here with the meanings of the acronyms provided.

1. **REAP.**
   R—Read.
   E—Encode.
   A—Annotate.
   P—Ponder.
2. **PARS.**
   P—Set a purpose.
   A—Ask questions related to purpose.
   R—Read to answer questions.
   S—Summarize in your own words what has been learned.
3. **OK4R**
   O—Overview.
   K—Key ideas.
   4R—Read, Recall, Reflect, Review.
4. **PQRST**
   P—Preview.
   Q—Question.
   R—Read.
   S—Summarize.
   T—test.

In comparing the various study techniques, similar elements can be observed. What are they? Elements that seem to be common to all of the methods are listed in the table under the heading *Step*. (It will be seen in Chapter 13 that these steps are actually elements of the directed reading lesson.) Three study techniques are then listed under *Method*. Think of the steps involved in each method. (Refer to the acronym meanings on previous pages if necessary.)

Do the methods in question have elements that correspond to the steps listed in the first column? If so, write in the step in the appropriate space. One is done for you.

Step	Method		
	SQ3R	PQRST	PARS
1. Overview	Survey		
2. Set purposes	Question		
3. Silent reading	Read		
4. Comprehension check	Recite		
5. Review	Review		

There are various study techniques available for use by students. The teacher should be aware that similarities exist among the strategies and should recognize these similar elements.

Dillner and Olson (1977) note the similarities of the various strategies.

Many of the strategies designed direct the student to follow a series of steps in approaching study-type reading tasks in an organized manner. Most of them provide instructions to *survey* the material to be read and then to *formulate questions* about the information before actually reading it. Following the reading, the students are given a way to *assess their understanding* of the content. Often the steps are labeled and form an acronym to assist the student in remembering the sequenced steps involved in carrying out the technique. In this way the acronyms are readily employed: SQ3R, PARS. (Can you recall the steps?) Thus the procedures, practices, and repetition are built into the system and are theoretically supported by many of the sound principles of learning psychology.

Since the strategies seem to be based on similar elements, the teacher can select the technique deemed most appropriate for his or her students, based on an understanding of their needs and abilities. If the teacher feels comfortable with a certain technique (perhaps it fits his teaching style), he might teach it rather than another technique. The fact that the teacher understands and feels confident with a particular procedure might help in motivating the students. Enthusiasm on the part of the teacher often stimulates the students themselves. If one acronym seems to appeal to the students or lends itself readily to their memory, that particular technique might be chosen. Level of the students should also be considered. A formula too cumbersome to commit to memory might not be suitable for intermediate students even though it could be useful at the high school level.

Attempting to teach all methods to the students could confuse them and defeat the purpose of better understanding and retention of information. As the teacher, you might select one technique, learn it, provide much opportunity for teacher-directed practice, and allow the students to apply it in content area subjects and independent study.

Adjusting Rate to Purpose

The term *rate of reading* actually refers to *rate of comprehension*. (Dallmann et al., 1978.) Rate of reading should be determined by the *purpose* for which one reads and the *type of material* he or she is reading. For example, it is often necessary to skim material to get an overview of its content instead of reading it word for word.

Children need considerable guidance from the teacher and supervised practice in adjusting rates in order to acquire flexibility and perform the skill independently. Simply telling students to read faster or slower without providing them with the "how" of the task will be of little benefit. Dallmann et al. (1978) present a set of guidelines for improving reading rates. The guidelines are listed and summarized here.

1. *Growth in ability to read at appropriate rates is subject to training.* There is reason to think that almost all readers could make valuable increases in the speed with which they read, without loss of comprehension, if they received appropriate help. Emphasis on the increase of reading rates

should usually be postponed until pupils have gained proficiency in reading skills basic to the development of greater speed. This gain ordinarily takes place by the intermediate grades.

2. *Reading rates should vary with the purpose of the reader and the type and difficulty of the material.* It is possible that the desirable rate may vary even within a given selection from one part to another. This should be understood by both the teacher and the learner. When the teacher sets the purpose for reading in first grade, he may ask a pupil to read a page to find out what Katie did when she saw the new kitten on the sidewalk. Then the pupil is asked to glance over the next page to find the new word *kitten.* Here the teacher may point out that in the second task it was not necessary to read every word on the page, so it should not take the student long to read the page. In this way, learning to read at different rates and for different purposes can be begun early in reading instruction.

In later stages of reading, the learner should be given more and more opportunity to decide on suitable purposes and determine what rate of reading will be needed to accomplish his objective. Children may be shown three categories into which reading rates may be divided to help clarify the ways of adapting speed to nature of material and purpose for reading it. The categories of reading rates are: rapid reading, moderately rapid reading, and slow reading.

Skimming and scanning can be thought of as two kinds of rapid reading, but a person can be reading rapidly without using either technique. A reader may *scan* if he is looking at a table of contents for the title of a given chapter to find the page on which it begins. He scans when he looks over the words on a page or two of a dictionary in order to locate an entry word. The reader is *skimming* when he rapidly reads a paragraph or longer selection to get the main idea and a few supporting facts.

A person is using rapid reading when he reads a newspaper to get a general picture of what is going on or when he reads a magazine article or fiction just for fun.

Slow reading should usually be done in a study-type situation or at times such as when the readers desires appreciation of the author's style. Moderately fast reading is done when the reader wishes to note some details.

3. *Teachers and pupils should have clearly defined goals for the improvement of reading rates.* The teacher should determine the needs of the pupils and have *specific* purposes for reading different selections. The learner should have a clear understanding of the purpose(s) set by the teacher and should also have his own objectives for reading.

4. *Development of ability to read at appropriate rates should not interfere with development of other reading skills.* Increase of rate should not be stressed at the expense of comprehension. When the pupil is reading

slower than his purposes for reading require, his rate should be increased.

Nor should increased rate be done at the expense of other reading skills. Greater speed in locating information (e.g., finding an entry in an index) should not cause a reader to become less accurate. He should spend less time in finding the entry without interfering with accuracy.

5. *Neither haste nor undue tension should characterize the efforts to read at appropriate rates.* Harmful effects can occur if pressures are created that result in anxiety and fear of failure. This does not mean that a person should not be prodded at times if poor achievement below the expected level is due to dawdling habits or lack of effort. A child should be encouraged to do his best without becoming frantic when he fails to accomplish his goal.

6. *The marked differences in children's ability to read at appropriate rates should be recognized.* Individual differences in children can result partly from training and experience and in innate capacities. The teacher must know the needs and abilities of the students in order to work out an effective program for acquiring skill in reading at appropriate rates. Some children reading with less than average speed in all types of reading situations may be working up to capacity or even pushing themselves to work. Others who are above the norm in reading rates may still be reading below their own potential.

Summary   Although slow, careful reading may be needed to understand each detail of an algebra problem, textbook reading is often done at a more rapid rate when the student is reading continuous running material such as history. This rate is slow enough for the reader to pay attention to the main points and details and retain much of what is read (this rate can be utilized in the *read* step of SQ3R and other study techniques presented on pp. 179–180) (Dillner and Olson, 1977).

It is easy to see then that the rate of reading depends on the *purpose* for reading and the *difficulty of the material*. In reading a novel at a rapid rate, the reader may slow down to read a section that is humorous or otherwise meaningful to him. In reading a textbook, the reader may come to a section already familiar to him and increase his rate accordingly (Dillner and Olson, 1977).

✳ Activities

1. Learn how reading rate is dependent on purpose for reading by completing these activities. Choose two selections from the graded passages in Appendix B.

   (a) Write in the title or number of the first passage here. _____

   _____

(b) Your *purpose* is to read to determine the main idea of the first passage. What *rate* of reading is appropriate for this task? _____

_____

_____

_____

(c) Now read the passage. What is the main idea? _____

_____

_____

_____

(d) Why would slow reading be inappropriate for this purpose? _____

_____

_____

_____

(e) You probably have found that if you read too slowly, you may not be able to synthesize the sentences into a meaningful whole.

(f) Write in the name of the second selection. _____

_____

_____

_____

(g) Read to note some of the details of the selection. You should know that a moderately fast rate is appropriate for this task.

(h) Now read the selection. What are some of the details of the selection?

_____

_____

_____

_____

(i) Why would rapid reading probably be inappropriate for this purpose?

_____

_____

_____

_____

_____

Often you would need to use various rates with the same selection, depending on your purpose. You could go back to this same selection and change your purpose. In doing so, your rate would change.

2. Mr. Meticulous insists that every word in a passage is important; if it weren't, the author wouldn't have bothered to write it. He can frequently be heard admonishing his sixth-grade pupils, "Slow down! Slow down! Give every word a chance to be absorbed. The good reader is one who responds to every word."

(a) What error is Mr. Meticulous making? _____

_____

_____

_____

(b) What effect will his philosophy probably have on children who comply? _____

_____

_____

_____

_____

Specialized Skills

In order for the student to derive meaningful information from maps, graphs, diagrams, charts, and other pictorial material, he or she must become competent to use and interpret these materials. Specialized skills are required for effective reading in the content areas, such as social studies or science. They are also necessary for successful independent study projects and for life-coping situations of everyday adult living. Samples of pictorial material and the specialized reading skills required for accurate interpretation are presented here. Complete the activities for each sample.

Maps   Can you use maps to derive the information that they represent? Study the maps and use them to answer the questions.

The following exercises on coordinates, pictorial maps, road maps, directions, symbols, and tables are from *Reading 2700,* by Sam V. Dauzat, Jo Ann Dauzat, Wayne Otto, and Burton W. Kreitlow.[1] For answers to the exercises, check pp. 192–194.

[1] From *Steck-Vaughn Adult Reading 2700* by Sam V. Dauzat, et al. Copyright © 1978, Steck-Vaughn. Reprinted by permission of the publisher.

Coordinates

A This lesson will help you learn how to locate places on maps.[2] Read the story. Look at the drawing.

Sam Harvey bought a small grocery store. He wanted to redo the arrangement of foods on the shelves. He made a drawing of the store to help him plan how to do it. This is what it looked like.

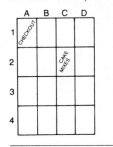

Notice the numbers and letters Sam used to help him describe where to put things. He put the checkout stand at 1-A. He put the cake mixes at 2-C.

To tell what number and letter go with a space, look across from the space to the number and up from the space to the letter.

B Use the drawing in part A to write your answers.

1. Sam put canned drinks at 4-A. Put a *D* in that space.
2. Flour is at 2-C. Put an *F* in that space.
3. Ice cream was put at 1-D. Put a *C* in that space.
4. The frozen foods section is 2-D. Put *FF* there.
5. Paper goods are at 1-B. Put a *P* there.
6. Sam put canned goods at 2-B. Write *CG* there.
7. The meat counter is at 4-B and 4-C. Write *meats* across those spaces.
8. At 3-D, Sam put the dairy case. Write *milk* in that space.
9. School supplies are at 1-C. Write *S* in that space.
10. Sam put aspirin and such at 4-D. Write an *A* there.

> Sam's drawing is a **grid system**. The rows have numbers. The columns have letters. Rows go across. Columns go up and down.

[2] From *Steck-Vaughn Adult Reading: 2700* by Sam V. Dauzat et al. Copyright © 1978 by Steck-Vaughn Company.

Pictorial Maps

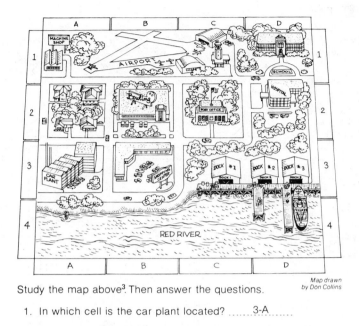

Map drawn
by Don Collins

Study the map above[3]. Then answer the questions.

1. In which cell is the car plant located? .... 3-A ....

2. Where is the hospital located? ....

3. What is in 1-D? ....

4. Where are the houses located? ....

5. What is in 1-C? ....

6. Where is the post office located? ....

7. Where are most of the river docks located? ....

8. Where is the ship docked? ....

9. Where is the bowling alley? ....

10. How far is the school from the river? ....

11. How far is the car plant from dock #3? ....

12. How far is it from the airport to the shopping area? ....

13. How far is it from the machine shop entrance to the airport

    entrance? ....

[3] From *Steck-Vaughn Adult Reading: 2700,* Sam V. Dauzat, et al. Copyright © 1978 by Steck-Vaughn Company.

Road Maps

A Read the story[4]. Find the places on the map.

Hugh just got a job transfer. He had been working the night shift at the paper mill in Scottsville. But next week he will begin as night foreman at the mill in Cane City.

This weekend, Hugh plans to make his first trip to Cane City to check out the plant and find a house. Since he has not been there before, he will use a road map. This is what the map of the area looks like. Each • on the map shows a city. The lines show the roads. The numbers and letters (the coordinates) can be used to tell where things are located.

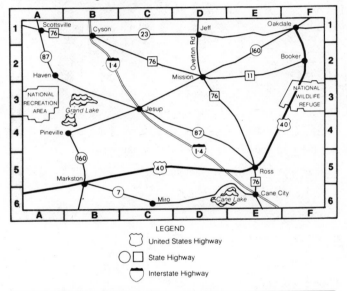

LEGEND

⬡ United States Highway

◯▢ State Highway

⬣ Interstate Highway

B Use the map to answer these questions.

1. Where is Scottsville located? ....

2. Where is Cane City located? ....

3. If Hugh took the shortest way, how many cities would he go

   through on his way from Scottsville to Cane City? ....

4. Where is Haven located? ....

5. Which city is nearest the recreation area? ....

[4] From *Steck-Vaughn Adult Reading: 2700,* by Sam V. Dauzat et al. Copyright © 1978 by Steck-Vaughn Company.

C Read the story below[5].

As supervisor for a cosmetics distributor, Gena will visit many cities and towns each month. Her home base is Jesup. But she will have to visit each local salesperson once every two months. The map for Part A shows the cities to which Gena must travel.

D Use the map for Part A to answer these questions.

1. What town is located in cell 6-E? ....

2. What town is located in cell 3-C? ....

3. What town is located in cell 2-D? ....

4. What is located in cells 3-B and 4-B? ....

5. In which cell does Highway 160 intersect I-4? ....

6. Which two towns are connected by Overton Road? ....

....

7. Gena plans to go from Jesup to Oakdale. Which road should she use? ....

8. She plans to go from Oakdale to Ross. Which road should she take? ....

9. She plans to go from Ross to Miro. Where will she need to change roads? .... Which road will she take from there? ....

10. Which two cities are farthest from Gena's home? ....

E Maps often have an **index** to help you locate places. If you know the name of the place, find it in the index. The grid numbers will tell you where to look on the map. Complete the sample index below.

Booker ...2-F...	Jesup	Oakdale ....
Cane City ...6-E...	Markston	Pineville ....
Cyson	Miro	Ross ....
Haven	Mission	Scottsville ....
Jeff		

[5] From *Steck-Vaughn Adult Reading: 2700,* by Sam V. Dauzat et al. Copyright © 1978 by Steck-Vaughn Company.

Directions

We need to know how to tell directions many times every day[6]. When we tell someone how to get to a certain place, we may need to tell them to go north, or south, or east, or west. Advertisements in newspapers and on radio and television often tell us things like, "Drive north on Main Street until you see the River Oaks sign." When we watch the television weather report, a knowledge of directions can help us understand what kind of weather is moving toward where we live. And anytime we walk or drive in an area that is not familiar to us, we need to know directions in order to find our way to where we are going.

On many maps, north is at the top. But this is not always the case. When you look at a map, find the compass rose, the symbol which shows directions. (If there is none, north is probably at the top.) Some direction symbols you will see are shown below.

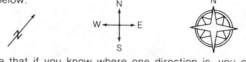

Notice that if you know where one direction is, you can also tell the other directions. When you are facing north, south is behind you, west is to your left, and east is to your right.

A Fill in the missing directions on these compass roses. Notice that north is not always in the same place.

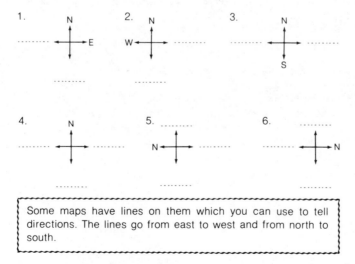

Some maps have lines on them which you can use to tell directions. The lines go from east to west and from north to south.

B Study the map below to answer the questions[7].

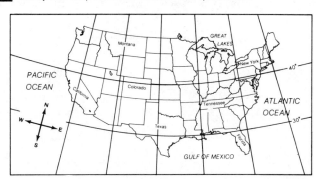

1. Find the lines on the map which run up and down. In which
   directions do they run? ....
2. Find the lines on the map which run across the page. In
   which directions do they run?...
3. Is the Pacific Ocean on the east or the west side of the
   United States? ....
4. In which direction is Montana from Colorado? ....
5. To go from Texas to Florida, in which direction would you
   travel? ....
6. To go from the Great Lakes to Tennessee, in which direction
   would you travel? ....
7. To go from the Gulf of Mexico to the Atlantic Ocean, in
   which direction would you travel? ....
8. Seven states are named on the map. Three of them are east
   of Texas, and three of them are west of Texas. Name the
   states east of Texas. .... Name
   the states west of Texas. ....
9. If there is no direction symbol on a map, what are two ways
   you can use to find directions? ....
   ....

[7] From *Steck-Vaughn Adult Reading: 2700,* by Sam V. Dauzat et al. Copyright © 1978 by
Steck-Vaughn Company.

Symbols

This page is about reading symbols on maps. Use the map to answer the questions[8]. Look at the example in the box before you begin.

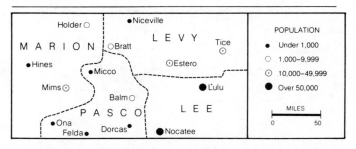

1. Which county has the most large cities?
   a. Marion   b. Levy
   c. Pasco   d. Lee

2. Which is the smallest city in Levy County?
   a. Tice   b. Niceville
   c. Bratt   d. Estero

3. What might be the population of Holder?
   a. 500   b. 7,000
   c. 12,000   d. 55,000

4. How far is it from Micco to Balm?
   a. 1 inch   b. 50 inches
   c. 1 mile   d. 50 miles

[8] From *Steck-Vaughn Reading: 2700,* by Sam V. Dauzat et al. Copyright © 1978 by Steck-Vaughn Company.

Answer Key

Page 186, Coordinates

	A	B	C	D
1	Chuck cut	P	S	C
2		CG	Cake mix F	FF
3				Milk
4	D	Meats		A

Page 187, Pictorial Maps

1. 3-A
2. 2-D
3. School
4. 2-A
5. Airport
6. 2-C
7. 3-D
8. 3-D (count 4-D correct, also.)
9. 2-B
10. 2 blocks
11. About 3 blocks
12. About 2 to 3 blocks
13. About 2½ blocks

Pages 188–189, Road Maps

B.
  1. 1-A, 2. 6-E, 3. 2
  4. 2-A, 5. Haven

D.
  1. Cane City   2. Jesup
  3. Mission   4. Grand Lake
  5. 3-C   6. Jeff and Mission
  7. State Highway 160
  8. U.S. Highway 40
  9. Cane City, State Highway 7
10. Booker and Oakdale

E.

Cyson—1-B, Haven—2-A,
Jeff—1-D, Jesup—3-C
Markston—5-B, Miro—6-C
Mission—2-D, Oakdale—1-F
Pineville—4-B, Ross—5-E
Scottsville—1-A

Pages 190–191, Directions

A.

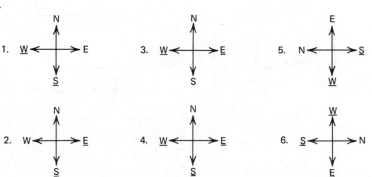

B.
1. North and south
2. East and west
3. West
4. North
5. East
6. South
7. East (or northeast)
8. Tennessee, Florida, New York;
   Colorado, Montana, California
9. North will usually be at the top of the map. Or, if
   the map has lines, the lines will run north-south and
   east-west.

Page 192, Symbols
1. d 2. b 3. b 4. d

Graphs   There are four kinds of graphs—pictorial, bar, line, and circle.
They all contain similar elements. Graphs usually have a title to tell what
the graph is about and a scale of measure. Graphs also present some type
of relationship. Therefore, when using graphs, the reader should:

1. Read the title to get an idea of what the graph is about.
2. Look for the scale of measure.
3. Look for and identify the type of relationship being presented.

Samples of pictorial, bar, line, and circle graphs are provided. Can you
derive information by interpreting the graphs? Study the graphs and use
them to answer the questions that follow each sample.

Sample Pictorial Graph

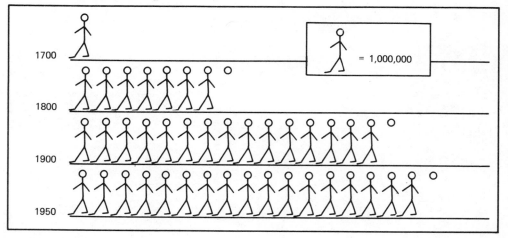

Population of the United States, 1700–1950

194

1. The population of the United States in 1700 was more than five times that in 1800.

_____ True

_____ False

2. Between 1900 and 1950, the population grew by about 15 million.

_____ True

_____ False

(Answers: 1. False   2. False)

Sample Bar Graph
Population of Selected Cities in State X, 1980

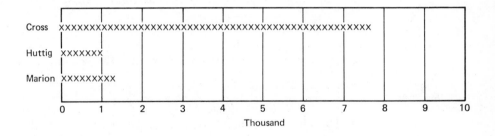

1. The population of Cross is about
   (a) 7,000
   (b) 70,000
   (c) 80,000
   (d) 8,000,000

2. The city of Cross has more people than the city of Huttig.

_____ True

_____ False

3. The city of Marion is more than twice as large as the city of Huttig.

_____ True

_____ False

(Answers: 1. a   2. True   3. False)

Sample Line Graph
Weight gain for patient X over a six-week period

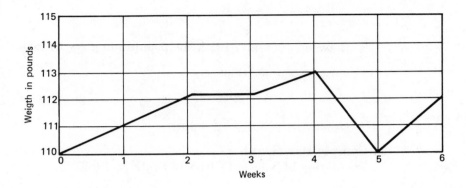

1. Patient X weighed the least during the fifth week.

   _____ True

   _____ False

2. Patient X weighed the most during the second week.

   _____ True

   _____ False

3. Patient X weighed 6 pounds more at the end of the 6 week period.

   _____ True

   _____ False

(Answers: 1. True   2. False   3. False, 1 pound more than first week)

Sample Circle Graph
Status of State Y High School Graduates, 1980

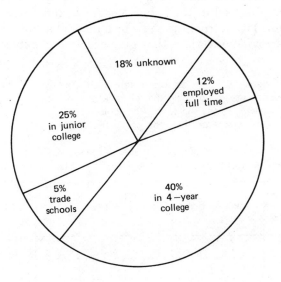

1. How many of the high school graduates attend 4-year college? _____

2. What percentage of graduates are unknown? _____
   (Answers: 1. 40 percent   2. 18 percent)

It can be seen from the samples that the circle or pie graph show the relation of various parts to the whole. The line graph shows changes between different quantities, while the bar graph compares the size of quantities. A pictorial graph contains units that are shown in a picture format.

Tables Tables consist of listing of information that must be read horizontally and vertically. In teaching students to read tables, have them note the title, headings, and subheadings for the rows and columns to find out what information is provided in the table. Verbalize the process involved in interpreting information from the table as a model for how the student should read a table. Provide questions that give practice in extracting information from tables.

Use the table below to form as many real words as you can[9]. Word beginnings are given down the left side of the table. Word endings are given across the top of the table.

Write the words you make on the lines below the table. One has been done for you.

Not every beginning and ending will make a real word. If necessary, check the words you have made in the dictionary.

ENDINGS ⟶ / BEGINNINGS	ick	ock	ay	ing	ap
tr					
st					
cl					
fl					
th					

fling
....
....
....
....
....
....
....
....
....
....
....
....

[9] From *Steck-Vaughn Adult Reading: 2700*, by Sam V. Dauzat et al. Copyright © 1978 by Steck-Vaughn Company.

Other Special Skills In addition to maps, graphs, and tables, authors frequently employ other devices to supplement textual material or to present ideas that cannot be accurately depicted by words. Devices such as pictures, illustrations, charts, diagrams, and schematic drawings are useful to explain ideas more fully. However, these are self-explanatory only if students have learned how to extract information from them. Teachers should guide study of the special forms by helping students focus attention on titles or other verbal information, by asking questions that require interpretation of the diagram, drawing, or other pictorial material, and by discussing the information conveyed in the material.

Special skills and abilities involved in reading special types of printed material are presented here.

I. Ability to Use and Interpret Maps and Globes
  A. Locating Desired Information
    1. Interpreting Key or Legend and Other Symbols
    2. Using Scales
    3. Interpreting Directions
  B. Recognizing Type of Projections or Map Distortions
II. Ability to Use and Interpret Graphs, Tables, Charts, Diagrams, and Other Illustrative Material
  A. Interpreting Tables—Single cell, Multiple cell, Schedules
  B. Interpreting Graphs
    1. Bar Graphs
    2. Circle Graphs
    3. Line Graphs
  C. Interpreting Tables
  D. Interpreting Timelines
  E. Interpreting Other Pictorial Material
  F. Interpreting Charts

Activities

Use what you have learned in the chapter and your own outlining skills to complete the skeleton outline. The topics are listed here.

Using Almanac	Organizational Skills	Specialized Skills
Note-taking	Using Indexes	Skimming
Using Atlas	Using Newspapers	Using Diagrams
Using Graphs	Summarizing	Interpreting Charts
Using Appendixes	Using Encyclopedias	Using Card Catalogs
Using Glossary	Scanning	

Outline of Work-Study Skills

I. Adjusting Rate to Purpose

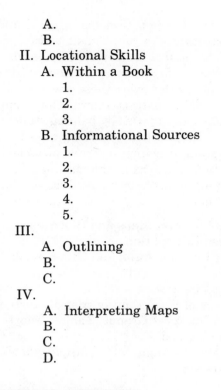

         A.
         B.
    II. Locational Skills
         A. Within a Book
              1.
              2.
              3.
         B. Informational Sources
              1.
              2.
              3.
              4.
              5.
   III.
         A. Outlining
         B.
         C.
   IV.
         A. Interpreting Maps
         B.
         C.
         D.

ADDITIONAL ENABLING ACTIVITIES

1. This is a reading-study activity. Read and take notes on the set of sources listed. You should read *at least one* source from each lettered section. That is, read at least one from part a, one from part b, and one from part c.
   (a) Locational and organizational, and specialized skills.
        (1) Colden, Outline of Study Skills, pp. 288–289.
        (2) Harris and Sipay, Chapter 12, pp. 333–364.
        (3) Zintz, Chapter 12, "Study Skills", pp. 305–311, 318, 323.
   (b) Study techniques.
        (1) Dillner and Olson, "Using a Study Technique," pp. 71–73.
        (2) Burmeister, "SQ3R" (and other study techniques), pp. 104–108.
   (c) Adjusting rate to purpose.
        (1) Dallmann et al., "Reading Rate and Comprehension," pp. 207–216.
2. An activity of your choice.
3. An activity selected by your instructor.

READING RESOURCES / REFERENCES

1. Burmeister, Lou E. *Reading Strategies for Secondary School Teachers,* 2nd ed. Reading, Mass.: Addison-Wesley, 1978.
2. Colden, Garland. *Developing Competence in Teaching Reading.* Dubuque, Ia.: William C. Brown, 1978.
3. Dallmann, Matha, Roger L. Rouch, Lynette Y. C. Chang, and John J. DeBoer. *The Teaching of Reading,* 5th ed. New York: Holt, Rinehart & Winston, 1978.
4. Dillner, Martha H., and JoAnne P. Olson. *Personalizing Reading Instruction in Middle, Junior, and Senior High Schools.* New York: Macmillan, 1977.
5. Harris, Albert J., and Edward R. Sipay. *Effective Teaching of Reading,* 2nd ed. New York: David McKay, 1971.
6. Otto, Wayne, and Robert D. Chester. *Objective-Based Reading.* Reading, Mass.: Addison-Wesley, 1976.
7. Tadlock, Delores Fadness. "SQ3R—Why it works, Based on an Information Processing Theory of Learning," *Journal of Reading* (November 1978), pp. 110–112.
8. Van Dongen, Richard D. An Analysis of Study Skills Taught by Intermediate Grade Basal Readers. Masters thesis, University of New Mexico, August, 1967.
9. Zintz, Miles V. *The Reading Process,* 2nd ed. Dubuque, Ia.: William C. Brown, 1975.

Chapter 11
Teaching Work-Study Skills

RATIONALE

Although word recognition and comprehension skills are basic to reading ability, the work-study skills are basic to school success. The importance of the prospective teacher having knowledge of the work-study skills was emphasized in Chapter 10. Since the ability of students to use the skills is important to school success and future daily life-coping situations, the teacher must also become competent in teaching the skills. The acquisition of work-study skills enables students to become independent, mature readers. In order for teachers to lead students toward this independence, they must become knowledgeable of the skills and competent in teaching them.

OBJECTIVES

This chapter will enable you to demonstrate competence in teaching work-study/specialized skills. After completing this chapter, you will be able to:
1. Design a plan (that includes introduction and reinforcement) for teaching a given work-study or specialized skill.
2. Teach a selected work-study or specialized skill to a peer group or small group of children.
3. Critique the teaching behaviors of a peer who is implementing a plan for a given work-study skill.
   (Criteria will be provided.)
4. Complete an objective identified by the instructor.

PREASSESSMENT

See Appendix A-11.

Instructional Activity 1

Designing Plans for Teaching Work-Study Skills

A Sample Teaching Plan

Study the steps involved in preparing a plan for teaching a work-study skill at the sixth-grade level.

1. State the *objective*. The overall objective is for the learner to understand the concept of outlining and to complete a simple outline. To meet this objective, the learner must be able to identify subtopics in a paragraph and supporting details for the subtopics (from material at the 4.5 reading level).
2. List the *materials* needed for the lesson. Graded paragraphs.
3. Outline the *procedure* for the lesson.
   (a) Be able to provide students with a reason for the lesson. Tell them why it is important. For example, outlining is a way of organizing our thinking. It can help us get into focus the main ideas and supporting points of paragraphs or longer units. It allows us to organize information so that we can get a clearer understanding of it. Outlining can help us remember key ideas of material read. It also helps us organize our thoughts before we begin writing paragraphs, reports, and the like.
   (b) Identify the steps necessary for completing the task. As the teacher, list the steps necessary for completing an outline in random order as they occur to you.
      (1) Identifies the main idea of a paragraph.
      (2) Identifies subtopics that support the main idea.
      (3) Identifies supporting material for the subtopics.
      (4) Diagrams a two-step outline form.
      (5) Reads independently at the 4.5 level.
      (6) Writes with ease.

Now that the tasks involved in completing an outline have been listed, a logical sequence of the tasks must be arranged. In order for the student to complete an outline, he or she must have these skills, in the given order.

1. Reads independently at the 4.5 level.
2. Writes with ease.
3. Identifies the main idea of a paragraph.
4. Identifies subtopics that support the main idea.
5. Identifies supporting material for the subtopics.
6. Diagrams a two-step outline form.

Inability to perform one of these tasks may prevent the student from successfully completing an outline. It might be necessary for the teacher to provide instruction for some students in some of these skills.

It is possible that you, as the teacher, might want to give a pretest to determine student mastery of the skills necessary for outlining. Perhaps you already know the needs of your own students. Assuming the students have previously demonstrated proficiency in steps 1 and 2, a pretest could be given on steps 3 to 6. The test itself might be to outline a given paragraph and write a title for it. The writing of a title tests the main idea, while other skills are tested in the construction of the paragraph.

Results can be recorded in checklist form.

	Identifies main idea of paragraph	Identifies subtopics to support main idea	Identifies supporting evidence for subtopics	Diagrams a two-step outline
Betty	✓			
Georgia	✓	✓		
Herman	✓			
Maria	✓			
David	✓			
Jay	✓	✓		
Carlita	✓			

From the information gathered on the test it is seen that the students were able to name the main idea of the paragraph. Instruction then should begin with identifying subtopics that support the main idea. An easy way to begin this instruction is to relate something of significance to the children to the task. For example, how many meals do we usually have each day? What do we call these meals? (Write them down, spaced apart.)

Meals We Eat.
I. Breakfast.
II. Lunch.
III. Dinner.

Name two things we eat at breakfast.

Meals We Eat.
I. Breakfast.
    A. Bacon.
    B. Toast.

Name two things we eat at a noon meal. (Add the items to the outline.)
II. Lunch.
    A. Soup.
    B. Sandwich.

Name two things we eat at an evening meal. (Add the items to the outline.)
III. Dinner.
    A. Meatloaf.
    B. Peas.

Focus the students' attention on the form of the outline, on the three items that support the title, and on the items that support the subtopics. Emphasize that outlining helps us to organize information. With the students' aid, write a paragraph from the outline. Then have them outline the paragraph just written.

When students have mastered the procedure for constructing a simple outline, further subdivisions may be introduced and reinforced at the appropriate level. To keep the lesson meaningful, expansion of the original outline may be accomplished.

    (c) Prepare for *practice*. Another topic may be chosen for the students to complete in outline form. If helpful, students might work in pairs before independent practice is done.
    (d) Prepare for *reinforcement*. Provide a simple paragraph for the students to outline main ideas and supporting ideas.
    (e) Plan for *evaluation*. The same task can be done for postassessment as was done for preassessment.

Results of the postassessment will help you to make decisions concerning individual instruction or temporary small group instruction. Additional instruction and practice can be given to students who need help.

The following condensed sample lesson can be expanded in the same manner as the previous sample lesson and may be used in preparing your own plan (see pp. 205–206).

Skill: Using maps, graphs, and tables.
Objective: Given a map, graph, or table, the student will be able to read and answer questions related to it at the appropriate grade level.
Procedures:
Maps: Give the students a map and stress the facts that all maps have legends. Explain the meanings of the symbols on different legends. Then give the students an unfamiliar map and ask them to answer several questions about it that require the use of the legend. Discuss the procedure used to answer the questions.

Preparing Your Plan
When you have carefully studied the steps in preparing the sample lesson and the design for a successful lesson in Appendix E, prepare your own plan for teaching a specific work-study skill.

Use the sample lesson as a model. Refer to Chapter 10 for an outline of the work-study skills and choose a skill on which to base your planning.

Read the remaining sections of this chapter for teaching suggestions that may be helpful.

General Teaching Suggestions

If possible, teach the skill selected in an inductive manner or at least include some inductive teaching techniques when appropriate in the presentation. For example, as you go through the steps in introducing the SQ3R study method, ask the students to summarize what is being done. Lead them through the method and assist them in verbalizing the steps. A selection may be reproduced on transparencies and shown with an overhead projector so the students can see each step being demonstrated. A selection from a textbook being used by the students in a content area subject might be used to demonstrate the steps involved in the study method.

Suggestions for Teaching Pictoral Material (Graphic Aids)

You should present the use of pictorial material in your content classes if they apply in your area. The use of graphic aids such as graphs, charts, diagrams, and pictures probably is most relevant in content areas such as social studies, mathematics, science, agriculture, home economics, and health.

Interpreting maps requires several subskills. A student must be able to read physical and political maps and must understand the use of scales, legends, and map symbols.

The initial presentation of map interpretation should use actual maps found in a content textbook and placed in an opaque projector or maps drawn on transparencies. The following areas should be covered: studying the title of the map, noticing the legend, noticing the directions on the map, and using the map scale. For further practice, construct worksheets that require your students to apply map interpretation. Each of these graphic aids requires that a student understand what is given directly (literal comprehension) and what is implied (interpretive comprehension.)

Sources of Additional Suggestions for Teaching

Some suggested topics and sample plans for teaching outlining can be found in Zintz (1975, pp. 311–318).

For additional suggestions for teaching work-study skills, see the Reading Resources/References.

Instructional Activity 2

Teaching Work-Study or Specialized Skills

Teach the lesson you have prepared on Objective 1 in order to introduce or reinforce a specific work-study skill. You may choose to teach your lesson or any of the sample lessons provided in the chapter or the Reading Resources/References. Refer to Appendix C, checklist 3, "Criteria for Teaching a Lesson."

Instructional Activity 3	**Critiquing Work-Study or Specialized Skills Lessons** Critique (orally or in writing) the teaching of another student (Objective 2). Use checklist 4 in Appendix C as a criterion to critique the teaching of a peer. This employs the same checklist used in teaching Objective 2, with a rating scale added for critiquing.

SUGGESTED TEACHING ACTIVITIES

1. *Skill:* Organizing information.[1]

   Objective: The student will be able to organize information in a variety of ways at the appropriate grade level—outlining, note-taking, and summarizing.

   Preassessment: The teacher gives students reading materials that they are capable of reading as part of their assignment and asks them to outline one paragraph, take notes on a second paragraph, and summarize a third one.

   Procedures: Students may want to indent and to letter and number the headings. Roman numerals represent major headings; headings of next-highest significance, or second-order headings, are indented and prefaced by capital letters; points that support second-order headings, which are third-order headings, are preceded by Arabic numerals; last, fourth-order headings are preceded by lowercase letters.

   Example:

   ```
   I. XXXXXXXXXXXXXXXXXXXXXXXXXXXXXX
      A. XXXXXXXXXXXXX
      B. XXXXXXXXXXXXX
      C. XXXXXXX
         1. XXXXXXXXXXX
            a. XXXXXXX
            b. XXXXXXXXXXXXX
         2. XXXXXXXXXXX
   ```

   Underlining is another method of outlining, if you own the book.

   Note-taking: A child may draw illustrations (see example) before he has mastered outlining.

   Summarizing: This requires the selection of the main points. The complete sentence pattern is the best one for summarizing. Fragmented sentences are likely to be of little use later.

[1] Adapted from *To The Rescue,* Creative Teaching Ideas, Bulletin 1503, 1978, Louisiana Department of Education.

2. *Skill:* Locating information.
Organization: Individual/small group.
Materials: Posterboard or construction paper, marks-a-lot or crayons, and scissors.
Procedure: The teacher cuts out several egg shapes from the posterboard or construction paper. He or she cuts the eggs so they appear cracked. On one-half of each egg, he writes a question such as: What movie is showing downtown this Saturday? What is the largest lake in South Dakota? Does this book contain information on rice farming? On the other half he writes the sources in which answers to the questions could be found. The student selects a question and matches it up with the correct source of information by putting the egg parts together. The exercise may be made self-checking by numbering the backs of the egg parts.

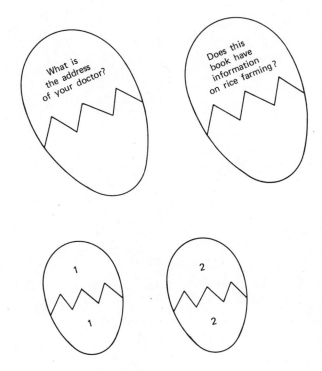

ADDITIONAL ENABLING ACTIVITIES

1. Attend class session(s) Time _____ Date _____ .
2. An activity of your choice.
3. An activity selected by your instructor.

READING RESOURCES/REFERENCES

1. Dauzat, Sam V., Jo Ann Dauzat, Wayne Otto, and Burton W. Kreitlow. *Reading 2600* (Locating and Organizing Information), and *Reading 2700* (Maps, Graphs, and Tables), Steck-Vaughn Adult Reading, 1978.
2. Otto, Wayne, director. *The Wisconsin Design for Reading Skill Development, Teacher's Resource File: Study Skills.* Wisconsin Research and Development Center for Cognitive Learning, The University of Wisconsin, Madison, Interpretive Scoring Systems, 1972.
3. Zintz, Miles V. *The Reading Process,* 2nd ed. Dubuque, Ia.: William C. Brown, 1975.

Section 6

Teaching Reading: Approaches, Procedures, Materials

In order to be successful, the teacher must understand how all of the reading skills fit into the larger picture of a developmental and functional reading program. The competencies for this section relate to the understanding of approaches for teaching reading.

The teacher:

- Is knowledgeable about techniques for teaching reading such as the basal reading approach and the language experience approach.
- Uses the organizational plan of a directed reading activity to improve reading skills.
- Uses the organizational plan of a directed reading activity to promote application of reading skills in the content areas.
- Identifies appropriate settings for oral and silent reading and adjusts activities accordingly.
- Identifies components of other approaches and selects an approach appropriate for given students.

Using the Chapters in Section 6

The chapters in Section 6 need not be pursued in the given sequence. In fact, they may be pursued after those in Section 7. Follow the listed steps to complete the chapters.

1. Read the rationale for an overview of the contents and a sense of why it is important.
2. Read the objectives.
3. The preassessment is optional. If you take it, score it to discern your strengths and weaknesses.
4. Read the information provided in the text and do the activities as directed.
5. Select additional enabling activities for those objectives in which need extra help. Use the Reading Resources/References as suggested by your instructor.
6. Schedule a meeting with your instructor and take the postassessment. If you choose, retake the preassessment to determine your readiness for postassessment.
7. Evaluate your performance and move to the next chapter in your sequence or repeat steps 4 to 6 accordingly.

Chapter 12
Basal Reader Approach

RATIONALE

The developmental reading program is one aspect of a total reading picture. In the developmental program the focus is on sequential introduction, reinforcement, and mastery of the range of reading skills discussed in previous chapters. The basal reader approach is one vehicle for implementing the developmental reading program. In fact, the basal reading approach is the primary system of reading instruction in America. It provides for the planned, sequential development of a wide range of reading skills.

Because of the prominence of the approach, it is highly likely that you will be expected to implement a basal reading approach in your own classroom during your teaching career. This chapter will help you develop the competencies necessary for your success in such a venture.

OBJECTIVES

After completing this chapter, you will be able to:
1. Identify major characteristics of a basal reading approach.
2. State at least two advantages and two disadvantages of a basal approach.
3. Explain how different grouping plans relate to the basal approach.
4. Identify the major teaching procedure in a basal approach.
5. Complete an objective identified by the instructor.

PREASSESSMENT

See Appendix A-12.

Instructional Activity 1

Characteristics of the Basal Reading Approach

Basic to the basal reading approach is the belief that the best way to teach reading is by providing children with instruction in word recognition and comprehension skills in planned sequential lessons. These lessons are developed through a series of books, or *readers,* that are graded by difficulty of the reading passages and interest level of the content.

Think about your experiences in elementary school when you were learning to read. Visualize the book you used in the first, second, or third grade. List some of the names of the characters.

If you can do this, you probably were taught to read through a basal reading approach. Most American children still are! In fact, the predominant tool for reading instruction in America is the basal reader series, although various other supplementary materials are used also.

A *basal reader series*[1] consists of a number of books containing passages written at increasing levels of difficulty. These books usually begin with materials for developing reading readiness skills and incorporate all word recognition, comprehension, and some work-study skills into books that range upward to at least the sixth reading level. A series may contain a readiness book, one to three preprimers, a primer, and one to two readers for each grade level. In addition to the basal readers, the series will usually contain a number of workbooks to accompany the readers, mastery tests, and a teacher's guide for each text.

The basal readers cover the entire range of reading skills, as discussed in previous chapters. They form the core for the entire developmental reading program in a given school system. The individual reading skills are introduced, developed, and reinforced sequentially in the readers and accompanying workbooks. The readers themselves are carefully controlled for the introduction of vocabulary items and written language complexity.

Some of the basal readers are identified by levels; others are identified by grades to indicate the complexity of the skills and the language included in the book. For instance, a book at level 7 or G means that there are six levels of skills that should be prerequisite to entry at this level. Or a book identified as 3^2 reader indicates that there are other materials of lesser difficulty that should be mastered prior to entry into this book. The designation further indicates that the book is of the difficulty level usually associated with the second semester of the third grade.

The teacher's guides that accompany the readers provide the overall philosophy of the program and help the teacher use the materials as intended by the authors. The guides usually have carefully developed, detailed lesson plans for each of the selections in the reader. These plans follow the directed reading lesson detailed in Chapter 13.

---

[1] There are about a dozen different basal reader series; they are identified by the name of publishing company; for example, Scott-Foresman, Houghton Mifflin, Macmillan, Harper & Row; and Holt, Rinehart and Winston.

Activities

1. Use the curriculum section of your library to locate basal readers. List the publishers and the number and range of readers (e.g., from readiness to sixth grade) for at least three reading series.

Publisher	Date	Number of Readers	Range

2. If you are a visitor in fifth-grade classroom during the reading lesson, how might you know whether or not a basal reading approach is used?

   Give evidence other than asking the teacher or children. _____

   _____

   _____

   _____

Instructional Activity 2

Strengths and Weaknesses of the Basal Reading Approach
Before you read the instructional material, do the following activity. It will help you discover some of the strong and weak points of basal readers.

   Carefully look through at least one of the basal series. Choose one with the most recent copyright date. Then respond to these items. Compare your responses with those of a peer.

1. Roles of the female characters tend to be _____

   _____

2. Roles of the male characters tend to be _____

   _____

3. The sentence structure tends to be _____

   _____

4. The racial characteristics of the characters tend to be _____

   _____

5. The socioeconomic conditions of the characters tend to be _____

   _____

215

6. The topics of the selections tend to be _____

_____

7. If you were an elementary student, how would you feel about learning

to read from this series? _____

_____

Strengths and Weaknesses of Basal Reader Programs

Even though a basal approach dominates reading instruction, the approach is not without its critics. Some of the positive and negative features are presented here.

STRENGTH	WEAKNESS
1. The systems are well planned and carefully sequenced. The vocabularies are controlled so that the child does not encounter too many unknown words in a selection and so that the words can be repeated in new selections and mastered by the student.	1. The controlled language complexity results in stiff language patterns. The controlled vocabulary results in boring selections with poor literary style.
2. The teacher's guides provide valuable suggestions for teaching, thereby saving much preparation time.	2. Many teachers are not selective about activities from teacher's guides and try to do everything. The guides may decrease the creativity of the teacher and create sterile reading lessons.
3. The systems usually contain all components for developing, reinforcing, extending, and evaluating skills.	3. Teachers may not alter the approach and materials to fit the needs of their specific groups.
4. The basal reading systems facilitate organization of groups for instruction.	4. The selections tend to have middle-class, ethnic majority biases, at least in older editions.
5. Basal materials are usually authored by reading experts.	5. The characters tend to show sex-role stereotyping, at least in older editions.
	6. Complete materials tend to be expensive.

Are the criticisms of basal reading programs valid in view of what you found in activity 2? Why? _____

216

Authors of basal reader series are putting forth much effort to improve the readers in content and format. In fact, the more recent series have tried to negate criticisms 1, 4, and 5, with some positive results. The weaknesses that relate to teacher use (or misuse) of the materials are more difficult to correct. Teachers may need to be reminded that the teacher's guide provides many activities as *suggestions,* not prescriptions. The wise teacher should select the activities that correspond to the needs and interests of the particular children. This also applies to the workbooks that accompany the basal readers.

 Activities

Apply what you have learned to these situations. Compare your responses with those of a peer.

1. Shirley September just got started on her first teaching job. She is so dedicated to her work that she does not want her students to miss anything. She uses a basal reading program as the heart of her reading instruction. She calls the teacher's guide her Ten Commandments for teaching, and she has her students do everything the guide lists. Since school began in late August, her better students have completed three "stories" in their basal readers. This is the middle of October.

   (a) What common error is Shirley making? _____

   _____

   _____

   (b) What advice would you give her? Why? _____

   _____

   _____

2. Ms. E. Conni Me is never wasteful. She always has every child do every page in every workbook they get. As her friend, what would you tell her? Why? _____

   _____

   _____

Instructional Activity 3

Grouping for Basal Reading Instruction
Basal reading instruction does not mean that every fifth-grade child must be reading from the fifth-grade reader. The approach facilitates grouping on the basis of one or more factors. In most instances the students have

been assigned to a particular book on the basis of some criteria—norm-referenced tests, criterion-referenced tests, informal reading inventories, cloze tests, or some other means, as discussed in Chapter 17. The intent is to match the student's reading level to the book at the appropriate level of difficulty. This usually results in a class of students being grouped in three to five subgroups for instructional purposes. This is a type of *achievement grouping*, or reading-level grouping.

For certain parts of the lesson the teacher may form other grouping patterns. For instance, students may be grouped for skills instruction in patterns different from the reading-level grouping. In this pattern, all children who have common reading skills needs may be grouped for instruction, regardless of the level of the reader in which the child is placed. This is referred to as *skills grouping* and is discussed further in Chapters 17 and 18.

Children can also be grouped on the basis of *interest* in the basal approach. Students who share a common interest can be grouped together to do enrichment-type activities after the teacher-directed activities have been completed.

The basal reading approach can accommodate any of the three given types of grouping—achievement or reading-level grouping, skill needs grouping, and interest grouping. The grouping pattern should reflect the purposes of the teacher and the needs of the students. Note, however, that there are some inherent dangers in sole reliance on one type of grouping and adherence to rigid groups. For instance, when the teacher groups solely on reading level, the students quickly learn their "place in the scheme of things" even if the books are not marked. They may begin to think of themselves as slow readers, poor readers, and the like. In such cases, poor self-concepts can develop and inhibit progress in reading. But, when the groups are flexible and the student is sometimes grouped with the better readers, or even the poorer readers, the student is less locked into a category of good, average, or poor reader. Varying the grouping patterns also allows students to stimulate the learning of their peers in ways not possible in grouping that is lock-step.

Activity

Apply what you learned to these situations. Compare your responses with those of a peer.

Jerry Germaine teaches sixth-grade students. He has three groups of students for reading instruction. Each group is reading from a different textbook.

(a) What type of pattern is Jerry using in his classroom?

_____

(b) On Wednesday, Jerry called three people from Reader 6 Group, five people from Reader 5 Group, and six people from Reader 4 Group together. He presented a lesson to them on how to use the guide letters on the card catalog. What type grouping is Jerry using? _____

_____

Instructional Activity 4

Teaching Procedures for the Basal Reading Approach

Although there are minor variations, the basal reading approach relies heavily on a directed reading activity as the main lesson format. This procedure is described in some detail in the teacher's guide that accompanies the basal reader series. The main features of the lesson include the following steps. (The teaching procedure is further developed in Chapter 13.)

1. Building readiness by:
   (a) Helping students relate background experiences to new learning.
   (b) Presenting new vocabulary.
   (c) Setting purposes for reading.
2. Silent reading by students (students read from the basal readers).
3. Checking and stimulating comprehension by teacher questions.
4. Silent or oral rereading by students in response to new purposes set by teacher.
5. Developing new skills or refining those previously learned.
6. Reinforcing skills or concepts (students may work in accompanying workbooks).
7. Extending activities into other related areas or independent practice.

The basic lesson format provides a balance between activities that require direct teacher involvement and those that require minimal teacher direction. This facilitates simultaneous meaningful activity of multiple groups in the classroom. While one group of students is engaged in steps 1 to 5 of the directed reading activity, other groups may be engaged in activities related to steps 6 or 7, which allow for more independent learning. This means that the teacher must be able to manage simultaneously the learning experiences of two to five groups.

It may require several class periods to complete a given directed reading activity. This depends on the maturity of the students, the length of the given reading passage, and the complexity of the skills to be developed.

 Activity

1. Mrs. Master has her fifth-grade students divided into three groups based on their instructional reading level, which ranges from 4.0 to 6.0.

   (a) Would the children be reading from the same basal reader? _____
   (b) The following figure depicts the reading class in groups. Look at the

activity in which the group is engaged; then decide which step of the DRA each group is pursuing.

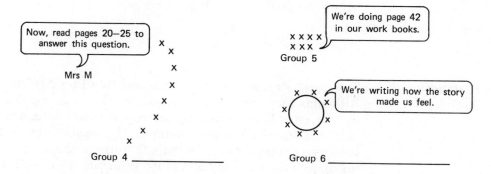

2. Observe in a classroom where the teacher uses a basal reading approach. See if you can identify the steps of the DRA as the teacher works.

ADDITIONAL ENABLING ACTIVITIES

1. Read and take notes on at least two of the following texts for each of the objectives.
   (a) Lapp and Flood, pp. 441–458 (Objective 2).
   (b) Ransom, Chapter 4 (Objectives 1 and 2).
   (c) Burns and Roe, pp. 250–262 (Objectives 2 and 4).
   (d) Dallmann, pp. 60–65 (Objectives 1, 2 and 4).
2. For extra work on Objectives 1, 2, 3, and 4, interview a classroom teacher. Turn the objectives into questions to ask.
3. Observe a reading class that uses a basal reading approach. Use "Observation Guide 5," Appendix C-5 (Objectives 1, 3 and 4).

4. Attend class session(s) Time _____ Date _____ .
5. An activity of your choice.
6. An activity selected by your instructor.

READING RESOURCES / REFERENCES

1. Burns, Paul C., and Betty D. Roe. *Teaching Reading in Today's Elementary Schools.* Chicago: Rand McNally, 1976.
2. Dallmann, Martha, Roger L. Rouch, Lynette Y. C. Chang, and John J. DeBoer. *The Teaching of Reading,* 5th ed. New York: Holt, Rinehart & Winston, 1978.
3. Lapp, Diane, and James Flood. *Teaching Reading to Every Child.* New York: Macmillan, 1978.
4. Ransom, Grayce. *Preparing to Teach Reading.* Boston: Little, Brown, 1978.
5. Spache, George D., and Evelyn B. Spache. *Reading in the Elementary School,* 4th ed. Boston: Allyn and Bacon, 1977.

Chapter 13
Teaching A Directed Reading Activity

RATIONALE

Reading has no body of content; it exists as a language arts skill, a medium of communication between author and reader. Therefore the goal of reading instruction in the elementary school is to help children develop reading skills that will enable them to become independent learners.

The passages included in basal reading series are placed there not because of their body of content but because they lend themselves to the teaching of specific word recognition, comprehension, and work-study skills. Each reading lesson is designed or directed for teaching selected reading skills. Each reading lesson should be a directed reading lesson, planned to ascertain that the children receive the teacher guidance necessary for them to develop the reading skills of appropriate complexity and in an appropriate sequence. A directed reading lesson consists of a series of activities in a prescribed sequence. This chapter will acquaint you with the directed reading lesson and help you become competent in teaching reading skills according to the given plan. It will also help you develop competence in utilizing a directed reading approach for teaching in the content fields.

OBJECTIVES

Both knowledge and application-level objectives are developed in this chapter. After completing this chapter, you will be able to:
1. Identify the teaching-learning activities included in a directed reading activity.
2. Sequence the elements of a directed reading lesson and provide a rationale.
3. Prepare a written plan for teaching a directed reading activity that meets given criteria.
4. Identify elements of the directed reading activity that adapt for reading in the content fields.

5. Implement a directed reading activity that satisfies given criteria in peer or actual classroom settings.
6. Critique according to given criteria a directed reading activity taught by a regular teacher or a peer.
7. Complete an objective identified by the instructor.

PREASSESSMENT

See Appendix A-13.

Instructional Activity 1

Major Activities in Directed Reading Lessons

The directed reading lesson, also referred to as a directed reading thinking activity, involves a number of activities that are the explicit responsibility of the teacher.

Preteaching Tasks

1. Selecting and stating worthy objectives for the activities.
2. Becoming thoroughly familiar with the content of the passage to be read.
3. Determining how to stimulate interest in the selection and designing activities to use.
4. Determining which words in the selection will cause difficulty for the students both in terms of pronunciation and meaning.
5. Deciding how to introduce the new words in context.
6. Deciding how much of the passage the children should read at a time.
7. Preparing for prereading questions and postreading questions that will check on and extend the comprehension of the students.
8. Determining how the new skills will be introduced and reinforced and designing activities to use.
9. Deciding on how much guided practice is needed and designing activities to use.
10. Determining how much and what type of independent practice is needed and designing activities to use.

Teaching Tasks

1. Getting the students ready to read. Getting their attention. Developing necessary concepts.
2. Introducing new words.
3. Providing reasons for reading the selection.
4. Asking stimulating questions and encouraging thinking at more complex levels.
5. Setting purposes for rereading.
6. Introducing new skills.

7. Providing guided practice for skills.
8. Providing independent activities.

The directed reading activity also involves the reader in a number of activities, such as:

1. Verbalizing experiences that relate to the passage.
2. Pronouncing the new words.
3. Silent reading at an appropriate rate to accommodate the purpose.
4. Answering questions.
5. Rereading orally or silently in response to new purposes.
6. Learning new skills.
7. Engaging in guided practice activities.
8. Engaging in independent practice activities.

✳ Activities

Apply what you have learned in these situations. Compare your responses with those of a peer.

1. Mr. Paul has a group of third-level children who are slow readers and have short attention spans. Therefore he decides to guide their reading page by page.

   (a) Identify the preteaching task Mr. Paul performed. _____

   _____

   (b) Do you agree with his decision? Why? _____

   _____

2. Cindy is preparing to teach a selection that deals with a trip to the zoo. She puts pictures of different animals on display before the lesson. Then she uses the pictures to stimulate a discussion.

   (a) Identify the teaching task Cindy performs. _____

   _____

   (b) Do you think this is a good activity for the purpose? Why? _____

   _____

3. Mr. Brandon is busy engaging the sixth-year students in a discussion of their experiences with spiders. In the discussion he provides this dialogue. "Spiders are members of a class called *arachnids*. Ticks are arachnids, too. They have four pairs of legs." As he says *arachnids*, he holds up a card with the word written on it.

   (a) Identify the task Mr. Brandon is performing _____

   _____

225

(b) Do you think this is a good activity? Why? _____

_____

Sequence of Activities in Directed Reading Lessons

The activities described in the previous material are placed in a specified sequence for presentation. The sequence involves prereading activities that are based on sound principles. The activities include building readiness for the lesson (providing an anticipatory set) by providing the necessary background to allow the student to be successful in the lesson and establishing purposes so that the learner's behaviors are goal oriented. The sequence involves postreading activities that are educationally sound. These activities include checking on understanding and extending understanding of the selection.

The skill development aspect of the DRA may be sequenced either for prereading or postreading activities. The format that follows presents skill development as a postreading activity. The rationale for this is that the skill development aspect is a minilesson in itself and facilitates a type of grouping that cuts across the usual reading-level grouping pattern as discussed in Chapter 12. The placement of skill development activity after the directed reading of the selection permits grouping based on skills needs. Additional reasons include the fact that placement of skill development after reading the selection allows for uninterrupted reading of the selection without "sidetracking" for skill instruction, and this sequence permits the skill development to "spin off" from the content of the selection.

The procedure for presenting a directed reading activity is now presented in sequence.

Teaching a Directed Reading Lesson: A Recipe

I. Readiness for the lesson
   A. The teacher helps children verbalize experiences that relate to selection. Pictures or other stimuli may be used to capture student interest.
   B. The teacher introduces new words. This must be done in a context setting (either oral or written). The key is that the child glean the meaning of the word in a given context, the pronunciation of the word, and the graphic (letter arrangement) representation of the word.
      1. May use word cards.
      2. May use pictures with labels.
      3. May draw definitions and synonyms from the students in part A.
      4. May use glossary or dictionary (ascertain that this is *not* too

time consuming and is *not* the major manner in which new words are introduced). Also be certain to list the word in a context illustrating the desired meaning.

  C. The teacher gives the student some major purpose for reading the selection. "Read to find out . . . ," or "Read to answer these questions." Be sure that the questions are general enough that the student does not answer the question by reading only a part of the selection. You may want to state your comprehension objective for the lesson at this point and let the children know why it is important to learn.

II. Directed Silent Reading
  (Distribute books to children)

  A. Direct the children to read the selection (or part of the selection, depending on the students' reading abilities, attention spans, and the difficulty of the material and length of the materials.)

  B. Encourage the children to adjust reading rates in terms of the type of selection, style of the selection, understandings desired from the selection, and the child's own experiences related to the selection. For example, you may ask the students to read slowly because you want them to use all of the facts to draw a conclusion or quickly scan the material to predict what it is going to be mainly about.

III. Comprehension Check

  A. Comprehension checks may be oral, written, or both, depending on the needs of the children and the organizational patterns in the classroom.

  B. Determine if the purposes established for silent reading have been accomplished.

  C. The comprehension check should involve measuring the four types of comprehension skills: literal comprehension, inferential comprehension, critical comprehension, and vocabulary (word meaning in context).

  D. Use questions to promote comprehension at increasingly complex levels, as discussed in Chapter 8.

IV. Rereading

  A. Rereading may have been accomplished during the check on understanding.

  B. May be either oral or silent, but it must be done in response to specific purposes set by the teacher. "Read the part that substantiates your opinion." "Read the part that tells. . . ."

V. Skill Development

  A. Teach and/or reinforce a specific reading skill at this point. The skill will usually be one based on the reading of the selection.

  B. Specific skills to be taught here include word recognition, comprehension, or work study.

VI. Follow-up or Application (Guided practice)

At this point, have the children apply the new skill to new reading materials or reinforce the skill in a variety of ways.

VII. Additional Activities (Independent practice)
   A. Encourage the children to read supplementary information related to the topic.
   B. Encourage creative expressions stimulated by the selection.

Instructional Activity 3

Planning A Directed Reading Activity

You must have a passage in order to develop your plan. You may select one from a basal reader or you may use one included in the appendix. After you decide on the passage, follow these steps.

1. Read the passage yourself.
2. Answer this question. What reading skills can be taught through this lesson? Write them down.

   (a) Word recognition? _____

   (b) Comprehension? _____

   (c) Work-study? _____

3. Restate these reading skills as objectives to be developed. Identify at least two objectives.

   _____ and

   _____

4. Scan the passage again as you look for words that would probably cause difficulty for the reader. Write them down. _____

   _____

5. Determine which of the words you should introduce to the students.
6. Put the words in a context for introduction to the children. Be sure that the context gives meaning to the word and that the meaning is the one used in the selection. Write your words in context here.

   _____

   _____

   _____

7. Identify at least one prereading question or purpose that will help the student determine the type reading he or she should do. _____

   _____

8. Construct comprehension questions in each of the areas given. You should have some questions that clearly relate to the stated objective.

You need not ask the questions in the sequence given here when you implement the plan.

(a) Vocabulary _____

_____

(b) Literal _____

_____

(c) Inferential _____

_____

(d) Critical _____

_____

9. Identify the purposes for oral rereading. _____

_____

_____

10. Decide how you will introduce the skill identified in the objective. (If it is a phonics skill, use the procedure identified in Chapter 7. If it is another word recognition skill, use the procedure identified in Chapter 5. If it is a work-study skill, use the procedures identified in Chapter 11.) Write the steps you will use. _____

_____

_____

_____

11. Decide which skill you want to reinforce. Tell what you will do to guide practice in it. (You may want to select one of the activities identified in Chapters 5, 7, 9, or 11 for reinforcement. Be sure that the activity is in agreement with your objectives.) _____

_____

_____

12. Decide which independent practice activities you want the students to pursue. Write at least two here. _____

_____

_____

13. Decide what you will do to gain the students' interest in the whole lesson. Write how you will do it. _____

_____

_____

14. Now organize the items you listed in the sequence for teaching a directed reading activity. Write it according to the seven major steps. This is your teaching plan. Submit it to a peer for critique before submitting it to your instructor.

Instructional Activity 4

Adapting the Directed Reading Activity for Content Area Reading

Anytime the teacher utilizes reading material as the source of information for students, there are certain steps he or she should follow, regardless of the content being taught. The DRA for content area reading incorporates steps basic to good teaching in science, mathematics, social studies, English, or whatever the subject may be. The DRA for content reading includes both prereading and postreading activities, just as the DRA does for teaching reading.

The DRA for content reading is designed to be used in a group situation. Best results occur when the reading materials are at the students' instructional level, but use of the DRA can help bridge a gap for students for whom the materials would otherwise be too difficult. The DRA approach is appropriate for guiding reading as a classroom activity and a homework assignment.

Steps for a DRA in the content areas include the following.

Step I. Build readiness
Purpose: To bridge the gap between the students' backgrounds of experience and the new concepts presented in the materials.
A. Background
　1. Finding out what the students already know and clarifying any misconceptions that may exist.
　2. Supplying information for students to expand their background of experience.
　3. Creating an awareness of the significance of the materials.
B. Introduce new vocabulary
　1. Teaching words not in the reader's listening vocabulary that might confuse the student, particularly when those words express key concepts.
　2. Clarifying meanings of words as used in the text, particularly the meanings unique to the content. For example, consider the meanings of the word *square:* the *square* root of 49 is 7; the *square* of 7 is 49; a *square* is a four-sided closed

figure with equal-length sides that meet at 90 degree angles; the window frame was out of *square*; a *square* dance was held; she needs to *square* things with me; I think that the Charleston is a *square* dance; they met on the courthouse *square*.

3. Clarifying unusual, colloquial, slang terms or figurative language.
4. Clarifying meanings of key abbreviations such as DNA, RDA, BTU, MPH, RPM, mg, and g or math and science formulas.

C. Preview selection
1. Directing attention to the author's style of presentation or the author's purpose.
2. Directing attention to graphic aides such as maps, charts, tables, graphs, diagrams, and pictures.
3. Directing attention to study aides such as questions, summaries, underlined words, italicized words, side headings, titles, and subtitles.

D. Establish purposes for reading
1. Giving reasons that the material is important to the student.
2. Setting prereading purposes in the form of general statements or as prereading questions.

Step II. Guide silent reading
Purpose: To help students adjust rate to purpose as they read the selection to accomplish the purposes set in step I.

Step III. Develop comprehension
Purpose: To extend the students' understanding of the important aspects of the subject matter.
A. Discussing answers to prereading questions.
B. Clarifying responses to postreading questions.
C. Assisting students in sorting relevant facts, understanding main ideas, forming generalizations that correspond to key concepts, and identifying important relationships in the materials.
D. Determining the need for rereading all or part of the materials to accomplish redefined purposes.

Step IV. Guide rereading (either silent or oral)
Purpose: To refine and reinforce the students' comprehension of the key concepts and facts about the subject matter.
  Guiding students to extend understanding of the subject matter by rereading in response to new purposes either a part of the selection or the entire selection.

Step V. Application of information
Purpose: To provide opportunities for students to apply important

information to solve problems or to other situations. This may include one or more of the following tasks.

A. Setting up problems
1. Identifying the problem to be solved.
2. Locating supplemental information—this may be new information from reference books.
3. Reading for additional information.
4. Selecting the information that related to the problem and organizing it as a written report, an oral presentation, or the like.

B. Extending interest and appreciations by choosing supplementary recreational reading materials.

C. Analyzing new information for relevance to own lives.

Independence in Content Reading

The teacher who uses the DRA approach to content area reading helps the student achieve greater comprehension of the information and also helps him or her form a pattern for achieving academic independence. The steps in the DRA closely correspond to the steps in the study techniques discussed in Chapter 10. The teacher who establishes the DRA pattern for reading can help the student begin to complete some of the steps.

For instance, step I of the DRA Building Readiness parts A-C corresponds to the survey or preview step of the SQ3R. Step I, part D—(establishing purposes) corresponds to the Q (or questions) step of the SQ3R study plan. Step II (silent reading) corresponds to the first R in the SQ3R plan. Step III (develop comprehension) corresponds to the second R (recite in the study plan). The third R (review) corresponds with step IV (guide rereading) of the DRA.

Because of the similarities in the steps as presented in the following table, the teacher should be able to help the student become independent by gradually having the student assume the responsibility for getting ready for reading by using previewing techniques, setting purposes for reading, independent silent reading, answering self-developed questions, and rereading parts that are important.

Comparison of DRA and SQ3R Independent Study Plan

DRA		SQ3R	
I.	Build readiness • Expanding backgrounds • Presenting new vocabulary • Previewing selection • Set purposes for reading	S	Survey material to get an idea of what it is all about • Note italicized vocabulary • Note special features
		Q	Turn side headings into questions to be answered
II.	Guide silent reading	R	Read selection
III.	Develop comprehension	R	Recite Answer the questions raised in step 2

DRA	SQ3R
IV. Guide rereading Clarify concepts/facts	R Review • Check to be certain of under-standing. • Reread any part necessary

Activities

1. Select a content area textbook or use a 6-to 8-level passage from Appendix B-4. Prepare a plan for teaching a particular chapter or chapter part that follows the DRA content plan steps.

2. Observe a classroom teacher present a lesson using a content textbook. Match the procedures used to the steps in the DRA content plan.

3. Compare the two plans for the DRA. List the similarities here. _____

_____

_____

_____

_____

_____

4. Contrast DRA content with DRA for reading. List the major differences here. _____

_____

_____

5. (a) Which major steps of the DRA for reading are omitted from DRA content plan? _____

_____

(b) Provide a rationale for these omissions. _____

_____

_____

_____

Check: Your answers should include these ideas.

   • The two plans are very similar. The major difference is found at step V.

- The DRA content plan fails to include any provision for skill development or reinforcement because of the difference in the purposes of the two plans.
- The DRA approach to reading is designed to facilitate the teaching of reading skills, whereas the DRA content plan is designed to facilitate the teaching of the subject matter.

ADDITIONAL ENABLING ACTIVITIES

You may want to engage in several of the supplementary learning activities listed here in order to accomplish the stated objectives.

1. Read and take notes on at least one of the following sources for each objective indicated.
   (a) Burns and Roe, pp. 252–262 (Objective 1).
   (b) Karlin, pp. 156–162 (Objecitve 1).
   (c) Smith and Bayett, Chapter 6 (Objective 4).
   (d) Burmeister, Chapter 5 (Objective 4).
2. Observe as a classroom teacher presents a directed reading activity. Utilize the DRA checklist included in Appendix C-6 as your observation guide (Objectives 1 and 6).

   Time _____ Date _____ Place _____
3. Observe and critique the directed reading activity taught by a peer. Use the DRA checklist for criteria in Appendix C-6 for critique (Objectives 1 and 6).
4. Attend class session(s) Time _____ Date _____
5. An activity of your choice.
6. An activity selected by your instructor.

READING RESOURCES / REFERENCES

1. Burns, Paul C., and Betty D. Roe. *Teaching Reading in Today's Elementary Schools.* Chicago: Rand McNally, 1976.
2. Burmeister, Lou. *Reading Strategies for Secondary School Teachers.* Reading, Mass.: Addison-Wesley, 1974.
3. Karlin, Robert. *Teaching Elementary Reading,* 2nd ed. New York: Harcourt, Brace, Jovanovich, 1975.
4. Smith, Richard J., and Thomas C. Barrett. *Teaching Reading in the Middle Grades.* Reading, Mass.: Addison-Wesley, 1974.

Chapter 14
Oral and Silent Reading

RATIONALE

Although oral and silent reading are not approaches to teaching reading, all approaches to teaching reading are founded on these processes. One technique may rely more heavily on silent reading processes, while others utilize extensive oral reading. Because of this dependence a discussion of oral and silent reading is included in this section.

Observation of practices in elementary, junior, and senior high schools as well as comments made by parents, children, and in-service teachers point to the fact that there is a misunderstanding of the processes involved in oral and silent reading. This misunderstanding frequently manifests itself in questionable classroom teaching procedures. This chapter will help you understand these processes so that you may competently deal with them in the classroom.

It will also give you the knowledge base to make appropriate decisions about using oral and silent reading and will provide you with an opportunity to apply this knowledge to teaching situations.

OBJECTIVES

After completing this chapter, you will be able to:
1. Contrast oral and silent reading processes.
2. Distinguish between appropriate and inappropriate practices for teaching oral reading.
3. Identify skills involved in oral reading.
4. Model good oral reading skills.
5. Complete an objective identified by the instructor.

PREASSESSMENT

See Appendix A-14.

Instructional Activity 1

Contrast Between Oral and Silent Reading

For some years oral reading was considered to be the overt operation of the silent reading process—the audible counterpart of mental activity. In fact, as indicated in Chapter 16, this assumption forms the base for several diagnostic practices. More recent thinking on the topic reflects some doubts about the accuracy of the assumption, however.

Oral reading requires attention to correct pronunciation, careful enunciation, and voice inflections to indicate punctuation and volume. Use of the voice to reflect the action or tone of the passage or mood of the author is also important in oral reading.

In *silent reading,* the reader translates the print into meaning, bypassing many of the intermediate steps that are obvious in oral reading. In silent reading there is no need to vocalize or subvocalize (pronounce mentally) any of the words. The reader focuses on association of meaning with the printed words instead of association of sound with the printed symbols.

In addition to the differences in the processes of oral and silent reading, there is also a difference in the rate at which they take place. Think through the information just presented on the nature of oral and silent reading. Which do you think would require relatively more time? Why?

Carefully attending to each component word and translating the print into its oral counterpart require time. In terms of the mechanics of reading as discussed in Chapter 1, the oral reader engages in more fixations, longer fixations, and more regressions per passage than the silent reader, particularly if the reader is beyond the beginning stages in reading development. The reading rate is restricted by the need to pronounce each word. Even with the most proficient oral reader, the reading rate is reduced to the rate at which he or she can articulate words.

These facts about oral and silent rates may not be particularly meaningful at the initial states of reading development, but they become significant as the student progresses. When the student is just beginning to develop an association between reading and his oral/aural language skills, his oral reading rate approximates his silent reading rate. However, by the time he has reached the sixth grade, his silent reading rate should be about double his oral reading rate.

Activity

Apply what you have learned to these situations. Compare your responses with those of a peer.

1. Sal's teacher constantly has to remind him to "read with your mind, not with your lips" when he is doing silent reading. What characteristic of

   oral reading is interfering with Sal's silent reading? _____

   _____

2. Miss Yester firmly believes in the importance of oral reading. In her

fifth-grade classroom, reading means reading orally. What characteristic of oral reading is Miss Yester overlooking? _____

_____

Check: Your responses should include these ideas.

- Sal is transferring the oral reading behavior of pronouncing each word to silent reading. This results in the subvocalization.
- Miss Yester is overlooking the fact that fifth-grade students can read much more rapidly in a silent reading activity than in an oral reading activity. She is causing the students to waste valuable class time.

Instructional Activity 2

Appropriate and Inappropriate Oral and Silent Reading Practices
The differences in the processes of oral and silent reading have some instructional implications, one of which is that practice in one will not produce proficiency in the other. The skills involved in proficient oral reading will not transfer to proficient silent reading. In fact, they may interfere with silent reading proficiency. Silent reading involves a telegram-type reading in which unimportant words may be omitted entirely and in which substitution of synonyms is acceptable. Oral reading demands deliberate attention to each word, a behavior that, if applied to silent reading, could hinder comprehension of ideas. The child who omits words or substitutes synonyms in oral reading is labeled a poor reader, although such behaviors are acceptable, even desirable, in silent reading.

Another implication relates to the classroom practice of having one child read orally while others follow along, reading silently. Because of the rate differential, students "reading along" silently develop habits of slow reading, with more fixations, longer fixations, and more regressions. They are being encouraged to pronounce each word mentally. All of these behaviors are detrimental to proficient silent reading. Additionally, since there is a discrepancy between the student's rate of thinking and rate of reading, he or she has time to spare to wander mentally to extraneous topics. The result is poor silent reading behaviors with poor comprehension.

There are other classroom practices that fail to acknowledge the powers and limitations of oral and silent reading. Not only do "read along" situations interfere with proficient silent reading, they may also contribute to poor listening skills and even poor pronunciation of words. In such settings the child who knows that his turn to read is coming may not follow along but may read ahead to be prepared when his turn comes. Consequently, he is listening only marginally, if at all. The child who listens as the oral reader stumbles over unfamiliar words may develop incorrect sound associations for the words as a result. Children who hear poor oral reading *modeled* by others are not strengthened in their reading development. In fact, their own poor oral reading habits may be reinforced.

Another instructional implication centers around the time devoted to oral reading. The following activity will help you to understand this implication.

Survey at least five people. Ask these questions.

1. About how much time did you spend in oral reading today?

a. _____ b. _____ c. _____ d. _____ e. _____

2. About how much time did you spend in silent reading today?

a. _____ b. _____ c. _____ d. _____ e. _____

What conclusion can you make about the importance of oral reading in

daily life? _____

_____

As your quick survey probably showed you, oral reading has limited application in real life. The amount of time spent in silent reading exceeds the time spent in oral reading many times over. Yet, in many classrooms, a disproportionate amount of instructional time is devoted to oral reading. In view of life-related reading demands, such practices clearly are unjustified.

 Activities

Extend your learning by responding to these activities. Compare your responses with those of a peer.

1. Use the passage with the "peep" in Appendix B-1. Observe as a person reads the passage orally, then silently. Time the reading under both conditions. Fill out the following chart.

	Type of Reading	
	Oral	Silent
Number of fixations	_____	_____
Number of regressions	_____	_____
Time	_____	_____
Rate, words per minute[a]	_____	_____

[a] The formula used for determining the number of words read per minute is number of words ÷ number of seconds × 60. For example, assume that someone read the passage of 124 words in 30 seconds, the words per minute = 124 ÷ 30 = 4.1 × 60 = 246 words per minute. The reading rate is 246 words per minute.

2. Observe at least three reading lessons at different levels. Make a note of the amount of time devoted to oral reading at each of the levels.
   (a) Primary grades (1 or 2)

   Oral reading time _____

   Silent reading time _____

   Total lesson time _____
   (b) Intermediate grades (4 and 5)

   Oral reading time _____

   Silent reading time _____

   Total lesson time _____
   (c) Upper grades (6 to 8)

   Oral reading time _____

   Silent reading time _____

   Total lesson time _____
   Did you notice discrepancies? If so, use the information in the packet to

   explain them. _____

   _____

   _____

3. Respond to this situation that takes place in a sixth-grade social studies class. The students are taking turns reading orally from the textbook as others follow along. Each student gets to read two paragraphs before the next student reads. Most of the reading is faulty, with the teacher having to supply many words. When questioned about the procedure, the teacher responded, "Most of these students are poor readers. So, if I have them read orally, I can give them the correct pronunciation of the words. Anyway, how else can I be sure that they really read the chapter?" Is this

   a good instructional procedure? Why? _____

   _____

   _____

4. Using what you have learned in this and previous chapters, suggest a

   sound alternative to the preceding procedure. _____

   _____

Check: These critical points should be reflected in your answers.

   • The oral reading rates of children at primary levels approxi-
     mates the silent reading rates; therefore instructional time is

not lost during oral reading situations. Furthermore, young children really enjoy oral reading activities. However, as the children progress in skill, their silent reading rates overtake the oral rates and instructional time is lost by focus on oral reading. In addition, the student's rate of thinking supercedes the rate of oral reading, thereby allowing time for thinking of things other than the materials. When this happens, comprehension suffers.

- The instructional procedure failed in its goal to facilitate comprehension. The teacher is making these faulty assumptions: (a) oral reading means that comprehension has occured, and (b) oral reading skills transfer to silent reading. The teacher has set up a situation that may result in poor listening behavior; as one child reads, others may read ahead to be prepared for their turns. The situation also provides a *poor* reading model for students who are already poor readers and need good models.

    The teacher has also set up a situation that interferes with the potential comprehension of the oral reader. The reader has to focus energies that could have been employed for comprehension on correct pronunciation and the like and also has to get a "teacher assist" on some words; this, in itself, interrupts strands of meaning.

- The teacher could structure a DRA for this chapter that would teach the correct pronunciation of words *before* reading, give the pupils reasons for silent reading, and check their understanding and guide their discussion of key concepts by questioning. If the teacher really wanted some oral reading in the lesson, he could use it as children prove their answers to questions.

Appropriate Uses for Oral Reading

Even though many classroom practices are unsound, oral reading has some legitimate goals in the total reading program. There are circumstances in which oral rather than silent reading is required to attain a goal. This is the case with children in the initial stages of reading development who delight in reading orally to others or listening as others read orally to them.

Most oral reading should take place in functional sharing situations. In order to meet this goal, there are two basic requirements. First, there should be an audience of one or an entire group of people who will be listeners. This generally means that the listeners do not have copies of the materials and do not read along. The second requirement is that the reader has had an opportunity to prepare. This means that he or she is not asked to read orally any material that he has not yet read silently. This provides the reader with an opportunity to decode unfamiliar words and to understand the meaning of the passage before he is to use his oral reading skills to interpret that passage for others.

Some suggestions for oral reading in functional situations include the following.

1. Supply children with a copy of a group or individual experience story. Have them take the story home to read to parents or siblings. Have them read the story to children in other classes.
2. Allow children to read orally the page or two of their library book that represents their favorite part.
3. Provide passages for choral reading. This is particularly helpful for shy children who can participate in choral reading without embarrassment.
4. Ask children to interpret poetry or other rhythmic material through oral reading.
5. Encourage children to use their voices to interpret the mood and feelings of characters through dialogue in a passage from the basal readers. Have other children narrate important parts that have no conversation.
6. Have students give a puppet play in which the dialogue is read. This activity is also especially good for shy children who feel self-conscious in oral reading situations. In puppet shows, the attention is on the puppet and not on the oral reader.
7. Provide situations in which the student must read orally to prove a point. This could be incorporated into the DRA, as described in Chapter 13.
8. Allow students to read individual reports on a content area topic.
9. Have students read a passage silently. Then ask comprehension questions and have the student read orally to prove his answers. This could be part of a DRA in the basal reader or in a content area text.
10. Allow well-prepared readers to tape-record a short story for later use at a listening station.

Activities

Apply what you have learned to these situations. Compare your responses with those of a peer.

1. Choose one of the appropriate practices just identified. Implement a plan that employs that practice in a real or simulated classroom setting while being videotaped or observed. Critique the lesson.
2. Mr. Pal uses a buddy system for oral reading. The children have partners to whom they may orally read their favorite passage from their library books or the stories they wrote in creative writing. Through this system, Mr. Pal is certain that everyone can do some oral reading in a 15-minute period. Is this an appropriate practice? Why? _____

_____

3. Unless he is testing, Mr. Gold always has the student read a passage silently before he can read it orally. Is this a good practice? Why? _____

_____

_____

Instructional Activity 3

Skills Involved in Oral Reading

As mentioned previously, oral reading requires some special skills. One way of apprising students of what these skills are is through modeling by the teacher in daily oral reading to the children. Modeling sets the standards for oral reading fluency to which the students may aspire. The skills that should be modeled include the following.

1. Standard pronunciation.
2 Clear enunciation.
3. Adequate phrasing.
4. Observation of punctuation.
5. Appropriate volume.
6. Appropriate use of voice inflection.
7. Use of the voice to convey meaning such as mood or emotion of characters or excitement or solemnity of the scene.
8. Appropriate rate.
9. Correct handling of books.
10. Sensitivity to audience needs, interests, and responses.

There are some common behaviors that interfere with the student's development of oral reading skills. Deficiencies such as the following become evident as the student engages in oral reading.

1. Small sight vocabulary.
2. Inaccurate, careless guessing at words.
3. Poor knowledge of sounds.
4. Poor blending of sounds.
5. Poor enunciation.
6. Word-by-word reading.
7. Poor phrasing.
8. Excessive repetitions.
9. Hesitations and halting reading.
10. Finger pointing.
11. Poor reading posture.
12. Poor handling of the book.

13. Lack of voice expression; monotonous reading.

14. Poor volume—too loud or too soft.

Oral Reading and the Divergent Speaker

Language variations have implications for instruction in oral reading. The oral reading of divergent speakers may be characterized by pronunciation of words that do not match the standard pronunciation but do match their dialect or by reconstructions of the written sentence to conform better to their dialect. Teachers should not interpret these behaviors as errors but as manifestations of the student's ability to process a different form of language while maintaining meaning. This topic receives greater attention in Section 7.

Instructional Activity 4

The Oral Reading Model

The activities included here should enable you to accomplish the stated objective.

 Activities

1. Choose one of the passages from the appendix or a passage of at least 300 words from another source, preferably one with dialogue. Read the passage while you taperecord. Critique your performance according to Checklist C-7 in Appendix C.

2. Select a passage from a children's or adolescent's fiction book that you think would be appropriate in level of difficulty and interest to a given group of students. Read that passage orally to the students as a way of interesting them in reading the book for recreation. Have a peer critique your reading using Checklist C-7.

ADDITIONAL ENABLING ACTIVITIES

1. Read and take notes on the following for each objective indicated after the reference.

    (a) Spache and Spache pp. 244–256 (Objectives 1 and 2).

    (b) Dallmann, et al., Chapters 8A and 8B (Objectives 1 and 2).

    (c) Durkin, Chapter 4 (Objectives 1 and 2).

2. Attend class session(s) Time _____ Date _____

3. An activity of your choice.

4. An activity selected by your instructor.

READING RESOURCES / REFERENCES

1. Dallmann, Martha, Roger L. Rouch, Lynette Y. C. Chang, and John J. DeBoer. *The Teaching of Reading,* 5th ed. New York: Holt, Rinehart Winston, 1978.
2. Durkin, Delores. *Teaching Them to Read,* 2nd ed. Boston: Allyn and Bacon, 1974.
3. Spache, George D., and Evelyn B. Spache. *Reading in the Elementary School,* 4th ed. Boston: Allyn and Bacon, 1977.

Chapter 15
The Language Experience Approach

One day I saw a fly rocket.
It made white lines in the sky.
It went over my tree.

Mat

RATIONALE

Reading is one aspect of language development. The normal sequence of language development proceeds from listening to speaking to reading to writing, as discussed in Chapter 1. A child's speaking development depends largely on his or her listening experience. The child's reading development is greatly influenced by his development in listening and speaking aspects of language. Therefore oral and aural experiences, the bases for the primary language system, form a foundation for success in reading skill development. An approach to reading instruction that draws on the language experiences relevant to the child has much merit. This is particularly true when children are in the process of arriving at an understanding of what reading is, when the basal reader materials are inappropriate for the child's interest level, and when the child's own primary language patterns are not reflected in textual materials.

This chapter will help you gain competence in using a language experience approach for teaching reading.

OBJECTIVES

Both knowledge and application objectives are set for this chapter. After completing this chapter, you will be able to:
1. Identify the philosophy supporting the language experience approach.
2. Identify major characteristics of the language experience approach.
3. Identify arguments against and supporting use of the language experience approach.
4. Identify at least three special uses of the language experience approach.
5. Identify the major procedures in a language experience approach.
6. Prepare a plan for teaching a language experience lesson.
7. Implement a language experience lesson in simulated or actual teaching situation.
8. Complete an objective identified by the instructor.

PREASSESSMENT

See Appendix A-15.

Instructional Activity 1

Philosophy Supporting the Language Experience Approach

The language experience approach is based on the primacy of the oral/aural language system. It capitalizes on the language facility of the child and provides the milieu in which the child can apply what he or she already knows about language to learning how to read. This approach focuses on reading as one of the processes of communication. Learning to read is therefore a part of the process of language development.

The language experiences that the child has had, whether meager or wealthy, form the backdrop from which he may learn to read with the least difficulty. The language experience approach allows the child to learn to read the language as he already uses it. He does not have to learn the language as set down in textbooks as the content for learning to read.

The approach can be tailored to suit the individual. The child with a language pattern that is more mature than the one found in basal readers may learn to read with ease the complex language he dictates for a language experience story. Likewise, the child with an immature language pattern or dialectal speech is likely to learn to read with ease the language he dictates for a language experience story. This is so because the approach maximizes the correspondence between the child's own language and the printed word. The fewer the mismatches between the printed words and the child's own language, the greater the likelihood of success in reading for the child.

The language experience approach incorporates the learner's language and personal experiences in the creation of reading materials that highlight the interrelationship of the language arts. This approach is harmonious with the definition of reading (Chapter 1) as a communication process.

Lee and Allen (1963, pp. 1–2) identify the following as premises for the language experience approach.

- Communication skills of listening, speaking, reading, and writing are closely interrelated.
- Reading is completely interwoven with all the other language arts.
- Reading is concerned with words that arouse meaningful responses that reflect the individual experiences of the learner.
- Words have no meaning in themselves.
- The spoken word is a series of auditory symbols that arouse meaning in the mind of the listener.
- The written word is a series of visual symbols that correspond to sound

symbols. If the sound symbols are known, the corresponding visual symbols arouse meaning in the mind of the reader.

- Reading is developing meaning from patterns of symbols that one recognizes and associates with meaning. Reading arouses meanings in the reader. It does not provide meanings.

Instructional Activity 2

Characteristics of the Language Experience Approach

There are three major characteristics of the language experience approach (Hall, 1976).

1. The major reading materials are composed by the students themselves. These reading materials emerge as the pupils talk about their experiences, many of which are planned by the teacher. The experiences, either group or individual, are recorded in print and form the content for reading instruction.

2. Interrelationships among all language and communication skills are stressed. The student's listening, speaking, and writing skills are incorporated into reading instruction. As the child's listening skills develop and his or her speaking skills mature, so does the student-produced content for his reading instruction. Therefore the student receives reading instruction from content at an appropriate level of difficulty.

3. There are no externally imposed vocabulary controls. Unlike the basal reading approach, the language experience approach places no constraints on the complexity of the vocabulary used or on the complexity of the language patterns, nor does the approach plan for the repetition of vocabulary for mastery in a reading context. Still, there is repetition of many of the words usually found on sight word lists or basic vocabulary lists simply because of the nature of the words.

Instructional Activity 3

The Language Experience Approach: Pros and Cons

As with any of the other ways of teaching, the language experience approach has had educators who support it and others who oppose it. There is still disagreement concerning its use at beginning and subsequent stages of reading development. There are educators who see the approach as a total developmental reading program and others who limit its use to a supplementary approach. Some educators visualize the approach as a totally individualized technique, while others put it in the perspective of a large-group or small-group context. The approach is many things to many teachers. You will have to decide what the language experience approach has to offer you and the children you will teach after you examine both its advantages and disadvantages.

Advantages of the Language Experience Approach

Some of the arguments in favor of using the language experience approach include the following.

1. The approach helps students develop a sense of what reading is all about, as given in this framework adopted from Lee and Allen (1963).
    *   What he thinks about he can talk about.
    *   What he can talk about can be expressed in painting, writing, or some other form.
    *   What is written can be read.
    *   Books contain the message the author would say if he were here.
2. The vocabulary is more meaningful to the child than that used in a basal approach.
3. The language is more meaningful and less stilted than that used in a basal approach.
4. The approach avoids the mismatches between one's spoken language and that found in commercially prepared materials. This is especially important in dealing with linguistically different children.

Criticisms of the Approach

Some of the frequently cited criticisms of the language experience approach are listed next.

1. Children may not develop a satisfactory reading vocabulary, since there is no vocabulary control and planned repetition.
2. There is no sequential plan for skill development; therefore skills may be taught haphazardly.
3. There are no structured teachers' guides with suggested lesson plans.
4. It is possible for children to memorize the stories without really learning to read.
5. It provides no criteria for evaluation of pupil progress.
6. It fails to encourage students to understand the ideas written by others.

Dealing with Conflicting Ideas

Even a cursory glance at the preceding criticisms of the language experience approach and the procedures for implementation of the approach would suggest that this is not an easy way of teaching reading. It does require flexible classroom management, personalized record keeping, and a teacher who knows what the reading skills are and when to teach them. It requires a dedicated, creative teacher. Unfortunately, not all of the extra effort always results in superior achievements for the students; research fails to indicate a clear superiority of the language experience approach over other approaches in terms of student achievement. However, there do seem to be some benefits that are supported by research data.

There is ample research evidence to support the following conclusions about the language experience approach.

1. The overall reading achievement of students taught through this approach is satisfactory if not superior to those taught by other approaches.
2. The reading vocabulary of students instructed through the language experience approach compares favorably and perhaps exceeds that of students taught through other approaches.
3. Students instructed through a language experience approach develop greater facility in written communication than those taught through a basal reading program. This increased language facility manifests itself in diversity of vocabulary, sentence length, mechanics of writing, and spelling.
4. Linguistically different students have, at the time of entrance to school, sufficient language backgrounds to cope with reading instruction.

 Activities

Use what you have read to respond to these situations. Compare your responses with those of a peer. Based on the information you now have, would you recommend the language experience approach in these situations:

1. To Mr. Re Pete, a fourth-grade teacher who believes that carefully planned repetitions of basic vocabulary is necessary for children to become successful readers? Why? _____

_____

2. To Miss Newly, a first-year teacher who has serious doubts about her ability to teach reading? Why? _____

_____

3. To Mr. Manual, who clings to the teacher's guide of his basal reader as if it were a life preserver? Why? _____

_____

_____

Instructional Activity 4

Special Uses of the Language Experience Approach
The language experience approach has been recommended for use for special populations. Some of these recommendations are based on research finding; others are based on personal experiences and point of view. Hall (1978) presents an extensive account of the research involving the language experience approach and special populations. These studies are synthesized here.

Beginning Readers (Readiness Level)

It seems that the language experience approach has its most widespread use at this level. It is sensible as an approach to helping the beginner to discover what reading is all about. It is also appropriate for teaching left-to-right and top-to-bottom orientation, auditory and visual discrimination, letter recognition, oral language usage, and social skills of cooperation and discussion.

Culturally Different Learners

Since textual materials rarely represent the experiences lived by learners of minority cultures, the language experience approach is attractive as an alternative for teaching. The approach has been used successfully to teach reading to Mexican-American students and North American Indians.

The culturally different learner frequently speaks a nonstandard dialect. Besides cutting down on the mismatch between the child's language and the language of print, the language experience approach also conveys a sense of respectability of his language. As indicated earlier, the clash between the child's language and the teacher's (and society's) attitude toward the language frequently results in poor learning in language areas by the child.

The Remedial Learner

The literature frequently mentions the benefits of using the language experience approach with older students whose progress in the acquisition of reading skills has been retarded. Spache and Spache (1977) report the results of using the language experience approach with academically disadvantaged students. They guided the content of the experiences into the areas of mathematics, science, social studies, and English. The discussions about the textual theme were organized and recorded and later duplicated and distributed to the members for reading. The results showed significant increases in reading, language usage, and social studies; there were some other positive factors, such as decreases in absences and school dropouts.

Other studies, as reported by Hall (1976), also attest to the benefits of using the approach with remedial students even at the junior and senior high school levels. Interestingly, several of them indicate increases in content learnings as well as in reading ability. Therefore it seems that the language experience approach could be used to reinforce and expand skills in the content areas of mathematics, science, social studies, and English if the teacher is selective about the stimulating experience provided in step 1 of the language experience approach.

The approach seems to apply to teaching reading to learners in any age group. In fact, we have been successful in teaching illiterate adults to read through a language experience approach. Because of the personalization of the learning materials involved, the approach has potentially successful application for a wide variety of learners, as indicated here and in Chapter 18.

※ **Activities**

Based on what you know now, would you recommend a language experience approach in these situations? Compare your responses with those of a peer.

1. To Ms. C. Cure, who is competent as a teacher of reading and who is seeking help for her sixth-grade remedial readers? Why? _____

_____

_____

_____

2. To Mr. Handy, who is working with a group of economically disadvantaged children who dislike the "stories" in the basal reader? Why?

_____

_____

Instructional Activity 5

Teaching Procedures for the Language Experience Approach
The creation of language experience "stories" can be either a group or an individual activity, depending on the objective of the teacher and the needs of the learner. Initially, the teacher may want to work with stories composed by the entire group as he or she assesses the language facility of the pupils. He may use the assessment as the basis for forming smaller, more compatible groups for dictation of stories. Later, as the pupils feel comfortable with dictating stories, the teacher may begin to encourage individually produced materials.

   Although there are many different variations, the following steps are a basic guide for using a language experience approach.

1. Plan real experiences around things that interest the children. Be alert to the relevant experiences the students have out of school and capitalize on them.
2. Talk about the experience. Stimulate a discussion about it. Ascertain that each child contributes to the discussion by adding facts or opinions about the experience.
3. Establish a purpose for composing the experience story. Try to provide good reasons and show the children the importance of the activity. The

story may be used in a class or school newspaper, a part of a book to be shared with another class, and the like.

4. Create the story. After the children have expressed their individual reactions, the teacher helps them decide what they would like to include in the written account. The pupils decide on the content, the exact sentences, the sequence, and the title. The teacher records the story as the pupils compose it.

At this stage in the development of the experience story, the teacher should be guided by the following ideas.

- Too much teacher direction defeats the purpose of the entire approach.

- Encourage each child to make a contribution.

- Resist the temptation to alter the language pattern, vocabulary, and grammar suggested by the children.

5. Read the story. The teacher may read the story orally first and then have the children read it together with him or her. This can be followed by oral reading of the story by individual children.

6. Practice on identification of sentences. The teacher may read a given sentence and have the students locate it in the story. The teacher may record individual sentences on sentence strips and have the students use them to reconstruct the story.

7. Develop word skills. The teacher may select a group of words from the chart to have the students master as *sight words*. The teacher may place them on word cards and have the students match these with the same word as it occurs in the story. These word cards may form a "word bank." The teacher may select a group of words that conform to a given pattern to help students develop *phonic skills* or *structural analysis skills*.

8. Reread the story. Individual children may be called on to reread the story.

9. Practice reading the story (copied onto a chart or page) periodically. Provide opportunities for the children to read the story to classmates, students from other classes, and parents or siblings.

10. Extend skills. Provide opportunities for students to illustrate the entire story, parts of the story, or individual words, as desired. When preparing the story for printing (e.g., in a newspaper or a class book) guide the students in revising the first draft to include more colorful or descriptive words, to vary the sentence structure, to make a more unified composition, and the like.

These steps may not be completed in a single lesson. In fact, it is desirable to extend the lesson over a period of several days to provide the reinforcement needed. Even if all steps are completed in a single lesson, the teacher should provide opportunities to repeat steps 6 to 10 on subsequent days.

List some real experiences that could be planned by teachers at various levels to stimulate interest and provide relevant content for group language experience stories.

1. Primary level

   (a) Visiting a farm _____

   (b) _____

   (c) _____

   (d) _____

   (e) _____

2. Intermediate level

   (a) Observing a puppet show _____

   (b) _____

   (c) _____

   (d) _____

   (e) _____

3. Upper grades

   (a) Visiting a newspaper office and observing the press operations _____

   (b) _____

   (c) _____

   (d) _____

   (e) _____

List some real experiences that the students at various levels could possibly have outside of school that might form the basis of individualized language experience stories.

1. Primary level

   (a) A new baby at home _____

   (b) _____

   (c) _____

2. Intermediate level

   (a) A new pet _____

   (b) _____

   (c) _____

3. Upper grades

(a) A recent trip _____

(b) _____

(c) _____

Also, a television program enjoyed by all of the children, such as "Little House on the Prairie" or "Spider Man," might be used as the basis of either a group or individualized language experience story.

 Activities

Use what you have learned to respond to these situations. Compare your responses with those of a peer.

1. A group of first graders have produced the following story from a language experience activity with their teacher.

We have a pet fish at school and his name is Fred. Fred is a goldfish. His house is really an aquarium. Chris gave Fred some fish food at breakfast time. Fred swims in his aquarium all day. He even swims when Miss Embers tells us to sing our good morning song.

List some words that could be taken from the story and taught as sight words (you may refer to the sight word list in Chapter 4).

_____

The teacher could write the sight words on cards and have the students match the cards with the words from the story on the chalkboard, pocket chart, or flip chart. When they have received sufficient practice with this, the teacher would have the students listen as she or he reads the story orally. The students could then stand or hold up the appropriate card when they *hear* the word read.

2. Read the preceding story. Decide what common elements or patterns appear that may be used to develop phonic skills or structural analysis skills.

Instructional Activity 6

Planning for Teaching Language Experience Lessons
In previous instructional activities, you learned about the steps for implementing a language experience lesson. A model teaching episode depicting the use of the language experience approach follows. As you read the episode, decide which step the teacher is employing. The episode is placed within the framework of the elements of a successful lesson as illustrated in previous chapters and outlined in Appendix E.

Teaching Episodes LEA

Day 1

Anticipatory Set

Teacher: Carlos has been out with the flu all week and he has missed some of the excitement in our class. If only we could get in touch with him to share at least one exciting thing! I wonder how we could do it. Think for just a second of a way we could to it. Give me a "thumbs up" signal when you know one.

(Calls on various students for suggestions. Elicits response that the class could share through writing to him.)

Objective

Great! That's just what we can do today. We can make a story about something in our class to share with Carlos. It's important that we think about what to share and how to share it so that Carlos can read about it.

Input

I'm thinking of something Carlos would like to know. It is something we just got in our room. We just gave it a name yesterday, can you guess what it is? Right, it's our fish.

Let's talk about it. What would we want to tell Carlos about our fish?

(Continues to ask questions. Encourages participation by all children.)

Good! All of you have such interesting things to add. But we can't tell everything. Let's decide which things we want to put in for Carlos to read about.

(The children finally arrive at the following story. The teacher records it on the chalkboard pointing out capital letters and punctuation as she does so.)

We have a pet fish at school and his name is Fred. Fred is a goldfish. His house is really an aquarium. Chris gave Fred some fish food at breakfast time. Fred swims in his aquarium all day. He even swims when Miss Embers tells us to sing our good afternoon song.

Fine. Now listen as I read the story.

Modeling

(Orally reads the story.)

Check on Understanding.

Now will someone read the story alone?

(Allows two or three children to do so and then numbers the sentences 1 to 6.)

Now I am going to read a sentence from the story. I want you to show me which sentence I read by holding up that number of fingers.

(Reads: Fred is a goldfish.)

Great! You held up two fingers because I read sentence number two. Now let's have someone else read and you respond.

(Allows several children to read individual sentences.)

259

Guided Practice

Now read the story to your partner as I come by to listen.

Independent Practice

I am going to write the story on a paper to give each of you. I want you to make a picture at the top that tells more about the story. Then you may take the story home to read to someone there. I'll send a copy to Carlos by his sister. Would someone like to make the picture for Carlos' copy?

Day 2

Set

Yesterday we made a story about Fred and all of us read it. What did we have to do to read it? Raise fingers to show me the number of things you know.

(Accepts all responses. Elicits response that we need to know words.)

That's right. We need to be able to recognize words to read.

Objective

That's what we will do today—work on some words so that you can know them in a flash. You won't even have to stop and think about them. Then you can read faster and better.

Input

I have some words on these cards that I want you to learn to recognize fast. As I hold up one, I want you to take it and match it with the word in our story. I've written our story on this large chart so that you can match the words. When you match the word, read that sentence.

Modeling

I'll do this one for you. Here is my card ⌐is⌐ . I match it in the first sentence. Then I read the sentence: "We have a pet fish at school and his name is Fred." Then I say the word on my card: *is.*

Check Understanding

Could my word match in another sentence? Look carefully. Hold up the number of fingers to tell me which ones! Good. Now someone come match it in one of those sentences, then read the sentence and the word.

(Repeats process with other word cards.)

Guided Practice

I'm giving each of you a set of the cards. One will say the word as his or her partner holds the card. Then switch jobs. I'll come to hear you.

Independent Practice

Take your word cards home and say them to someone there.

 Activities

Apply what you have learned to these situations. Compare your responses with those of a peer.

260

1. Look carefully at the story. Then make the following required decisions. Which other words were probably on the word cards? Why do you think so? _____

   _____

   _____

2. The children in the episode were ready to learn some phonics. Read the story and decide which common elements or patterns appear.

   Pattern A _____ Pattern B

   Examples _____ Examples

3. The children in the episode were ready to learn some structural analysis skills. Read the story and decide which common patterns are illustrated.

   Pattern A _____ Pattern B

   Examples _____ Examples

4. The teacher wants to teach comprehension of phrases that tell where something happens. Read the story and identify the examples to be used.

   Phrase 1 _____

   Phrase 2 _____

5. What conclusions can you form about word skills in a language experience approach? _____

   _____

6. List an alternative way that the teacher could have worked with identifying sentences. _____

   _____

7. Preparing your plan

   (a) Identify the motivating experience you will provide. _____

   _____

   _____

   (b) State the reasons you will use to show the children importance of the activity. _____

   _____

   _____

   (c) Write the steps to be included in your plan. (You may want to refer to instructional Activity 5.)
      (1)
      (2)

(3)

(4)

(5)

(6)

(7)

(d) Now incorporate these items into a complete plan that follows the format in Appendix E and includes the seven steps just identified.

Submit the plan for critique by a peer and your instructor. Note that in order to complete a language experience lesson, you may need to make two daily plans, one which is done after the story has been constructed.

Check: Your work should incorporate these ideas.

- Words from a sight word list probably were on the word cards, since the teacher was teaching for immediate recognition of words. These would include: we, have, a, at, and, his, gave, some, in, all, even, he, when, us, to, our, and good.
- The following patterns can be seen in the story.
  1. Phonics-consonants
     Initial h—his, house
     Initial s—some, sing, song
     Initial f—fish, food
  2. Phonics-vowels
     Short i—his, fish, is, Chris, swims, sing
     Short e—pet, Fred, tells
     Digraph
     Long ŏŏ—school, food, afternoon
  3. Structural analysis
     Compound words—goldfish, breakfast, afternoon
  4. Structural analysis
     "s" on verbs—swims, tells
  5. Phrases—"at school," "at breakfast time"

Instructional Activity 7

Presenting Language Experience Lessons

You will need a real classroom or a simulated classroom setting for these activities. The teaching should take place in two phases, perhaps on consecutive class sessions as shown in the teaching episode in the Instructional Activity 6.

In phase 1 of your plan, you will complete steps 1 to 5 as identified in Instructional Activity 5. Steps 6 and 7 should be completed in the second phase. This will enable you to examine the contents of the story to find patterns for word skills or comprehension skills that will be taught in phase 2, as you did in Instructional Activity 7. Try to focus on skills other than sight words if possible.

Implement your plan and critique your performance with a peer and your instructor. You may want to use the plan format as a guide for critique.

ADDITIONAL ENABLING ACTIVITIES

1. Read and take notes on at least one of the following sources for each objective. Notice that the objectives that are dealt with in the source are listed in parentheses.
   (a) Lapp, and Flood, pp. 464–474 (Objectives 1 and 6).
   (b) Hittlemann, pp. 187–201 (Objective 1).
   (c) Dallmann, et al., pp. 54–60 (Objective 3).
   (d) Hall, *Teaching Reading as a language Experience* (Objectives 1, 2, and 4).
   (e) Hall, 1978, (Objectives 3 and 4).
   (f) Spache and Spache, Chapter 5 (Objectives 2, 3, and 4).
2. Observe a teacher implementing a language experience lesson. (Objectives 5 and 6) Time _____ Place _____
3. Implement a plan for a language experience approach.

   Time _____ Date _____ Place _____
4. Attend class session(s) Time _____ Date _____ .
5. An activity of your choice.
6. An activity selected by your instructor.

READING RESOURCES / REFERENCES

1. Dallmann, Martha, Roger L. Rouch, Lynette Y. C. Chang, and John J. DeBoer. *The Teaching of Reading,* 5th ed. New York: Holt, Rinehart & Winston, 1978.
2. Garman, Dorothy. "So They've Dictated A Story . . . Now What?" *Teacher* (December 1978), pp. 53–54.
3. Hall, Maryanne. *Teaching Reading as a Language Experience,* 2nd ed. Columbus, Ohio: Charles E. Merrill, 1976.
4. Hall, Maryanne. *The Language Experience Approach for Teaching Reading: A Research Perspective,* 2nd ed. Cosponsored Urbana, Ill.: ERIC Clearinghouse on Reading and Communication Skill, National Institute of Education; Newark, Del.: International Reading Association, 1978.
5. Hittlemann, Daniel R. *Developmental Reading: A Psycholinguistic Perspective.* Chicago: Rand Mcnally, 1978.
6. Lapp, Diane, and James Flood. *Teaching Reading to Every Child.* New York: Macmillan, 1978.
7. Lee, Doris M., and R. V. Allen. *Learning to Read Through Experience.* New York: Appleton-Century-Crofts, 1963.
8. Spache, George D., and Evelyn B. Spache. *Reading in the Elementary School,* 4th ed. Boston: Allyn and Bacon, 1977.

Chapter 16
Additional Approaches, Programs, and Materials

RATIONALE

Just as "there's more than one way to skin a cat", there is more than one way to help people become mature readers. Some "ways" are designed to form the core of the developmental reading program while others are best used as supplements.

Being an effective teacher of reading demands selecting (when the decision rests with the teacher) and implementing a basic program which can be altered to accommodate the particular needs of the learner and "teaching style" of the teacher. An essential ingredient in wide selection and use of approaches, programs, and materials is knowledge of what is available. This chapter is designed to acquaint you with some of the other approaches, programs, and materials for teaching reading.

OBJECTIVES

After completing this chapter, you will be able to:
1. Identify the basic features of an individualized reading approach.
2. Identify the major features of code-emphasis programs or materials.
3. Identify the major characteristics of skill-management systems.
4. Complete an objective identified by the instructor.

Instructional Activity 1

The Individualized Reading Approach

An individualized reading approach, based on the principles of seeking, self-pacing, and self-selection (Olson, 1949), can be implemented once students have acquired a basic sight vocabulary and word identification techniques sufficient to allow them freely to select and read a variety of reading materials. In this approach, students select and read materials at their own interest and ability level and thereby refine their reading skills.

The key to success in a program where every child in a class or a group may be reading from different materials is careful management by the teacher, both before and during implementation of an individualized reading program. Before the program can begin, the teacher must have access to a wide variety of materials at a broad range of difficulty and interest levels, including trade books, newspapers, magazines, brochures, and even basal readers. Deciding on how to keep records, securing material for teaching and reinforcing new skills, determining whether to involve the whole class or just a few of the more independent pupils, and strategizing for introducing the approach to students and their parents all comprise major preparatory tasks to be undertaken. Once the preliminary decisions and introductions have been made, the teacher may implement the program in steps parallel to the following.

1. Allow students to select their own materials—books from the library or their home libraries, magazines, basal readers.
2. Have students read from their self-selected materials at their own pace during the reading period while recording difficult words. This uninterruped, sustained, silent reading (Hunt, 1970) continues throughout the time normally allotted for reading instruction until the child is ready for a conference.
3. Hold periodic conferences with individual students during which student skill and progress are assessed. The conference time (10 to 15 minutes) may include checking on student comprehension of the materials by asking questions or allowing the student to retell what was read, encouraging the students to broaden his or her scope of reading materials, having the student orally read a favorite section, or analyzing word recognition problems the student may be having.
4. Keep records of the student's reading development, including number and types of books read, skills mastered and skills needed, and lists of difficult words for the student.
5. Provide specific skill instruction based on need of the student. You will need to use some type of scope and sequence chart or checklist as an aid in sequencing skill instruction. (See Appendix C-7 for examples.)
6. Provide opportunities for creative sharing of materials read in small group or whole class settings.

Organizing and implementing an individualized reading program is demanding on teacher time and energy, since there is no packaged material or set "how-to" materials to guide the daily operation. Much of the success or failure of an individualized program is left to the teacher. Success is possible only if the teacher can diagnose the individual reading needs of each child, plan and implement an effective sequential word recognition/comprehension program, find time to confer with each student regularly, and manage the physical environment of so many children doing so many different things all at the same time. Even so, the basic features of the program can be woven into a suitable approach for all students to foster love of reading and continuation of the development of reading skills. For a detailed description of this individualized approach to reading, see Spache and Spache (1973).

 Activities

Apply what you have learned. Compare your responses with those of a peer. Based on the information you now have, would you recommend:

1. The individualized reading approach to Mr. I. Deal, who believes that all learning in school should be based on the child's interests? Why?

_____

_____

2. The individualized approach to Mr. Z. Ro, who thinks that reading skills are hogwash and that people learn to read by reading? Why?

_____

_____

Instructional Activity 2

Code-Emphasis Materials

There are specialized materials available that stress decoding skills in the initial stages of reading development. Among these are phonics series and linguistic series.

Intensive Phonics Materials

Phonics materials may be intended as supplementary to other approaches, such as basal readers or individualized reading, or as replacements for other approaches. These programs emphasize learning sound-symbol associations and applying phonic generalizations and, therefore, usually employ rigorous control over word usage and language structure at the initial stages of learning to read. Intensive phonics programs tend to disagree on approach, whether synthetic, analytic, or a combination; on sequence for introducing phonemes, such as which consonants or which vowel sounds to teach first; on how many and which phonics generalizations to develop; and on when to introduce more meaningful non-stilted language structure. The phonics programs, which are intended as basic for the reading program, include:

Keys to Reading (Economy Company)—a synthetic approach.

Basic Reading (Lippincott)—a phonic-linguistic approach.

Open Court Basic Reader (Open Court)—a synthetic approach.

If one believes that students need to develop an entire repertoire of word recognition techniques, then programs that provide intensive phonics almost exclusively would be viewed as deficient. Furthermore, some of the phonics principles taught are of questionable value. There is the danger that children instructed in such programs will become slow, laborious readers, "sounding out" words that they could otherwise identify at sight or through context. Perhaps the gravest danger is that children will develop the concept that reading is converting print into its oral counterpart and will become word callers instead of readers.

Linguistic Materials

These materials also place their main emphasis on recognizing the correspondencies between written language symbols and oral language symbols in the beginning stages of reading. Although there are great variations, linguistic materials tend to present only one regular pattern at a time, usually a CVC word with a common phonogram or word families such as an: can, fan, Nan, Dan, ran, and the like. The materials avoid drill on rules but focus on common spelling patterns that should facilitate learning. Initially, only a few high-frequency irregular words are introduced so that sentences can be constructed. Linguistic materials include:

Merrill Linguistic Readers (Charles E. Merrill).

SRA Basic Reading Series (Science Research Associates).

Miami Linguistic Readers (D. C. Heath).

Palo-Alto Program (Harcourt).

These programs represent a phonological approach and embody stilted language patterns, facts that puzzle and perplex some linguists who focus on the meaning aspects of reading. Such linguistics contend that even beginning reading material should reflect the natural language of speech (Wardhaugh, 1975). Certainly, the listed linguistic materials would fall far short of the goal.

Instructional Activity 3

Skills-Management Systems

Based on the intent to provide reading instruction that is directly in keeping with the specific needs of individual students, skill-management systems can provide the organizational framework for such diagnostic-prescriptive teaching of reading. Skills-management systems attempt to break the act of learning to read and becoming a proficient reader into skills components; this results in numerous behaviorally stated reading objectives to be diagnosed, taught, and tested for mastery. In addition to placement devices and criterion-referenced inventories, most systems provide record-keeping devices, individual or group charts, or special key-sorting cards whereby the teacher can quickly determine which of the sets of reading skills a student has mastered and those in which he or she still needs instruction (see Appendix C for a sample). Once skills needs have been determined and recorded, the student is given instruction, either as an individual or in a group, in the skills yet to be mastered. The specific teaching techniques and materials are not prescribed by the system, but several systems do provide information matching skills with published materials appropriate for teaching them. Skills-management systems include the following:

Fountain Valley Teacher Support System (Zweig).

The Wisconsin Design for Reading Skill Development (National Computer Systems).

Prescriptive Reading Inventory (McGraw-Hill).

Read On (Random House).

Although there are obvious advantages to providing students with individually prescribed instruction made possible through the use of skill-management system, there are also some concerns. One is that the attempt to segment the reading act into what seems to be components may result in the omission of some important skills and fragmentation of a process that may be "more than the sum of its parts." Furthermore, some of the skills may be unnecessary (Lawrence and Simmons, 1978). Other concerns include the danger that mastery of the skills will be an end in itself and not a means to apply them in a reading setting. For a detailed description of skills-management systems, see Otto, Rude, and Spiegel (1979).

 Activities

Apply what you have learned to these situations. Compare your responses with those of a peer.

Based on what you now know, would you recommend:

1. An intensified phonics program for a child who taught himself or herself to read before beginning school? Why?

   _____

   _____

2. A linguistic program for a child who seems to become confused if expected to learn too many different words in a short time? Why?

   _____

   _____

3. A skills-management system to a teacher who is convinced that a holistic approach to reading is superior? Why?

   _____

   _____

Combining Approaches: An Eclectic Program

Each approach, program, and set of materials has its advantages and disadvantages, its proponents and its opponents. What is a teacher to believe? Generally, if the teacher believes that each person is an individual in needs, desires, skills, interests, abilities, and disposition to learning, he or she will select the best from each program, approach, or material and mix them into a reading approach uniquely suited to the students, classroom environment, and teacher. Most teachers utilize a basal reading approach as the core of the reading program and supplement it with language experience, particularly at the initial stages of reading development or with special learners, and with individualized reading once the students have acquired a basic level of independence as readers and learners and with gifted learners. Other teachers dedicated to a language experience approach, especially for young children and those whose language patterns and experiences may not be suitable for a basal approach, may use that approach as the core of the developmental reading program and supplement it with individualized reading to extend the students' interests and broaden their experience. In classrooms where individualized reading is the focus of the reading program, teachers may develop skills lessons as presented in basal readers, use the basals as supplementary reading materials, and use a student interest-based language experience approach to give students group-oriented experiences and to augment the reading materials collection. Specific skills materials can be used in any of the basic approaches as student needs dictates.

The results of extensive research also seem to support eclectic approaches to teaching reading. The task of selecting approach and material would certainly be simplified if research could support clear superiority of one over the others, but this is not the case (Bond and Dykstra, 1967). Until research proves that one method or approach is significantly better than another in producing mature readers both in terms of skill and motivation to read, teachers will need to search for the approach that works best for them and their students.

 Activities

1. Compare and contrast a beginning book from a linguistic reader series with one from a basal series.

Likenesses   Differences

_____   _____

_____   _____

_____   _____

2. Compare and contrast a third-grade book from a linguistic reader series with one from a basal series.

Likenesses	Differences
_____	_____
_____	_____
_____	

3. Which of the two levels represent the greatest contrast between linguistic and basal readers? Give a statement to account for this.

_____

_____

4. Select a teacher's guide from one of the synthetic phonics series. Compare the teaching steps given in the guide to those given in Chapter 7, Instructional Activity 4.

5. (a) Write at least four phonics generalizations taught in one level of one of the books listed under intensive phonics material. Use the guide in Appendix F to assess each one as to utility.

	Utility		
Principle	Clymer	Bailey	Emans
_____	_____	_____	_____
_____	_____	_____	_____
_____	_____	_____	_____
_____	_____	_____	_____

(b) What conclusions can you form? _____

ADDITIONAL ENABLING ACTIVITIES

1. Read and take notes on the following sources for supplementary information on the objectives given in parentheses.
   (a) Alexander, ed., Chapter 14 (Objectives 1 and 2).
   (b) Farr and Roser, Chapter 10 (Objectives 1 and 2).
   (c) Otto, et al., Chapter 4 (Objectives 3).
   (d) Spache and Spache, Chapter 5 (Objective 1).
2. Observe in a reading class where the teacher employs one of the approaches or programs.

3. Attend class session(s) Time _____ Date _____
4. An activity of your choice.
5. An activity selected by your instructor.

READING RESOURCES / REFERENCES

1. Bond, Guy L., and Robert Dykstra, "The Cooperative Research Program in First-Grade Reading Instruction." *Reading Research Quarterly* (Summer 1976), pp. 1–42.
2. Breen, Leonard G., "Additional Approaches and Materials," in *Teaching Reading,* J. Estill Alexander, et al., eds. J. Estill Alexander, General Editor, J. Estill Alexander, Leonard G. Breen, Arnold R. Davis, Mona M. Donnely, Betty S. Heathington, Phyllis E. Huff, Lester N. Knight, Brenda Kolker, Nancy B. Tanner, Thomas N. Turner, Sammye J. Wynn. Boston: Little, Brown. 1979, Chapter 14.
3. Farr, Roger, and Nancy Roser. *Teaching A Child to Read.* New York: Harcourt Brace Jovanovich, 1979.
4. Hunt, Lyman C., Jr., "The Effect of Self-Selection, Interest and Motivation Upon Independent, Instructional and Frustration Levels," *The Reading Teacher* (November 1970), pp. 146–151.
5. Lawrence, Paula Smith, and Barbara Mathews Simmons, "Criteria for Reading Management System," *The Reading Teacher,* (December 1978) pp. 332–336.
6. Olson, Willard C., *Child Development.* Boston: D. C. Heath, 1949.
7. Otto, Wayne, Robert Rude, and Dixie Lee Spiegel. *How to Teach Reading.* Reading, Mass.: Addison-Wesley, 1979.
8. Spache, George D., and Evelyn Spache. *Teaching Reading in the Elementary School,* 3rd ed. Boston: Allyn and Bacon, 1973.
9. Wardhaugh, Ronald, "Linguistics and Reading," in *Teacher's Resource Book* Series R, Carl B. Smith and Ronald Wardhaugh, New York: MacMillan, 1975, pp. 32–44.

Section 7
Diagnostic-Prescriptive Teaching of Reading

This section deals with competencies necessary for the teacher to identify needs of students and to respond to these needs with appropriate instruction. The teacher:
- Identifies individual differences in readers.
- Uses various types of instruments to measure the individual differences.
- Plans learning situations and experiences that are responsive to learner needs in reading.
- Is aware of the varying rates of reading development and provides reading material for several developmental groups.
- Prescribes learning experiences based on diagnosis of reading needs.

Using the Chapters in Section 7
The chapters in Section 7 can be pursued in any order after completion of Section 5. Follow the listed steps to complete the chapters.

1. Read the rationale to get an overview of the contents and a sense of its importance to teachers.
2. Read the objectives.
3. Take the preassessment if you desire, or go to step 4. If you take the preassessment, score it and identify your areas of strength and weakness.
4. Read the information in the text for each objective and complete the activities as directed.
5. Select additional enabling activities that correspond to your determined areas of weakness. Use the Reading Resources/References as suggested by your instructor.
6. Schedule a meeting with the instructor and take the postassessment.
7. Evaluate your performance and repeat steps 4 to 6 and go on to the next chapters in your sequence.

Chapter 17
Assessing Reading Behaviors

RATIONALE

Students at any age or grade level can only learn the next reading skill in the heirarchy of the learning sequence. The student can build securely on building blocks that are well-placed, but the tasks of the teacher are to determine which learning block follows and the student's preparedness for that instruction.

This chapter is concerned with how the teacher will determine (diagnose) the blocks of learning the student has mastered or has not mastered and which block of learning the student is now ready to acquire (prescription).

OBJECTIVES

After completing this chapter, you will be able to:
1. Define formal and informal measures of reading achievement.
2. List the general contents of standardized reading achievement tests.
3. Identify the major categories of skills measured through most standardized reading readiness tests.
4. Utilize the definition of formal and informal measures of reading achievement to make decisions about the type of test to use in given situations.
5. Utilize an informal reading inventory to analyze students' reading strengths and weaknesses.
6. Utilize a cloze test and analyze the results.
7. Utilize a reading skills checklist as a diagnostic instrument.
8. Utilize teacher-made instruments to evaluate a subskill of reading.
9. Prepare and utilize criterion-referenced inventories for reading skills.
10. Identify the influence of dialectal variations and miscue analysis on the interpretation of diagnostic data.
11. Identify the reading interests and attitudes of children and youth.
12. Complete an objective identified by the instructor.

PREASSESSMENT

See Appendix A-17.

Instructional Activity 1

Formal and Informal Reading Tests

What is meant by the terms formal and informal testing? They certainly have nothing to do with the manner in which we are attired yet, in the school setting, we hear these terms used frequently.

Before continuing, write your definitions of formal and informal tests.

_____

_____

_____

_____

_____

Tests that have been administered to many students in a certain grade and age level and from which an expected performance can be determined for other students of the same age and grade level are formal, or standardized, tests. [These tests are generally administered schoolwide or system-wide at a specified time (or times) during the school year or possibly only at certain grade levels during the school year.]

The formal test may be administered to a group of students or to an individual student. Because the test has been standardized, you know the kind of performance to expect of the student(s) to whom you administer it.

Standardized reading tests fall into one of three categories: survey tests, semidiagnostic tests, and diagnostic tests. The survey test is used to assess the reading achievement of both many students and even an individual student. The standardized survey test cannot be used diagnostically because it yields only one or two scores.

The standardized reading test that is similar to the standardized survey test is the semidiagnostic test. This test yields several subscores that indicate strengths or weaknesses of the students. Therefore it can be used more diagnostically than the survey test.

A diagnostic test is designed for individuals or small groups of students who have reading problems. These diagnostic standardized tests appraise the specific skills needs of the student and are very useful in diagnosing and planning remediation for the student.

There are other formal examinations. Some of them are general achievement tests of which reading is only a part. Also, standardized readiness tests are available to help determine a student's readiness to begin reading instruction.

Standardized Tests and Children of Divergent Cultures

Standardized testing seems to be another area in which sociological factors intervene. Many children who do not speak standard English also tend not to perform well on standardized tests, whether the tests be of intelligence or of reading ability. Many of the instruments are inappropriate for testing nonmainstream culture children. In fact, many tests are standardized using samples of primarily mainstream culture (standard English-speaking) children.

Children who are unlike the norm group, then, are judged by standards that are not truly representative. Cultural interferences may inhibit the performance of such children (Cullinan, 1976).

Again, write a definition of a standardized test. Compare your second definition with the first. Did you improve in defining that term? Did your second definition include these points?

1. The test is administered to many students.
2. The scores are used as a measurement device to determine expected performance from other students who take the test.

Name the three kinds of standardized reading tests and then two other kinds of standardized tests. Check your responses in Instructional Activity 1.

Informal tests are measurement tools that have not been standardized. They may be used to augment standardized tests and test areas that the standardized tests did not examine. Also, they measure areas in reading that are difficult to approach objectively.

Some informal tests include skill tests, checklists, inventories (interest, attitude), questionnaires, the cloze technique, and self-appraisals. An informal measure can also be a teacher-made test.

One type of informal measurement tool with which you will become familiar is the informal reading inventory, which tests the functional reading levels of students. It is a diagnostic instrument that reveals areas where the student is having reading difficulties.

 Activities

1. Rewrite your definition of an informal test. _____

   _____

   _____

   _____

2. Name a type of informal reading test. _____

   _____

3. List some other types of informal tests that are used by teachers. _____

   _____

   _____

Check back in the instructional materials to determine the accuracy of your responses.

277

Instructional Activity 2

General Content of Standardized Reading Tests

Standardized reading achievement tests generally provide three scores: a vocabulary score, which is usually word meaning and not word recognition, a comprehension score, and a total score, which is a combination of vocabulary and comprehension. The teacher can readily see where, in these broad areas, the student is weak.

The standardized reading achievement tests will also generally provide subskill test achievement levels. These give an indication of the student's strengths and weaknesses, which is helpful to the teacher in planning reading subskill groupings and activities.

Some subskill areas you might expect to find on a reading achievement test are: restating material, being able to summarize material, drawing inferences from the written page, getting the sequence of story events, getting the main idea of a story, and defining words as they are found in the context of a phrase, sentence, or paragraph.

All of the areas tested in a reading achievement test are broad. The scores provide an indication of general strengths and weaknesses.

Instructional Activity 3

Major Categories of Standardized Reading Readiness Tests

Primary-grade teachers (and first-grade teachers in particular) need to know with assurance that a student is ready to begin formal instruction in reading. To do this, teachers often administer a standardized reading readiness test.

The standardized reading readiness tests generally test some or all of the child's ability to (1) follow directions, (2) discriminate visually (3) recognize words and/or letters, (4) indicate motor control or coordination, and (5) recognize numbers.

While following directions, the student might be asked to do a series of tasks; of course, just taking the test, keeping up, and marking on the correct line will also indicate to the teacher the child's ability to follow directions.

To test for visual discrimination, the student may be asked to identify the item in a series that matches the key item. For a student to indicate that he or she knows the letters of the alphabet, he may be asked to mark a certain letter in a given series. From a series of pictures, the student may be asked to determine which picture matches an orally expressed word. To check the student's motor control, he may be asked to copy a pattern.

Many factors contribute to a child's readiness to begin reading instruction, as discussed in Chapter 2. Health, visual acuity, hearing acuity, and background of experiences combine to propel the child toward the readiness for reading or work to delay preparedness for reading instruction. Knowing when the child is ready for reading is important.

In addition, some checks should be made on the child's significant concepts of printed language. These concepts include that print relays a message, understanding what a letter is and what a word is, identification of the first letter in a word, capital and lowercase letter equivalency, function of space on a page, and the function of punctuation marks (i.e., the period, question mark, and quotation marks) (Clay, 1978). These checks have been converted to "Sand," a test by Marie Clay that can be quickly administered. Pupil performance on the test can help the teacher plan future instruction for the child.

Without looking back, name five skill areas that might be found on standardized reading readiness tests.

Instructional Activity 4

Using Formal and Informal Reading Tests

 Activities

Use the information you gained in the previous two activities to decide successfully the course of action to follow in the following situations.

1. The school year has just begun and you feel the need to get quickly a general idea of the levels where your students are reading. Describe the kind of test you would administer to get this type of information. _____

_____

_____

_____

2. You teach in a self-contained classroom. Discuss the type of test you would administer to get a broad picture of your students' general abilities. _____

_____

_____

_____

_____

3. Johnny is having some difficulty with reading. You want to know exactly what type of problems he is having. Discuss the kind of test you would administer to Johnny. _____

_____

_____

279

_____

_____

4. Mary does not indicate a liking for reading. She often refuses to get her books out. She seldom checks a book out of the library. Discuss the type of test you might use to help you motivate Mary to read. _____

_____

_____

_____

5. As the teacher, you want to know if the students can apply their skills in multiplication to everyday situations. Discuss the kind of test you would use. _____

_____

_____

_____

6. You need to know how well your students compare with students from other parts of the country in their social studies work. Discuss the type of test you would use to get that information. _____

_____

_____

_____

7. Last year the school administered a reading test to all the students. Now you want to know how much your students have gained in reading skills since they were tested a year ago. Discuss the kind of test you would select to get this information. It will have to be the same test administered a year ago. _____

_____

_____

_____

8. Carolyn is really struggling in the reading class. You are not certain of her difficulties and, too, you want to know how Carolyn measures up to other students in the country that are her age and at her grade level.

Discuss the type of test you would administer to Carolyn. _____

_____

_____

_____

_____

Check: Your responses should include these ideas.

1. (a) Standardized test.
   (b) Survey test.
2. (a) Standardized test.
   (b) Achievement test.
3. (a) Diagnostic test.
   (b) Formal or informal test.
4. (a) Informal test.
   (b) Interest inventory.
5. (a) Informal test.
   (b) Teacher-made test.
6. (a) Standardized test.
   (b) Achievement test.
7. (a) Standardized test.
   (b) Reading test.
8. (a) Standardized test.
   (b) Reading test.
   (c) Semidiagnostic test.

Instructional Activity 5

Utilizing Informal Reading Inventories

The informal reading inventory consists of a series of graded selections with accompanying comprehension questions, or free-response comprehension checks in which the student relates what he or she reads, or a combination of both. The student reads selections at the same level, one orally at sight as the test administrator records errors, and one silently. The reading and comprehension check process continues until the test administrator has secured the necessary data from which to identify reading needs.

Levels of Reading Identified in an Informal Reading Inventory

To provide appropriate reading instruction for students, the classroom teacher must be able to identify the needs of each student. An informal reading inventory allows the teacher to ascertain quickly the independent, instructional, frustration, and capacity levels of the student. It also provides insight into the student's ability to comprehend what he has read and the strengths and weaknesses of his word attack skills.

From the test results, the teacher is able to prescribe reading instruction suited to the individual student's needs.

An informal reading inventory yields four reading level scores. The highest reading level is the *independent reading level,* where the student reads fluently and the words pose practically no difficulty in pronunciation or meaning. The student usually makes no more than one error per 100 words and has no problems with comprehension.

The next level is the *instructional level.* The student makes no more than five errors per 100 words and indicates at least 75 percent comprehension of what he reads.

At the *frustration level,* the student has many difficulties and misses more than five words per 100 read. Also, there is very little or no understanding of what has been read.

At the *capacity level,* the student can understand 75 percent of the material read by the teacher.

Without looking back into the material, complete the following table.

Reading Level	Number of Word Recognition Errors	Percent of Comprehension
1.		
2.		
3.		
4.		

Use this text to determine the accuracy of your work.

 Activities

Use what you have learned to help determine the reading levels of the following students.

1. John has read to Miss Jones. She notes that John was reading in the seventh-grade reader, that he made six errors in reading a 200-word selection, and that he answered correctly six out of the eight questions she asked to check his comprehension. At what reading level was this

   for John? Why? _____

   _____

2. Missy was eager to have her turn at reading for the teacher because she liked the looks of the third-grade reader. Missy read only a few words of the 100-word passage, and then she skipped a word. She read on, then make up a word to use in place of one she did not know. Later, she asked the teacher to pronounce a word for her. Missy made some other errors, too. She said "had" for "have," "as" for "ask," and "do" for "does." When the teacher asked six comprehension questions about the passage, Missy knew the correct answers for only three. At what reading level was this for Missy? Why? _____

_____

3. Susie reached the frustration level in reading when she read from fifth-grade material. Susie's teacher then began reading to Susie from other fifth-grade material. She asked Susie comprehension questions that Susie answered with 100 percent accuracy. The teacher then read to Susie from sixth-grade material, and Susie answered the comprehension questions with 85 percent accuracy. The teacher then read from a seventh-grade reader, and Susie answered the comprehension questions with less than 75 percent accuracy. What grade reading material was Susie's capacity level? Why? _____

_____

_____

Check: Your responses should contain some of these ideas.

- John was at the instructional level because he read with less than 100 percent but more than 74 percent comprehension and made only three errors out of 100 words read (97% accuracy).
- Missy was reading at the frustration level. She made more than five reading errors, and she did not comprehend 75 percent of the material. Missy was not attending to the endings of words.
- Susie read at the instructional level somewhere below fifth grade. Susie's frustration level was at fifth grade. Susie's capacity level was at the sixth-grade level.

Types of Comprehension Questions on an Informal Reading Inventory

As a part of the informal reading inventory, the teacher asks questions to check the student's understanding of what was just read. The questions generally fall into certain reading comprehension skill categories. For instance, one question will check the student's knowledge of the vocabulary used in the passage. The teacher could ask for an antonym of a word in the story or for the meaning of a word by the way it was used in the sentence (context clue for meaning).

A second type of question will check the student's ability to recall details in the passage that was read. This type of question is the easiest to develop. It will begin with "Where was the . . . ?". "How many . . . ?", and the like. The answers to these questions are always stated in the passage.

Another question asked on informal reading inventories is the main idea question. This is easily done by asking directly, "What was the main idea of the story?" Another way is to ask the student to give a title to the story.

There is always at least one question on an informal reading inventory that will check the student's ability to infer information or make judgments about the passage just read. This question goes beyond the story. It asks for information that is not stated in the story but that is implied there. Students can be quite creative with their answers to this question! There is generally no right or wrong answer to this question.

The teacher may also ask questions that require the student to think critically of the material just read. For the purposes of this instructional unit, however, you will need to know only the four types of questions discussed earlier and illustrated later.

Name the four types of comprehension questions discussed in the text. Use the information in the text to check your responses. For each type of question cited, note a few words that will help you remember the meaning of the terms. Use the information in the text to check your responses.

Identifying types of Questions on an Informal Reading Inventory

For the nursery rhyme "Mary Had a Little Lamb" the teacher might ask the following questions.

Vocabulary. Can you give me another word for *fleece?*

Recall of Details. What was the size of Mary's lamb?

Main Idea. What would be another good title for this rhyme?

Inference. Where have Mary and the lamb been today?

 Activities

Apply what you have learned to these situations. Read each nursery rhyme and complete the activity by labeling each set of questions following the rhyme as (1) vocabulary, (2) recall of details, (3) main idea, and (4) inference question.

1. Humpty-Dumpty sat on a wall
   Humpty-Dumpty had a great fall.
   All the king's horses and all the king's men
   Couldn't put Humpty-Dumpty together again.

(a) Who tried to help the king's men put Humpty-Dumpty back together? _____

(b) What was the weather like the day this rhyme took place? _____

(c) Give a new title to this rhyme. _____

(d) What does the word *together* mean in the rhyme? _____

(e) How did Humpty-Dumpty get on the wall? _____

Now check your work. Did you identify question c as being the main idea? Good for you! Did you identify questions b and e as inference questions? Hurrah! Did you write "vocabulary" beside question d? Wonderful! Then, of course, you answered the first question correctly—recall of story details!

2. Jack and Jill went up the hill
To fetch a pail of water
Jack fell down
And broke his crown
And Jill came tumbling after.

_____ (a) What caused Jack and Jill to fall down?

_____ (b) What is a synonym for the word *fetch?*

_____ (c) In this rhyme, to what does the word *crown* refer?

_____ (d) Give a homonym for the word *pail*. Write it.

_____ (e) If you needed to send this message in a telegram and could use only five or six words, what words would you use in the telegram?

_____ (f) How did Jill get down the hill?

3. Jack Sprat could eat no fat
His wife would eat no lean
So betwixt them both
They licked the platter clean.

_____ (a) What could Jack Sprat eat?

_____ (b) What does the word *licked* mean as it is used in this rhyme?

_____ (c) Give another word for *betwixt*.

_____ (d) If this were to be a newspaper article, give a good headline for the article.

_____ (e) What did the Sprat's get clean?

4. Jack be nimble
Jack be quick
Jack jump over
The candlestick.

———— (a) Give a word that is opposite in meaning to *nimble*.

———— (b) Why would Jack need to be quick?

———— (c) What would be a good title for this rhyme?

———— (d) What is Jack to jump over?

Check: Compare your responses to the questions about rhymes 2, 3, and 4 with these responses.

2. "Jack and Jill,"
   (a) Inference question.
   (c) Vocabulary in context question.
   (b, d) Vocabulary questions.
   (e) Main idea question.
   (f) Detail question.

3. "Jack Sprat."
   (a) Inference question
   (b, c) Vocabulary questions.
   (d) Main idea.
   (e) Detail question.

4. "Jack Jump over the Candle Stick."
   (a) Vocabulary question.
   (b) Inference question.
   (c) Main idea question.
   (d) Detail question.

Writing Comprehension Questions for an Informal Reading Inventory

You have learned to identify the types of comprehension questions. Now try your hand at writing some.

✳ Activities

You will have to work with a peer and evaluate the questions you have written. If you feel you need additional assistance, ask your instructor for help. You may want to refer back to Chapter 8 to do this activity. Use the nursery rhyme "Hey Diddle Diddle."

Hey Diddle Diddle
The cat and the fiddle
The cow jumped over the moon
The little dog laughed to see such sport
And the dish ran away with the spoon.

_____

_____

_____

_____

_____

Diagnosis of Comprehension Errors

You have learned some of the kinds of questions that are asked following the oral reading of a given passage. Now you will learn how to determine or diagnose the instructional needs of the student in the area of reading comprehension.

Your student has read the Humpty-Dumpty rhyme to you and you have asked these questions. You have placed a check mark beside the ones that were answered correctly and placed an X mark beside the questions to which the student responded incorrectly.

1.　x　(a)　Who tried to help the king's men put Humpty-Dumpty back together?
　　　√　(b)　What was the weather like the day this rhyme took place?
　　　√　(c)　Give a new title to this rhyme.
　　　x　(d)　What does the word *together* mean in this rhyme?
　　　√　(e)　How did Humpty-Dumpty get on the wall?

In what two areas of comprehension does this student indicate a weakness? What is your diagnosis? _____

_____

_____

Did your response show (1) detail, and (2) vocabulary? Good for you. Try this next exercise.

2.　x　(a)　What caused Jack and Jill to fall down?
　　　√　(b)　What is a synonym for the word *fetch?*
　　　√　(c)　In this rhyme, to what does the word *crown* refer?
　　　√　(d)　Give a homonym for the word *pail*. Use it in a sentence.
　　　x　(e)　If you needed to send this message in a telegram and could use only five or six words, what words would you use in the telegram?
　　　√　(f)　How did Jill get down the hill?

What is your diagnosis? _____

_____

_____

_____

3. Do another exercise.
    √ (a) What could Jack Sprat eat?
    x (b) What does the word _licked_ mean as it is used in this rhyme?
    c (c) Give another word for _betwixt_.
    √ (d) If this were to be a newspaper article, give a good headline for the article.
    √ (e) What did the Sprats get clean?

What is your diagnosis? _____

_____

Did your responses have some of these ideas in them?

1. The errors on comprehension questions about Humpty-Dumpty could be identified as (a) recalling details of the story, and (b) lack of vocabulary.
2. The errors on the comprehension questions about Jack and Jill are (a) inference, or failure to read between the lines of the story, and (b) main idea, or condensing or summarizing.
3. The comprehension errors on the rhyme Jack Sprat are (a) vocabulary as used in context, and (b) vocabulary as it pertains to synonyms.
4. Do you recall the percentage of correct responses necessary on comprehension questions for the independent reading level? Write it here.

_____

5. What is the percentage of correct responses necessary on comprehension questions for the instructional reading level? Write it here.

_____

6. What is the percentage of correct responses necessary on comprehension questions for the capacity level? Write your response here.

_____

Look back in the chapter to check your answers.

Marking Reading Errors on an Informal Reading Inventory
When an informal reading inventory is being administered, the teacher must listen carefully to the student read and simultaneously mark the kinds of errors the student makes while reading orally.

To record the student's errors, the teacher marks her or his copy of the test in the following manner (or one that is comfortable for the teacher) while the student reads orally.

Item	Symbol	Example
Words the teacher pronounces for the student	Write a "P" above the word	The story is very P interesting.
Words the student inserts or parts of words the student adds	Write in the word or word parts	He pulled on his shoes his and ∧ socks.
Words the student substitutes for the printed word	Write in the substituted word	black He went back to the store
Words the student omits when reading	Draw a ring around the omitted word or words	The cat and ⟨the⟩ fiddle
Words the student actually mispronounces	Draw a line through the word and/or write it in phonetically.	mō/nà/gam′/ŭs monogamus
Words that the student hesitates or pauses over for 3 seconds or more	Write an "h" above the word	h He made an appropriate speech.
A word or group of words the student repeats	Draw a wavy line under the word or words	His appearance was startling
Punctuation that the student ignores	Write an "x" above the disregarded punctuation	x Mary, the cat, and the dog went home

You will note in a later section of this chapter that there is not a complete consensus on what constitutes a reading error. For example, a hesitation may be considered a symptom of poor oral reading but not necessarily an error; the same is true for ignored punctuation. Some teachers record repetitions as errors while others do not, and some consider the quality of the deviation from what appears in print. We will consider these ideas later, but for now you need only concern yourself with the preceding items.

Activity

Without looking back, list the kinds of oral reading errors students might make. _____

_____

_____

_____

Go back and draw the appropriate symbol beside each term. Use the information in the text to check your work.

Diagnosing Oral Reading

This section is concerned with using a marking system for oral reading miscues to analyze a student's oral reading behaviors. Using such a system can help you reconstruct the way a student read a passage orally so that you can study it to plan possible teaching objectives.

✳ ### Activities

Read the following poem. Determine the kinds of errors made when it was read by the student.

```
                    bitty   lamp
Mary had a little∧lamb
   it is fun
Its fleece was⟨white⟩as snow.ˣ
        p
And everywhere that Mary went
     lamp        h
The lamb was sure to go.
```

1. List the errors made by the student beside the correct term.

   Omissions _____

   Hesitations _____

   Repetitions _____

   Mispronunciation _____

   Substitutions _____

   Teacher pronounced _____

   Disregarded punctuation _____

   Insertions _____

2. Check your work to see if it listed these oral reading errors.
   Insertions—bitty
   Disregarded punctuation—the period following snow
   Teacher pronounced—everywhere
   Repetitions—that Mary went
   Mispronunciation—it is for it's, fun for fleece, lamp for lamb
   Hesitations—sure
   Omissions—white

3. Beside each symbol, write the type of oral reading error it signifies.

   P _____

   _____

the _____

O/ver _____

h _____

x _____

Return to the first part of this unit and check your work. Note that substitutions of words has been omitted from the review list.

4. In the following rhyme you will notice that the student made several oral reading errors. (They have been marked for you.)

Beside the given symbols, write the error made on the test and identify the type of error using words.

Old king Cole was a merry old soul   ou as in

              he   (plow)

And a merry old soul was he.^{x}

        p

He called for his fife

(And) he called for his drum

     asked

And he called for his fiddlers three.

	Write in the Error	Identify Error with Words
P	fife	teacher pronounced
⬭		
～～～		
the		
o/vér		
h		
x		

Return to the text to check your responses.

Developing an Informal Reading Inventory

Making an inventory for classroom use is an easy task. Locate a set of graded readers in an elementary school or in Appendix B. From a book at each primary-grade level, select a passage of about 100 words that contains enough information that questions can be asked to determine the student's comprehension. For upper elementary grades, the passage selected needs to be close to 200 words long.

Formulate questions for each passage; include vocabulary questions, main idea questions, inferential questions, and detail questions.

For silent reading by the student followed by comprehension questions from the teacher, a second set of reading passages and comprehension questions at each grade level is necessary.

After the test has been assembled, the teacher administers the test to students individually.

Introduce the student to the testing situation and tell him or her what to expect. The student will orally read a passage while the teacher records reading errors on a copy of the passage. Next, the student is asked the comprehension questions created for the passage, and the teacher records the errors and accuracy of those responses.

The student then reads silently from the silent reading passages, which are at the same grade level. Prepared comprehension questions are asked by the teacher when the student indicates completion of the silent reading passage. Errors are recorded.

The teacher continues through the sequence of graded material in this same manner until the errors in reading and comprehension indicate frustration on the part of the student. At this point, the teacher might read to the student and then ask the comprehension questions. The students' capacity level is indicated when he or she is able to listen to the teacher read a passage and can answer 75 percent of the comprehension questions correctly.

✳ Activity

Your task at this point is to develop a certain portion of an informal reading inventory. You are to select oral and silent reading passages at four consecutive grade levels and write comprehension question for these eight passages. For example, you might select grade levels 1, 2, 3, and 4, or you might select grade levels 3, 4, 5, and 6. When you have completed this task, have a classmate review your work before submitting it to your instructor.

Administrating an Informal Reading Inventory

When you have completed the informal reading inventory that was assigned in the previous activity, administer it to an elementary student and record the oral reading errors and the comprehension errors. If possible, by only using your small portion of the inventory, determine the four reading levels of your subject and diagnose the needs of the student; write out the areas that you find need improvement.

You might want to record the oral reading by the child so that you can recheck your markings of oral reading errors. You may also want to have a classmate record errors from the taped oral reading and compare your markings.

Instructional Activity 6

Administering and Analyzing Cloze Tests

Identifying Reading Levels with Cloze Tests

Another informal device useful in determining reading levels is the cloze technique. This device determines how the textual materials correspond to the child's reading levels.

In this technique, the student is supplied with a passage from which words have been replaced by blanks. The student's task is to supply the deleted word by completing the thoughts as suggested from the context clues inherent in the passage.

For instance, as you _____ through this sentence, you _____ able to determine the _____ that the writer would use _____ of the ideas that _____ expressed in the words _____ are available. You show _____ ability to use context _____ .

How did you do? Did you supply these words in order? *read, are, words* (ideas), *because, are, that, your, clues.*

The steps given next, based on those suggested by Taylor (1953), should be followed in constructing a cloze test to assess reading levels.

1. Select a passage of 250 to 300 words.
2. Delete every *n*th word (e.g., fifth, eighth, tenth) except first and last sentences. (You may keep proper nouns, numbers, and dates. Remove the next word.)
3. Retype the passage with 10 spaces left for each blank. (You do not want the length of the blank to provide a clue to word length.)
4. Administer the passage to the class.
5. Score the passage, giving credit for exact replacements. (In some instances, you may choose to give credit for synonyms also. But the technique is based on credit for exact replacements only.)
6. Divide the number of correct replacements by the total number of blanks. (This will yield a cloze percentage score.)
7. Compare the cloze percentage score to the following criteria to determine reading level (Rankin and Culhane, 1969).

Score Range, percent	Reading Level
40 below	Frustration
41 to 60	Instructional
61 above	Independent

The cloze technique is adaptable to other teaching-testing situations. For instance, the teacher may determine the students' proficiency in replacing verbs only by deleting every nth verb in a passage. Or only nouns may be omitted, depending on the information desired.

Constructing and Administering Cloze Tests

Using the steps for constructing a cloze test identified in Instructional Activity 6 and one of the graded passages in Appendix B, prepare a cloze test. You may want to number the blanks. Mount the cloze passage on heavy paper (or laminate it) so that it will not be limp. Then prepare your key of exact replacements. (You may also want to list acceptable synonyms.)

Administer the cloze test to a peer. Score it and apply the criteria identified in Instructional Activity 6. What level of difficulty was the passage? At what reading level did the peer perform? What conclusion can you make about the reading level of the peer?

Submit the cloze test and the results of the first administration to your instructor for critique.

Make any necessary revisions in the cloze test or your testing technique.

Administer the test to a student whose reading level corresponds to the level of difficulty of the passage. Score the test and apply the criteria. At which reading level did the student perform? What conclusion can you form about the reading level of the student?

Instructional Activity 7

Reading Skills Checklists As Diagnostic Instruments

Using Reading Skills Checklists

How do you, as the classroom teacher, know if a student has been introduced to a reading skill, had practice with the skill, and mastered it? A checklist of reading skills will help answer the question.

Skills checklists provide the teacher with information regarding the students' previous learnings. It indicates which skills have been mastered, which skills have been taught but not mastered, and which skills have not been taught.

Reading skill checklists also provide the teacher with informaion that is helpful in grouping the students for learning. Only students in need of instruction on a specific reading skill would be presented a lesson designed to develop that specific skill.

Most reading skill checklists have a marking system. One mark might indicate that the student had had the skill lessons but had not mastered the skill; another mark indicates that the student mastered the skill. A blank space tells the teacher this is a skill the student needs to learn. Often, too, a date is placed in the checklist indicating at what time in the student's school experience the skill was mastered. This information is helpful to the teacher.

Reading skill checklists help the teacher with lesson planning. Review or practice lessons can be planned for a skill with some students, and introductory lessons might be planned for another group.

Keeping the skills checklist records is an important part of successfully utilizing the instrument. It is a diagnostic tool that the teacher will want to keep current and readily assessible.

Classroom teachers can make their own reading skills checklist by using the information found in scope and sequence charts of publishers of reading textbooks; also, the teacher might simply study the reader and the teacher's manual that accompanies it to develop a reading skills checklist. Of course, there are prepared skills checklists available to the teacher.

How do you determine whether or not a student has mastered a skill? A set of tests usually accompanies a skills checklist. On the tests the number of items that must be completed correctly to achieve mastery will be found.

Also, a manual might accompany the checklist and, in it, there will be instructions for test administration, scoring, and marking the skills checklist. Answer keys will also be included.

Activities

1. Name one way you as the teacher might use a reading skills checklist as a measurement instrument. _____

_____

_____

_____

2. Interview an elementary teacher and learn the different ways the teacher utilizes a reading skills checklist. Write a summary of the interview. _____

_____

_____

_____

295

_____

_____

_____

_____

Check: Your response to the first item should include some or all of these ideas.

- To determine the skills mastered by students.
- To determine the skills needed to be learned by student.
- To determine when, in the student's school experience, the skill was mastered.
- To determine the necessary grouping for instruction.
- To help determine objectives for future lessons.

Evaluating Scores on Checklists

	de	anti	pre	semi	Key	
Mary	gr 5	gr 5	gr 6		⊠	Skill mastered
Sam	gr 5	gr 6				
Jane	gr 5	gr 5			◺	Skill taught, tested, but not mastered
Elmer	gr 5	gr 6				
Reed	gr 5	gr 5	gr 6		▭	Skill not tested
Joe	gr 5	gr 6			gr	Grade level

Prefixes Grade 6 Level

Activities

The preceding is a small section of a reading skills checklist with student's names and the symbol key to the checklists. Answer the questions and then compare your responses with those of a peer.

1. What information does this checklist provide you? _____

_____

_____

_____

2. What groups would you create for teaching one of the specific prefixes?

_____

_____

_____

_____

Check: Your responses should include some or all of the following ideas.

- Sam, Elmer, and Joe had been taught and tested on the prefix *anti* but had not mastered it. They need to be taught this prefix again and tested again.
- Mary and Reed had been taught and tested on the prefix *pre* but had not mastered it. They need to be taught that prefix again and tested on it again for mastery.
- The prefix *semi* will need to be taught to all this group of students and tested, too, on this skill.
- These students are well prepared for grade six because they mastered some sixth-grade skills the prior year.

You have now diagnosed these students' needs based on a reading skills checklist and have prescribed this next need in the sequential learning of skills.

Instructional Activity 8

Using Teacher-made Instruments as Diagnostic Devices

A Teacher-Made Instrument for Testing Skills
A task of the teacher is to prepare tests that help determine students' knowledge and understanding of reading skills and their ability to apply those skills in new situations.

Study the following example of a teacher-made test on study skills—using an index.

Knowledge (recall)
1. Where in a book would you look for an index?
   (a) Front.
   (b) Middle.
   (c) Back.
2. You would use an index to:
   (a) Locate the page numbers of the chapters in the book.
   (b) Locate the page number of a certain topic found in the book.
   (c) Locate the page numbers of the illustrations in the book.

3. Which of the following is from an index?
   (a) Allen, John, 210
       antiques, 102
       bells, 97
       bonnets, 37
       chimes, 156
   (b) Taming the Land   75
       Gaining Independence   92
       The Migration   107

Application
4. Turn to the index in your science book. Beside each item below, write where in the text you could locate information about the item.

   (a) Why hot air rises _____

   (b) Air takes up space _____

   (c) The names of the planets _____

   (d) The kinds of levers _____

   (e) The scientific method _____

When the teacher scores the test, knowledge will be gained immediately about the students' ability: they can or cannot recognize an index; they know or do not know what an index is for; they can or cannot tell where in the book an index is located; and they can or cannot apply their knowledge of indexes. This means that the teacher is measuring more than mere recall on the test. Items that measure comprehension or understanding of the recalled facts and application of the knowledge are also important in a teacher-made test. Be certain that you include items at these levels of thinking as you prepare teacher-made tests for reading skills.

Developing a Measurement Instrument for a Subskill in Reading

Now, prepare a teacher-made test on a subskill of reading. Be certain to include and label (1) a recognition and/or knowledge level question, and (2) an application level question. Have at least five questions.

Here are some suggestions for subskill areas.

1. Consonants.
2. Vowels—long or short.
3. Consonant blends.
4. Silent consonants.
5. Controlled vowels.
6. Changing *y* to *i*.
7. Plurals.
8. Possessives.
9. Contractions.
10. Compound words.
11. Syllables.
12. Story detail.
13. Story sequence.
14. Word meaning.
15. Main idea.
16. Fact and opinion.
17. Inferences.
18. Alphabetize.
19. Dictionary.
20. Uses charts, maps, and the like.

Hint: Nonsense words are helpful in testing certain skills. Exchange your completed work with a classmate and check one another's questions against the given criteria. If there are questions, check with your instructor.

Instructional Activity 9

Preparing and Utilizing Criterion-Referenced Inventories

Criterion-Referenced Inventories

A criterion-referenced inventory or test is based on objectives that have been stated in behavioral terms. Performance of the student is then measured against these specifically stated objectives. A performance objective may be stated as follows.

Given a word and four additional words from which to choose, the student will correctly select the homonym for the word.

or

Given samples of an index, a table of contents, a bar graph, and a dictionary, the student will correctly identify the index.

or

Given a word of three or four syllables and four numerals from which to choose, the student will correctly circle the numeral representing the number of syllables in the word.

The tests, then, are made to evaluate the objectives that have been determined. They also test that objective in the manner in which the objective is stated.

Let us return to the behaviorally stated objectives and see what a criterion-referenced measurement instrument would look like.

Circle the word in the box that is a homonym of the word on the left of the box.

fair	fare far for four	wait	watt weight what wheat
pear	Peer par prey pair	made	mead mied maid media

Circle the number that represents the number of syllables in each word.

Alphabet	2	3	4	5
Dictionary	2	3	4	5
Recently	2	3	4	5
Expression	2	3	4	5

The criterion-referenced test needs at least four items per skill to determine if the student really has knowledge of the skill or has just guessed well.

Developing a Criterion-Referenced Inventory

As the teacher, you may wish to use criterion-referenced tests or they may be assigned to you to use. In this period of accountability, criterion-referenced tests have come to the forefront. You must be prepared to write examples of test items so that you can assist your students in getting ready to take such a test.

You will be given seven behaviorally stated objectives. You are to develop four test items for each reading subskill objective. When you have completed the task, have two of your classmates evaluate your work.

Several behaviorally stated objectives on subskills of reading are presented next. Use these as a basis for your test item development.

- Given four pronouns, one of which is a possessive pronoun, the student will identify the possessive pronoun.
- Given four words, including one word with a suffix, the student will identify the word with the suffix.
- Given a group of nonsense words, the student will identify the nonsense word that would show a long vowel sound.
- Given a series of letters from the alphabet, the student will identify the letter named by the teacher.
- Given a group of vocabulary words from a fifth-grade reader, the student will identify the word stated by the teacher.
- Given a word definition and four words from the science vocabulary, the student will match the definition with the word.
- Given a simulated guide strip from a dictionary and a series of words, the student will identify the words that would appear on that page in the dictionary.

Instructional Activity 10

Adjusting for Dialectal Variations and Other Factors

In previous instructional activities you learned about administering informal reading inventories and dealing with oral reading errors. The information contained therein dealt with identifying children's levels of reading so that they might be grouped for instruction with materials at an appropriate level of difficulty. The word recognition criteria, established for determination of reading levels, considered only the quantity of oral reading errors; however, there have been some pleas within the last decade to consider the quality of the reading errors also.

Kenneth Goodman, one of the persons prominent in the movement, based his ideas on miscue analysis, which he began as a research tool for describing the reading process. As a result of his research, he found that the miscues—observed responses that mismatch the expected response—had two dimensions. One dimension related merely to the number of miscues, but the other related to the quality of the miscues.

An analysis of the miscues made by the reader can help the teacher judge how proficiently a reader uses reading as a communication process.

In analyzing miscues, the teacher may use the following procedure as identified by Goodman (1975).

1. Count the reader's miscues.
2. Subtract the miscues that are all shifts to the reader's own dialect. According to Goodman, these are not really miscues at all. They are expected oral responses to the written message. They are results of the reader's attempt to convert print into its oral counterpart.
3. Count all the miscues that result in acceptable meaning before correction. The acceptable meaning does not have to correspond to that originally intended.
4. Count all miscues that result in unacceptable meaning but that the reader corrects.
5. Add the miscues from steps 3 and 4. This represents the total number of miscues that are acceptable for meaning or are self-corrected.

If the teacher is more concerned about the quality of the miscues (as they affect comprehension) than about the quantity of miscues, then he or she may want to include these additional steps before applying the word recognition accuracy criteria as given for an informal reading inventory.

6. Subtract the number arrived at in step 5 from the number obtained in step 1. Use the adjusted score to determine reading level.[1]

There are some important teaching implications of quality analysis of oral reading miscues. One relates to the dialect-speaking child. Research has indicated that dialect-speaking readers frequently translate what they read aloud into their own dialect.[2] However, there is inconclusive evidence as to how the translation affects meaning. Even so, an analysis of oral reading miscues that counts dialectal variations as errors will yield an unreliable estimate of the child's reading level. For these children "errors"

[1] For a complete discussion on miscue analysis, see Goodman, 1975.
[2] For further information on these topics, see Cullinan, 1976, Harber and Beatty, 1978, Lamberg, 1979, Lucas and Singer, 1976, and Seitz, 1977.

may be reflections of the child's primary language system and not of poor reading skill. This, in itself, has an implication for teachers. Dialect is an organized form of language. Although it differs from standard English, non-standard dialect is not really inferior. This means that teachers of the non-standard dialect reader will have to be "educated" about that dialect to determine which miscues are dialect and which are genuine miscues.[3]

Another implication is that teachers may need to broaden their perspectives on oral reading responses. They should be more concerned with the quality of reading miscues than the quantity. Perhaps they should consider errors based on words such as graphic similarities, sound similarities, and errors based on context of the materials.

 Activities

Apply what you have learned to these situations. Compare your responses with those of a peer.

1. Use the informal reading inventory you developed for Objective 5. Use the oral reading responses from the child to whom you administered the Informal Reading Inventory. Reevaluate the oral reading of the passages according to the steps in this instructional unit. Then fill in the following table.

	Original WR Accuracy, percent	Adjusted WR Accuracy, percent
Passage 1	_____	_____
Passage 2	_____	_____
Passage 3	_____	_____
Passage 4	_____	_____
Passage 5	_____	_____
Passage 6	_____	_____

(a) Did you change the reading levels because of the adjustment? _____

(b) What conclusion can you make about analysis of oral reading for quality of miscues? _____

---

[3] For further information on dialectal variations and differences between selected languages and English, see Lapp and Flood, 1978, pp. 497–527.

2. Using one of the selections you developed or one in Appendix B, have a dialect speaker read the passage orally as you record errors according to the types identified in Activity 10. After the reading, have the reader retell what he read. Then fill in the following information. (Be certain to supply the reader with a passage that according to your best judgment, is at his instructional level.)

Step 1. Total miscues. _____

Step 2. (a) Total dialect shifts. _____

(b) Total miscues − dialect shifts. _____

Step 3. Total acceptable meaning miscues. _____

Step 4. Total unacceptable meaning but self-corrected miscues. ___

Step 5. Total step 3 + step 4. _____

Step 6. Total step 2b − total step 5. _____

What conclusion can you make about dialectal variations as miscues? _

Instructional Activity 11

Assessing Affective Dimensions of Reading
Among the affective dimensions of reading are attitudes, interests, and values. These are important, because the goal of reading instruction is to develop students who have the ability and skills necessary for reading and who also have a love for reading and the habit of reading.

Analysis of student attitudes indicating how they feel about reading can help the teacher in making decisions about instructional procedures and materials to use. Information that certain students dislike reading or think it unimportant can alert the teacher to the necessity of making some provisions in the reading program that might help the student alter a negative attitude toward reading. Some ways to assess attitudes are presented here.

Teacher Observation
Observing students in informal situations such as in the library, during independent study or free reading periods, or in conversation with peers and noting behaviors related to reading in anecdotal form can provide a valuable technique for making inferences about attitude. Heathington and Alexander (1978, p. 770) suggest the following observational checklist to

obtain information that reflects attitude toward reading. Observations should span at least a 2-week period.

1. Seemed happy when engaged in reading activities.
2. Volunteered to read aloud in class.
3. Read a book during free time.
4. Mentioned reading a book at home.
5. Chose reading over other activities.
6. Requested to go to library.
7. Checked out books at library.
8. Talked about books read.
9. Finished most books begun.
10. Mentioned books has at home.

Questionnaires and Interviews

A measure of attitude toward reading can be obtained by structuring questions or incomplete sentences to which the student will respond either orally or in writing. The questions can form the basis of a questionnaire or the structure for interviewing a student. Samples of responses about school in general, books and reading, the reading environment, study habits, class activities, and the teacher can be gleaned through statements such as:

The hardest thing about reading is . . . .

Reading comic books is . . . .

Studying in school is . . . .

Assessing Reading Interests

Most people know from experience that they are more motivated to do and more persistent in doing things that interest them regardless of the difficulty of the task. For this reason, it is helpful for the teacher to know what interests the student has to facilitate a better match between student interest and topics to be read. An interest inventory can be structured to ascertain pupil interest. The inventory can be administered orally or in written form. A sample inventory is shown here.

Name: _____ Grade: _____ Date: _____

1. What is the best book you have ever read?

2. What is the best book someone has read to you?

3. What do you like to do when you have free time? After school? On Saturdays?

4. What are your favorite TV programs?

5. What are your hobbies?

6. Which of these places have you visited? Library? Art museum? Circus? Concerts? Zoo? Theater? Parks?

7. Which is your favorite school subject?

8. Which subject do you like least?

9. What can you do best?

10. Which places would you like to visit?

ADDITIONAL ENABLING ACTIVITIES

1. This is a reading-study activity. Read and take notes on all of the following sources.
   (a) "Primary Reading Skills" and "Upper Elementary Grade Level Reading Skills" in Barbe, 1.
   (b) "Finding the Appropriate Level of Materials for Each Student" in Burmeister, 1.
   (c) Goodman (Objective 10).
   (d) Ransom, "Diagnosis of Instructional Needs," Chapter 6, pp. 139–187.
   (e) Zintz, "The Informal Reading Inventory," Chapter 4, pp. 73–89.
   (f) Zintz, "Learning to Anticipate Meaning," Chapter 11, pp. 292–299.

2. This activity will provide additional information for Objectives 1, 5, 6, 7, 8, and 9. Schedule an observation and conference with a teacher who is administering:
   (a) A standardized reading test.
   (b) A diagnostic reading test.
   (c) An informal reading inventory.
   (d) A teacher-made reading test.
   (e) A cloze test.
   (f) A criterion-referenced reading test.
   (g) A reading skills checklist.

3. Study copies of commercially prepared reading tests and accompanying manuals. Where possible, administer these tests to a peer or child at the appropriate level. This activity will provide additional work on Objectives 2, 3, 5, 9, 10, 11, and 12.
   (a) Standardized reading test.
   (b) Informal reading inventory.
   (c) Criterion-referenced reading test.
   (d) Interest inventory test.

4. Attend class session(s) Time _____ Date _____.
5. An activity of your choice.
6. An activity selected by your instructor.

READING RESOURCES / REFERENCES

1. Barbe, Walter B. *Educator's Guide to Personalized Reading Instruction.* Englewood Cliffs, N.J.: Prentice-Hall, 1961.
2. Burmeister, Lou E. *Reading Strategies for Secondary School Teachers.* Reading, Mass.: Addison Wesley, 1974.
3. Clay, Marie. *A Diagnostic Survey.* London: Heinemann Educational Books, 1978.
4. Cullinan, Bernice, ed. *Black Dialects and Reading.* Urban, Ill.: National Council of Teachers of Reading, 1976.
5. Goodman, Kenneth S., ed. *Miscue Analysis.* Urban, Ill.: ERIC Clearinghouse on Reading and Communication Skills, 1975.
6. Guszak, Frank J. *Diagnostic Reading Instruction in the Elementary School,* 2 ed. New York: Harper & Row, 1978.
7. Heathington, Betty S., and J. Estill Alexander, "A Child-based Observation Checklist to Assess Attitudes Toward Reading," *The Reading Teacher,* (April 1978), pp. 769–771.
8. Harber, Jean R., and Jane N. Beatty, compilers. *Reading and the Black English Speaking Child.* Newark, Del.: International Reading Association, 1978.
9. Hood, Joyce. "Is Miscue Analysis Practical for Teachers?", *The Reading Teacher* (December 1978) pp. 260–266.
10. Lamberg, Walter J. "Assessment of Oral Reading Which Exhibits Dialect and Language Difference," *Journal of Reading* (April 1979), pp. 609–615.
11. Lapp, Diane, and James Flood. *Teaching Reading to Every Child.* New York: Macmillan, 1978.
12. Lucas, Marilyn, and Harry Singer. "Dialect in Relation to Oral Reading Achievement: Recoding Encoding, or Merely a Code," in *Theoretical Models and Processes of Reading,* 2nd ed., Harry Singer and Robert Ruddell, ed. Newark, Del.: International Reading Association, 1976.
13. Rankin, Earl F., and Joseph W. Culhane. "Comparable Cloze and Multiple-Choice Comprehension Test Scores," *Journal of Reading* (December 1969), pp. 193–198.
14. Ransom, Grayce A. *Preparing to Teach Reading.* Boston: Little Brown, 1978.
15. Seitz, Victoria. *Social Class and Ethnic Group Differences in Learning to Read.* Newark, Del.: International Reading Association, 1977.
16. Shuy, Roger, ed. *Linguistic Theory: What Can It Say About Reading?* Newark, Del.: International Reading Association, 1977.
17. Taylor, Wilson. "Cloze Procedure: A New Tool for Measuring Readability," *Journalism Quarterly* (Fall 1953), pp. 414–438.
18. Thonis, Elanor Wall. *Literacy for America's Spanish Speaking Children.* Newark, Del.: International Reading Association, 1976.

19. Tortelli, James Peter. "Simplified Psycholinguistic Diagnosis," *The Reading Teacher* (April 1976), pp. 637–639.
20. Zintz, Miles V. *The Reading Process,* 2nd ed. Dubuque, Ia.: William C. Brown, 1975.

Chapter **18**
Diagnostic-Prescriptive Teaching

RATIONALE

In order to help students gain independence in reading skills, teachers often use an approach that employs medical terminology. They diagnose needs and prescribe for these needs. These prescribed lessons and activities provide strength to the student in the specific skills area. It is certainly a more scientific approach then simply teaching and hoping that the students need the lesson. The prescriptive approach saves the time and energy of both the teacher and the students. It provides for teachers and students to see growth graphically and to know with certainty which skills need to be emphasized, which need reviewing, and which have been mastered.

This chapter will enable you to use a diagnostic-prescriptive approach as you teach reading skills.

OBJECTIVES

After completing this chapter, you will be able to:
1. Identify the major advantages of a diagnostic-prescriptive teaching skills program.
2. Identify the essential steps in diagnostic-prescriptive teaching.
3. Identify at least two complete commercially prepared scope and sequence charts of reading skills.
4. Identify at least three different types of record-keeping systems that facilitate diagnostic-prescriptive teaching.
5. Convert given teaching material into a diagnostic aid.
6. Establish initial teaching groups from given diagnostic data.
7. Demostrate a diagnostic-prescriptive technique in an actual or simulated setting.
8. Identify accommodations in approach, procedures, and materials for teaching reading to students with special needs.
9. Complete an objective identified by the instructor.

**Instructional
Activity 1**

Advantages of Diagnostic-Prescriptive Skills Programs

If you had a severe pain and cramping in your leg and you went to a physician, would you think it wise to be given medicine that cures itching skin? Of course not! You expect to be treated for the pain and cramping in your leg.

Teachers, too, must be specific in diagnosing the "reading skills ailments" of students and then be specific in providing appropriate prescriptions for alleviating those ailments and increasing the students' reading skills and abilities. The advantages for teachers and students in this diagnostic-prescriptive procedure are many.

In this approach, the teacher uses a reading skills checklist. It might be one developed by the school system, by a book publisher, or by an authority on reading. It will be based on the sequential instructional skill needs of students at specific grade levels and chronological and mental age levels. If the teacher develops a skills checklist, he or she should be mindful of the age, grade, and instructional needs of the students while doing so.

Of course, in using a checklist, it is also necessary to use pre- and post-testing procedures. This testing program provides information for reteaching or advancing to the next higher level of skills.

Through the use of the diagnostic-prescriptive approach to skill development, the teacher is able to identify easily definite goals and objectives to which the teaching efforts are exerted. All energies are diverted toward definite, identified needs of specific students.

The diagnostic-prescriptive approach provides an opportunity for charts, graphs, or other visual records of progress to be maintained. The teacher and/or students might see growth and development at all times. This provides feedback of progress to goals, which is essential to continued improvement.

Records that are maintained in a diagnostic-prescriptive program are easily transferred from teacher to teacher as the student moves through the grades. This provides a continuous growth record of the student; each teacher is able to build on work previously mastered by the student. This assures that learning occurs in appropriate increments, that the new skills are placed on a firm foundation. No time is wasted on the teaching and learning of a skill that is already being skillfully applied by the student, or is precious instructional time lost by presenting a skill that is too difficult for the student to master. The approach helps the teacher keep instruction at appropriate levels of difficulty.

When using the diagnostic-prescriptive approach, the teacher is able to group students for instruction based on common needs. The approach facilitates grouping across existing group lines formed for reading ability levels or pulling together students from various reading groups to work on specific skills that meet the individual needs.

Activities

Use what you have learned to respond to these situations. Compare your responses with those of a peer.

1. Can you name four advantages of the diagnostic-prescriptive approach to the skills development program in a classroom? Try it.

   (a) _____

   (b) _____

   (c) _____

   (d) _____

Check: Your responses should include some or all of these ideas.

   - Useful in grouping students with common needs.
   - Provides a checklist of skills in an orderly sequence of development.
   - Provides teachers with definite objectives toward which they can direct their teaching.
   - Provides student growth records that move easily from teacher to teacher.
   - Provides for records that help students witness their own growth.

2. Visit a school. Inquire if a reading skills checklist is used in the school. Ask to look at a copy of the checklist if one is available. Make notes on what you see on the checklist.

Instructional Activity 2

Essential Steps in Diagnostic-Prescriptive Teaching

The pattern for a diagnostic-prescriptive program is quite simple, as illustrated in these steps.

1. *Establish Objectives.* Decide exactly which reading skills are to be mastered by the children at the level you teach. This is the scope of your program. Also decide the order in which the skills should be mastered. This is the skill sequence. This step can be made easy for the teacher who used a skills checklist such as the one provided in Appendix C-8. The skills are already provided in an appropriate sequence. The prescriptive teacher only has to select the skill that is appropriate for the student at this particular level of difficulty and state it in behavioral terms.

2. *Diagnose.* Determine by pretesting exactly which of the skills the children already possess and those in which they need instruction. In some

instances assessment instruments may accompany the checklists. If so, the teacher may use these instead of constructing them.

3. *Select Learning Activities.* Decide which introductory and reinforcement activities can best be used to help the students meet the objectives. These activities should account for the different learning styles of the children and should involve the use of films, tapes, pictures, and other media to make the lessons meaningful.

4. *Organize for Instruction.* Decide which grouping patterns seem best in terms of (a) the nature of the skill to be taught, (b) the available teacher time, and (c) the common needs and interests of the students.

5. *Implement Instruction.* Utilize the previously planned teaching/learning activities in the appropriate grouping pattern. Be certain to include initial instructional activities (usually teacher directed), guided practice activities, and independent practice activities, as described in Appendix E.

6. *Postassessment.* Determine if the student has mastered the skill identified in the objective.

7. *Implement Remedial Procedures.* For students who fail to demonstrate proficiency on the postassessment, provide additional teaching/learning activities. This allows the student to develop the necessary skill at one level before facing the impossible task of succeeding at the next higher level of difficulty. In other words, this step helps to prevent subsequent failures.

The diagnostic-prescriptive teaching process provides for continuous progress of students through the reading curriculum, as illustrated in the following diagram.

Diagnostic-Prescriptive Process

Establishing → Diagnosing → Selecting → Organizing →
objectives   learning   for instruction
                                       activities

Prescriptive → Giving → Implementing
teaching   postassessments   remedial
                                              procedures

Record-keeping is an important aspect of the diagnostic-prescriptive program. After the preassessment and postassessment are administered and scored, the teacher must record these scores in some manner so that information can be easily retrieved. A class or group chart is handy for this. Also, an individual profile card is generally available to accompany a checklist and allows information to be recorded.

To illustrate, consider the sample class chart shown here.

	Maps	Skill: Locating Information: Graphs	Encyclopedias
Adam			
Amy			
Carol			
Doug			
Gail			
Jim			
Lon			

A symbol system indicating mastery might be employed. For instance, an X in a box beside a name and under a specific skill would indicate mastery. A diagonal line through a box could indicate that the student had been tested but had not mastered the skill. Dates can be entered in the box if desired.

By glancing at the class or group chart, the teacher immediately knows who has mastered a skill and who has not. This tells the teacher who can move on to a new skill and who needs additional work on the skill just tested.

For students needing additional work, the teacher must plan additional or supplemental lessons to assist them in mastering the skill.

 Activities

Answer the following questions. Compare your responses with those of a peer.

1. Some words and/or phrases follow. Place a check mark after each phrase that refers to a step in the diagnostic-prescriptive teaching process.

    _____ (a) Reteaching _____

    _____ (b) Reinforcement _____

    _____ (c) Postassessment _____

    _____ (d) Criterion-referenced test _____

    _____ (e) Recording data _____

    _____ (f) Selecting objectives _____

    _____ (g) Predicting outcomes _____

    _____ (h) Preassessment _____

    _____ (i) Teaching strategies _____

    _____ (j) Mainstreaming _____

Check: Which ones did you place a checkmark after? You are correct if you checked letters a, c, e, f, h, and i.

2. Now go back, correct your errors and, using ABCs, label in *sequential order* the steps of the diagnostic-prescriptive process.

Check: Did you place them in this order?

1—F
3—D
5—E
6—A
8—B
9—C

3. Shotgun Sharon teaches everything to everyone. She shoots out her pellets of wisdom to the whole class. Fortunately, they hit a few of the intended targets, but many go unscathed by the pellets. Does Sharon use a diagnostic-prescriptive approach? How do you know? _____

_____

_____

_____

Compare your responses with those of a peer.

4. Rory Rifle targets his teaching. His sights are always set on specific reading skills. Furthermore, he tries to match those skills with pupils who need them. Does Rory use a diagnostic-prescriptive approach? How do you know? _____

_____

_____

_____

Instructional Activity 3

Using Scope and Sequence Charts

Publishers of reading texts develop and print large charts that show the scope and the sequence of the skills taught in their reading series. Scope refers to the kinds and numbers of skills, sequence refers to their order of introduction, maintenance, and mastery.

In some instances, publishers have the scope and sequence charts printed in the teachers' manual that accompanies the reading series. This is a convenient and handy method that provides a quick reference.

Whether in manual or on a large wall chart, a scope and sequence chart will have a format somewhat like the following example.

	Word Analysis	Comprehension	Study Skills
Primary grades	Phonics—initial sounds of b, d, f, h, j, k, l, m Blends fl, st, fr, sm, sm Vowels—short and long	Main idea of story Sequence of story Draw conclusions Predict outcomes	Table of contents Titles Locate specific information
Upper Elementary	Rules for syllabication Rules for accent Prefixes and suffixes	Main ideas Story details Interprets story ideas	Dictionary Glossary Outlining

The chart might also be broken down into grade levels. It will also have additional headings such as recreational reading, vocabulary, oral reading (poetry), and the like.

Keep in mind that a commercially prepared scope and sequence chart from a specific reading text book publisher will be limited to the grade levels for which the publisher has written the series of books. If the book series is for grades one to six, these are the levels covered in the scope and sequence chart.

Various school systems have developed their own scope and sequence charts of skills that they want to be taught to the students. These are similar to the reading skills checklists.

Some commercially prepared scopes are not charts, but lists of objectives for the student. For example, one might appear as follows.

Scope and Sequence of Skills
Second Reader

The student will:

1. Recognize and use compound words.
2. Recognize and use punctuation marks.
3. Add the *ing* ending to short words.
4. Add *s* endings to verbs.
5. Alphabetize to the second letter.
6. Classify words.
7. Recognize homonyms.
8. Recognize antonyms.
9. Recognize synonyms.
10. Recognize basal read vocabulary.

Note that such a listing will probably be for skills taught in a specific book or basal reader of a given publishing company.

Activity

Locate the curriculum librarian or a teacher friend who would have a commercially prepared scope and sequence chart. Borrow the chart and make notes of the topics listed on the chart.

See if you can find an example of a wall chart and a scope and sequence within a reading manual. Note the similarities and the differences in the two. Which do you like better?

Be prepared to identify a commercially prepared scope and sequence chart if your instructor would ask you to do so.

Instructional Activity 4

Diagnostic-Prescriptive Record-Keeping Systems

In order to function efficiently in a diagnostic-prescriptive program for students, the teacher must have a system of record-keeping. That system must provide for recording all pertinent information easily and quickly. Also, the system must be manageable in terms of size and storage. Most important, it must provide needed information on an individual student at a glance and information on a group of students with little investment of time.

One method of record-keeping is utilized in the group check sheet or profile sheet for each skill of concern. On this profile sheet, the teacher lists the major skills and its subsets of skills, either in a row or a column. Then the individual pupil names are listed. Throughout the day, the teacher may record instances of student performance in a given skill. This is especially useful when employing diagnostic techniques such as structured teacher observations, individual response methods, oral reading segments, and sample products as mentioned in previous instructional packets. The information on a group profile may be analyzed quickly to identify children who need specific skills instruction. An example of a group record sheet is on p. 317. This card lists the skills and provides spaces for students' names. Recording mastery or nonmastery of administered tests aids in quickly developing reading skills groups for instruction.

Another method of keeping records involves the use of individual profile sheets. On these profiles, a complete record of skills is kept for each individual. This method requires more investment of teacher time than does the group profile both to record data and to use them in the formation of skills groups. It does, however, have the advantage of accompanying the individual as he or she moves from one teacher to the next. Two samples of individual profile sheets are presented on pages 318 and 319. The second is an example of an individual profile method that has been adopted for ease in establishing skills groups.

The record-keeping card on page 319 lists the skills around the edge of the card. The individual students' name, grade, and other vital information

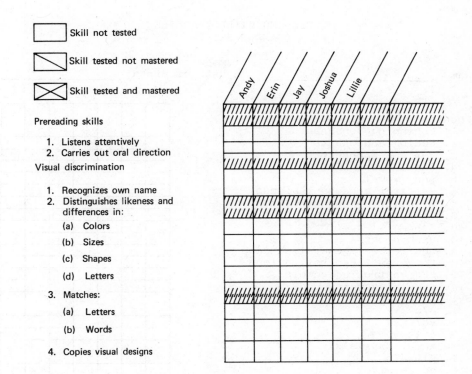

□ Skill not tested

◫ Skill tested not mastered

⊠ Skill tested and mastered

Prereading skills

    1. Listens attentively
    2. Carries out oral direction

Visual discrimination

    1. Recognizes own name
    2. Distinguishes likeness and
       differences in:

       (a) Colors

       (b) Sizes

       (c) Shapes

       (d) Letters

    3. Matches:

       (a) Letters

       (b) Words

    4. Copies visual designs

are recorded in the center of the card. Near the outer edge of the card there are small holes, one corresponding to each listed skill. When the student masters the skill, the hole is pulled out. The teacher can then insert a stylus through a hole in a stack of cards corresponding to a given skill; the cards that fall off indicate the students who have mastered the skill. The cards remaining on the stylus belong to students who need additional instruction.

Of course, there can be variations on the theme of any one of the already discussed record-keeping cards. Therefore you, as a student, must be prepared to identify a skills checklist-type record-keeping system for a diagnostic-prescriptive skills program if your instructor presents you with such a task.

✳ **Activity**

Which of the three type cards did you like best? Why?

_____

_____

_____

_____

READING SKILLS PROFILE
(SAMPLE SKILLS)

Name _____   Date of Birth _____

	K	1	2	3	4	5	6	7	8
Phonics									
1. Beginning consonants									
2. Ending consonants									
3. Variant consonants									
4. Short vowels									
5. Long vowels									
6. 2-letter consonant blends									
7. 3-letter consonant blends									
8. Consonant digraphs									
9. Schwa									
10. Diphthongs									
11. Short vowel generalizations									
12. Long vowel generalizations									
13. "R" controlled vowels									
14. Special vowel sounds									
Syllabication									
1. v/cv									
2. vc/cv									
3. c+le									
Structural Analysis									
1. plurals									
2. possessives									
3. contractions									
4. prefixes									
5. suffixes									
6. compound words									
Comprehension									
1. word meaning									
prefixes									
suffixes									
synonyms/antonyms									
homophones									
multiple meanings									
2. Sentence/paragraph									
context clues									
facts/details									
main ideas									
sequence									
relationships									
conclusions									
fact/opinion									
fact/fiction									
propaganda									
Special Skills									
1. Locating information									
newspapers									
guide letters-words									

◪ = skill tested, not mastered   ☐ = skill not tested

⊠ = skill mastered

Individual Profile (Selected Skills)

	Word Recognition			Comprehension	
	Phonics			Literal	
O	initial consonants			facts/details	O
O	ending consonants			stated sequence	O
O	variant consonants			directions	O
O	short vowels			Inferential	
O	long vowels			makes inferences	O
O	2-letter consonant blends			main idea (implied)	O
O	3-letter consonant blends			sequence (implied)	O
O	consonant digraphs			relationships	O
O	silent letters			Critical	
O	schwa			outcomes	O
O	special vowels			conclusions	O
O	diphthongs			generalizations	O
O	short vowel generalizations			fact/opinion	O
O	long vowel generalizations			fact/fiction	O
	Syllabication			propaganda	O
O	accent			author's purpose	O
O	vc/cv			Study Skills	
O	v/cv			outlining	O
O	c+le			summarizing	O
	Structure			note taking	O
O	plurals			underlining	O
O	possessives			locating information	O
O	tense markers			using special resources	O
O	prefixes			Specialized Skills	
O	suffixes			maps	O
O	contractions			charts	O
O	compounds			tables	O

Date of Birth

Name

Instructional Activity 5

Converting Teaching Materials into Diagnostic Aids

For the diagnostic-prescriptive approach to be successful, diagnosis must be continuous, must be provided for every child in the program, and must form the cog around which the entire reading program rolls. Such expectations can be heavily demanding on teacher time unless the teacher has access to rapidly implemented procedures that yield relatively accurate data. The accomplishment of the task can be greatly facilitated if the teacher converts teaching materials into diagnostic aids.

Much of the evidence gathered in the diagnosis step of the diagnostic-prescriptive procedure can, and probably should, be based on informal procedures.

A passage in a basal reader, for instance, can become a very good informal inventory for assessing proficiency in oral and silent reading. As the student reads the passage orally at sight, the teacher might lightly mark in the manual copy of the reader the number and kinds of miscues the student makes. The teacher can use these data for initial placement of the student in instructional materials by applying the criteria for word recognition accuracy identified in Chapter 17. The types of miscues made yield diagnostic data for analysis of skills needs.

A scope and sequence chart can be converted to a checklist by identifying the skills appropriate at a given level of difficulty and placing them on charts. The checklist can structure the teacher's observation of the students' reading performance in a variety of settings. The purposeful observations enable the teacher to collect data on specific aspects of the students' reading skills.

A workbook lesson on a specific skill might be used as a pretest. The teacher must, however, analyze the workbook page to determine the skill on the page and the level of its difficulty. By doing so, the teacher can use the workbook page as a type of criterion-referenced inventory, provided that proficient performance on the page indicates application of the specific skills.

Most teaching activities can be converted to diagnostic aids when individual pupil response cards or other individual response methods are used. In order to use the technique, the teacher must structure an activity that focuses on a specific skill. For example, to determine the students' ability to auditorily distinguish between hard and soft sounds represented by *g,* the teacher may use the following procedure.

Diagnostic Teaching Segment

Teacher working with entire class: I am going to say some words to you. Some will have the soft sound represented by the letter *g.* Others will have the hard sound. You will use your response cards (two strips of different colored paper) to show me which sound I have said.

For the hard sound, you will hold up your yellow strip. For the soft sound, you will hold up your green strip.

For example, if I say the word *goat,* what would you do? Show me. Great! You would hold up your yellow card because the sound is hard.

Suppose I say *gem,* what will you do? Show me.

Fine. You held up the green card. You knew that the sound was soft.

Now respond as I say each of these words. (Teacher goes through a series of illustrative words.)

The teacher carefully observes the color-coded responses of the students, making notes of who responds haltingly with uncertainty, whose responses are consistently correct or incorrect, and whose responses are inconsistent. Through this activity the teacher can identify the children who are proficient in the skill and those who need further work. This information provides the basis for instructional decisions about grouping and skills instruction.

Sample products of students' work over a period of time provide valuable diagnostic data. From these samples, the teacher may note patterns of errors and areas of progress in specific reading skills. The sample products can be placed in individual folders or in folders identified by specific reading skills.

 Activities

1. Locate a reading workbook for a middle grade level. Select a page in the workbook, identify the skill being stressed on the page, and write a paragraph indicating how you would or could use the material to determine the specific skill needs of students.

2. In some of your past work you have written learning/teaching activities for a small group of students. Use these activities again now and be prepared to show a peer group how this material might be used in a diagnostic manner.

3. Write a plan that indicates the use of a teaching activity for diagnostic purposes. Use the individual pupil response technique.

4. Corey the complainer has often been heard to blast the diagnostic-prescriptive reading program his school implemented this year. "Diagnostic-Prescriptive! That's a laugh! Diagnostic-descriptive is a better term. All I have to do anymore is test and tell what's wrong with the kids. I don't have any time left over to prescribe and teach."

   (a) What fact does Corey seem to be overlooking? _____

   _____

   _____

   (b) What would you tell him that will help him have time to teach?

   _____

   _____

321

Instructional Activity 6

Forming Teaching Groups Based on Diagnostic Data

The diagnostic procedures provide information that is the base for three teaching decisions: content in terms of the objectives that should be accomplished and the materials presented; methodology or the teaching techniques and procedures to be employed; and organization or how the students will be grouped to accommodate their individual needs. The organization decision is treated in this instructional activity.

As you learned in previous chapters, there are several ways to group students. Certain diagnostic data are helpful in deciding which way suits a specific need. One type of grouping employs achievement data as its base. Although standardized reading achievement tests provide limited diagnostic data, they may be utilized as diagnostic tools with some adaptations. For instance, a composite score on a reading achievement test has limited value unless the teacher has analyzed the items on the test and established the skills that are actually being measured by each. Then the teacher can determine which skills the student does or does not possess in relation to the score.

The standardized test scores of a group of students within a classroom are presented here. These students all have standardized test scores in comprehension below the fourth-grade level, and they are fifth-grade students. Look carefully at the information in the column marked Comprehension.

	Comprehension	Main Idea	Details	Sequence	Draws Conclusion
Shonda	3.0	2.7	3.5	2.9	3.9
Scott	3.5	3.2	3.9	3.8	3.1
Carol	2.2	2.2	2.7	2.1	1.8
Jeff	3.5	3.9	3.1	3.2	3.8
Gerald	2.8	3.4	3.6	2.2	2.1
Hollis	2.9	3.2	3.7	3.2	1.5
Chris	3.2	3.5	3.8	3.4	2.1
John	2.9	3.4	3.5	2.7	2.0
Mathew	3.5	3.5	4.2	3.3	3.0
Roberto	2.9	2.1	4.0	3.3	2.2

What does this information show you? Only that no student is doing as well as the average fifth-grade student. It tells you nothing about the students' skill needs. As such, these data cannot help you begin a diagnostic-prescriptive program. They are much too general to be useful.

If you find the type of skills tested on the instrument in the comprehension area, you may get some useful information. Study the comprehension subtest scores to determine exactly where strengths and weaknesses lie. Look at the information in the column marked Main Idea, Details, Sequence, and Draws Conclusions to see what information we might gather about this small group of students.

1. Which comprehension skills were measured? _____

2. In which skill does the group appear most competent? _____

3. In which skill does the group appear weakest? _____
4. Rank the comprehension skills by performance of the group from strongest to weakest.

    Strongest _____

    _____

    _____

    Weakest _____
5. Using the information from Chapter 9, explain why this pattern makes

    sense. _____

    _____

Check: When you look at subskill scores you begin to get information detailed enough to help you plan specific lessons for the students. Overall scores are not too helpful. From the information given on these students, you are able to see right away that their greatest strength is in being able to identify or select details in a story. The second strength is in selecting or identifying the main idea. The third strength is in putting parts of a story in the correct sequence. This group's greatest weakness is the comprehension subskill area—being able to draw conclusion from material they read. The pattern makes sense in terms of the relative difficulty of the comprehension skills. Facts, details, main idea (when stated), and sequence of events are all at literal comprehension levels. Drawing conclusions is at the critical comprehension level and would be more difficult (notice that every child except Jeff and Shonda had their highest score in details and weakest in conclusions).

6. You made the decision to teach sequence skills first, since all of the

children need them, as shown by their performance. However, you want to teach them in two groups. Examine the data and list your groups.

I	II
_____	_____
_____	_____
_____	_____
_____	_____
_____	_____
_____	

(a) Why did you divide them this way? _____

_____

(b) Check your responses.

I		II	
Shonda	2.9	Scott	3.8
Carol	2.1	Jeff	3.2
Gerald	2.8	Hollis	3.2
John	2.7	Chris	3.4
		Mathew	3.3
		Roberto	3.3

The basis for this division was achievement score in sequence skill. Notice that in Group II, the scores are clustered except for Scott. He may need to work separately.

Factors to Consider

When setting up groups based on diagnostic data, there are some points to consider. Teachers should use them to help formulate organizational decisions.

1. Some children need multiple skills and can work in only one group at a time.
2. Some skills should be prerequisite to others. For example, short vowel sounds should be mastered before working on special vowel sounds.
3. The composition of the class suggests possibilities for peer tutoring.
4. In setting up groups, one must attend to these variables: individuals, skills, and skills that have prerequisites.

 ## Activities

Apply what you have learned in these situations. Check your responses with those of a peer.

1. (a) Study the diagnostic data given in the following class profile. Set up three skills groups and identify the skill and the members.

Group 1   Skill: _____   _____
    Members   _____   _____
                _____   _____
                _____   _____
                _____   _____
                _____   _____

Names	short vowels	long vowels	diphthongs	schwa	"r" controlled	a + l, w, u
Larry				X		X
Marie						X
Angela				X		
Wayne						X
Susan					X	
John			X			
Will				X		
Michael		X		X	X	
Bob						X
Rachel					X	
Bert				X		
Jim	X		X	X	X	
Marcia			X			
Richard	X			X	X	X
Jerry			X		X	

Group 2   Skill: _____   _____
   Members   _____   _____
                          _____   _____
                          _____   _____
                          _____   _____
                          _____   _____

Group 3   Skill: _____   _____
   Members   _____   _____
                          _____   _____
                          _____   _____
                          _____   _____
                          _____   _____

(b) Give a justification for your decision.

2. Identify an appropriate instructional sequence of skills for Jim. You may want to consult a scope and sequence chart.

(a) _____   (b) _____   (c) _____

(d) _____   (e) _____   (f) _____

Instructional Activity 7

Demonstrating Diagnostic-Prescriptive Techniques

This is to be a demonstration lesson. It will have all the parts of the diagnostic-prescriptive approach. Study the lesson outline carefully; you will be expected to demonstrate a similar lesson in a peer group or actual classroom setting.

Sample Teaching Episode

1. *An Objective.*   Alphabetizing By Second and Third Letter.
2. *Pretest.*
    Placed on chalkboard: ax-back
    Class, these are guide words from a page in the dictionary. I will show you some words. If that word goes on this page of the dictionary, turn your thumbs up. If it does not go on this page in the dictionary, turn your thumbs down.
    away—show your thumbs (watch the students)
    aye—show your thumbs
    azure—show your thumbs

able—show your thumbs
bit—show your thumbs
buck—show your thumbs
azalea—show your thumbs

Some of you did this easily. Let's do one a little more difficult.
Place on chalkboard: ghost-glove
grove—show your thumbs
gladness—show your thumbs
give—show your thumbs
glance—show your thumbs
gentle—show your thumbs
glare—show your thumbs
gloom—show your thumbs

Some of you are having more difficulty with this task. It is because you are having to think about the second and third letters in the word. In the first quiz we worried only about the second letter.

The teacher has noted the students who were unsuccessful with one or both tasks and has listed their names. The task is to plan and implement lessons to teach the students the dictionary skill of alphabetizing to the second and third letter.

3. *Implement Teaching/Learning Activities*[1]

   (a) *Set* Why is it easy to find your Dad's name in the telephone book? Yes, the book is arranged in alphabetical order and you find names easily when they are arranged that way. Do you know of something else that is arranged in alphabetical order?

   (b) *Objective.* At the end of this lesson you are going to be putting things in alphabetical order when the first letters are the same. This will help you use the dictionary, the telephone book, and the encyclopedia. It will also help you as you develop your own dictionary of new words you learn this year.

   (c) *Input.* Do you remember the alphabet song your teacher taught you in grade one? Let's sing it together.

   Now, that little song told the letters of your alphabet in exact alphabetical order. You know the song and you know the alphabet, so we do not have too far to go to learn to alphabetize to the second letter.

   It is getting close to Halloween. Here are some pumpkins with Halloween words on them. How can I put these in alphabetical order? Watch as I work through some.

   When we alphabetize to the second letter we must look at the

---

[1] Notice how the elements in this lesson correspond to the lesson design in Appendix E.

second letter of the word and decide where that letter comes in the alphabet. The first letters, of course, are alike.

(d) *Modeling.* Let's practice with these name tags. You three wear these name tags around your necks and stand in front of the group. The names are Jerry, Jay, Joshua. All begin alike. We must look at the second letter to alphabetize.

When you know which name is first, raise one finger. When you know which name is second, raise two fingers. When you know the alphabetical order of all three, raise three fingers.

You were first, so place the first name tagged person in alphabetical order under the one on the blackboard. Now you place the second, and so on. That wasn't difficult. Let's try another task.

Here are some word cards. I'll put them on the chalktray. Decide the first word in alphabetical order, and so forth. The words are door, desk, day, dime, and dump.

(e) *Check for Understanding.* Raise your fingers again when you can alphabetize words one, two, three, four, and five.

Let's check your work again by one person at a time placing the word in the correct alphabetical order.

(f) *Guided Practice.* Here are some Halloween words on a piece of paper. Tear the paper apart and move the words around until they are in alphabetical order. I'll be walking around checking. The words are ghost, gray, gloom, goblin, and gnats. You may glue them on your paper after I have checked them for accuracy.

(g) *Independent Practice.* Here is another sheet with more Halloween words. Tear the paper apart and put these words in alphabetical order. The words are spook, shake, scare, suit, squeal, silent, skip, and sad.

When you have them in order, copy them on the remainder of the sheet of paper. Copy them in alphabetical order. Put your name and date on the paper.

4. *Postassessment.* Here are five words, one each on a card for each of you. Line these words up in alphabetical order and copy them on your paper in alphabetical order.

5. *Remediation.* Plan more manipulative work with alphabetizing to the first letter and then more work with alphabetizing to the second letter.

 ### Activities

1. In the preceding diagnostic-prescriptive episode performance of the students on the preassessment suggested that some grouping is necessary. Use the information on the following class profile to determine the teaching groups.

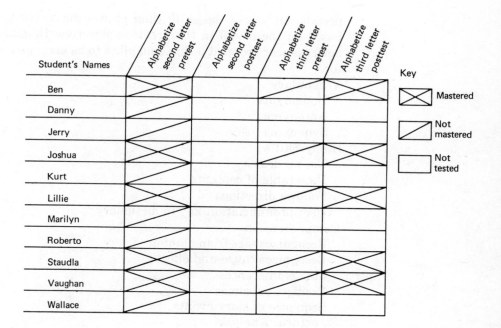

Student's Names	Alphabetize second letter pretest	Alphabetize second letter posttest	Alphabetize third letter pretest	Alphabetize third letter posttest
Ben				
Danny				
Jerry				
Joshua				
Kurt				
Lillie				
Marilyn				
Roberto				
Staudla				
Vaughan				
Wallace				

Key:
- ⊠ Mastered
- ◺ Not mastered
- ☐ Not tested

(a) Identify the students who need instruction in alphabetizing to the second letter.

_____   _____

_____   _____

_____   _____

(b) Identify those students who were pretested for alphabetizing to the third letter.

_____   _____

_____   _____

_____   _____

(c) Of those students who were taught the lesson in the teaching episode, how many mastered the objective?

_____

What skill are these students ready to pursue?

_____

(d) How many skills groups should you probably have in this class now?

_____

2. This activity requires you to apply your knowledge.
   Some reading skills are listed here. Select a skill. Get your instructor's

permission to use the skill; then plan a diagnostic-prescriptive lesson based on the model in the previous objective. Demonstrate this lesson before a peer group at a time and place to be arranged with your instructor.

Vocabulary
  Homonyms
  Antonyms
  Synonyms
Study Skills
  Uses index
  Uses table of contents
  Follows directions
  Uses pronunciation key in dictionary
Comprehension
  Recognizes fact from opinion
  Recognizes cause and effect
  Makes inferences
  Predicts outcomes
  Sequence of story events
Structural Analysis
  Plurals (nouns)
  Possessives
  Contractions
  Compound words
  Prefixes
  Suffixes
  Syllables (number)
  Syllables (accented)
Phonetics Analysis
  Initial consonants
  Final consonants
  Medial consonants
  Consonant digraphs
  Vowels—long
  Vowels—short
  Vowels—digraphs
  Vowels—controlled

Instructional Activity 8

Prescriptive Teaching for Children with Special Needs
Recent changes in policies and procedures for education of handicapped children and youth have resulted in fewer special education settings and more regular education classes for students with mild problems who can profit from regular classroom participation. Such developments accentuate

the need for diagnostic-prescriptive teaching of reading so that teachers can identify where each child is in terms of skills, decide how he or she might learn best, and implement instruction that moves each child progressively closer to attainment of the full level of potential. Special instructional accommodations may have to be made for children with special needs because those needs are not frequently addressed by most reading programs. Although an inclusive treatment of reading for all types of special-needs students is beyond the scope of this book, suggestions for adjusting reading instruction to the needs of some special groups are included here. Other special help can be secured from service personnel in the schools such as the resource teacher, the itinerant teacher with training in special handicaps, and the reading specialist.

The Auditorily Impaired Student

Some special accommodations within the classroom and attention to some special needs can help students with sensory impairment profit from instruction within the regular classroom. Environmental provisions include seating the student near the source of instruction, facing the student and maintaining eye contact during instruction to facilitate the student's ability to use lipreading as a communication aid, alternating periods of oral instruction with other activities that require careful attending with less demanding work, providing a supportive environment that encourages participation by all but, at the same time, indulges the student when she or he wants to remain inconspicuous, and assigning a friend to help with directions. Instructional provisions such as showing the visual form of key words and using other visual aids to reinforce skills and to promote retention of information and, at beginning stages of reading, altering or abandoning phonics instruction for word recognition techniques with a visual base (sight words, context clues, structural analysis), and/or highlighting tactile and kinesthetic features of language may enable the auditorily handicapped student to use visual modes as a means of compensation. When students have progressed in the basic auditory skills that support reading, an analytical approach to phonics instruction can be implemented (Savage and Mooney, 1979).

Because impairment in auditory acuity and auditory perception interfere with the student's total language development, an approach to teaching reading that takes into account the interrelatedness of language skills seems to be most appealing for auditorily impaired students. The usefulness of the language experience approach to teaching reading to deaf and hearing impaired children at both the beginning and intermediate levels was reported by Stauffer (1979).

Children who began with the approach at a preschool level showed growth in oral and reading vocabulary and in complexity of language generated. Although the children seemed to enjoy participation in and communicating about an experience (mostly through hand signs), the teachers noted that for the younger children, better responses were generated if the children dictate individual accounts. At the intermediate-grade levels, the approach involved using both signed and vocalized language for dictation. Teachers at these levels found that once students become familiar with the dictation process, they can accept and "read back" the connecting words (prepositions, articles, conjunctions) supplied by the teacher even though they are absent from the dictation of the hearing impaired child. It seems then that the language experience approach, which stresses active participation in experiences and the use of language (sign, oral, or both) to communicate about those experiences, offers a great boost to the overall language development of such children.

Visually Impaired Students

It is quite likely that the visually impaired child will receive instruction in the regular classroom with special services provided by a resource teacher. Whereas methods used for instructing the partially sighted child are "substantially the same as for normally seeing children" (Hanninen, 1975), there are some special classroom accommodations and some modifications in materials and equipment that must be considered. For example, the student needs a constant physical environment in order to learn his or her way around in the room. Illumination should be adequate, with great efforts to control glare. Since partially sighted students tend to have difficulty with figure-ground contrasts, paper should be matte finished and off-white or buff with black print. Diagrams, pictures, and other visual materials should be clear and uncluttered, perhaps with prominent features outlined in dark felt-tip pens. Visual displays should have sharply contrasting colors.

Some students may require the use of low-vision aids such as distance magnifiers, fixed-focus stand readers, large-type print materials. The American Printing House for the Blind provides such services to the visually handicapped and can be contacted at the following address for a list of special services.

American Printing House for the Blind
1839 Frankfort Avenue
Louisville, Kentucky 40206

As far as reading instruction is concerned, it may be wise to teach to the strengths of the visually impaired, to their other senses that help them compensate. For word recognition, this might mean early focus on phonics instead of sight words. Furthermore, a tactile/kinesthetic method that uses raised print or otherwise textured letters to be touched and traced as an aid to word recognition may prove helpful to the visually handicapped child, whether the problem is visual acuity or visual perception (Savage and Mooney, 1979).

Students with Receptive Language Disorders

A problem with serious implications for learning to read, receptive language disorders interfere with language development at its very foundation—understanding language itself. Students with such disorders have difficulty in attending to what is being said, comprehending what is said to them, learning meanings of words, and forming concepts; they learn from oral presentations unless they are supplemented with visual aids and demonstrations (Savage and Mooney, 1979).

Students who have such a disorder need extensive work in language development, both from the semantic and syntactic perspectives. Since a language experience approach spotlights receptive and expressive language development, it is particularly suitable for children with receptive language problems. Even so, special considerations must be made when using the approach with students with language disorders, as expressed by Mooney and Savage (1979). For instance, the child must be constantly supervised and, therefore, requires large expenditures of teacher time for listening to, recording, and reading what the student dictates. Special attention must be given to sentence structure, with efforts to expand the sentence patterns used by the child.

Bilingual Students and Reading

Students who come to school speaking a native language other than English have particular problems in learning to read English materials. They lack the semantic and syntactic "rules and regulations" for English, even though they may have mastered the code in their native language.

Modified language experience approaches seem to be successful with bilingual children, both those who are initially learning to read (Wiesendanger and Birlem, 1979) and those who are reading far below their ability. Because the approach emphasizes language development through expansion of vocabulary (semantic development) and structure of sentences (syntactic development) in the student's second language, it provides numerous opportunities for extensive oral activities. Steps in the modified approach include the following.

1. Develop a theme by involving the students in a high-interest activity that is relevant to them. Have the students discuss the activity, perhaps even repeating sentences using the teacher's sentences as a model (Wiesendanger and Birlem, 1979).
2. Relate the activity to experiences in the child's personal background. "How is what we have done similar to something you have done?"
3. Compile lists of words generated by students during the discussion. Have students group them into categories.
4. Structure open-ended questions that relate to the theme established. "Suppose that . . . ?", "What would you do if . . . ?"
5. Have students develop a story around the theme and dictate to the teacher for recording. Provide duplicated copies for each child.
6. Select words from the story for mastery as sight words. Provide oppor-

tunities for the students to learn the words by sight (see Chapter 5 for suggestions).

7. Put individual sentences on sentence strips. Have students read sentences and reconstruct the story.
8. After students have three to five sight words that illustrate a pattern, teach the phoneme-grapheme relationships inductively (see Chapter 7 for a plan).

When using textual materials with bilingual students, it is especially important to prepare them to cope with possible trouble spots. This might include discussing specialized vocabulary, focusing attention on words indicating important relationships, and clarifying the meaning of figurative language. Another special technique that may prove helpful for bilingual students who, in most instances, are also minority students, is described next.

Minority Students and Reading

Reading educators advocate that the teacher accept the minority child, his or her culture, speech patterns, and experiences. An adaptation of the directed reading activity (discussed in Chapter 13), for minority children that actually utilizes their experiences to promote reading has yielded positive results in increased comprehension. Developed and tested by Au (1979), the experience-text-relationship method (ETR) utilizes discussion to relate what the student already knows to what will be presented in the textbook. Textual materials are broken into short sequences of one to two pages for reading; comprehension checks on content follow. Short sequences with checks for understanding help clear up any misconceptions that will interfere with cumulative comprehension. In the final step, the teacher focuses on the relationship between the textual content and the experiences that the students have had and the knowledge they now possess.

Questioning strategies may be altered as a means of relating the experiences and linguistic patterns of minority students to traditional materials used for reading instruction. Turner (1979) suggests that questions that focus on comparisons and contrasts between lives of the students and their reading are especially beneficial. Specifically, the altered questioning strategies should target the following.

1. Challenge values found in reading materials that strongly contrast with predominant values in the students' culture.
2. Identify language patterns and words that are rare in the students' culture and provide suitable substitutions or translations.
3. Probe cultural bias reflected in the material.
4. Comparing the motives, feelings, and personality of a story character to those of a cultural hero.

Although there is inconclusive evidence that minority children develop reading skills more successfully through materials that directly relate to their ethnic experiences, common sense suggests that this might be true. Regardless of whether or not multiethnic materials foster better reading skills, it is sensible to incorporate some reading materials that relate specifically to the experiences of minority children as a way to validate the value of their own cultural heritage and to help them maintain a positive self-image.

The Gifted Child and Reading

Although the gifted student can learn to read through any type of approach and some probably learn to read without any formal instruction at all, some instructional adaptations for these students seem warranted if they are to continue accelerating their reading skills. A rapid rate of learning with need for few exposures to the materials is characteristic of gifted learners. Acknowledging this, the teacher should allow these students to read at their own rapid rate, eliminating many activities that call for rereading, and omit activities that are solely for reinforcement, since the students do not need them for an optimal degree of learning. This means that the teacher who relies on a basal reader as the core of the reading program will have to reconsider how to use that program and to modify some of the repetitive phases of a directed reading activity (as described in Chapter 13) to accommodate the gifted student.

An individualized reading program (IRP) may be better suited for the gifted student. In such a program the students are allowed to select their own reading materials and to read them at their individual rates, recording difficult words encountered in the reading (see Chapter 16). An individualized reading program enables teachers to avoid the pitfalls in educating the gifted student, as pointed out by Harris and Sipay (1979): failure to free the gifted student from the review and repetition so necessary for slow learning and average children and the tendency to put the gifted student in nonreading situations such as with a library helper or a peer-tutor during reading instruction, neither of which promotes continued growth in reading.

The individualized approach capitalizes on the usual strengths of the gifted student, wide range of interest in various topics with intensive interests in some topics, ability to proceed through a learning activity at a rapid rate, ability to accept large measures of responsibility for learning, and ability to read extensively. Although not exclusively designed for gifted students, the individualized reading approach does seem uniquely useful in facilitating the reading growth of such students.

ADDITIONAL ENABLING ACTIVITIES

You may want to select at least one additional enabling activity for each objective.

335

1. Read and take notes on at least two of the following sources for each of the objectives indicated in parentheses. Note that all objectives for the chapter cannot be attained through this enabling element.
   (a) Olson, and Dillner, "Diagnostic and Prescriptive Teaching," in 4 (Objectives 2, 3, and 7).
   (b) Burron, and Claybaugh, "Grouping for Instruction," in 1 (Objective 6).
   (c) Ransom, Chapter 7 (Objectives 2 and 7).
   (d) Dauzat, "Informal Diagnosis: The Nucleus of Individualized Reading," in Earle (Objectives 1, 2, and 4).
2. Observe a teacher who uses a diagnostic/prescriptive approach (Objective 8).
3. Attend class session(s) Time _____ Date _____ .
4. An activity of your choice.
5. An activity selected by your instructor.

READING RESOURCES / REFERENCES

1. Au, Kathryn Hu-Pei. "Using the Experience-Text-Relationship Method with Minority Children," *The Reading Teacher* (March 1979), pp. 677–679.
2. Burron, Arnold, and Amos L. Claybaugh. *Basic Concepts in Reading Instruction: A Programmed Approach.* Columbus, Ohio: Charles E. Merrill, 1972.
3. Degler, Lois Sauer, and Victoria J. Risko, "Teaching Reading To Mainstreamed Sensory Impaired Children," *The Reading Teacher* (May 1979), pp. 921–925.
4. Earle, Richard, ed. *Classroom Practice in Reading.* Newark, Del.: International Reading Association, 1977.
5. Guszak, Frank J. *Diagnostic Reading in the Elementary School,* 2nd ed. New York: Harper & Row, 1978.
6. Hanninen, Kenneth A. *Teaching the Visually Handicapped.* Columbus, Ohio: Charles E. Merrill, 1975.
7. López, Sarah Hudelson. "Children's Use of Contextual Clues In Reading Spanish," *The Reading Teacher* (April 1977), pp. 735–740.
8. Olson, Joanne P., and Martha H. Dillner. *Learning to Teach Reading in the Elementary School.* New York: McMillan, 1976.
9. Oñativia, Oscar V., and Mariá Alejandra Reyes Donoso. "Basic Issues in Establishing a Bilingual Method," *The Reading Teacher* (April 1977), pp. 727–734.
10. Ransom, Grayce A. *Preparing to Teach Reading.* Boston: Little, Brown, 1978.
11. Ross, Alan O. *Psychological Aspects of Learning Disabilities and Reading Disorders.* New York: McGraw-Hill, 1976.

12. Savage, John F. and G.F. Mooney. *Teaching Reading to Children with Special Needs.* Boston: Allyn and Bacon, 1979.
13. Stauffer, Russell G. "The Language Experience Approach to Reading Instruction for Deaf and Hearing Impaired Children," *The Reading Teacher* (October 1979), pp. 21–24.
14. Trezise, Robert L. "What About A Reading Program for the Gifted?", *The Reading Teacher* (April 1978). pp. 742–747.
15. Turner, Thomas N. "Questioning Techniques: Probing for Greater Meaning," *Teaching Reading,* Alexander, J. Estill, general editor. Boston: Little, Brown, 1979, pp. 149–171.
16. Wisendanger, Katherine Davis, and Ellen Davis Birlem. "Adapting Language Experience to Reading for Bilingual Pupils," *The Reading Teacher* (March 1979), pp. 671–673.

Appendixes

Appendix A
Preassessments and Keys for Chapters

APPENDIX A-1

PREASSESSMENT: Chapter 1

1. Which of the following is least important in an adequate definition of reading?
   (a) Communicating with the author.
   (b) Pronouncing words.
   (c) Converting print into meaning.
   (d) Understanding meaning intended.

2. In which situation is reading taking place?
   (a) Bill orally read the recipe as his mother made a pie. He could not gather the ingredients, however, because he did not know what cream of tartar, cinnamon, nutmeg, and confectioner's sugar were.
   (b) Sandi read a paragraph to the class. When asked to tell about it in her own words, she could only think of a few bits and pieces.
   (c) Jan read Chapter 6 of a social studies text to prepare for a test. After she read, she correctly answered a series of questions.
   (d) Her dad reads the same story to Mollie each night. Last night, the 4-year-old decided to read it herself. She said every word correctly, even if they did not match the page.

3. For each situation in question 2, justify your response.

   (a) _____

   (b) _____

   (c) _____

   (d) _____

4. One of the first steps in the reading process is:
   (a) The eye reacts to the printed stimuli.
   (b) The reader reacts to the message.
   (c) The reader makes correspondencies between the graphic stimulus and its oral counterpart.
   (d) The reader converts words into meaning.

5. Sequence the steps in the reading process given in question 4 as they occur in the act of reading.

   (a) _____

   (b) _____

   (c) _____

   (d) _____

6. The mechanical process of reading refers to:
   (a) Making matches between written symbols and the sounds they represent.
   (b) Responding emotionally to the printed material.
   (c) Gathering meaning from individual words.
   (d) Moving the eyes across the page in a predetermined order.

7. Which of the following factors have limited influence on the development of reading ability?
   (a) Vision.
   (b) Auditory acuity.
   (c) Chronological age.
   (d) Self-concept.

8. The child who is insensitive to differences in the pronounced words *rag* and *rig* may lack skill in:
   (a) Auditory acuity.
   (b) Visual discrimination.
   (c) Language development.
   (d) Auditory discrimination.

9. Place these language skills in the sequence in which they normally develop.

   (a) Reading _____ .

   (b) Speaking _____ .

   (c) Writing _____ .

   (d) Listening _____ .

10. Which statement best describes the relationship of reading with other language skills?
    (a) Development of reading ability is strongly influenced by the person's primary language system.
    (b) Development of reading ability is independent of the other language aspects.
    (c) The child's secondary language system forms the base for development of reading skills.
    (d) All of these.

KEY: Chapter 1

1. b (Objective 1).
2. c (Objective 1).
3. (Objective 1).
   a Could not get meaning from words, was calling words only.
   b read orally, pronounced words but did not get meaning.
   c read for meaning and was able to answer questions correctly.
   d was not getting meaning from page, just reciting words recalled from hearing story read—print was not necessarily the stimuli.
4. a (Objective 2).
5. (Objective 2).
   (a) a.
   (b) c.
   (c) d.
   (d) b.
6. d (Objective 2).
7. d (Objective 3).
8. d (Objective 3).
9. (Objective 3).
   (a) 4.
   (b) 2.
   (c) 1.
   (d) 3.
10. a (Objective 3).

APPENDIX A-2

PREASSESSMENT: Chapter 2

Directions. Read each statement carefully, then decide if it is true or false. Write T or F in the blank.

1. If a child is physically mature, he is ready for beginning instruction.
   _____F_____

2. If Jane and Sue have the same mental age and Jane is ready to begin reading, then Sue is also. _____F_____

3. It is desirable for a pupil to have a mental age of at least six years when beginning reading instruction. _____T_____

4. When a child turns 6 years old, she should already have started, or should start now, a program of formal reading instruction.
   _____F_____

5. It is generally believed that for a child's efforts at learning to be successful, physiological needs must be met. _____T_____

6. Every child should have a complete physical examination before entering school. _____T_____

7. The child's attitude toward his teacher will not affect his learning.
   _____F_____

8. Most first graders are eager to start reading. _____T_____

9. Reading is only as effective as the experiences brought to the printed page. _____T_____

10. Children from impoverished backgrounds tend to have language that mismatches that of textbooks. _____T_____

11. It is not necessary to administer a test for visual acuity to young children unless a problem is suspected. _____F_____

12. The audiometer is a reliable device for measuring auditory acuity.
    _____T_____

13. Complaints of buzzing in the head may indicate that a child has a hearing problem. _____T_____

14. When helping a child learn to discriminate auditorily, it is better to use nonsense words than words she is familiar with. _____T_____

15. Following directions involves the skill of listening comprehension.
    _____T_____

16. The left-to-right eye movement used in reading comes naturally for children. _____F_____

17. The Keystone Telebinocular is a device that can check both nearsightedness and farsightedness. _____T_____

18. Squirming about may be a sign of visual disability. _____T_____

19. The whisper test is a good method for detecting minor hearing difficulties. _____T_____

20. Memory is involved in listening comprehension. _____T_____

KEY: Chapter 2

1. F (Not necessarily, other factors involved) (Objective 1).
2. F (Mental age not sole determiner, individual differences exist) (Objective 1).
3. T (desirable, but not essential) (Objective 1).
4. F (age not sole determiner) (Objective 1).
5. T (Objective 1).
6. T (Objective 1).
7. F (his attitude toward self, teacher, and the subject all affect the child's learning) (Objective 1).
8. T (Objective 1).
9. T (Objective 1).
10. T (Objective 1).
11. F (a reliable screening device should be administered that can detect potential factors that influence reading) (Objective 2).
12. T (Objective 2).
13. T (this may be temporary and coincide with colds) (Objective 2).
14. T (Objective 2).
15. T (Objective 2).
16. F (this is a learned behavior) (Objective 2).
17. T (Objective 2).
18. T (or other physical factors) (Objective 2).
19. T (Objective 2).
20. T (Objective 2).

APPENDIX A-3

PREASSESSMENT: Chapter 3

1. Knowledge.

    (a) Read each statement carefully, then decide if it is true or false.

        (1) To insure readiness for reading instruction, allow time for mental maturation. _____

        (2) Discussing good nutrition with young children is beyond their level of experience and should be avoided. _____

        (3) A definite time for the child to go to the bathroom should be strictly adhered to. _____

        (4) Special jobs for the child only teach him to dislike work.

        _____

        (5) Reading readiness is a maturational phenomenon; therefore readiness skills cannot be taught. _____

    (b) Match the factor with a procedure for fostering readiness in that area.

        (1) Intellectual development

        (2) Physical condition

        (3) Social and emotional development

        (4) Experiential background

        (a) Free play with other children

        (b) Handling books properly

        (c) General readiness activities, with little emphasis on reading

        (d) Allowing frequent rest periods

        (e) Field trips

    (c) Match the skill with a procedure for fostering readiness in that area.

        (1) Visual discrimination

        (2) Auditory discrimination

        (3) Listening comprehension

        (4) Left-to-right orientation

        (5) Color discrimination

        (a) Using crayons

        (b) Recognizing rhymes

        (c) Writing

        (d) Assembling puzzles

        (e) Recalling details of a story orally to the children

2. Performance.

    (a) Describe an activity to develop visual discrimination. _____

    _____

    (b) List those things needed in a plan to teach a reading readiness skill.

    _____

(c) Select one of the skills listed in part 2. Using the essential parts of a plan, develop a plan to teach that skill. Implement the plan in a real or simulated setting.

KEY: Chapter 3

1. Knowledge.
   (a) (Objective 1).
       (1) T.
       (2) F.
       (3) F.
       (4) F.
       (5) F.
   (b) (1) c.
       (2) d.
       (3) b, a.
       (4) e.
   (c) (Objective 2).
       (1) d.
       (2) b.
       (3) e.
       (4) c.
       (5) a.
2. Performance.
   Submit these to your instructor for evaluation.
   (a) (Objective 3).
   (b) (Objective 3).
   (c) (Objective 4).

APPENDIX A-4

PREASSESSMENT: Chapter 4

Your performance on the pretest will indicate to you the objectives that need further attention. You can become more competent in those areas by completing at least one activity under the appropriate objective.

1. What are the five broad categories of word recognition skills? _____
_____

2. What is meant by the term *sight word?* Give two meanings. _____
_____
_____

3. What are some sources of words to include in a sight vocabulary? _____
_____
_____

4. Identify the types of context clues. _____
_____
_____

5. What are the elements (or subskills) involved in structural analysis?
_____

6. What are the subskills involved in the use of the dictionary? _____
_____
_____

KEY: Chapter 4

1. Sight words, context clues, structural analysis, use of the dictionary, and phonics (Objective 1).
2. Words recognized immediately on sight; specific words categorized in lists and those designated to be sight words in the basal text list (Objective 2).
3. Word lists: Dolch, Kuĉera-Francis, Gates' list, lists from basal texts (Objective 3).
4. Verbal context clues, picture clues (Objective 4).
5. Inflectional endings, compound words, contractions, prefixes, suffixes, base words (or root words) (Objective 5).

6. Alphabetization, use of guide words, use of diacritical markings, pronunciation guide, selection of meanings to fit a given context (Objective 6).

APPENDIX A-5

PREASSESSMENT: Chapter 5

1. Knowledge.
    (a) Which of the following should form the base for word analysis instruction?
        (1) Phonics.
        (2) Structural analysis.
        (3) Dictionary use.
        (4) Sight words.
    (b) In determining the sequence for introduction of word recognition skills:
        (1) Grade level is the most reliable guide.
        (2) Consideration should be given to student achievement levels.
        (3) Consideration should be given to arranging the skills from simple to complex.
        (4) The number of syllables in the words should be a prime consideration.
    (c) The student unlocks the word *implant* by identifying the known sight word *plant* and a known prefix. The student is demonstrating:
        (1) A phonics skill.
        (2) A context clue skill.
        (3) A structural analysis skill.
        (4) A sight word skill.
    (d) In teaching context clues:
        (1) Visual context skills should be developed before verbal context skills.
        (2) Visual context and verbal context skills should be developed simultaneously.
        (3) Visual context skills should be taught after verbal skills.
        (4) Visual context clues have no place in the reading program.
    (e) In teaching the use of the dictionary, the teacher should:
        (1) Put lists of words for students to look up on the board.
        (2) Give words to be looked up in context.
        (3) First teach rules for dividing words into syllables.
        (4) All of these.
2. Performance.
    (a) Prepare a plan for teaching a structural analysis skill that contains the five essential steps.
    (b) Name at least three criteria that should be met in teaching word recognition skills.
    (c) List criteria that should be used to critique the teaching of a word recognition skill.

KEY: Chapter 5

1. Knowledge.
   (a) 4 (Objective 1).
   (b) 3 (Objective 1).
   (c) 3 (Objective 2).
   (d) 2 (Objective 2).
   (e) 2 (Objective 2).
2. Performance.
   Submit this section to your instructor for evaluation.
   (a) (Objective 3).
   (b) (Objective 4).
   (c) (Objective 5).

APPENDIX A-6

PREASSESSMENT: Chapter 6

This preassessment will serve as a diagnostic instrument whereby your instructor may determine your areas of weakness and strengths in the content of phonics.

An overall score on the instrument has little meaning in accomplishing the diagnostic purposes. Therefore your score in each item will be assessed to determine whether or not you should pursue supplementary learning activities relative to the item.

Use your preassessment as a study guide. You may want to retake the test to determine your own readiness for taking the post assessment.

1. A _____ is a unit of sound in spoken words.

2. A _____ is a graphic unit.

3. Circle the consonant digraphs in the following words.

bush	shelves	laugh
chateau	whistle	goat
ringing	Thursday	beautiful
elephant	beat	church

4. Write a definition of a consonant digraph. _____

5. Label each of the underlined graphemes according to appropriate phonetic terms and/or its function in the word.

(a) shirt _____   (k) head _____

(b) toil _____   (l) also _____

(c) stripe _____   (m) car _____

(d) cluster _____   (n) fir _____

(e) boy _____   (o) saw _____

(f) grape _____   (p) where _____

(g) boat _____   (q) were _____

(h) day _____   (r) dwell _____

(i) yellow _____   (s) grow _____

(j) jelly _____   (t) pitcher _____

6. Write a definition of a consonant blend. _____

   _____

7. Underline the vowel digraphs in the following words.
   maybe   easy

foot	great
could	goat
ceiling	window
vein	donkey

8. Circle the diphthongs in the following words.

vowel	grow	soybean
loud	growl	choice
rejoice	hoist	proud

9. Write a definition of a diphthong. _____

_____

10. Circle the short vowels in the listed words. Use initial position only in multisyllabic words.

eager	operative	ambulance
order	indignant	clock
rich	rigorous	right
ignore	attitude	orchard
upset	rumble	
	etch	

11. Circle the words that contain the soft sound of *g*.

gypsy	girl	gamble
age	generation	wagon
guest	giraffe	give

12. Circle the words that contain the soft sound of *c*.

citadel	cease	cycle
cyst	appreciate	common
cabbage	incisors	sincere
character	cuticle	

13. Give the conditions under which *c* and *g* have a soft sound. _____

_____

14. Circle the silent consonants in the following words.

fight	wreath	talk	island
catch	climb	dumb	calm
debt	itch	doubt	gnat
psychology	knife	knight	wrong
ghost	walk	aisle	pneumatic
	comb		

15. (a) Give the conditions under which *y* functions as a consonant.

_____

_____

_____

(b) Give an example of *y* as a consonant. _____

(c) Give at least three conditions under which *y* functions as a vowel.

_____

(d) Give an example of *y* as a vowel. _____

16. (a) Give the conditions under which *w* functions as a consonant. _____

_____

(b) Give an example of *w* as a consonant. _____

_____

(c) Give the conditions under which *w* functions as a vowel. _____

_____

(d) Give an example of *w* as a vowel. _____

17. If *aip* were a word:

(a) How would the *a* sound? _____

(b) How would the *i* sound? _____

(c) State the generalization that applies. _____

18. If *tatle* were a word:

(a) Where would you divide it into syllables? _____

(b) State the reason for the division. _____

(c) How would the *a* sound? _____

(d) State the generalization which applies. _____

19. If *motlid* were a word:

(a) Where would you divide it into syllables? _____

(b) State the reason for dividing it this way. _____

_____

(c) How would the *o* sound? _____

(d) State the generalization that applies. _____

_____

20. If *ame* were a word:

(a) How would the *a* sound? _____

(b) How would the *e* sound? _____

(c) Why would the vowels sound this way? _____

_____

21. If *oazzle* were a word:

(a) Where would you divide it into syllables? _____

_____

(b) Why would you divide it this way? _____

_____

(c) How would the *o* sound? _____

(d) How would the *a* sound? _____

(e) State the generalization that applies. _____

_____

22. (a) Divide *symbol* into syllables. _____

(b) Why is it divided this way? _____

(c) How does the *y* sound? _____

(d) Why does the *y* make this sound? _____

_____

(e) What sound does the *o* make? _____

_____

(f) Why does the *o* make this sound? _____

_____

KEY: Chapter 6

1. phoneme

2. grapheme
3. bu(sh)   (sh)elves   lau(gh) (*f* sound)
   (ch)ateau (*sh* sound) w(h)istle   goat
   ri(ng)i(ng)   (Th)ursday   beautiful
   el(eph)ant (*f* sound) beat   (ch)ur(ch)
4. A consonant digraph is a two-consonant letter combination that produces one that is different from the sound represented by either letter
   in isolation.
5. (a) shirt—consonant digraph.
   (b) toil—diphthong.
   (c) stripe—three-letter consonant blend.
   (d) cluster—two-letter consonant blend.
   (e) boy—diphthong.
   (f) grape—two-letter consonant blend.
   (g) boat—long vowel digraph.
   (h) day—long vowel digraph.
   (i) yellow—y as a consonant.
   (j) jelly—y as a vowel (ĭ, or ē sound).
   (k) head—short vowel digraph.
   (l) also—special a sound.
   (m) car—r-controlled vowel.
   (n) fir—r-controlled vowel.
   (o) saw—special a sound.
   (p) where—consonant digraph.
   (q) were—w as a consonant.
   (r) dwell—two-letter consonant blend.
   (s) grow—w as part of vowel digraph.
   (t) pitcher—consonant digraph.
6. A consonant blend is a two- or three-consonant letter combination in
   which the sounds merge but are still distinguishable.
7. maybe   easy
   foot (oo sound)   great
   could (o͝o sound)   boat
   ceiling   window
   vein   donkey
8. vowel   grow (ow is digraph here)   soybean
   loud   growl   choice
   rejoice   hoist   proud
9. A diphthong is a two-vowel letter combination in which the sounds
   merge but are still distinguishable.
10. eager (long e)   operative   etch
    order (r-controlled)   indignant   ambulance
    rich   rigorous   clock
    ignore   attitude   right (long ī)
    upset   rumble   orchard (r-controlled)

11. (gypsy)   girl (hard *g*)   gamble (hard *g*)
    (age)   (generation)   wagon (hard *g*)
    guest (hard *g*)   (giraffe)   give (hard *g*)

12. Soft *c*
    (citadel)   (cease)   (cycle) (both hard and
    (cyst)   appreciate (sh sound) soft)
    cabbage (hard c)   (incisors)   common (hard)
    character (hard c) cuticle (both hard)   (sincere)

13. *c* and *g* have their soft sound when they are followed by *e, i, y.*

14. fight   wreath   talk   island
    catch   climb   dumb   calm
    debt   itch   doubt   gnat
    psychology   knife   knight   wrong
    ghost   walk   aisle   pneumatic
                   comb

15. (a) *y* is a consonant when it occurs in initial position in a syllable or
        word.
    (b) yes, yell, yarn, young, etc.
    (c) *y* is a vowel when it (1) occurs at the end of a word or syllable; (2)
        occurs midsyllable; (3) occurs with another vowel as part of a vowel
        digraph; (4) occurs as part of a diphthong.
    (d) (1) cry, baby; (2) lynx; (3) play; (4) toy.

16. (a) *w* is a consonant when it occurs at the beginning or a word or
        syllable.
    (b) wish, wear, want, were, etc.
    (c) *W* is a vowel when it (1) occurs as the second letter of a vowel
        digraph; (2)occurs as the second letter of a diphthong.
    (d) (1) know, knew, few, etc.
        (2) crowd, how, now, etc.

17. (a) Long a—ā.
    (b) Silent—aɪ.
    (c) When two vowels occur side by side in a syllable, the first is usually
        long and the second is silent.

18. (a) ta tle.
    (b) When a word ends in *le,* the *le* plus the preceding consonant form
        the final syllable.
    (c) Long *a.*
    (d) This is an open syllable and the vowel sound in an open syllable is
        generally long—*table.*

19. (a) mot lid.
    (b) When two consonants are between two vowels, divide the word be-
        tween the two consonants—*vccv.*
    (c) short *o.*
    (d) The *o* occurs in a closed syllable and the vowel sound in closed
        syllables is usually short.

20. (a) Long $\bar{a}$.
    (b) Silent e.
    (c) When a word ends in silent e, the preceding vowel sound is generally *long.*—came, name.
21. (a) oaz zle.
    (b) When the word ends in *le,* the preceding consonant plus *le* form the final syllable.
    (c) Long o.
    (d) Silent a.
    (e) When two vowels occur side by side in the same syllable, the first is usually long and the second silent.
22. (a) sym bol.
    (b) When a word has two consonants coming between two vowels, the syllabic division is usually between the two consonants.
    (c) Short i.
    (d) Because it is the only vowel in the closed syllable.
    (e) The schwa (ə) sound.
    (f) Because it occurs in an unaccented syllable.

APPENDIX A-7

PREASSESSMENT: Chapter 7

1. Knowledge.
    (a) Which of the following represents the attitude of most authorities about sequence of phonics skills?
        (1) The order of presentation is immaterial.
        (2) The most logical sequence is alphabetical order.
        (3) The sounds represented by single consonants in initial position should be taught first.
        (4) The sounds of the long (glided) vowels should be taught first.
    (b) One useful source for determining the order for teaching skills is:
        (1) The table of contents for a basal reader.
        (2) The scope and sequence chart that accompanies the basal reader series.
        (3) Commercially prepared phonics charts.
        (4) The index of any basal reader.
    (c) Which of the following statements reflects research findings about phonic principles?
        (1) Instructional materials contain only the phonic generalizations of greatest use to children.
        (2) Some phonic generalizations frequently taught to children are useless.
        (3) Phonic generalizations commonly taught have at least 90 percent utility.
        (4) Phonics rules should not be taught in elementary grades.
    (d) The synthetic phonics method refers to:
        (1) The technique of teaching letter sound-symbol relationships and combining them into words.
        (2) The predominant technique for teaching phonics today.
        (3) The process of teaching little words in big words.
        (4) The technique of presenting whole words and breaking them into component sounds.
    (e) One advantage of an analytic approach to teaching phonics is that:
        (1) The repetitive drills result in fast learning.
        (2) It avoids distortion of sounds.
        (3) It helps children build words from isolated sounds.
        (4) It enables children to learn phonics so completely that instruction in other word recognition techniques is unnecessary.
    (f) One advantage of an inductive approach to phonics instruction is that:
        (1) The teacher states the phonic principle for the child.
        (2) It focuses on memorization of rules.

(3) It approximates what is required of the pupil in an actual reading situation.

(4) It enables the child to build words from isolated sounds.

(g) Which of the following is not a step in the recommended procedure for teaching phonics?

(1) Auditory discrimination.

(2) Blending sound on known sight words.

(3) Visual discrimination.

(4) Production of the key sound(s) in isolation.

2. Performance.

(a) Select a phonic element or generalization and design an inductive lesson for teaching it. Do this on a separate page.

(b) Using the phonic element you selected, design a reinforcement activity for it. The activity can be either inductive or deductive. Do this on a separate page.

(c) Teach the lesson you prepared in a setting identified by your instructor.

KEY: Chapter 7

1. Knowledge.
   (a) 3 (Obj. 1)
   (b) 2 (Obj. 1)
   (c) 2 (Obj. 2)
   (d) 1 (Obj. 3)
   (e) 2 (Obj. 3)
   (f) 3 (Obj. 3)
   (g) 4 (Obj. 4)
2. Performance.
   Submit this section for evaluation by your instructor. (a)–(c) (Objective 4).

APPENDIX A-8

PREASSESSMENT: Chapter 8

1. Knowledge.
   (a) The basic units for comprehension include:
      (1) Word meaning, phrase meaning, syllable meaning.
      (2) Word meaning, phrase meaning, paragraph structure.
      (3) Phrase meaning, sentence meaning, paragraph meaning.
      (4) Word meaning, word pronunciation, sentence meaning.
   (b) Understanding phrases involves:
      (1) Comprehension of the meanings of each component word.
      (2) Comprehension of the component words and their relationships to each other.
      (3) Focusing on the explicit meaning of the individual words.
      (4) Application of structural analysis techniques to word meanings.
   (c) Sentences written in passive voice tend to be:
      (1) Useful in teaching comprehension to young children.
      (2) Easier for children to understand than other structures.
      (3) Good exercises for teaching the importance of word order to sentence meaning.
      (4) Difficult to comprehend for young children who focus on word order.
   (d) Which level of comprehension is the least complex?
      (1) Critical level.
      (2) Literal level.
      (3) Inferential level.
      (4) Vocabulary level.
   (e) Determining the correctness or potential value of written material corresponds to comprehension at the:
      (1) Literal level.
      (2) Inferential level.
      (3) Critical level.
      (4) Vocabulary level.
   (f) Determining implied meanings of written material corresponds to comprehension at the:
      (1) Literal level.
      (2) Inferential level.
      (3) Critical level.
      (4) Vocabulary level.
   (g) Receiving surface messages from written material corresponds to understanding at the:
      (1) Literal level.
      (2) Inferential level.

(3) Critical level.

(4) Vocabulary level.

(h) Identifying facts and details from a passage corresponds to understanding at the:

(1) Literal level.

(2) Inferential level.

(3) Critical level.

(4) Vocabulary level.

(i) Written signals such as *finally, while, next,* and *soon* cue:

(1) A main idea.

(2) A written direction.

(3) An implied meaning.

(4) A sequence.

(j) The student who can predict a logical outcome to a passage is demonstrating:

(1) A literal comprehension skill.

(2) A vocabulary skill.

(3) Skill in understanding implied meanings.

(4) A critical comprehension skill.

2. Performance.

This portion deals with identifying comprehension skill from the questions used. The questions are about the story of the "Three Little Pigs." Read each question and decide the level of comprehension and the comprehension skill that one must have in order to answer the questions.

(a) What did the first pig build his house of?

Level _____ Skill _____

(b) Could this story really have happened? Why?

Level _____ Skill _____

(c) Do you think the third pig cared about his brothers? Why?

Level _____ Skill _____

(d) What happened just after the wolf called, "Little pig, little pig, let me come in."

Level _____ Skill _____

(e) Why do you think the author used the same sequence of the wolf calling to the pigs, the pigs giving the same reply, and the wolf making his threat?

Level _____ Skill _____

KEY: Chapter 8

1. Knowledge.

(a) 3 (Objective 1).

(b) 2 (Objective 1).
(c) 4 (Objective 1).
(d) 4 (Objective 2).
(e) 3 (Objective 2).
(f) 2 (Objective 2).
(g) 1 (Objective 3).
(h) 1 (Objective 3).
(i) 4 (Objective 3).
(j) 4 (Objective 3).
2. Performance (Objective 4).
(a) Literal, facts/details.
(b) Critical, distinguishing fact from fiction.
(c) Critical, drawing conclusion, making a judgment.
(d) Literal, sequence.
(e) Critical, author's mood, tone, purpose.

APPENDIX A-9

PREASSESSMENT: Chapter 9

1. Knowledge. Multiple choice: Circle your response.
   (a) Comprehension questions serve which two main purposes?
      (1) To stimulate understanding and to establish a purpose for reading.
      (2) To measure understanding and to identify students with deficient comprehension ability.
      (3) To establish purposes for reading and to identify students with deficiencies in comprehension ability.
      (4) To check on understanding and to help the reader retain information.
   (b) Prereading questions serve to:
      (1) Help the reader form a purpose for reading and match a reading style with his or her purposes.
      (2) Measure the depth of the reader's understanding.
      (3) Stimulate literal comprehension.
      (4) Check on reader's understanding of the reading materials.
   (c) When using preread questions, the teacher should:
      (1) Match them to the level of post reading questions asked.
      (2) Be sure to require critical comprehension ability.
      (3) Insist that the reader read the material slowly and carefully.
      (4) Assign only a short reading passage.
   (d) When preparing comprehension questions, the teacher should:
      (1) Structure true/false questions.
      (2) Structure questions that measure the student's background information.
      (3) Keep questions brief and to the point.
      (4) Avoid questions that require evaluation on the part of the reader.
   (e) When asking comprehension questions, the teacher should:
      (1) Let the first child that raises his or her hand respond.
      (2) Name a child to answer before asking the question.
      (3) Identify an incorrect response and reject it.
      (4) Allow students time to think about answers.
   (f) When teaching comprehension skills, the teacher should:
      (1) Select materials of interest to the child.
      (2) Have materials at the child's independent reading level.
      (3) Use difficult materials so that the reader will be challenged.
      (4) Insist that each child attempt to answer all the comprehension questions.
2. Performance.
   (a) Use the following passage to structure comprehension questions that relate to the skill identified.

367

The unseasonably warm air hung heavy and still about the town, creating discomfort for the people. A feeling that something was about to happen shrouded the countenance of even the most sturdy inhabitant. At 2:00 AM house lights could be seen throughout the town as the restless people yielded to their insomnia. Only the children, devoid of the sense of danger so obvious to the seasoned adult, slept.

At 2:05 AM the stark silence was broken by a distant rumbling. Heartbeats quickened and spines tingled as the rumble magnified to the sound of a runaway locomotive thundering its way toward the town. The people knew what their eyes could not confirm in the dense blackness. Their town lay in the path of inevitable destruction. A blood-thirsty twister was winding their way.

(1) Fact or detail. _____

_____

(2) Main idea. _____

_____

(3) Cause-and-effect relationship. _____

_____

(4) Predicting outcome. _____

_____

(5) Comparison and contrast. _____

_____

(b) Choose one of the skills named and, on a separate sheet, prepare a lesson plan for teaching the skill that contains the critical elements.

(c) Present the lesson in a real or simulated setting while being observed and rated by the instructor.

KEY: Chapter 9

1. Knowledge.
   (a) 1 (Objective 1).
   (b) 1 (Objective 1).
   (c) 1 (Objective 1).
   (d) 3 (Objective 1).
   (e) 4 (Objective 4).
   (f) 1 (Objective 4).
2. Performance.
   Submit these items to your instructor for evaluation.
   (a) (Objective 2).
   (b) (Objective 3).
   (c) (Objective 4).

APPENDIX A-10

PREASSESSMENT: Chapter 10

1. In scanning, the reader:
   (a) Quickly reads the most important words to get the main idea.
   (b) Quickly moves the eyes in a vertical pattern to isolate key words.
   (c) Quickly summarizes what the material is about.
   (d) None of these.
2. In searching an index to find where a topic is discussed in a book, the reader would most appropriately:
   (a) Scan.
   (b) Skim.
   (c) Use the SQ3R method.
   (d) Read every word.
3. Outlining is one type of:
   (a) Organizational skill.
   (b) Locational skill.
   (c) Specialized comprehension skill.
   (d) All of these.
4. An alphabetical listing of special words and their meanings found in a book is:
   (a) An index.
   (b) An appendix.
   (c) A glossary.
   (d) A contents page.
5. A source giving daily astronomical data is:
   (a) An index.
   (b) An atlas.
   (c) A card catalog.
   (d) An almanac.
6. Which of the following is not a study technique?
   (a) SSSR.
   (b) SQ3R.
   (c) PQRST.
   (d) OK4R.
7. All study techniques have in common:
   (a) The survey.
   (b) The comprehension check.
   (c) The reading.
   (d) All of these.
8. A student's reading rate should:
   (a) Be as rapid as possible.

        (b) Vary according to purpose.

        (c) Be accelerated by mechanical devices.

        (d) None of these.

9. Reading various types of graphs is:

        (a) A skill exclusive to reading textbooks.

        (b) Important only in mathematics.

        (c) A specialized study skill.

        (d) Inappropriate for instruction in elementary grades.

10. Locational skills involve:

        (a) Use of SQ3R.

        (b) Use of outlining.

        (c) Learning to summarize.

        (d) Use of encyclopedia.

KEY: Chapter 10

1. b
2. a
3. a
4. c
5. d
6. a
7. d
8. b
9. c
10. d

APPENDIX A-11

PREASSESSMENT: Chapter 11

1. Performance.
    (a) Design a plan for teaching an outlining skill. Include both introductory and reinforcement activities. The plan should include elements of a lesson design.
    (b) Implement the plan in a real or simulated setting.
    (c) Observe as a peer teaches a work-study skill. Critique according to criteria in Checklist C-3 and C-4.

KEY: Chapter 11

1. Performance.
    Submit your work for instructor evaluation.
    (a) (Objective 1).
    (b) (Objective 2).
    (c) (Objective 3).

APPENDIX A-12

PREASSESSMENT: Chapter 12

1. The predominant approach for teaching reading in America is:
   (a) The language experience approach.
   (b) The individualized reading approach.
   (c) The diagnostic-prescriptive approach.
   (d) The basal reading approach.
2. A basal reader series consists of:
   (a) Graded reading textbooks of increasing difficulty with accompanying workbooks.
   (b) Consumable worktexts containing stories at increasing levels of difficulty.
   (c) A number of paperbound books for prereading lessons.
   (d) A number of reading books of increasing difficulty that contain only phonetically regular words.
3. One feature frequently cited as a weakness of basal reader programs is:
   (a) The teacher's guide.
   (b) The controlled vocabulary and controlled language complexity.
   (c) The authorship of the programs.
   (d) The evaluation component of the programs.
4. In the basal reading approach:
   (a) Grouping for instruction is irrelevant.
   (b) Basic grouping is done to match reading level to book level.
   (c) Flexible grouping is impossible.
   (d) Grouping for skills instruction is unnecessary.
5. The main lesson format for the basal approach consists of:
   (a) Diagnosis and prescription based on needs.
   (b) Oral reading of the selection paragraph by paragraph.
   (c) Assignment of workbook lessons to reinforce skills.
   (d) The directed reading activity.
6. The teacher who is introducing new vocabulary to the students before they read is likely to be:
   (a) Teaching an individualized reading lesson.
   (b) Following the steps of a DRA.
   (c) Violating the intent of the basal reading approach.
   (d) Using a language experience approach.

KEY: Chapter 12

1. d (Objective 1).
2. a (Objective 1).
3. b (Objective 2).
4. b (Objective 3).
5. d (Objective 4).
6. b (Objective 4).

APPENDIX A-13

PREASSESSMENT: Chapter 13

1. Knowledge.
    (a) Which of the following is not a major activity in a directed reading activity?
        (1) Introducing new words in context.
        (2) Setting purposes for reading.
        (3) Classifying word recognition techniques.
        (4) Providing guided practice.
    (b) Which of the following is not a teaching task in a DRA?
        (1) Stimulating interest in the selection.
        (2) Reading the selection to the students.
        (3) Introducing new reading skills.
        (4) Asking comprehension questions.
    (c) Which of the following is the first activity in a DRA?
        (1) Presenting new words to the students.
        (2) Silent reading of the selection.
        (3) Helping children verbalize experiences related to the topic.
        (4) Establishing purposes for silent reading.
    (d) Sequence the following activities as they should occur in a directed reading activity.

        (1) Building readiness. _____

        (2) Rereading. _____

        (3) Skill development. _____

        (4) Follow-up or guided practice. _____

        (5) Silent reading. _____

        (6) Independent practice. _____

        (7) Comprehension check. _____
    (e) Which of the following steps does not apply to content area reading?
        (1) Building readiness.
        (2) Silent reading.
        (3) Comprehension check.
        (4) Skill development.
    (f) Using the DRA approach in the content fields:
        (1) Is unjustifiable in terms of time.
        (2) Prepares the students for academic independence.
        (3) Is appropriate only in the science and social studies areas.
        (4) Prevents giving reading as a homework activity.

2. Performance.
   (a) Select a passage. Prepare a plan for teaching that passage that includes the essential steps in a directed reading activity.
   (b) Implement the plan in a real or simulated setting while being observed.
   (c) Observe as another person implements a DRA. Critique according to Checklist C-6.

KEY: Chapter 13

1. Knowledge.
   (a) 3 (Objective 1).
   (b) 2 (Objective 1).
   (c) 3 (Objective 2).
   (d) (Objective 2).
      (1) 1.
      (2) 4.
      (3) 5.
      (4) 6.
      (5) 2.
      (6) 7.
      (7) 3.
   (e) 4 (Objective 4).
   (f) 2 (Objective 4).
2. Performance.
   Submit this section to your instructor for evaluation.
   (a) (Objective 3).
   (b) (Objective 5).
   (c) (Objective 6).

APPENDIX A-14

PREASSESSMENT: Chapter 14

1. Knowledge.
   (a) Which of the following is a true statement about oral and silent reading?
      (1) Both require identical reading skills.
      (2) The rate differential between oral and silent reading is in favor of oral reading.
      (3) As a practice, instruction in oral reading should predominate.
      (4) Generally, the oral reader engages in more and longer fixations than the silent reader.
   (b) Which of the following is not a characteristic of oral reading?
      (1) Requires focus on association of meaning with print instead of association of sound with print.
      (2) Requires attention to careful enunciation.
      (3) Requires use of the voice to reflect passage action or tone.
      (4) Requires attention to voice inflection to correspond to punctuation.
   (c) Which of the following statements concerning oral and silent reading is correct?
      (1) The skills involved in proficiency in one transfer to proficiency in the other.
      (2) Practice in silent reading will result in improvement in oral reading.
      (3) Practice in oral reading will result in improvement in silent reading.
      (4) Skills involved in proficiency in one may interfere with proficiency in the other.
   (d) Having one child read orally while others follow along, reading silently, is:
      (1) Viewed as a poor instructional practice.
      (2) A good practice in improving listening skills.
      (3) An educationally sound instructional procedure.
      (4) Rewarding for both sets of readers.
   (e) The greatest proportion of instructional time for oral reading is justified:
      (1) At intermediate reading levels.
      (2) At beginning stages of reading development.
      (3) When reading in the content fields.
      (4) At upper grade levels.
   (f) Which of the following is a functional situation for oral reading?
      (1) When one student orally reads from a selection as others read along silently.

(2) When each child orally reads a paragraph from the text in turn.
(3) When children interpret poetry through oral reading.
(4) When all reading instruction is devoted to oral reading.
(g) Which of the following interfere with proficiency in oral reading?
(1) Small sight vocabulary.
(2) Finger pointing.
(3) Word-by-word reading.
(4) All of these.
2. Performance.
Choose a short passage. Orally read it while being rated by your instructor according to Checklist C-7.

KEY: Chapter 14

1. Knowledge.
(a) 4 (Objective 1).
(b) 1 (Objective 1).
(c) 4 (Objective 2).
(d) 1 (Objective 2).
(e) 2 (Objective 2).
(f) 3 (Objective 2).
(g) 4 (Objective 3).
2. Performance.
Submit this section to your instructor for evaluation. (Objective 4).

APPENDIX A-15

PREASSESSMENT: Chapter 15

1. Knowledge.
   (a) The language experience approach is based on:
      (1) The child's facility with written language.
      (2) Philosophically dubious assumptions.
      (3) The oral-aural language facility of the child.
      (4) A rigorous vocabulary control.
   (b) The language experience approach stresses:
      (1) The interrelationship of reading and other language skills.
      (2) The primacy of the written word.
      (3) That reading provides meaning for the reader.
      (4) That immature language patterns interfere with reading development.
   (c) Which of the following is not a characteristic of the language experience approach?
      (1) Externally imposed vocabulary controls.
      (2) Major materials composed by students.
      (3) Listening, speaking, writing skills incorporated into the instruction.
      (4) Repetition of many function words.
   (d) Which of the following is viewed as an advantage of the language experience approach?
      (1) Children can memorize the stories easily.
      (2) The language is less stilted than that in basal readers.
      (3) Lack of structured teacher's guides.
      (4) Requires no specified criteria for evaluation of student progress.
   (e) Research supports which of the following claims about the language experience approach?
      (1) The reading vocabulary of students instructed in the language experience approach is inferior to that of students taught by other methods.
      (2) Children instructed in the language experience approach fail to show any greater facility in written communication than those taught by other approaches.
      (3) Linguistically different children fail to have the necessary language backgrounds at the time of school entry to cope with reading instruction.
      (4) Overall reading achievement of students taught by the language experience approach is satisfactory if not superior to those taught by other approaches.

    (f) The language experience approach has been shown to be effective with which of these populations?

       (1) Beginning readers.

       (2) Remedial learners at junior and senior high school levels.

       (3) Learners with diverse linguistic backgrounds.

       (4) All of these.

    (g) Which of the following is not an essential step in a language experience approach?

       (1) Talk about experiences.

       (2) Create a story.

       (3) Read the story.

       (4) Practice until students commit the story to memory.

2. Performance.

    (a) Prepare a plan for teaching a language experience lesson that includes, in sequence, the 10 steps.

    (b) Use the plan to teach a language experience lesson in a real or simulated setting while being observed by your instructor.

KEY: Chapter 15

1. Knowledge.

    (a) 3 (Objective 1).

    (b) 1 (Objective 1).

    (c) 1 (Objective 2).

    (d) 2 (Objective 3).

    (e) 4 (Objective 3).

    (f) 4 (Objective 4).

    (g) 4 (Objective 5).

2. Performance.

Submit this section to your instructor for evaluation.

    (a) (Objective 6).

    (b) (Objective 7).

APPENDIX A-16

PREASSESSMENT: Chapter 16

1. All of the following are descriptive of an individualized reading program except:
    (a) Employs a series of high-interest low-vocabulary readers.
    (b) Employs self-selected reading materials.
    (c) Requires lessons for development, extension, and refinement of reading skills.
    (d) Requires extensive record-keeping.
2. Most intensive phonics programs:
    (a) Employ a directed reading approach.
    (b) Focus heavily on comprehension at the early stages of reading acquisition.
    (c) Utilize a synthetic approach to teaching principles.
    (d) Focus on relatively few highly useful phonic principles.
3. Skills-management systems generally:
    (a) Focus on reading as a unitary activity.
    (b) Focus on sets of separate skills assumed as components of the reading act.
    (c) Focus on ways to divide classes into ability groups.
    (d) Provide the necessary instructional materials to be a complete reading program.
4. Which of the following is not a characteristic of linguistic readers?
    (a) Stress phoneme-grapheme relationships.
    (b) Have highly-controlled initial vocabulary.
    (c) Are written in a language style that closely approximates the oral language of children.
    (d) Focus on word patterns or families.
5. An approach that blends elements of several different approaches is called:
    (a) An individualized reading approach.
    (b) A linguistic approach.
    (c) An eclectic approach.
    (d) A code-emphasis approach.
6. Strong emphasis on silent reading is a component of:
    (a) An intensive phonics program.
    (b) An individualized reading program.
    (c) A code-emphasis program.
    (d) Initial instruction material in linguistic programs.
7. Individualized reading approaches are based on the belief that:
    (a) Learners themselves are the best judges of how fast they should progress in reading.

383

(b) There are more differences than commonalities among students.

(c) Independent reading periods allow students to practice their reading skills.

(d) Sustained silent reading produces superior comprehension.

8. Which of the following are not code-emphasis approaches?

(a) Basal reader approaches.

(b) Linguistic approaches.

(c) Intensive phonics approach.

(d) Both a and b.

KEY: Chapter 16

1. a
2. c
3. b
4. c
5. c
6. b
7. a
8. a

APPENDIX A-17

PREASSESSMENT: Chapter 17

1. Knowledge.
    (a) Which of the following is a type of standarized reading test?
        (1) Informal reading inventory.
        (2) Survey test.
        (3) Criterion-referenced test.
        (4) Cloze test.
    (b) A diagnostic test:
        (1) Should be administered exclusively in individual settings.
        (2) Is designed to appraise the specific skills needs of students.
        (3) Is one type of survey test.
        (4) Should be administered at the end of each school year.
    (c) Two broad skills generally tested on a reading achievement test include:
        (1) Word recognition and comprehension.
        (2) Word recognition and vocabulary.
        (3) Comprehension and vocabulary.
        (4) Summarizing material and word recognition.
    (d) Which of the following categories would not be found on a standardized reading readiness test?
        (1) Visual discrimination.
        (2) Following directions.
        (3) Letter recognition.
        (4) Auditory sequencing.
    (e) Which of the following types of tests would you administer to Perry, who is experiencing some difficulty in reading, but you are not sure of the type of problem?
        (1) Standardized reading achievement test.
        (2) A diagnostic test.
        (3) An interest inventory.
        (4) A cloze test.
    (f) Which of the following reading levels can be obtained from an informal reading inventory?
        (1) Independent, instructional, frustration, capacity.
        (2) Interest, independent, basal, frustration.
        (3) Recreational, independent, instructional, capacity.
        (4) Independent, frustration, potential, capacity.
    (g) Which of the following types of comprehension questions should be asked on an informal reading inventory?
        (1) Vocabulary, main idea, predicting outcomes.

   (2) Recall of details, main idea, sequence of events.
   (3) Cause-and-effect relationships, vocabulary, details.
   (4) Vocabulary, details, inference.
(h) Which of the following symbols indicate that the student repeated something in his oral reading?
   p
   (1) word.
   (2) today and yesterday.
   (3) This oppossum.
        ran
   (4) He can do. . . .
(i) A cloze test is used:
   (1) To determine reading levels.
   (2) To determine oral reading fluency.
   (3) As a standardized test of reading achievement.
   (4) To determine students' reading rate.
(j) A reading skills checklist is:
   (1) A useful device for diagnosing student needs.
   (2) A formal measurement instrument.
   (3) A component of all basal reader series.
   (4) A self-administered inventory.
(k) Criterion-referenced tests:
   (1) Are one form of standardized tests.
   (2) Are used to determine pupil performance in relation to other pupils.
   (3) Are used to measure pupil performance against specifically stated objectives.
   (4) Have little diagnostic value.
(l) Miscue analysis:
   (1) Makes provisions for dialectal variations in oral reading.
   (2) Refers to a procedure for determining oral reading fluency.
   (3) Is a procedure for reducing the quantity of reading errors.
   (4) Requires silent reading of graded passages.

2. Performance.
(a) Using the story of the Three Little Pigs, write one comprehension question at each of these levels.

   (1) Vocabulary. _____

   (2) Inference. _____

   (3) Facts or details. _____

   (4) Main idea. _____

(b) Read the selection, noting the errors marked, then answer the questions.

is named   can   X

My dog's name is Spots. I'll tell you why. When he

doors   all over

comes inside, he makes spots on the floor.

List the oral reading errors.

Omissions _____

Hesitations _____

Mispronunciations _____

Substitutions _____

Insertions _____

Disregarded punctuation _____

(c) Using the preface at the beginning of this book, prepare a cloze test. Administer it to a peer and score it. Give the reading level.

(d) Prepare a test for a main idea skill that includes at least five questions with at least one knowledge level and one application level question.

KEY: Chapter 17

1. Knowledge.
   (a) 2
   (b) 2
   (c) 3
   (d) 4
   (e) 2
   (f) 1
   (g) 4
   (h) 3
   (i) 1
   (j) 1
   (k) 3
   (l) 1
2. Performance.
   Submit this section to your instructor for evaluation.
   (a) (Objective 5).
   (b) (Objective 5).
   (c) (Objective 6).
   (d) (Objective 8 and 9).

APPENDIX A-18

PREASSESSMENT: Chapter 18

1. Knowledge.
   (a) One advantage of a diagnostic-perscriptive approach is that:
      (1) There is no need for evaluation.
      (2) Teaching efforts are geared toward definite goals.
      (3) Skills instruction can be geared to large groups rather than in-
         dividuals.
      (4) The level of difficulty of the reading materials is immaterial.
   (b) Which of the following is not a step in a diagnostic-prescriptive ap-
      proach?
      (1) Select learning activities.
      (2) Establish objectives.
      (3) Administer standardized tests.
      (4) Implement instruction.
   (c) Scope and sequence charts:
      (1) Provide information on the kinds of skills taught and their order
         of introduction.
      (2) Provide an index of the growth of individual pupils.
      (3) Provide suggestions for teaching specific skills.
      (4) All of these.
   (d) Diagnostic-prescriptive teaching requires:
      (1) Use of group profile sheets.
      (2) Use of sustained silent reading.
      (3) A system for record-keeping.
      (4) Use of structured oral reading samples.
   (e) Which of the following can be used diagnostically?
      (1) Oral reading passages.
      (2) A checklist.
      (3) Individual response cards.
      (4) All of these.
2. Performance.
   (a) Use the following data to complete this section.

	Initial consonants, %	Short vowels, %	Consonant digraphs, %
Cherie	85	80	50
Mike	70	80	70
Kate	50	70	60
Scott	85	80	60

The students took a mastery test and the scores are represented in percentages of correct responses.

    (1) Knowing the performance of the students, divide them into two groups.

_____   _____

_____   _____

_____   _____

    (2) Give rationale for the division. _____

    (3) Which skill should Kate be taught first?

        Why? _____

    (4) Which skill should you begin teaching Scott?

        Why? _____

(b) Demonstrate a diagnostic-prescriptive teaching technique while being evaluated by your instructor.

KEY: Chapter 18

1. Knowledge.
    (a) 2 (Objective 1).
    (b) 3 (Objective 2).
    (c) 1 (Objective 3).
    (d) 3 (Objective 4).
    (e) 4 (Objective 5).
2. Performance.
Submit this section to your instructor for evaluation.
    (a) (Objective 6).
    (b) (Objective 7).

Appendix B
Passages for Use with Chapters

Use this passage with Chapters 1 and 14.

EDITORIALS

Most publishers and journalists uphold a code of ethics which distinguishes between objective news coverage and opinion. They believe that only unbiased stories should be in the news section of a paper or magazine. The editorial pages are for the expression of the publisher's opinions.

An editorial contains personal comments on some subject, usually a current event or well-known person. It may criticize or praise the actions of some public official or group.

Editorials usually begin by stating an issue or recounting briefly some recent news event. They may end by giving advice or making a plea for some type of action. Many editiorials contain facts as well as opinions. A good writer uses facts to reinforce the ideas expressed in the editorial.

From *Steck-Vaughn Adult Reading 2800* by Sam V. Dauzat et. al. Copyright © 1978 by Steck-Vaughn Company.

APPENDIX B-2

MAN OF "MIDDLING PEOPLE"

Benjamin Franklin was born in Boston in 1706, of what he called the "middling people." His father was a candlemaker. His grandfathers before him had been honest farmers of Oxfordshire, England. Ben's mother was a tidy Nantucket woman. Her mother had come to this country as a servant. Ben grew rich and famous without ever feeling that he need rise higher than the honest folk who made him.

No learned man ever learned less from school. He had only two years in school. Later, he taught himself mathematics, French, Spanish and Italian.

In fact, Franklin taught himself almost everything that ever entered his mind—except printing. He learned printing while working for his older brother James, who was then the best printer in America. Ben was soon an expert, too. Because James was jealous and Ben was independent, the younger brother ran away to Philadelphia at the age of 16.

Ten years later Benjamin Franklin was the best and biggest printer in America. He printed almanacs, religious books, textbooks, reprints of classics and the best in current English literature. He did all the government printing for Pennsylvania, Delaware, Maryland and New Jersey. He had founded the first German-language newspaper in this country. He was editing the magazine that later became *The Saturday Evening Post.*

Citizen and Inventor

Within 20 years Ben Franklin became Philadelphia's most important citizen. He was clerk of the colony's Assembly, alderman of the city's Common Council, and organizer of the first fire brigade. A few years more, and he was founder of the Philadelphia Academy, the colony's postmaster and its most powerful politician behind the scenes.

He had started the American Philosophical Society, formed to link scientists together. Many of the most famous names in our scientific history are on its rolls.

Franklin also had invented a stove that gave twice as much heat for a fourth as much fuel. The Franklin stove made the inventor's own name as familiar as that of Poor Richard.

When he was 40, world fame burst upon him. From a traveling "professor," he bought a bit of parlor magic. It was a jar for condensing electricity produced by rubbing with the hand. Only a small boy would have taken the "magic" apart to see what made it work. Only a philosopher would have succeeded. With so much of both in him, Ben Franklin in a few months found out more about electricity than all scientists before him.

From *Help Yourself to Improve Your Reading Part I,* by Ruth B. Herin. Copyright © 1962 by Reader's Digest Services, Inc., Educational Division, Pleasantville, N.Y. 10570.

APPENDIX B-3

FRANCIS DRAKE—KNIGHT OR DRAGON?

His mother would have preferred to raise him on a farm. But his father was appointed pastor to the seamen in the shipyards of Rochester, an English port. So the boy Francis grew up among sailors, learning everything he could from them. The most important thing he learned was that if his country was to survive, it must establish its sea power.

The year was 1567 and Spain reigned supreme over the seas. The Spanish controlled most of the ocean trading routes and enjoyed special privileges in the New World, where its galleons loaded up with treasure. As a result of the Spanish naval power, sea travel was hazardous for English ships.

At sixteen, Francis eagerly joined the crew of his older cousin, English trading captain, Jack Hawkins, who was planning a daring trading expedition into Caribbean waters. At a Mexican port the Hawkins fleet stopped to scrape the ships of barnacles and fill leaking seams. "Spanish galleons sighted starboard, Sir!" cried a sailor suddenly. The ships were Spanish, indeed, but their captains gave friendly greeting and offered assistance. It was only after Hawkins' men lowered their guard that, without warning, the Spanish galleons opened fire, killing Hawkins' sailors and scattering his ships, which returned to England battered.

Francis never forgot that experience, and he swore to return to the Caribbean and take revenge. The chance came when he took command of his own ship, and for two years he troubled Spanish ships in the New World seas. He and his men would approach by night in small, oared boats. They would board the sleeping Spanish vessels, loot them, and burn them as they withdrew, only to strike again the next night. Drake relied on the sailing knowledge he acquired from boyhood and from his cousin. He used quick maneuvers and gave precise commands. To the Spanish captains, he became known as El Draque—meaning the Dragon!

Queen Elizabeth I was very proud of Drake's success, even though some of her advisors, like the cautious Lord Burghley, thought him a dangerous pirate. He would have had Drake imprisoned for risking war with Spain. Drake reminded the Queen how much her country needed the booty from his conquests, and, indeed, she sent him on a secret expedition to the Pacific Ocean, where no English ship had ever ventured. He sailed around South America and then north along its western coast, raiding Spanish settlements in Chile and Peru for spices and treasure. Then, to escape the alerted Spanish fleet, he crossed the Pacific, Indian, and southern Atlantic oceans to arrive in England—three years after his departure—the first Englishman to have sailed around the world!

During the long and risky voyage around the world, Drake lost many sailors who died from combat, starvation, and disease. But his crew so respected and cherished him for his vitality and boldness that they returned again and again, eager to sail under such an experienced sailor— a great sea dog, as they say in sailing lingo.

The King of Spain demanded Drake's head, but Queen Elizabeth rewarded him with knighthood, bestowing on him a large country estate. Later she appointed him Vice-Admiral of the English Navy. In 1588, Drake tasted complete victory when he led the historic sea fight against the "invincible" Spanish Armada, whose final defeat made England ruler of the seas.

From *Riders on the Earth,* Teachers' Edition Workbook, by Bernard J. Weiss et al. Copyright © 1973, Holt, Rinehart & Winston, Publishers.

APPENDIX B-4

GRADED PASSAGES

Readability levels for these passages were determined by using the Fry Graph for Estimating Readability.

Level 1 (107 words)

MY TEACHER

Today was my first day at school. My name is Julia Hill. My teacher's name is Miss Buford. She is nice. She let me sit in the first row. Miss Buford is smart. She knows everything. She showed us how to count. I can count up to 10 now. Miss Buford let us play games. She cut out some paper dolls. She gave me one. I colored my doll with crayons. Miss Buford said I colored good. She printed letters on the blackboard. I told her I knew some letters. Miss Buford said that was good. I like school. I like Miss Buford. She is my teacher.

Level 2 (167 words)

A TRIP TO THE ZOO

Tom's birthday was on Saturday. He was 7 years old. His dad had a surprise for him. He took the whole family to the zoo. They all got up early. Tom's mother packed a picnic basket.

At the zoo his father took them to see the elephants. Tom was afraid of the big elephants. But he didn't say so. He wasn't a sissy. His sister Sarah was scared of the snakes. The snakes were all in cages. One of the snakes looked right at Sarah. It struck the glass door of the cage. Sarah screamed.

Tom's dad took them next to the monkey house. The monkeys were funny. Tom watched the monkeys play. After a while Tom's mother fixed the picnic lunch. After they ate, they went to see the lions and tigers. One of the lions roared. Tom saw his great big teeth.

Tom's dad bought them all some ice cream cones. The whole family had a good time. It was a good birthday for Tom.

Level 3 (131 words)

THE BAT

The bat flies, but it is not a bird. It is an animal and doesn't have feathers like a bird. Instead, the bat has skin stretched between its arms and legs. The bat is really a mouse that flies. Bats don't like bright light, and they do their flying at night. During the day they hang upside down in caves or holes in trees. Most bats come out just before dark and then begin flying around. Most kinds of bats live on insects that they catch in the air. Some bats live on fruit. But one kind of bat is dangerous. That one is the vampire bat. It lives on blood. It sinks its teeth into an animal and drinks the blood. They are not good bats to have around.

Level 4 (200 words)

TRICK OR TREAT

Nobody wanted to do it. Martha didn't want to. Nolan didn't want to. Neither did Ricky or Patty. But this was the last house. Someone had to do it. Someone had to go up and knock on Mr. Racker's door. The kids' sacks were almost full. They had been given candy and fruit. The other grown-ups had been good to them, but now there was Mr. Racker's door. He was a mean old man. He always seemed to be mad at the world.

Finally Martha told Patty they would have to go themselves; the boys were too scared. Nolan told Ricky to come on; no girls were going to show them up. Nolan knocked on the door. A voice inside called out, "What do you want?" Nolan swallowed hard and said, "Trick or treat."

The door opened a little. Mr. Racker looked down at them, and he said, "I didn't expect anyone; nobody ever stops here. I don't have any candy." The kids just looked at him. He got out his little coin purse and gave each one a dime. He said, "Don't you be telling anybody I gave you anything."

Nolan looked back as they left. Mr. Racker was smiling.

Level 5 (203 words)

HENRY FORD'S MODEL T

Henry Ford was the founder of the Ford Motor Company. He began making cars in the early 1900s. There were many small car companies then, and most cars were built by hand. But Ford had a better idea. He believed cars could be mass-produced. By making a great many cars, he could bring the price down. Everybody, not just the rich, could afford to buy one.

So, Henry Ford built his plant. His plant had the first production line where each worker did one small thing to the unfinished car as it came by him. At the end of the production line, the car was complete. Soon, Henry's Model T was selling by the thousands. The price of a new one dropped to $400. The workers at the plant kept turning them out faster and faster. They worked hard because Henry realized that workers worked better if they were well paid. He paid his workers $5 a day. At that time most factory workers made only $2 or $3 a day. By paying so much more, Ford got the best workers.

His model Ts sold in the millions. The last one was made in 1927. They are now collector's items.

Level 6 (187 words)

THE BULLDOZER

The bulldozer is one of man's most useful machines. With a bulldozer a man can alter one landscape into another. If he wants to build a house, he has a bulldozer level off the area, and if he wants to build a pond, he has a bulldozer put up the dam. The bulldozer scrapes up a load of dirt with its blade and then pushes the dirt to where the dam is going to be. When it gets enough dirt pushed up, it levels off the top and sides. At the same time the bulldozer is packing the dirt down.

It is powerful and is a very efficient machine. Most use diesel fuel, which is cheaper than gasoline. The big blade on the front of the bulldozer can be turned at various angles. In this way the bulldozer can do such things as dig trenches. With a special kind of blade in front, the bulldozer can clear land for farming.

The bulldozer is a real time and work saver. With it, man can do a great deal of work in a very short time.

Level 7 (222 words)

WRIST WRESTLING

Wrist wrestling is a fast growing sport. A few years ago the only competition was between men, when they usually got into an argument in a bar as to which one was stronger. Usually a bet was made, the two men went at it. But now wrist wrestling is very popular as a competitive sport, with national championships being held every year in California. There are championships for men and championships for women held now. There are several weight divisions. Each division has a champion, just like in boxing.

Although wrist strength is important, other strengths are, too. A good wrist wrestler has to have good back and leg strength to go along with arm strength. Technique and concentration are also important.

In the official matches, each of the two wrestlers grabs the other's hand. The forearms are in upright position. Each tries to bend the other's arm back down. If he can do this, he wins. Sometimes the matches are over in a couple of seconds. Sometimes, the match goes on for minutes until someone wins.

It is a sport that everybody can do. There is no expensive equipment to buy, and wrist wrestling can be practiced anywhere. However, it can be dangerous. People have torn muscles and even broken arms in wrist wrestling. It is definitely not a sport for the fainthearted.

Level 8 (207 words)

THE FUNERAL PROCESSION

Aunt Elizabeth had passed away on Monday, and today, Wednesday, the services had been held at the sanctuary. We were now in a long procession of automobiles on our way to the cemetery. As was customary, all of us who were driving had our lights on. As we slowly drove down the highway, most of the people in automobiles approaching us pulled off the highway and stopped. It is a practice that is followed by people in this part of the country. Some approaching cars, I noticed, did not pull over because, evidently, the drivers were not aware of the customary procedure.

It was about 10 miles down the highway before we turned off onto a country road that led past some farms to the cemetery. I noticed that spring had arrived, bringing renewed life to all that had seemed dead during the winter. The trees were greening in their annual ritual of rebirth.

Shortly after the turn was made, we passed by a field being plowed. I glanced over and saw that the farmer had stopped plowing. He had gotten off his tractor and was standing there. He had his hat off, and his head was bowed. It was just as if he were saying, "God speed." I know Aunt Elizabeth appreciated his gesture.

Appendix C
Checklists

APPENDIX C-1

CHECKLIST FOR READING READINESS FACTORS

Checklist for Classroom Observation. As well as yes or no answers, include other comments about the child from your observation.

1. Intellectual Development

Answer with
yes or no

   (a) Can the child draw something to demonstrate an idea as well as other children of his own age? _____

   (b) Is his memory span sufficient to allow memorization of a short poem or song? _____

   (c) Can he tell a story without confusing the order of events? _____

   (d) Does he interpret pictures? _____

   (e) Does he grasp the fact that symbols may be associated with pictures or subjects? _____

   (f) Can he anticipate what may happen in a story or poem? _____

2. Physical Condition

   (a) Do the child's eyes seem comfortable? (Does he squint, rub eyes, hold material too close or too far away from eyes?) _____

   (b) Does he respond to questions or directions, and is he apparently able to hear what is said in class? _____

   (c) Does he speak clearly and well? _____

   (d) Does he make his hands work together well in cutting, using tools, or bouncing a ball? _____

   (e) Does he give an impression of good health? _____

3. Social and Emotional Development

   (a) Does he work well with a group, taking his share of the responsibility? _____

(b) Does he cooperate with the other children in play activities? _____

(c) Does he work things through for himself (or is he always asking for assistance)? _____

(d) Does he take good care of materials assigned to him? _____

(e) Does he see a task (such as drawing, preparing for an activity, or cleaning up) through to completion? _____

4. Educational Factors and Experiential Background

(a) Does the child seem interested in books and reading? _____

(b) Does he ask the meanings of words or signs? _____

(c) Does he speak in sentences? _____

(d) Can he correctly name objects around the room? _____

(e) Does he know the letters of the alphabet and most of the sounds associated with them? _____

(f) Can he recognize his own name in written form? _____

Note. It may take more than one observation to become familiar with the true characteristics of the child. If you cannot answer some of these questions through observing, find out what you can learn when you work with the child on an individual basis. After getting a good idea as to what factors are affecting his behavior, examine some of his work and, if possible, discuss his readiness for reading with his classroom teacher. Draw some definite conclusions about the relationship between the factors affecting him and his readiness for reading instruction.

APPENDIX C-2

CHECKLIST FOR READING READINESS SKILLS

Checklist for classroom observation. As well as yes or no answers, include other comments about the child from your observation.

Answer with yes or no

1. Auditory and Visual Discrimination
   (a) Is the child sensitive to similarities and differences in pictures, words, letters? _____
   (b) Can she draw or copy simple drawings and letters? _____
   (c) Can she recognize rhymes?
   (d) Is she sensitive to similarities and differences in word beginnings or word endings? _____
2. Left-to-right Orientation
   (a) Has she established the habit of looking at a succession of items from left to right? _____
3. Listening Comprehension
   (a) Can she follow simple directions?
   (b) Can she anticipate what may happen in a story or poem? _____
   (c) Can she remember the central thought of a story as well as important details? _____
4. Color Discrimination
   (a) Can she name the color of different objects presented to her? _____
   (b) Can she associate a color with a certain word (e.g., grass-green, snow-white)? _____

Note. It may take more than one observation to get all the information you need to draw some conclusions. If you cannot answer some of these questions through observing, find out what you can learn when you work with the child on an individual basis. After getting a good idea as to how well developed her skills are, examine some of her work and, if possible, discuss her readiness for reading with her classroom teacher. Draw some definite conclusions about the relationship between her skills and her readiness for reading.

401

APPENDIX C-3

CRITERIA FOR TEACHING A LESSON

Check if your response is yes.

Objectives

_____ 1. Are the objectives of the teaching plan clearly stated?

_____ 2. Are the objectives *realistic* ones that the students should be able to achieve?

_____ 3. Is the skill appropriate for the level to be taught?

Material

_____ 4. Are all needed materials prepared beforehand?

Procedure

_____ 5. Is the introduction meaningful to the students?

_____ 6. Is a strategy worked out to allow the students to form generalizations about the information presented?

_____ 7. Are the students allowed to participate?

_____ 8. Is sufficient practice provided for understanding?

_____ 9. Do the activities provide for individual differences?

_____ 10. If applicable, is the whole word presented first, then analyzed, then presented again as a whole word?

_____ 11. Is practice provided for reinforcement of the skill(s)?

_____ 12. Are alternate activities (work sheets, games) available if needed to keep up interest?

Evaluation

_____ 13. Can student mastery and needs be determined from class participation and/or results on written activities?

Before Teaching

If you have not checked all the items, do some additional planning to meet the criteria before attempting to teach the lesson. Refer to the sample lessons in the respective chapters for help.

Self-Evaluation

When you have completed teaching your lesson, write down how you feel about the lesson. Note which of the criteria were not effectively met and what areas you would change before teaching again. Make notes next to the criteria on the checklist and fill in general comments here.

Comments

_____

_____

_____

_____

_____

_____

What do you see as your strongest area(s)? _____

_____

Your weakest area(s?)_____

_____

How would you change?_____

APPENDIX C-4

CHECKLIST FOR CRITIQUING A PEER

Critique orally or in writing the teaching of another student according to given criteria.

1. Use Checklist C-3, Criteria for Teaching a Lesson.
   Instead of placing checkmarks in the spaces before the numbers, use the following code.
   4 = excellent
   3 = above average
   2 = average
   1 = weak
   0 = unsatisfactory
2. Write in any remarks in the space following the criterion that you wish to comment on. Also write in any remarks in the spaces provided at the end of the checklist.
3. Share the evaluation with the peer-teacher you observed.

405

APPENDIX C-5

OBSERVATION GUIDE / CHECKLIST   BASAL READING APPROACH

1. How many groups of children are in the room? _____
2. What is each group *doing*?

   (a) Group 1. _____

   (b) Group 2. _____

   (c) Group 3. _____

   (d) Group 4. _____

   (e) Group 5. _____

3. Why are the children grouped that way? _____

   _____

4. What teaching materials are used? Identify the group.

   (a) Group 1. _____

   (b) Group 2. _____

   (c) Group 3. _____

   (d) Group 4. _____

   (e) Group 5. _____

5. (a) With which group does the teacher spend most time? _____

   (b) What is happening in that group? _____

6. If the teacher is doing a directed reading activity, check the aspects you see. If possible, match the group activity with a section of the plan. Write in the group number, also.

   (a) Readiness for lesson. _____

      (1) Builds new concepts. _____

      (2) Introduces new words. _____

      (3) Gives *prereading* purposes. _____

   (b) Directs silent reading. _____

   (c) Stimulates comprehension. _____

      (1) Asks literal questions. _____

      (2) Asks inferential questions. _____

      (3) Asks critical questions. _____

(d) Sets purpose and directs rereading.

    (1) Oral. _____

    (2) Silent. _____

(e) Teaches new skills. _____

(f) Guides practice of skills. _____

(g) Independent practice of skills or extended activities. _____

Appendix C-6

DIRECTED READING CHECKLIST

NAME OF TEACHER:_____ DATE _____

NAME OF OBSERVER/CRITIQUER: _____

GRADE LEVEL _____

NO. OF CHILDREN_____

Teaching Behavior	Superior	Above Average	Average	Below Average	Unsatis-factory	No Evidence
1. Builds Readiness for reading (a) Motivates the children (b) Introduces new words in context (c) Sets purpose for reading						
2. Guides silent reading						
3. Provides comprehension check (a) Asks literal questions (b) Asks inferential/ critical questions (c) Asks vocabulary (using context) questions						
4. Provides opportunities for rereading (a) Sets new purposes (b) Asks for reading response to purpose						
5. Provides for skill development (a) Introduces skill (b) Provides appropriate reinforcement of skill						
6. Provides (a) Activities for follow up and application (b) Provides for extended activities						

APPENDIX C-7   SKILLS CHECKLIST

Excerpted from the *Fountain Valley Teacher Support System in Reading*, Copyright © 1971, Richard L. Zweig Associates, Inc., 20800 Beach Boulevard, Huntington Beach, Calif. 92648. Reprinted by permission of the publisher.

Continuous Pupil PROGRESS PROFILE in READING

DIRECTIONS TO THE TEACHER: These profiles are to be used as a continuous record of the pupil's progress in reading. There is a separate profile for each skill area: Phonetic Analysis, Structural Analysis, Vocabulary Development, Comprehension and Study Skills. In recording the results of each test, make sure you are using the correct skill profile. Each one indicates the objectives on individual tests.

Count the number of incorrect responses for each behavioral objective. Based on the scoring instructions, write the date of the test beside the skill in the "Proceed" or "Reteach" column. At the beginning of the Phonetic Analysis profile is a list of letters representing perceptual-type problems. If a skill number followed by one of these letters is circled, write the letter next to the date of the test beside the skill.

WORD ANALYSIS / Phonetic Analysis

	Reteach	Proceed		Reteach	Proceed
a. audio-visual reversals			1-24. long vowel 'u'		
b. m-n-h substitutions			1-25. regular vowel combination 'ee'		
c. r-l substitutions			1-26. regular vowel combination 'ay'		
d. f-th substitutions			1-27. 'y' as a vowel		
e. b-d-p reversals			1-28. irregular vowel combination 'ow'		
f. th-wh substitutions			1-29. irregular vowel combination 'ōw'		
g. s-f substitutions			1-30. irregular vowel combination 'ew'		
h. sh-ch substitutions			1-31. murmur diphthong 'ar'		
i. s-th substitutions			1-32. murmur diphthong 'er'		
p-1. initial consonant 'b'			1-33. murmur diphthong 'ir'		
p-2. initial consonant 'c'			1-34. murmur diphthong 'ur'		
p-3. initial consonant 'd'			1-35. initial consonant 'k'		
p-4. initial consonant 'f'			1-36. initial blend 'sp'		
p-5. initial consonant 'g'			1-37. initial blend 'st'		
p-6. initial consonant 'h'			1-38. initial blend 'sl'		
p-7. initial consonant 'j'			1-39. initial blend 'sm'		
p-8. initial consonant 'l'			1-40. initial blend 'sw'		
p-9. initial consonant 'm'			1-41. initial blend 'spr'		
p-10. initial consonant 'n'			1-42. initial blend 'fl'		
p-11. initial consonant 'p'			1-43. initial blend 'bl'		
p-12. initial consonant 'r'			1-44. initial blend 'cl'		
p-13. initial consonant 's'			1-45. initial blend 'tr'		
p-14. initial consonant 't'			1-46. initial blend 'gr'		
p-15. initial consonant 'w'			1-47. initial blend 'cr'		
p-16. initial consonant 'y'			1-48. initial blend 'fr'		
p-17. initial digraph 'sh'			1-49. phonetic part 'qu'		
p-18. initial digraph 'wh'			1-50. initial digraph 'ch'		
1-1. final consonant 'd'			1-51. initial digraph 'kn'		
1-2. final consonant 'k'			1-52. initial digraph 'th' (voiced)		
1-3. final consonant 'l'			1-53. initial digraph 'th' (unvoiced)		
1-4. final consonant 'm'			2-1. initial consonant 'z'		
1-5. final consonant 'n'			2-2. initial consonant 'v'		
1-6. final consonant 'p'			2-3. hard 'g'		
1-7. final consonant 'r'			2-4. soft 'g'		
1-8. final consonant 't'			2-5. regular vowel combination 'ai'		
1-9. final consonant 'x'			2-6. regular vowel combination 'ea'		
1-10. final phonetic part 'st'			2-7. regular vowel combination 'oa'		
1-11. final phonetic part 'ng'			2-8. initial digraph 'ch' (k)		
1-12. final phonetic part 'ch'			2-9. irregular vowel combination 'aw'		
1-13. final phonetic part 'ck'			2-10. phonetic part 'sch'		
1-14. final phonetic part 'll'			2-11. initial digraph 'gu'		
1-15. short vowel 'a'			2-12. final consonant 's'		
1-16. short vowel 'e'			2-13. final blend 'nk'		
1-17. short vowel 'i'			2-14. final blend 'nd'		
1-18. short vowel 'o'			2-15. final blend 'nt'		
1-19. short vowel 'u'			2-16. final digraph 'sh'		
1-20. long vowel 'a'			2-17. phonetic part 'igh'		
1-21. long vowel 'e'			2-18. phonetic part 'ight'		
1-22. long vowel 'i'			2-19. phonetic part 'ear'		
1-23. long vowel 'o'			2-20. diphthong 'oy'		

Pupil's Name: _____

Age: _____   Grade: _____   1 2 3 4 5 6

RED PART 1   RED PART 2   RED PART 3

RED PART 4   RED PART 5   RED PART 6

ORANGE PART 1   ORANGE PART 2

Appendix C: Checklists

		Reteach	Proceed			Reteach	Proceed	
YELLOW PART 1	2-21. diphthong 'oi'			3-8. final digraph 'ph'				**YELLOW PART 2**
	2-22. murmur diphthong 'or'			3-9. irregular vowel combination 'au'				
	3-1. final blend 'ld'			3-10. silent 'b'				
	3-2. final blend 'lt'			3-11. vowel 'o' (love)				
	3-3. final blend 'mp'			3-12. phonetic part 'sc' (scene)				
	3-4. hard 'c'			3-13. irregular vowel combination 'ea'				
	3-5. soft 'c'			3-14. irregular murmur diphthong 'or'				
	3-6. initial digraph 'ph'			3-15. irregular vowel combination 'ie'				
	3-7. medial digraph 'ph'			3-16. phonetic part 'schwa'				

WORD ANALYSIS / Structural Analysis

		Reteach	Proceed			Reteach	Proceed	
RED PART 1	p-1. noun form 's'			2-10. suffix 'y'				**ORANGE PART 2**
	p-2. noun form 'es'			2-11. verb form 'n'				
	p-3. verb form 's'			2-12. verb form 'en'				
	p-4. verb form 'ed'			2-13. contractions				
	p-5. verb form 'ing'			2-14. syllables				
	p-6. compound words			2-15. accent marks-2 syllable words				
	p-7. rhyming words			3-1. noun form 'y'				**YELLOW PART 1**
RED PART 2	1-1. adverbial suffix 'ly'			3-2. noun plural '(i)es'				
	1-2. noun suffix 'er'			3-3. verb form 'y'				
	1-3. possessive form ''s'			3-4. verb form '(i)es'				
	1-4. adjective form 'er'			3-5. verb form '(i)ed'				
	1-5. adjective form 'est'			3-6. verb form 'ing'				
	1-6. compound words,			3-7. suffix 'tion'				
	2-1. prefix 'un'			3-8. suffix 'ward'				
	2-2. prefix 're'			3-9. suffix 'ment'				
	2-3. prefix 'dis'			3-10. suffix 'ous'				**YELLOW PART 2**
ORANGE PART 1	2-4. suffix 'ly'			3-11. suffix 'ern'				
	2-5. suffix 'ful'			3-12. suffix 'teen'				
	2-6. suffix 'less'			3-13. suffix 'ship'				
	2-7. suffix 'ness'			3-14. suffix 'some'				
	2-8. suffix 'er'			3-15. compound words				
	2-9. suffix 'th'							

VOCABULARY DEVELOPMENT

		Reteach	Proceed			Reteach	Proceed	
RED PART 1	p-1. recognizing unknown through pictures			3-5. antonyms				
	p-2. antonyms			3-6. homonyms				
	p-3. rhyming words			3-7. synonyms & synonymous phrases				**YELLOW PART 2**
RED PART 2	1-1. recognizing unknown through context			3-8. rhyming words				
	1-2. ident. words through definition & sentence			3-9. homographs				
	1-3. how, where, when, who & what			4-1. recognizing unknown through sentence use				
RED PART 3	1-4. antonyms			4-2. definitions and meanings				**GREEN PART 1**
	1-5. homonyms			4-3. homographs				
	1-6. synonyms & synonymous phrases			5-1. recognizing unknown through context				
	1-7. rhyming words			5-2. recognizing words through sentence				
ORANGE PART 1	2-1. recognizing unknown through context			5-3. how, where, when, who & what				**BLUE PART 1**
	2-2. ident. words through definition & sentence			5-4. definitions and meanings				
	2-3. how, where, when, who & what			5-5. multiple meanings				
	2-4. homonyms			6-1. how, where, when, who & what				
	2-5. rhyming words			6-2. definitions and meanings				**PURPLE PART 1**
YELLOW PART 1	3-1. recognizing unknown through context			6-3. understanding technical terms				
	3-2. ident. words through definition & sentence			6-4. multiple meanings				
	3-3. how, where, when, who & what			6-5. synonyms & synonymous phrases				**PURPLE PART 2**
	3-4. information from definitions			6-6. foreign root words				

412

COMPREHENSION

Level	Skill	Reteach	Proceed		Skill	Reteach	Proceed	Level
RED PART 1	p-1. main idea-pictures				3-14. recognizing absurdities			
	p-2. main idea-illustrating				4-1. main idea-titling			GREEN PART 1
	p-3. main idea-rephrasing				4-2. main idea-rephrasing			
RED PART 2	1-1. main idea-pictures				4-3. main idea-story parts			
	1-2. main idea-supporting ideas				4-4. main idea-key words and sentences			GREEN PART 2
	1-3. main idea-illustrating				4-5. detail-key words			
	1-4. main idea-rephrasing				4-6. recognizing tone, feeling, sadness			
	1-5. main idea-titling				4-7. creative reading-reacting personally			
RED PART 3	1-6. sequence in pictures				4-8. comparing and contrasting			GREEN PART 3
	1-7. arranging sentences-sequence				4-9. identifying and interpreting feeling, attitudes			
	1-8. arranging events & ideas-sequence				4-10. author's intent			
	1-9. matching picture with text				4-11. recognizing absurdities			GREEN PART 4
RED PART 4	1-10. answering questions-key words				4-12. fables, myths, and legends			
	1-11. identifying speaker, etc.				5-1. main idea-rephrasing			
	1-12. likeness and difference				5-2. main idea-composing paragraphs			
	1-13. creative reading-reacting personally				5-3. recognizing sequence			BLUE PART 1
	1-14. recognizing tone, feeling, sadness				5-4. detail through topical guides			
RED PART 5	1-15. comparing & contrasting-ideas				5-5. details supporting main idea			
	1-16. drawing conclusions				5-6. creative reading-reacting personally			
	1-17. inferences				5-7. likeness and difference			
ORANGE PART 1	2-1. main idea-supporting ideas				5-8. comparing and contrasting			BLUE PART 2
	2-2. main idea-rephrasing				5-9. identifying and interpreting feeling, attitudes			
	2-3. main idea-titling				5-10. vivid language			
	2-4. arranging sentences-sequence				5-11. cause & effect relationships			
	2-5. sequence within sentences				5-12. inferences			
ORANGE PART 2	2-6. answering questions-key words				5-13. recognizing absurdities			BLUE PART 3
	2-7. identifying speaker, etc.				5-14. figures of speech			
	2-8. recognizing tone, feeling, humor				5-15. fables, myths, and legends			
	2-9. creative reading-reacting personally				5-16. author's intent			
ORANGE PART 3	2-10. comparing & contrasting-ideas				5-17. evaluating bias			BLUE PART 4
	2-11. riddles and puzzles				5-18. identifying and interpreting irony, etc.			
	2-12. recognizing emotional reaction				6-1. main idea-supporting ideas			
	2-13. drawing conclusions				6-2. main idea-rephrasing			PURPLE PART 1
ORANGE PART 4	2-14. cause and effect relationships				6-3. main idea-composing paragraphs			
	2-15. figures of speech				6-4. recognizing sequence-sentences			
	2-16. author's opinion, intent				6-5. arranging sequence-events, ideas			PURPLE PART 2
YELLOW PART 1	3-1. main idea-supporting ideas				6-6. detail-matching picture with text			
	3-2. main idea-key sentences				6-7. detail-recall			
	3-3. arranging sentences-sequence				6-8. recognizing tone, feeling, sadness			
YELLOW PART 2	3-4. arranging events & ideas-sequence				6-9. creative reading-reacting personally			PURPLE PART 3
	3-5. answering questions-key words				6-10. identifying and interpreting feeling, attitudes			
	3-6. identifying speaker, etc.				6-11. vivid language			
YELLOW PART 3	3-7. verifying answer, opinion, hypothesis				6-12. cause & effect relationships			PURPLE PART 4
	3-8. recognizing tone, feeling, sadness				6-13. figures of speech			
	3-9. comparing & contrasting-ideas				6-14. evaluating bias			
YELLOW PART 4	3-10. riddles and puzzles				6-15. identifying and interpreting irony, etc.			PURPLE PART 5
	3-11. identifying & interpreting feelings				6-16. recognizing structure			
YELLOW PART 5	3-12. drawing conclusions				6-17. interpreting new ideas			
	3-13. cause & effect relationships							

413

STUDY SKILLS

Part	Skill	Reteach	Proceed
RED PART 1	p-1. table of contents		
	p-2. skimming or rereading-specific information		
	p-3. appropriate word for context		
RED PART 2	1-1. table of contents		
	1-2. alphabetical sequence		
	1-3. skimming or rereading-specific information		
	1-4. appropriate word for context		
RED PART 3	1-5. sources		
	1-6. generalization from facts		
	1-7. following directions		
	1-8. classifying-words and pictures		
ORANGE PART 1	2-1. table of contents		
	2-2. alphabetical sequence		
	2-3. skimming or rereading-specific information		
	2-4. finding personal pronouns		
ORANGE PART 2	2-5. appropriate word for context		
	2-6. judgment-fact, fancy, true, false		
	2-7. following directions		
ORANGE PART 3	2-8. classifying items-like or unlike		
	2-9. classifying-related ideas & subordinate details		
	2-10. summary sentence		
YELLOW PART 1	3-1. table of contents		
	3-2. charts, pictures, maps		
	3-3. encyclopedia, dictionary, glossary		
	3-4. alphabetical sequence		
	3-5. subtitles		
YELLOW PART 2	3-6. skimming or rereading-specific information		
	3-7. sources-relevant, irrelevant		
	3-8. judgment-fact, fancy, true, false		
	3-9. generalization from facts		
YELLOW PART 3	3-10. appropriate word for context		
	3-11. following directions		
	3-12. classifying items into categories		
GREEN PART 1	4-1. table of contents		
GREEN PART 2	4-2. charts, pictures, maps		
	4-3. timelines, flow-charts, diagrams		
GREEN PART 3	4-4. encyclopedia, dictionary, glossary		
	4-5a. radio, TV schedule		
	4-5b. newspapers		
	4-6. skimming or rereading-specific information		

Skill	Reteach	Proceed	Part
4-7. skimming or rereading-new ideas			GREEN PART 4
4-8. judgment-fact, fancy, true, false			
4-9. generalization from facts			
4-10. time & place relationships			
4-11. phrase meanings-dialect, idioms, colloquialisms			GREEN PART 5
4-12. classifying-stories and poems			
4-13. classifying-words and pictures			
4-14. classifying-related ideas & subordinate details			
4-15. summarizing-own words			GREEN PART 6
4-16. summarizing-story parts, ideas			
4-17. outlining			
5-1. table of contents			BLUE PART 1
5-2. charts, pictures, maps, graphs			
5-3. timelines, flow-charts, diagrams			
5-4. encyclopedia, dictionary, glossary			
5-5. radio & TV schedule, newspaper, etc.			BLUE PART 2
5-6. footnotes and bibliography			
5-7. skimming or rereading-specific information			
5-8. skimming or rereading-new ideas			BLUE PART 3
5-9. judgment-fact, fancy, true, false			
5-10. time & place relationships			
5-11. phrase meanings-dialect, idioms, colloquialisms			
5-12. classifying items into categories			BLUE PART 4
5-13. classifying-related ideas & subordinate details			
5-14. summary sentences			
5-15. topical outline			
6-1. table of contents			PURPLE PART 1
6-2. charts, pictures, maps			
6-3. timelines, flow-charts, diagrams			
6-4. card catalog-author, title, subject			
6-5. radio & TV schedule, newspaper, etc.			PURPLE PART 2
6-6. best source of information			
6-7. graphs and tables			
6-8. skimming or rereading-specific information			
6-9. judgment-fact, fancy, true, false			PURPLE PART 3
6-10. appropriate word for context			
6-11. phrase meanings-dialect, idioms, colloquialisms			
6-12. classifying-related ideas & subordinate details			
6-13. summary sentences			PURPLE PART 4
6-14. topical outline			

APPENDIX C-8

ORAL READING CHECKLIST

	Superior	Adequate	Needs Improvement
1. Sight vocabulary			
2. Word pronunciation			
3. Word enunciation			
4. Phrasing			
5. Observation of punctuation			
6. Volume			
7. Voice inflections			
8. Interpretation of mood or setting			
9. Rate			
10. Reading posture			
11. Handling of book			
12. Sensitivity to audience			

Read a passage of your choice to an audience of your peers as they use the checklist to critique your performance.

Appendix D
Word Lists

APPENDIX D-1

THE DOLCH BASIC SIGHT VOCABULARY OF 220 SERVICE WORDS[a]

a	could	had	may	said	under
about	cut	has	me	saw	up
after		have	much	say	upon
again	did	he	must	see	us
all	do	help	my	seven	use
always	does	her	myself	shall	
am	done	here		she	very
an	don't	him	never	show	
and	down	his	new	sing	walk
any	draw	hold	no	sit	want
are	drink	hot	not	six	warm
around	eat	how	now	sleep	was
as	eight	hurt		small	wash
ask	every		of	so	we
at		I	off	some	well
ate	fall	if	old	soon	went
away	far	in	on	start	were
	fast	into	once	stop	what
be	find	is	one		when
because	first	it	only	take	where
been	five	its	open	tell	which
before	fly		or	ten	white
best	for	jump	our	thank	who
better	found	just	out	that	why
big	four		over	the	will
black	from	keep	own	their	wish
blue	full	kind		them	with
both	funny	know	pick	then	work
bring			play	there	would
brown	gave	laugh	please	these	write
but	get	let	pretty	they	
buy	give	light	pull	think	yellow
by	go	like	put	this	yes
		little			you

	goes	live	ran	those	your
call	going	long	read	three	
came	good	look	red	to	
can	got		ride	today	
carry	green	made	right	together	
clean	grow	make	round	too	
cold		many	run	try	
come				two	

[a] Reprinted with permission of the Garrard Publishing Co. These basic service words and common nouns may be taught with the Basic Sight Vocabulary Cards, Group Word Teaching Game, and Picture Word Cards (published by the Garrard Publishing Co., Champaign, Ill. 61820).

APPENDIX D-2

THE DOLCH LIST OF NINETY-FIVE COMMON NOUNS[a]

apple	dog	horse	Santa Claus
baby	doll	house	school
back	door	kitty	seed
ball	duck		sheep
bear	egg	leg	shoe
bed	eye	letter	sister
bell			snow
bird	farm	man	song
birthday	farmer	men	squirrel
boat	father	milk	stock
box	feet	money	street
boy	fire	morning	sun
bread	fish	mother	
brother	floor		table
	flower	name	thing
cake		nest	time
car	game	night	top
cat	garden		toy
chair	girl	paper	tree
chicken	goodbye	party	
children	grass	picture	watch
Christmas	ground	pig	water
coat			way
corn	hand	rabbit	wind
cow	head	rain	window
	hill	ring	wood
day	home	robin	

[a] Reprinted with permission of the author and the Garrard Publishing Co. These widely used nouns may be taught with the Picture Word Cards, Garrard Publishing Co., Champaign, Ill. 61820.

KUČERA-FRANCIS CORPUS (ADAPTED)[a]

the	out	should	states	head	looked
of	so	because	himself	yet	early
and	said	each	few	government	white
to	what	just	house	system	case
a	up	those	use	better	John
in	its	people	during	set	become
that	about	Mr.	without	told	large
is	into	how	again	nothing	big
was	than	too	place	night	need
he	them	little	American	end	four
for	can	state	around	why	within
it	only	good	however	called	felt
with	other	very	home	didn't	along
as	new	make	small	eyes	children
his	some	world	found	find	saw
on	could	still	Mrs.	going	best
be	time	own	thought	look	church
at	these	see	want	asked	ever
by	two	men	say	later	least
I	may	work	part	knew	power
this	then	long	once	point	development
had	do	get	general	next	light
not	first	here	high	program	thing
are	any	between	upon	city	seemed
but	my	both	school	business	family
from	now	life	every	give	interest
or	such	being	don't	group	want
have	like	under	does	toward	members
an	our	never	got	young	mind
they	over	day	united	days	country
which	man	same	left	let	area
one	me	another	number	room	others
you	even	know	course	president	done
were	most	while	war	side	turned
her	made	last	until	social	although
all	after	might	always	given	open
she	also	us	away	present	God
there	did	great	something	several	service
would	many	old	fact	order	certain
their	before	year	though	national	kind

we	must	off	water	possible	problem
him	through	come	less	rather	began
been	back	since	public	second	different
has	years	against	put	face	door
when	where	go	think	per	thus
who	much	came	almost	among	help
will	your	right	hand	form	sense
more	way	used	enough	important	means
no	well	take	far	often	whole
if	down	three	took	things	matter

[a] From *Computational Analysis of Present-Day American English* by Henry Kučera and W. Nelson Francis, Brown University Press, 1967. Copyright © 1967 Brown University.

Appendix E
Design for a Successful Lesson

APPENDIX E

Seven steps in presenting a successful lesson are identified here. They are given in the sequence in which the lesson probably should be taught and are modeled in teaching episodes included in a number of the instructional units. They are an adaptation of the "Elements of a Successful Lesson" as presented by Dr. Madeline Hunter of the UCLA Laboratory School.

1. *Anticipatory Set*. This is a teacher-directed activity designed to focus student attention on the lesson to follow. It includes getting student attention and developing psychological readiness for the lesson.
2. *Objectives*. In this segment of the lesson, the teacher verbalizes what the students are expected to do at the end of the lesson and why the skill is important to learners.
3. *Input*. This is the instruction that will enable students to attain the objective. The information may be presented by films, pictures, discussion, demonstration, reading, or other teacher-directed strategies.
4. *Modeling*. In this phase of the lesson, the teacher provides a demonstration of a process or examples of the finished product so that students can visualize exactly what is involved.
5. *Checking for Understanding*. This aspect allows the teacher to be certain that the students profited by the input and modeling steps and can demonstrate that they understand the content.
6. *Guided Practice*. This step provides for practice of the newly acquired skill while the teacher is available to monitor and be certain that students do not practice an error.
7. *Independent Practice*. This step occurs after students can perform the task without errors. Then they can practice it without teacher supervision.

Appendix F
Utility of Phonics Generalizations

APPENDIX F

	Percent of utility		
	Clymer	Emans	Bailey
Vowel Principle			
1. When *y* is the final letter in a word, it usually has a vowel sound.	84	98	89
2. If the only vowel letter is at the end of a word, the letter usually stands for a long sound.	74	33	76
3. When there is one *e* in a word that ends in a consonant, the *e* usually has a short sound.	76	83	92
4. When a vowel is in the middle of a one-syllable word, ending in a consonant, the vowel is short.	62	73	71
5. When there are two vowels, one of which is final *e*, the first vowel is long and the *e* is silent.	63	63	57
6. When words end with silent *e*, the preceding *a* or *i* is long.	60	48	50
7. One vowel letter in an accented syllable has its short sound.	61	64	65
8. In many two- and three-syllable words, the final *e* lengthens the vowel in the last syllable.	46	42	46
9. The letter *a* has the same sound (o) when followed by l, w, and u.	48	24	34
10. When *a* follows *w* in a word, it usually has the sound of *a* in *was*.	32	28	22
11. When *y* is used as a vowel in words, it sometimes has the sound of long *i*.	15	4	11
12. When *y* or *ey* is seen in the last syllable that is not accented, the long sound of *e* is heard.	0	1	0
13 When the letters *oa* are together in a word, *o* always gives its long sound and the *a* is silent.	97	86	95
14. Words having double *e* usually have the long *e* sound.	98	100	87

15. In *ay* the *y* is silent and gives *a* its long sound.	78	100	88
16. When *ea* come together in a word, the first letter is long, the second silent.	66	62	55
17. The first vowel is usually long, the second silent in the digraphs *ai, ea, oa, ui.*	66	58	60
18. When there are two vowels side by side, the long sound of the first one is heard and the second is usually silent.	45	18	34
19. *W* is sometimes a vowel and follows the vowel digraph rule.	40	31	33
20. In the phonogram *ie,* the *i* is silent and the *e* has a long sound.	17	23	31

Vowel Dipthongs

21. The two letters *ow* make the long *o* sound.	59	50	55
22. When *e* is followed by *w,* the vowel sound is the same as represented by *oo.*	35	14	40

Vowels with *r*

23. The *r* gives the preceding vowel a sound that is neither long nor short.	78	82	86
24. When *a* is followed by *r* and final *e,* we expect to hear the sound heard in *care.*	90	100	96
25. When *c* and *h* are next to each other, they make only one sound.	100	100	100
26. When the letter *c* is followed by *o* or *a,* the sound of *k* is likely to be heard.	100	100	100
27. When *ght* is seen in a word, *gh* is silent.	100	100	100
28. When a word begins with *kn* the *k* is silent.	100	100	100
29. When a word begins with *wr,* the *w* is silent.	100	100	100
30. When a word ends in *ck,* it has the same last sound as in *look.*	100	100	100
31. When two of the same consonants are side by side, only one is heard.	99	91	98
32. When *c* is followed by *e* or *i,* the sound of *s* is likely to be heard.	96	90	92
33. *Ch* is usually pronounced as it is in *kitchen, catch,* and *chair,* not like *sh.*	95	67	87
34. The letter *g* often has a sound similar to that of *j* in *jump* when it precedes the letter *i* or *e.*	64	80	78

Phonograms

35. When the letter *i* is followed by the letters *gh,* the *i* usually stands for its long sound, and the *gh* is silent.	71	100	71
36. When *ture* is the final syllable in a word, it is unaccented.	100	100	95
37. When *tion* is the final syllable in a word, it is unaccented.	100	100	100

Glossary

Ability grouping Practice of placing students in groups within a class according to ability as shown by standardized and/or informal testing along with teacher observation. May also refer to a plan for determining student placement in a class.

Accent (stress) Marking that denotes emphasis to be placed on syllables in pronouncing words.

Achievement test An instrument designed to measure the level (grade equivalent/percentile) at which a person has attained knowledge.

Acuity Keenness of the senses, such as auditory acuity or keenness of the sense of hearing.

Affix A word that changes the meaning or tense of a word when attached to a base word. Affixes include prefixes, suffixes, and inflectional endings.

Analytical methodology Method of teaching word attack skills that begins with the whole word, then analyses it into its parts.

Antonym A word that is the opposite in meaning from a given word. For example, *light* can be an antonym for *dark*.

Aptitude Capacity for learning.

Articulation (enunciation) Pronunciation of sounds in words.

Ascending letters The letters of the alphabet that extend in height beyond the middle space of a line, such as *b, d, f, h, k, l,* and *t*.

Attention span Amount of time during which one can focus on a particular activity.

Audiometer An instrument used to screen a person's hearing ability by testing auditory acuity and discrimination.

Auditory discrimination Ability to recognize the likenesses and differences between and among sounds.

Basal reader method Method of teaching reading primarily through the use of graded reading texts specifically designed for the teacher to follow the sequenced steps of a directed reading lesson.

Base root. Basic word without suffixes or prefixes.

Behavioral objective. Instructional criteria stated in terms of the changes in behavior that are to take place in the learner after instruction.

Bibliotherapy Use of books as psychological therapy, mainly through the reader's identification with events or feelings of the main character(s) in the book.

Bilingual Having to do with two languages; a bilingual person is proficient in the use of two languages.

Blend Combination of two or more consonants that produce a blended sound when pronounced.

Breve Pronunciation mark that signifies the short sound of a vowel: *măn*.

Chronological age Age of a person in actual years.

Cloze procedure An informal procedure for determining reading comprehension in which the reader supplies missing words from a reading passage.

Compound A word formed from two or more words in which the individual meanings combine.

Concept Idea or thought; accumulation of experiences that can be represented in a generalization.

Configuration clues Cues that a reader may use to recognize a word by sight or in a reading passage; the reader might recognize the word because of its distinctive shape or structure or some other characteristics peculiar to the word that stimulate recognition in the mind of the reader.

Consonant A speech sound made by constriction in the breath channel.

Consonant blend or cluster Combination of two or more consonants that produce a blended sound when pronounced, such as the *str* in string.

Content words Words that make up the greatest part of our language and that possess most of the meaning in a sentence.

Context The given setting of a word in a phrase, or sentence, a sentence in a paragraph, or a paragraph in a longer selection that provides meaning peculiar to that word, sentence, or paragraph; the meaning of word, phrase, sentence, or paragraph in a given setting due to surrounding words.

Context clues Cues present within a phrase, sentence, or paragraph that alert the reader to meaning and sometimes pronunciation of an unfamiliar word by their structure, location, or use in the sentence.

Contraction A word formed from two words in which certain letters have been omitted. The omission of letters is signified by an apostrophe. For example, *don't* is the contraction for *do not*.

Controlled vocabulary A selected set of reading material words of a given difficulty level to be introduced gradually and thereafter repeated frequently so that the student may achieve word recognition mastery of the words.

Corrective reading A program of instruction designed to help the student develop reading skills in areas of noted deficiencies.

Criterion A set of predetermined skills, abilities, or knowledge against which ability of a person in those skills or abilities is measured.

Criterion-referenced test An evaluation instrument that measures a person's ability to perform a predetermined set of skills, abilities, or knowledge.

Decoding Translating written symbols into their corresponding speech sounds.

Deep structure The abstract underlying meaning of speech or writing.

Descending letter The letters of the alphabet that extend below the base line in writing, such as *g, j, p,* and *q.*

Developmental reading program A planned, sequential organization of instruction designed to introduce and reinforce reading skills systematically at ascending levels of difficulty.

Diacritical mark Symbols used in denoting pronunciation of words.

Diagnosis Process of securing information about factors that influence education for the purpose of matching educational experiences with student needs.

Diagnosis (informal) Process of securing data by nonstandardized instruments and/or teacher observation to determine specific instructional needs of the learner.

Diagnostic reading test An instrument designed to determine areas of needed instruction and specific skill needs in reading in order to prescribe compensatory instruction.

Dialect Speech patterns or pronunciations peculiar to certain geographic areas of the country that may not always conform to standard English but that are not necessarily considered incorrect due to their common local usage.

Dictionary skills The skills necessary to efficient use of the dictionary as a tool for unlocking word pronunciation and meaning. The skills consist of alphabetical order, use of guide words, use of pronunciation key, and selecting appropriate meanings.

Digraph A combination of two letters that represent one unique speech sound, such as *th* in think.

Diphthong Two vowels that, when sounded together, produce a somewhat blended sound, such as *ow* in cow.

Dominance The preference for use of either the right or left eye, hand, arm, and leg.

Eclectic approach A method of teaching that extracts desirable elements of various approaches to teaching reading and combines them into an integrated approach.

Experience background The accumulation of a person's knowledge, abilities, and the experiences gained from the environment that he or she brings to a learning task.

Experience chart Chart of words, sentences, or paragraphs derived from the speaking vocabularies of the learners. Experience charts are often used in the language experience approach to teaching reading.

Figure of speech A phrase whose meaning is not derived by the sum of individual word meanings contained in the phrase, but that represents a new meaning, such as "The job keeps me tied down."

Fixations The stops made by the eye during which the reader reacts to the printed words.

Fluency Ease of reading, extent to which a person reads smoothly with little difficulty.

Frustration level The reading level at which the reader recognizes 90 percent of the words encountered in a reading passage and comprehends 50 percent. At this level, the material being read is frustrating to the reader.

Generalization An assimilation of pieces of information by the reader into a concept. Making generalizations is a high-level reading skill.

Grapheme The written symbol that represents spoken sound.

Homograph Words that are spelled alike but have more than one pronunciation and meaning.

   content The child was *content* with the candy.
   The speech was poor in *content*.

Homonym Two or more words that sound alike but are spelled differently.

Homophone Two or more words that sound alike but are spelled differently; another name for homonym.

Independent reading level The reading level at which the reader recognizes 99 percent of the words encountered in a reading passage and comprehends 90 percent. At this level, the student can read with ease and without assistance.

Inferential comprehension Understanding written material on a higher level than literal comprehension. The second level of understanding in reading. The level of reading understanding in which the learner can infer and make generalizations and summaries from material read.

Inflectional endings Endings added to words that can change the case, tense, gender, mood, number, person, or voice of the words in order that they fit a given context without necessarily changing the basic meaning. For example, the inflectional ending *ing* has been added to the word *sing* in order to use *singing* to fit a given sentence context.

Instructional reading level The reading level at which the reader recognizes 95 percent of the words encountered in a reading passage and comprehends about 75 percent. At this level, the student can profit from reading instruction.

Informal reading inventory (IRI) An informal measurement of a learner's ability to recognize words and comprehend material read.

Kinesthetic methodology Approach to teaching reading based primarily on the use of the sense of touch, as in feeling of letter shapes.

Language experience method An approach to teaching reading in which the experience of the learners becomes the stimulus for reading instruction. (Experiences stated by the learner are recorded by the teacher and then read by the learner.)

Literal comprehension The lowest level of understanding in reading; that is, the level at which simple facts and details of a reading selection can be recalled.

Macron Pronunciation mark that signifies the long sound of a vowel; *nōte*.

Mastery test An instrument designed to measure amount or extent to which a learner has gained certain knowledge or acquired certain skills, that is, the extent to which that person has mastered learning.

Mental age The age for which a certain score on an intelligence test is average. The age of a person as reported by results of an IQ test.

Morpheme The smallest meaningful unit of language, such as prefixes and suffixes, inflectional endings and base words.

Motivation Incentive to approach a task.

Norms A percentile scale established by ranking a selected population based on their performance on a standardized test; norms do not necessarily represent desired levels of achievement.

Norm-referenced tests An evaluation instrument in which results are reported in norms (see *Norms*); that is, results are interpreted in reference to a set of preestablished rankings; a student's performance on a norm-referenced test is compared to the average score made by the sample population on which the test was standardized.

Perception Ability to discriminate with the senses.

Perceptual process Steps involved in realization of external objects or symbols through the use of the senses.

Performance test A test of ability to complete certain tasks instead of demonstrate knowledge.

Phoneme The smallest unit of speech that distinguishes one sound from another, such as *tap* from *top*.

Phoneme-grapheme correspondence Relationship of spoken sounds to their written spellings.

Phonic analysis Use of the knowledge of sound represented by letters in identifying a word.

Phonic generalizations Principles of sound-symbol relationships used in the process of identification of words.

Phonics A word recognition technique that utilizes correspondence between the written symbols (graphemes) and spoken sounds (phonemes).

Phonogram A speech sound represented by one or more letters.

Phrase A group of two or more words that are meaningful together but that do not constitute a sentence, such as "the little red truck." A sentence may contain several phrases.

Pitch The level of sound; the musical quality of speech.

Postassessment An instrument of evaluation given to an individual or group after instruction in a specific area has been received in order to determine amount or extent of learning.

Preassessment An instrument of evaluation given to an individual or group before instruction is begun in a certain area in order to determine specific needs.

Prefix A meaningful unit of letters added at the beginning of a base (root) that changes the meaning of the base. For example, *un* is a prefix that may be added to the word *kind* to form the new word *unkind*.

Pronunciation spelling The spelling of a word in phonetic symbols (as in the dictionary pronunciation of a word) instead of by its actual spelling. In the dictionary, a pronunciation key is given to provide words that contain the sounds represented by the key, also sometimes called respelling or sound spelling.

Psycholinguistics The study of language that involves both cognitive development and structure of a language.

Readability The grade level assigned to a reading passage after analysis of the number of syllables in the words and the length of sentences in the passage. These factors help to determine the level of difficulty of a selected passage.

Reading expectancy The level at which a person is capable of reading as indicated by achievement, background, discrepancy between scores of reading and listening tests, or computation of given formulas.

Reading miscue inventory An informal instrument for measuring the type of reading errors made, instead of the number of errors made.

Reading process Series of physical and mental activities that take place when a reader assimilates written symbols in the act of reading.

Reading readiness The stage of development at which a learner is ready to profit from formal instruction in reading; factors determining readiness include a person's intellectual, physical, and emotional maturity. The concept of reading readiness also applies to the level of preparation one must have before attempting any reading task, such as learning special vocabulary needed to understand a chapter in a book on maintaining a budget.

Redundancy The repetition of information in speech or writing that enables the receiver to understand the message even if only part of the actual words are comprehended.

Regression A reverting back of the eyes to reread a word or phrase in the reading process. A backward movement of the eyes to refocus on a word or phrase.

Remediation Instruction designed to improve reading skills in areas specified through evaluation.

Reversal tendency The inclination to read or write letters or words from right to left.

Reversals The tendency to transpose single letters or letters in whole words in reading, such as *d* for *b* or *was* for *saw*.

Root(word) A basic word without its possible prefixes, suffixes or derived forms. For example, *comfort* is the root of *comfortable*. A synonym for base(word).

Scanning Reading over a passage quickly in order to derive the overall meaning or main idea.

Schwa A vowel sound whose pronunciation is denoted by the symbol ə and that sounds like the *a* in about. The schwa sound is most often heard in the unaccented syllable of the word in which it is present.

Screening test An instrument designed to discern any gross problems, as in hearing or sight, in order to determine if further or more specific testing is needed.

Self-concept The way a person perceives himself or herself.

Semantics Study of the meaning of words in a language.

Sentence A complete thought in language containing at least a subject and a verb.

Sight approach A method of teaching reading by beginning with sight words (see sight words) rather than some analytical approach to word identification.

Sight reading Reading by recognizing words quickly on sight (see sight words); also, sight recognition.

Sight words (*a*). Any words that may be recognized quickly on sight because of previous repeated exposure of the words to the reader. (*b*). A set or core of selected words to be used as a basic vocabulary, as in a basal reading series.

Skimming Reading over materials quickly in order to obtain a general idea of their content.

Snellen chart An eye chart used in measuring visual acuity at far-point (20 feet).

Standard score A score expressed in the number of units a given score deviates from the norm.

Standardized reading test An evaluation instrument designed to test reading ability in the areas of comprehension, vocabulary, and word recognition.

Stress The amount of emphasis placed on a syllable of a word when pronouncing it.

Structural analysis A method of word recognition in which a word is identified by analyzing its known parts, such as root words, prefixes, suffixes, and inflectional endings.

Structure words Words whose primary functions are grammatical instead of meaningful or having content, such as determiners (articles), prepositions, and expletives.

Study skills Skills needed to obtain and retain information effectively from reading material such as textbooks and reference books. The abilities to locate, summarize, and outline information are considered study skills.

Subtest A test of a specific skill included under a broader category, such as a word recognition subtest, may be part of a standardized reading test.

Subvocal reading Reading in which the reader softly pronounces the words vocally when it is intended that he or she read silently.

Surface structure The arrangement of words grammatically, as in a sentence in speech or writing.

Survey test A test of general reading ability.

Sweep The movement of eyes from one line to the next in the reading process; also called return sweep.

Syllabication A process of breaking words into pronounceable units in order to recognize them in reading and to spell them.

Syllable The smallest word part, consisting of at least one vowel sound and sometimes consonant sounds.

Synonym A word that is close in meaning to another word and that may be used interchangeably with it. For example, *calm-tranquil*.

Syntax The structure of meaningful words of a language, as in a sentence.

Tachistoscopic devices The name given to quick-flash instruments used to expose letters or words rapidly to a reader in order to provide practice in visual perception and memory.

Teaching sequence The order in which skills are presented and taught; the mastery of some skills is prerequisite to the introduction of others.

Unvoiced sounds Sounds that are not produced from the vocal cords but from the breath, such as the *th* in think.

VAKT A method of learning that utilizes the visual, auditory, kinesthetic, and tactile senses of the learner. The method is useful in teaching students with poor visual memory to recognize words in print.

Visual acuity Keenness of the sense of sight.

Visual discrimination The ability to distinguish differences and similarities between letters or words.

Voiced, voiceless Distinction made between consonant sounds produced from the vocal chords (voiced) and those produced by the breath (voiceless). For example, the *g* in go is voiced, and the *th* in think is voiceless, or unvoiced.

Vowel A speech sound represented by the letters *a, e, i, o,* and *u.*

Word analysis Identifying a word in reading by breaking it into recognizable parts and sounds.

Word attack The process of recognizing words through context clues, structural analysis, phonics, or use of the dictionary.

Word calling Pronounciation of words without actual recognition or understanding of meaning.

CREDITS

Chapter 1:   Vincent Serbin from Leo de Wys, Inc.

Chapter 2:   Drawing by Mathew K. Dauzat.

Chapter 3:   Drawing by Mathew K. Dauzat.

Chapter 4:   Terrence Lennon

Chapter 5:   J. Gerard Smith

Chapter 6:   J. Gerard Smith

Chapter 7:   Terrence Lennon

Chapter 8:   J. Gerard Smith

Chapter 9:   J. Gerard Smith

Chapter 10:   J. Gerard Smith

Chapter 11:   J. Gerard Smith

Chapter 12:   Terrence Lennon

Chapter 13:   de Wys, Inc.

Chapter 14:   J. Gerard Smith

Chapter 15:   Drawing by Mathew K. Dauzat.

Chapter 16:   Mimi Forsyth from Monkmeyer Press Photo Service

Chapter 17:   Terrence Lennon

Chapter 18:   Hugh Rogers from Monkmeyer Press Photo Service

INDEX

Harber, Jean R., 301, 306
Harcourt, 268
Harris, Albert J., 22, 36-37, 54, 75, 79, 98, 116, 174, 200-201, 335
Harris, Larry A., 98
Harris-Jacobson Core List, The, 63
Hearing capacity level, 282
Heath, D. C., 268
Heathington, Betty S., 272, 303, 306
Heilman, Arthur W., 75, 79, 98, 116-117
Hillerich, R. L., 63, 75, 79
Hittleman, Daniel R., 169, 263
Homograph, 430
Homonym, 430
Homophone, 430
Hood, Joy, 306
Hood, Joyce, 54, 75, 79
Huebner, Mildred H., 116
Huff, Phyllis E., 272
Hunt, Lyman C., Jr., 266, 272
Hunter, Madeline, lesson plan, 423

Independent reading level, 282, 430
Index, 177
Individualized reading approach, 265-267, 335
Inductive approach, 130
Inductive teaching, 207
Inferences, 146
Inflectional endings, 430
Informal reading inventories, 281-283, 430
  administration, 292-293
  diagnosis, oral, 290-291
  diagnosis, written, 287-289
  levels identified, 281-228
  teacher-made, 291-292
  type questions, 283-287
Information, locating:
  book components, 177
  reference books, 117
  scanning, 175
  skimming, 175
  sources, 174-175, 177
Information, organization, 175-177
  note-taking, 176
  outlining, 176
  summarizing, 176

  underlining, 176
Instructional reading level, 282, 430
IRP, *see* Individualized reading approach

Johnson, Dale D., 31, 37, 75-76, 79, 89, 98, 169
Jongsma, Eugene A., 165, 169

Kales, Eva, 54
Karlin, Robert, 37, 54, 153, 234
Kerber, James E., 54
Keys to Reading, 267
Kinesthetic methodology, 430
Knight, Lester N., 272
Kolker, Brenda, 272
Kreitlow, Burton W., 185, 210
Kučera-Francis word list, 421-422

Laffey, James L., 22, 37, 125, 133
Lamberg, Walter J., 301, 306
Language experience approach, 89, 248-263, 331, 333
  advantages, 252
  characteristics, 251
  criticisms, 252
  culturally different, 254
  philosophy, 250-251
  planning, 258-260
  plans, 31
  presentations, 262-263
  procedures, 255-258
  readiness level, 254
  remedial learner, 254-255
Language experience method, 431
Language factors, 30
  competence (deep structure), 30
  listening, 30
  oral, 30
  performance, 30
Language system, primary, 8
  listening, 8
  speaking, 8
Lapp, Diane, 132-133, 138, 152-153, 220, 263, 302, 306
Larrick, James L., 36
Larrick, Nancy, 37
Lawrence, Paula Smith, 269, 272
Lee, Doris, 250, 263